PRINCIPLES OF SOFTWARE DEVELOPMENT LEADERSHIP: APPLYING PROJECT MANAGEMENT PRINCIPLES TO AGILE SOFTWARE DEVELOPMENT LEADERSHIP

KEN WHITAKER

Charles River Media

A part of Course Technology, Cengage Learning

COURSE TECHNOLOGY
CENGAGE Learning

Australia, Brazil, Japan, Korea, Mexico, Singapore, Spain, United Kingdom, United States

COURSE TECHNOLOGY
CENGAGE Learning™

**Principles of Software Development
Leadership: Applying Project
Management Principles to Agile
Software Development Leadership**

Ken Whitaker

**Publisher and General Manager, Course
Technology PTR:** Stacy L. Hiquet

Associate Director of Marketing:
Sarah Panella

Content Project Manager:
Jessica McNavich

Marketing Manager: Mark Hughes

Acquisitions Editor: Mitzi Koontz

Project Editor and Copy Editor:
Kim Benbow

Editorial Services Coordinator: Jen Blaney

Interior Layout: Jill Flores

Cover Designer: Mike Tanamachi

Indexer: Valerie Haynes Perry

Proofreader: Gene Redding

For product information and technology assistance, contact us at
Cengage Learning Customer & Sales Support, 1-800-354-9706

For permission to use material from this text or product,
submit all requests online at **cengage.com/permissions**
Further permissions questions can be emailed to
permissionrequest@cengage.com

PMI and PMBOK are trademarks of the Project Management Institute, Inc.,
which is registered in the United States and other nations.

All other trademarks are the property of their respective owners.

Library of Congress Control Number: 2008929232

ISBN-13: 978-1-58450-586-0

ISBN-10: 1-58450-586-9

Course Technology, a part of Cengage Learning
20 Channel Center Street
Boston, MA 02210
USA

Cengage Learning is a leading provider of customized learning solutions with
office locations around the globe, including Singapore, the United Kingdom,
Australia, Mexico, Brazil, and Japan. Locate your local office at: **international.
cengage.com/region**

Cengage Learning products are represented in Canada by Nelson Education, Ltd.

For your lifelong learning solutions, visit **courseptr.com**

Visit our corporate website at **cengage.com**

Printed in Canada
1 2 3 4 5 6 7 11 10 09

Here's What the Experts Are Saying

"They say it takes 10,000 hours to become an expert; if you don't have that long to wait to be a good software development leader, then here's your ticket. Ken has put together the topics and the experience that will help any aspiring software aficionado move beyond being just 'hard core' and into a role as a highly valued team leader."

—Charles Seybold, Co-founder and CEO, LiquidPlanner, Inc.

"Ken identifies many of the same problems I wrestle with as a programmer, manager, and owner of a software company. It took many years for me to even recognize these issues and many more to address them. Take a shortcut to less conflict and higher quality software by learning from Ken's fictional characters' pain, not your own!"

—Jeff Butterworth, CEO and Founder, Alien Skin Software

"Most books attempt to teach—and teach and re-teach—how to be a developer. Okay, we get it. Agile is good. Defects are bad. You should have meetings. While all the attention is spent on how to develop—estimating and charts and managing projects—*Principles of Software Development Leadership* shows how to manage technical teams of engineers and developers. Whitaker reminds us that being a vendor is about business and leadership. His book explains what executives need to know about building technology products, regardless of development methodology, such as how to create winning teams. (Hint: Winning teams create winning products.) What are the lines between products, projects, and programs? Organizing for success. Ultimately, Whitaker explains how to run development as the critical business function that it is. Get *Principles of Software Development Leadership* if you want to lead a technical team to success—or buy a copy for your boss if you want to work on a successful team."

—Steve Johnson, Vice President, Pragmatic Marketing

"You could spend 30 years learning what Ken knows about leading software engineering organizations, or you could buy this book and get 30 years ahead of your peers who don't.

Anyone who has 'been there, done that' will immediately recognize that Whitaker speaks with the voice of experience. He tackles everything that causes software projects and software project leaders to fail and tells you how to stay out of trouble and get to the finish line a winner. Even the most seasoned veteran will learn some tricks and techniques that could save the day—or their jobs."

—Rowland Archer, CTO, SVP Engineering, GSX, Inc.

"Ken Whitaker has neatly packaged some practical, no-nonsense leadership advice that will not only save some projects in these difficult economic times, but may well save some software development firms from going under. Highly recommended!

Principles of Software Development Leadership is chock full of well-organized advice that will reinforce several common-sense principles that you always knew but never articulated openly. But it will also provide you with some eye-opening 'aha!' insights that will explain (perhaps for the first time!) why some of your project managers get into trouble time after time.

Not every software development project will succeed during these next few difficult years of economic pressure; indeed, not every software product company will survive. The ones that do survive and succeed will be the ones that manage their projects aggressively, as if their lives depend on it. Ken Whitaker's excellent new book shows you how to do just that!"

—Ed Yourdon, software consultant and author

Dedication

For Gina,
I can't imagine a more loving partner in this life
and forever after . . .

Preface

The goal of *Principles of Software Development Leadership* is to provide an up-to-date reference of best practices leadership techniques for the following target audiences:

- **Project managers:** Apply Project Management Institute (PMI) fundamentals to the software industry using the *Project Management Body of Knowledge* (PMBOK) as a guide.
- **Software development managers, leads, and executives:** Teach software development professionals effective project management best practice tips and techniques.

I believe that there is an incredible opportunity to educate and motivate software development managers to become leaders based on PMI's best practices. Ultimately, every software development leader's primary responsibility is to lead his organization to deliver quality products on time and under budget. These guidelines are depicted as a balanced focus on managing the relationship between planning, processes, and people.

With so many books and seminars focused on process and technology methodologies, there are very few sources of information that really prepare software managers to be the "killer" leaders they strive to be. What is usually non-technical is forgotten, what is technical becomes unimportant, and what is the right thing to do becomes confused with office politics and arrogance. *You get the picture....*

According to the U.S. Bureau of Labor Statistics, in the U.S. alone there are over 612,000 computer software engineers and well over 250,000 managers in the computer/IT field. As an example of worldwide computer software growth, India has over 500,000 software and service professionals.

In addition, there are over 200,000 PMI members worldwide, including a large number of PMP-certified project managers, many of whom work in the software industry. However, there appears to be very few individuals in key software management roles who are PMP-certified or even professionally trained in project management skills. Typically, software organizations treat project management in one of the following ways:

- They cannot afford to invest in project management at all.
- They set up a separate project management organization that acts as a watchdog (some call it a "thorn in the backside") for software development.
- They incorporate non-technical project managers to lead technical teams, yielding mixed results.

Project managers need to be able to successfully facilitate software development teams while software development managers and executives must grasp fundamental project management skills. What better way than to teach how to apply PMBOK best practices specifically for modern-day, agile software teams? The style of *Principles of Software Development Leadership* will hopefully appeal to the analytical nature of the engineering reader and to the process nature of the project management professional.

Ken Whitaker
Seattle, WA USA

Acknowledgments

I would like to thank Kim Benbow for some amazing editing, Jill Flores for the quickest book layout I've ever seen, and Mitzi Koontz for allowing me to take on this project to begin with. To all of those maniacs who love to create software, I hope this book helps bridge the gap between project management best practices and the reality of agile software development. I'd like especially to thank Roy Sherrill and the entire team at Datalight who demonstrate a true passion for delivering first rate software and services to an ever-changing embedded marketplace.

About the Author

Ken Whitaker, PMP and CSM, has over 20 years of executive line management experience with leading technology companies in a wide variety of industries, including real-time embedded, healthcare, insurance estimating, marketing merchandising, real-time control, wireless, mobile GIS, presentation graphics (remember Harvard Graphics?), and led the software team who delivered the first PC-compatible, battery-powered laptop to market.

He graduated from James Madison University with an emphasis in mathematics and fine arts and attended Virginia Tech's Computer Science and Applications graduate school. He is Project Management Professional (PMP)–certified and an active member of the Puget Sound chapter of the Project Management Institute (PMI). Ken is also a Certified ScrumMaster. Ken is an active speaker at software industry events, including the following:

- Software Development Conferences (SD Expo) management track
- SQE (Software Quality Engineering) annual conference
- "Bug-Free" Software Success leadership seminars (www.softwaresuccess.com)
- American Electronics Association (AEA)
- Construx Software's Executive Summit and an active member of the Seattle-based Executive Council for Software Engineering (ECSE)
- Society of Technical Communications (STC)
- University of Washington's acclaimed Information Technology Leaders seminars (www.uwtv.org)
- Embedded Systems Conference (ESC)

Contents

Part 1

Taming the Soft Machine

The first chapter presents a rather humorous (but all too true) summary of the seven deadly habits of ineffective software managers. The second chapter, "Organizational Spring Cleaning," presents basic leadership steps you should take if you have just been promoted or have taken on a position at a different division or company. The remaining chapter in this section, "Relating PMBOK Best Practices to Software Development," introduces Project Management Book of Knowledge (PMBOK) concepts that apply to software development leadership.

1 Seven Deadly Habits of Ineffective Software Managers

This introductory chapter is written as a series of short stories and is quite different from the style presented throughout the rest of the book. These stories should introduce you to the trials and tribulations of software development management. Happy reading (and don't get too depressed)! The names used in these stories are made up to protect the guilty.

HABIT 1—RELEASING A PRODUCT BEFORE IT IS READY

Daniel is an experienced, high-powered software executive. He rose through the corporate ranks starting as a lowly software programmer for a major software corporation right out of college. He quickly demonstrated an amazing software programming talent along with a consistent ability to get things done. Daniel was always a sharp dresser and was recognized as having the ability to think on his feet with little or no warning. Programmers liked him because he was technical, executives liked him because he looked the part of a confident leader, and customers liked him because he was an honest communicator. The sales force, however, eyed Daniel with suspicion, since he wasn't interested in partying or golf, and anyone who didn't take every opportunity to play golf couldn't possibly be trusted.

Just six months ago he was promoted to director of software engineering, and, as a result, he spent more time in meetings and less time with his staff. Daniel believed that being the Head Engineering Honcho (HEH) allowed him to balance decisions that spanned both business and technical issues.

Now as a part of the management staff, he felt considerable pressure to find ways to manage and grow the company rather than just delivering great software.

To Daniel's surprise, the details of creating basic business assets (in other words, the software products) that consumed his time before were now less important. The software products that fueled the company's very existence had become nothing more than commodities that were expected to "just magically appear" completed. (Oh yeah, all delivered software was also expected to be 100% error free.)

On one beautiful wintry day in late February, management gathered into their chambers as they usually do on Mondays. This was, however, no ordinary Monday. This was the day when Tom, the CEO, proclaimed that the board wasn't happy. Tom was a solid executive and regarded as being very impactful—he had "The Look," the right three-letter name, the best haircut, and just enough gray hair to look sophisticated yet still be regarded as young (in Social Security terms). All in all, he was known as a "straight shooter."

"Guys, we have a problem," Tom proclaimed. "Were you wondering why our CFO sitting over there looks a little ragged? Unless we get our new integrated software suite delivered this quarter, I've been told that there is absolutely no way that we're going to make our financial results. Grace has been pouring over the financial statements and, no matter how the numbers are sliced, without this major software upgrade we may have to resort to Enronian measures." And for the finale, "The board members have made it clear to me that the prospect of not achieving our financial goals this quarter is not acceptable to them. That would be three quarters in a row of disappointing growth and earnings."

The silence was deafening. It was as if the air had been sucked right out of the room.

Thinking quietly to himself, Daniel remembered that he was recently told by his engineering manager that everything looked good for a release next month. Daniel was thinking to himself: "Let's see. January, March, April. Wait—that's wrong. January, February, and March. Yep, March is in this quarter after all." (Daniel was nervous, and when he gets nervous, he cross-checks things in his head just to be sure before he opens his mouth.)

"Folks," said Daniel, gathering his strength, "we can make that date. I have it on good authority from my team that the product suite will ship as planned in March."

All eyes were now on Daniel. "We *can* deliver the upgraded software suite this quarter."

That statement may have easily been interpreted as wishful thinking, but that one statement was just what everybody wanted to hear. As if a valve had been opened, oxygen rushed back into the room, and the management team huddled together and immediately launched into planning mode. This was great news, since the product release this quarter was just *confirmed* and *committed* to by the director of engineering himself.

The chatter started right up:

"Let's prepare for the launch."

"We gotta get sales geared up for this starting tomorrow!"

"I'll tell the board the good news."

Yep, there was no doubt—Daniel was today's hero.

Two days later, as if the devil himself had just arrived in Daniel's office, there stood Dante, the quality assurance (QA) manager. ("Odd," thought Daniel, "Dante did have a negative demeanor and piercing eyes of contempt. Perhaps he was the devil himself.")

"I don't care what Becky says. This software isn't even close to being ready." Daniel could tell that Dante was both exhausted and frustrated.

Not amused, Daniel demanded an explanation and immediately heard a barrage of reasons based on "missed deadlines," "engineering performs horrible unit testing," "features have been thrown in at the last moment," and the ever-popular "we never signed up for this schedule anyways." Daniel immediately invited Becky, the engineering manager, into his office so that all three could discuss this situation.

At first the meeting was civil. It became obvious to Dante that Daniel wanted to hear only good news, and it was obvious to Becky that Daniel needed to "get with it" and remember that "there was no software that was 100% error free."

"The customer can live with these issues, and they'll *never* find these problems anyways!" Becky was now pissed off. She tried to command the room by bringing a beaten-up World War II vintage army helmet with her. What appeared to be painted with blood was inscribed on the helmet "Born to Kill Microsoft." That helmet was one of her prized possessions, and she occasionally dragged it around to meetings where she thought it might come in handy. Daniel thought it somehow gave her super powers.

Now it was match point, and Dante delivered the final crushing blow: "This pig'll *never* ship!"

After facilitating this banter for what seemed like hours, Daniel threw his hands up and said, "Okay, okay. Let's simply go over the facts!"

The three of them painstakingly looked over the defect trends: new defects encountered, defects corrected, and completion of features and functions. The incoming defect rates had not trended downward, and unknown to Daniel, additional functionality had somehow snuck into the product over the past month. "Look-it," piped up Becky with authority. "We put those features in the suite for the customer!" These unexpected jewels, however, had the unwelcome result of further destabilizing the software. Besides, QA didn't even know these features were being added, and there was certainly no time for test development this late in the development cycle.

Lacking any energy to continue the debate, Daniel concluded the meeting with a motivating statement: "Do the best you can. This is going to be bad. Let's meet in a couple of days."

Becky and Dante left the meeting and went their separate directions, as if they had reached a draw in a boxing match. To signify engineering's confidence, Becky donned her helmet and wore it proudly throughout the halls. *This was war!*

Daniel asked for a meeting with Tom, the CEO, for first thing in the morning and left the office for the day utterly exhausted.

"This is going to be bad," he thought out loud.

The next morning he presented the new information to the CEO. Tom wasn't happy at all. He immediately gathered the management team. The team made the decision that in order to "save face," the software needed to be delivered at the end of March with the best possible quality and follow up the release sometime in early Q2 with a maintenance update. In other words, the product was going to be shipped—ready or not! Daniel's peers (especially the VP of Sales) felt lied to, and not one of the management staff took any responsibility in blindly accepting the state of the software a few weeks past.

Daniel was now all alone. "What have I done? I know better than to compromise what the customer pays good money for. And here I thought I was doing what was right for the company and for the management team, and now they all blame me. It just isn't fair!"

Daniel gathered his managers together to tell them the verdict. Becky felt vindicated, and Dante felt that all that talk about the importance of quality echoed by all of executive management in the past meant absolutely nothing.

Like Sales pushing for a dramatic quarter close, the software product was delivered the very last day of March, the fictitious 32nd of March. Due to the remaining product defects still open and unresolved, Dante and the QA organization refused to officially approve the product for release, even though they all knew it was going to be released anyway. The software worked pretty well, though, so perhaps customers wouldn't encounter major issues prior to the maintenance release after all. Needless to say, the teams were exhausted getting the product to a shippable state, and Daniel just crossed his fingers.

Outside of Engineering, everyone in the company was excited and motivated about the release. The thought crossed the executive team that "Hmm, perhaps this is how we should always rally the troops to get software delivered all of the time?" That's how the folks in Sales attempt to deliver results the last week of every quarter! *Same thing, right?*

About three weeks into April, the technical support phones started ringing. These calls were from customers, and they weren't calling to say, "Hello, how are you doing?" Customers were facing serious problems. Within about a week, customer support lines were *up in flames,* and Daniel was finding himself defending the incoming issues at escalation meetings. The company's sales team members, who just weeks ago celebrated the product release with nice commission checks, were upset due to the fact that their corporate accounts were questioning the product's quality and, most importantly to them, their personal integrity by selling it. Unfortunately, there was no simple workaround.

In order to stop the bleeding, the latest software product was removed from the shelves and from the company's web site. Customers were asked to use the prior version until the issues were resolved.

The company was in a meltdown state, and the teams were working around the clock to resolve product problems. The very fact that the software was released before it was ready for prime time caused anger and threats of cancelled contracts. In just a few weeks, the damage was getting worse as competitors snuck in and took away customers, one at a time. *Vultures going in for the kill!*

The board met privately with the management team to discuss the next steps. As Q2 came and went, the software was eventually updated in mid-Q3. In fact, the release four months later was more like what the original software should have looked like. The project was simply four months behind.

At the next company all-hands meeting, Tom delivered a somber presentation to the company. "We have lost a major customer due to product quality, and as a result, 30 of you will lose your jobs today."

Daniel, the software engineering executive, was terminated the day after the announcement. The California-based software company never recovered and eventually closed its doors.

Could this have been avoided? *Possibly. . .* Table 1.1 shows what went wrong in this story and what should have happened (summary tables are used for each habit throughout this chapter).

Table 1.1 Habit 1—Lessons Learned

What Went Wrong	What Should Have Happened
The management team was surprised.	Proactively set expectations and ensure that risks are understood (it does no one any good to be overly optimistic).
The software manager didn't gather and communicate the facts resulting in buy-in on inadequate information.	The "truth" in a project requires fact gathering and cross-functional buy-in.
The product was not ready to be released.	Execute to well-defined "checks and balances." (Otherwise, why even have them?)
The company lost credibility with customers, and everyone, especially employees, paid the price.	Knowing that you usually have a single chance to establish credibility with a customer, take the time to release a quality product and keep employees proud of the product they create.

HABIT 2—HIRING SOMEONE WHO IS NOT QUITE QUALIFIED (BUT WHO EVERYONE LIKES)

There's nothing like the hiring process, is there? Lots of résumés to review, phone screening that takes up a lot of personal time, and the drain on the organization during the interview process. To most managers, the hiring process is not something to look forward to but is instead a "royal pain."

Shelly had just been promoted to manager of the software engineering teams for a large software company in Austin (where most great software is created). She was well liked, a tremendous go-getter, and a positive influence within her team. Her team was highly regarded because they continually demonstrated the ability to deliver killer products on time. She needed to bring on another senior programmer who had experience with enterprise-wide software development programming and database programming skills.

In addition to the technical skills, she knew it was important to identify the attributes she expected from a senior-level contributor:

- Ability to design as well as implement solutions ("hands on")
- Ability to balance and prioritize in a heavily multitasking work environment
- Ability to communicate within the development organization, sales, customers, and partner companies
- Demonstrated experience in C#, Java, and mainstream Internet software tools to produce commercial software products and services

The position was posted on the company's web site and on the major job placement web sites.

Three months came and went. . . . Several interviews of candidates took place, and there were many disappointments. The need to fill this position was extremely high and getting more critical as time went by. Finally, an applicant named Brian interviewed for the job. He was presentable (unusual for a software engineer), smart, and definitely had the right credentials. Unfortunately, he didn't have recent hands-on experience, nor was he as current in the Internet software tools as he should be. Nonetheless, Shelly liked him and invited him back for a second round of interviews. He was thrilled for the opportunity and definitely wanted to pursue talking with them. Brian was still employed but had been miscast in his current company in a project manager role that he didn't like—he wanted to return to programming. *Hard to imagine why he wouldn't like being a project manager. . . .*

When he came back in for his second round of interviews, Shelly talked with him first to prime him for the interview process and how to position himself with the other interviewers. (She knew that some of the more technical interviewers could be merciless.) Initial interview feedback throughout the day was mixed. As Shelly expected, a couple of the interviewers weren't convinced of Brian's capabilities, though the less technical interviewers thought he would fit right in. *Well. . .nobody's perfect, right?*

At the end of the day, Shelly asked Brian how he thought the interviews went, and he stated that some of the interviews were "just okay," but for the most part he thought they went well. (He struggled with the "design how you'd program an elevator" question from the engineering architect on the team.) He again reiterated that he wanted the job, and even though he knew that he couldn't answer some of the technical questions, he would work hard to improve his technical skills. He knew he could do it; he had done it before.

The following day, Shelly got the entire interview team together, and they talked about the candidate. They couldn't come to a consensus, but they leaned more toward bringing him on board. Fundamentally, they all liked Brian and thought culturally he was a good match. Shelly had to do a fair amount of convincing—the prospect of starting a new round of interviews wasn't exciting to anyone, since the queue of other qualified candidates was at the moment slim. *Okay, there wasn't anyone lined up at the moment.*

Shelly didn't have time to call the references (she had programmers to manage, code to write, and non-work related Internet sites to look at!), so she asked Human Resources (HR) to do it for her this time. As you might expect, all of the feedback came back positive. Convinced this was a good thing, Shelly made the offer, he accepted on the spot, and he started two weeks later.

At first, everything went quite well—Brian was already very popular with the team and management, but he struggled at picking up technical concepts. It didn't take long for complaints of his lack of results became an undercurrent among the software engineers on the team.

Brian wasn't handling his workload and had unfortunately become more of a burden than an asset. It wasn't that Brian wasn't trying. He was working longer hours than most and really attempted to pick up the pace and do his fair share.

After two months, Brian was clearly behind on all of his assignments, and Shelly was forced to sit down with him and go over performance concerns. Although Shelly dreaded conversations like this, it was a necessary meeting. The meeting ended in a cordial way, and Shelly confirmed her support for his ability to perform in the role that the company needed. Brian did agree to do a better job. Unfortunately, the tempo of complaints from fellow teammates began to accelerate. He relied more on the other team members, and since he was in a key role, the project was now in trouble.

Around the third month after Brian was hired, Shelly had no alternative but to let Brian go. She prepared the performance background information necessary and filled out tons of paperwork for HR to approve. It almost seemed to Shelly that it took more work to terminate an employee than to hire an employee. Shelly called Brian into her office, and she told him that he was being terminated. Although they had a couple of prior performance conversations, Brian was surprised and angry saying that he wasn't given enough time to prove himself. "How is it going to look that I lost my job after only three months? I would have never left my other job if I had known this was going to happen."

> Don't misinterpret the term "bad hire" as an individual that is unsuitable for employment. Everyone has value, and oftentimes it is a matter of finding the right *opportunity*, at the right *time*, and under the right *management*.

As difficult and time-consuming as the hiring process can be, the after effects of a bad hire are far worse. Having a wrong new hire can

- Set a project back.
- Destroy team morale.
- Undermine the team's confidence in the hiring manager.
- Take a long time to rectify by either termination or job transfer, depending on the circumstances.

To avoid hiring mistakes, you may be inclined to adopt the philosophy of "try [out the candidate] before you buy [hire]." This will be discussed in Chapter 9, "Finding the Best Talent."

Could this have been avoided? *Possibly.* . . Table 1.2 summarizes what happened and what *could* have happened to avoid this situation.

Table 1.2 Habit 2—Lessons Learned

What Went Wrong	What Should Have Happened
The job requirements were not "requirements."	A clearly written job description should represent the minimum skills and knowledge required for anyone taking on that job.
The hiring manager didn't perform reference checks.	A hiring manager should never delegate all of the reference checks to someone less technical. Even though references tend to all be "candidate friendly," you can always find out possible issues that may impact whether a job should be offered (or not).
The hiring manager failed to listen to the interview team.	Even though the hiring manager should make the final decision on hiring a candidate, failure to listen to all of the interview team's feedback is oftentimes a fatal mistake (as in this example). There is no reason to ever be overly optimistic about a candidate's capabilities.

HABIT 3—MAKING EVERY DECISION A CONSENSUS DECISION

Everyone in the business community knows the opportunities available to software companies—with just a few engineers and a great idea, you can create an amazing line of products and services that could eventually become a cash bonanza or result in a complete meltdown. This is exactly the type of business and technical opportunity Tim had dreamed of.

Tim had grown from the ranks initially as a programmer, then a team lead, and was promoted to manager within the past year. He was well liked and was viewed as a great team player, mainly because he was a good listener. His company was small, his team had only three people, and there were high hopes for an IPO or acquisition. They were in a market, however, that wasn't alone. There were other startups with the same product idea, equally as aggressive, and just as eager for success. *Time to market meant everything....*

After his team's software project was delivered, it was time to get the team together to decide what should go into the next major upgrade. He addressed the team with a wonderful, well-constructed opening line:

"We need to decide on what goes into the next version of our software product."

The team was exhausted from the prior project's delivery, so there wasn't much interaction during the meeting. Tim decided, "OK, let's give it a rest. I'll gather up information from our product manager, Jody, and we'll meet again next week." Funnily enough, Jody was supposed to be at that particular meeting, but she was nowhere to be seen.

At the next team meeting, Tim had information this time:

■ List of defects (or as Tim liked to call them, "customer misunderstandings") from their bug tracking system
■ List of customer feature requests
■ List of customer support issues in priority order
■ Prioritized list of competitor's key features (causing Tim's company heartburn)

This meeting included a cross-section of participants: engineering management, engineering, quality assurance, technical documentation, project management, product management, and customer support. All told, 12 people were in attendance (which represented about one-third of the entire company). Tim, armed with lots of lists, set the meeting in motion:

"Okay, folks. Let's gather around and go through the details."

An hour later, the white boards were full of feature and defect lists that needed attention. No firm decisions had been made as to which of these the team should work on, but there was certainly a lot of healthy discussion. Over a month had gone by, and he knew it was time to get closure. The combined team met, and as Tim went over his notes, the team struggled at deciding what features to focus on.

Jody stated, "We need competitive features this year, or we're quickly going to lose our market share." Sam and Jeff, who seemed to always represent a united front, stated, "Those features would be nice, but we have some long-term defects that are making our lives miserable." Jody retorted, "Who ever heard of error-free software? We need more features!"

Sam then stated, "Well, what about our commitment to quality? It would be nice if we put our money where our mouth is." Tim, who had momentarily lost control of the meeting, proclaimed, "Look, we're all in this together. There must be a way to gain consensus with our decisions here."

Jody blew up: "I am so frustrated that I almost feel at the mercy of 12 people. We've been meeting for over two hours, and we can't ever decide on *anything*! I thought I had authority to make project decisions? It's *my* product and *I'm* responsible!" She stormed out of the meeting.

All eyes fell on Tim, the engineering manager. No one, including Tim, was quite sure who had the final decision. Based on company history of consensus-style management, there were still many meetings to go before any firm decisions would be made. Table 1.3 summarizes if this could have been avoided.

Table 1.3 Habit 3—Lessons Learned

What Went Wrong	What Should Have Happened
The engineering manager wasn't prepared with meeting agendas or how competing needs were to be prioritized.	When you chose to have a meeting, make sure to use standard meeting management techniques to make them into successful experiences. This may appear obvious, but failed meetings are generally due to poor planning.
Roles in this cross-functional organization weren't clear. In other words, who essentially makes the final decision? The engineering manager, the product manager, or the collective team?	The culture of the company can certainly dictate how decisions are made. Most software companies put the product manager in charge, since he is responsible overall for the success of a product. For many companies, the product manager has a role not unlike that of a brand manager at a consumer packaged goods (CPG) company—they have overall responsibility.
Consensus-style team management involved a lot of people, perhaps too many. Twelve people in multiple-product definition meetings can negatively impact the overall successful outcome of any meeting.	If you can reach consensus—great! Better still, the leader should gather cross-functional feedback but perform the act of prioritization of all of that information outside of meetings. A leader's role should be to transform all of the data into a meaningful project plan.

HABIT 4—PROMISING DEVELOPERS INCENTIVES

The medical devices company's software development team had been established for some time, with attributes that are fairly typical:

- Everyone enjoyed working with their teammates (it was almost a family).
- There was a strong team desire to build software the right way and to keep administrative activity at a distance.
- Everyone felt like they were working on the latest technology—learning is key to their culture.
- There has been a good history of high-quality releases, even if not always on time.
- There is general distrust of management of any kind.

The sales and marketing organizations believed that their own staff worked at 150%, and there was a perception that the software engineering teams didn't. *But you know those software guys....*

Do they really put in the effort? Do the financial results of the company really matter to them? Even the CEO noticed that there didn't seem to be any energy within the software development organization. All of this pressure was coming from all sides to Jason, the Director of Software Engineering. The development team was looking for strong leadership without compromising the set of attributes they valued most. Executive management and other organizations needed a higher sense of urgency from development.

Julie, the Sales VP, was pretty frustrated. "What other organization gets to come in whenever they want, scan the Internet all day, play online games, and then leave whenever they want? I don't see the accountability or dedication."

"And," Max, the company's CEO, chimed in, "it isn't unusual to walk by and see the engineers staring at e-mail or talking in the halls. I just don't see hands typin' on the keyboard writing code."

With the team focused on developing the largest software upgrade to date, Julie and Max had every right to be concerned. After talking on several occasions with Jason about the need for his team to pick up the pace, she convinced Max to institute similar motivational tools that she uses with her sales people. "Shoot, engineers are human, too. Right, Max?"

The concept that she had in mind was to offer incentives to get the engineers to become more inspired to kick in the extra hours, especially to finish this project. Max sat with Jason and made it sound like the idea just came to his head without any outside influence. "I know," stated Max, "let's motivate the programmers by dangling some killer incentives!" A little surprised, Jason wasn't sure what to say at first.

"This sure sounds like something Julie would instigate," thought Jason to himself.

"I suppose it could work. But it seems difficult to manage and could set a precedent that we won't want long term." Max wasn't amused. "We don't have much time left on our schedule, and we've got to do something. Paying a few dollars extra to guarantee on-time delivery is a small price to pay given the alternative. Jason, if we miss our delivery schedule, a delay could cost us millions in lost opportunities."

Max knew that the project was due August 15th. Jason still wasn't convinced. "The problem we'll have is setting expectations with the entire team. The strength of the team is quite frankly resting on the shoulders of two of my best engineers. I think if I can motivate them, then the rest will follow."

Max made it clear: "I have $50,000 I'm entrusting to you to get your organization motivated. Do as you see fit."

Jason met with both of his "select" engineers individually and gave the same speech to both. "Now, don't tell anyone about the loot. We need this product out quickly, and we need you to deliver."

Sumeer, one of the senior engineers, was pleasantly surprised and thought that additional compensation was a nice touch (especially since he was already wondering if he was underpaid by American standards). Peter, the lead software architect on the project, didn't really care one way or the other. "So, management feels like they have to pay us more to get things moving?

That figures." He gave it additional thought, reconsidered the situation, and believed that this was actually a real benefit. (He must have looked at his check book.) At that point, Jason informed them about the others in this special program. To some degree, the two of them felt as if they were one of the privileged few.

"Wow."

This was a good thing! Both engineers went back to their offices and pounded out code like they never had before. "I better buy a couple extra spare keyboards," mused Jason. "This one isn't going to last!"

Even though the scheduled deadline was in August, he knew that as long as it was delivered in Q3 the company would be more than happy.

But there was a catch. Jason told the executive staff at their next meeting what he had done to "engage" engineering. Julie sat back very pleased. The other VPs were a little surprised (especially since the CFO hadn't been told anything about this "transaction" from the CEO. Oh well—wasn't the first time.)

It was definitely upbeat, and this action could bring engineering into operating more like an incentive-based team, which the rest of the executive team wanted. Max asked, "Jason, what drop-dead date did you tell the other engineers?" Jason responded quite proudly, "I told them to deliver the project as soon as possible and that we needed this released in Q3."

Max was surprised. "Not *exactly* right. This has to be delivered with quality by August 15 or all bets are off! In other words, if this isn't shipped by then, the incentive is no longer going to be paid out."

"Oh, okay." (Did Sumeer and Peter know that?)

August 16th. . .

The team, despite heroics by the two key engineers, tried but didn't make its delivery date. The project was getting close to delivery but wasn't quite ready.

The executive team met. Max was noticeably upset. "This doesn't look good. Well, your team didn't make the date. There's no way we should give the team anything!"

Jason was frustrated. "I gotta give the team something—they put everything they have into getting this project released. We are *so* close."

Max stated, "This is against my better judgment, but I'll extend the date by another 30 days. Your team better come through."

"They will," responded Jason. "They will." Jason returned to his desk relieved—he didn't bother saying anything to the two engineers.

September 16th. . .

The product was not completed and, true to his word, Max withdrew the bonus incentive. Jason went to the two engineers and told them the news. Sumeer understood but was visually distressed—he was counting on the money. What will he tell his wife? He had worked many extra hours, and he hadn't seen much of his wife over the past few months. Peter, on the other hand, was not just distressed—he was angry. He had put in considerable overtime (OT) and was tired. Peter stormed out of the office right after Jason told him the news. He really had no idea that the incentive was tied to a specific scheduled date, since he had assumed that any time in Q3 would be acceptable.

Both engineers had put in an enormous effort to deliver the project. So had the rest of the team.

Meanwhile. . . A tired QA engineer whispered to another QA engineer. "Did you hear that software engineers were offered cash to stick to their schedule?"

"Yes, I heard. I assumed that it wasn't true. No way would one engineer be offered a special bonus without offering it to the rest of us."

"I think that's what happened. I think it's time to look for another job. This company isn't for me any longer."

"Couldn't agree more."

> Although *Merriam-Webster's Dictionary and Thesaurus* has some positive interpretations for the word *incentive*, there are two definitions that stand out: *inducement* and *bait*.

Avoid incentives at all costs—development is based on team dynamics, whereas sales is more individualized goal based! The negatives far outweigh the benefits:

- Incentives encourage project delivery shortcuts.
- Once you start incentives, you better be prepared to keep them as standard operations.
- Incentives discourage teammanship and encourage one-upmanship (politics).

As in the other habit examples, Table 1.4 summarizes what went wrong and what could have happened.

Table 1.4 Habit 4—Lessons Learned

What Went Wrong	What Should Have Happened
Management took extreme measures to change the behavior of the team by attempting to motivate the few. If there was ever a need to polarize a cross-functional software development team and to downgrade specific departments to second-class status, incentivize just the engineers!	The importance of transparency is critical to any organization, and this applies to rewards, benefits, and incentives. The word will get around (nobody's stupid, you know), and the secret will become common knowledge among the teammates. In this case, QA "got the message" that they weren't important (even if that wasn't the intention).

(continued)

What Went Wrong	What Should Have Happened
There was never any management discussion about alternatives to incentives. The easiest technique may have appeared to be "dangling money at the problem." As you can see, it had disastrous consequences.	If you must provide some additional benefits to key employees, reward and don't incentivize. There are better ways to motivate engineers. If money or incentives were actually a motivation for them, they'd most likely be in sales.
Engineering management didn't clarify the exact rules for the incentive with upper management, resulting in different expectations with the engineers that management wanted to motivate.	Any bonus program must have explicit guidelines that identify how the bonus is to be paid and how it is not. Keep in mind those risks that are out of the individual's control that could impact attaining the bonus.

HABIT 5—DELEGATING ABSOLUTE CONTROL TO A PROJECT MANAGER

Part of successfully running a company requires management to balance short-term and long-term needs. It is difficult for any organization to make those tradeoffs when there are so many tactical delivery requirements taking the lion's share of everyone's attention.

If a project appears to be getting behind or the true status is not exactly clear, it becomes anyone's guess when a project is going to be delivered. This lack of clarity has a direct impact on other organizations outside of development:

- Marketing and product management cannot properly plan a launch.
- Sales can't tell customers and partners when to expect the project delivery.
- Finance can't properly plan for revenue recognition.

> This dilemma isn't a curse of a specific software methodology: It applies equally well to traditional, structured waterfall projects as well as to those projects being developed using agile, iterative methodology.

The overall impact, however, is simple—the management of the organization isn't operating with any level of predictability.

There has traditionally been a division of power between the project manager and the software development manager roles (see Table 1.5).

Table 1.5 Comparing a Project Manager's Role with That of a Software Development Manager

If You Are a Project Manager	If You Are a Software Development Manager
How do you use your project management skills to facilitate development teams to deliver projects without resorting to command and control techniques?	How do you use your technical skills to ensure that your development teams deliver projects without you making the technical decisions? (Shoot, with all of the explainin' you have to do, you may as well do the work yourself, right?)

Let's get to the story... On a hot day in Research Triangle Park in North Carolina, Rowland was getting pretty frustrated with his development team. The engineers were a little too optimistic, the technical writers weren't getting any explanation as to how the product features worked, the customer support engineers were totally in the dark, and the quality assurance testers simply hated *everybody. Good times, good times...*

When Rowland asked anyone on the team what the status was for current projects in development, he'd invariably get a different response from different departments. "I don't trust I'm hearing the truth on any of our schedules."

As a reminder, PMI is the organization of project management professionals—the Project Management Institute.

Being a self-described technologist who abhorred needless process, he looked around and found a project manager, Lana. Lana had a very good reputation for being direct, objective, fair-minded, and most of all good at "rallying the troops." She was a project manager and a PMI member (but, dang it, she lost her PMI pin in the wash one day so she couldn't easily prove her PMI-ness in case she was asked).

Rowland couldn't wait to speak to her, and she was summoned into Rowland's office. He told her point blank, "I hereby appoint you Project Manager Emeritus (a PME, I guess)—find all of the dirt you can! I need your help to project manage our teams to success!"

"I'm good at it," she said. "I'll be glad to do it." Feeling a little giddy, she gave the oath that Rowland wanted to hear:

"As project manager of the Nerd Herd, I will find ALL DIRT, SO HELP ME GOD!"

She dove right in. Lana established herself as the team's project manager, set up meetings, and started tracking schedules. Yep, she was clearly in control. That's what a project manager should do, right?

One thing though... Issues came up, technical decisions had to be made, and she prided herself on getting things done without having to be knowledgeable about the products she was facilitating. She always had to defer to the team for product details, and her style was to get to consensus (which frustrated the product manager to no end), and that took time. Sometimes all it took was "one more question" to ask of the team in order to get to the right decision.

Table 1.6 is an example of what happened when Lana worked with the team and what could have happened if Rowland had had time to work with the team.

Table 1.6 How Additional Questions Can Influence Key Project Decisions

Project Manager's Dialog with the Team (What Took Place)	Software Engineering Manager's Dialog with the Team (What Could Have Taken Place)
Lana: So, we need to make a decision about getting our web services redefined. I've heard that we're missing a critical interface.	Rowland: We need to make a decision about getting our web services redefined. I've heard that we're missing a critical interface.
Engineers: Yep, in case the calling application needs to rollback a transaction in progress without impacting other transactions already queued.	Engineers: Yep, in case the calling application needs to rollback a transaction in progress without impacting other transactions already queued.
Lana: Great. Will that take long?	Rowland: Great. Will that take long?
Engineers: Nope, shouldn't take but a couple of days to implement.	Engineers: Nope, shouldn't take but a couple of days to implement.
Lana: Let's do it! I'll adjust the schedule by two days.	Rowland: Is the way that we're storing transactions suitable to handle this? I thought once a transaction was inserted, it couldn't be easily removed?
	Engineers: Now that you mention it, we should change out our method of storing transactions to use BEA's MessageQ instead of the round-robin engine we developed. Its recoverable messaging features are really what we've needed all along.
	Rowland: Changing out the queuing technology seems to require a considerable amount of work.
	Engineers: It is about a two month effort. If we don't do it now, we'll probably have to down the road. YOU make the decision!

(continued)

Project Manager's Dialog with the Team (What Took Place)	Software Engineering Manager's Dialog with the Team (What Could Have Taken Place)
	Rowland: I'm not happy about learning this at this point, but better now than trying to retrofit after we deploy. So we could do the quick two-day fix and limp by or correct it for the long term, and this is estimated at about two months of work? I'll meet with product management and will get back to you later today. Otherwise, keep on the track that you're on—we may not touch this capability until next release.

This example demonstrates that just knowing which questions to ask directly impacted making the right decision. In this case, what could have easily been interpreted as a two day impact was actually two months of work. The project manager must be aware of the technology (or have access to seasoned experts) in order to make the right project decisions. No wonder Microsoft's project managers are generally very technical with extensive software engineering background.

Even if the team had performed the two-day quick fix, eventually the engineers would have realized the necessity to replace the underlying technology. And that would have been too late in the project cycle, resulting in a major schedule impact. This caused Lana to rethink her ability to lead a highly technical project in the manner she was facilitating it. In fact, she was learning the hard way that managing schedules wasn't enough to keep a software project on track.

The team quickly lost confidence in Lana's ability to provide the necessary leadership and facilitation abilities.

Sob. "Everyone hates me, I'm just a glorified secretary, and I don't understand the technology I'm supposed to be monitoring."

Maintaining an objective project management role is a critical ingredient to the success of any software development organization, as long as this role is complemented with domain expertise to ensure that the right product and project decisions are made.

Otherwise, simply assigning a project manager will provide a schedule tracking function to the team and an "escalation agent" (otherwise affectionately known as "a tattle tail"). This is exactly why, to mitigate risk, the software development manager must have direct involvement in the project management activities throughout the software development life cycle (see Table 1.7). Could this have been avoided? *Possibly...*

Table 1.7 Habit 5—Lessons Learned

What Went Wrong	What Should Have Happened
The project manager had no mechanism in place to objectively evaluate technical dependencies and risks. In fact, without detailed technical or product knowledge, a project manager will tend to rely on team consensus to make decisions (which can be disastrous).	The importance of domain experts (whether technical or feature) is critical to making the right decisions during a software delivery. If the project manager doesn't have that background, it would be wise to enlist the help of an objective expert so that together the right decisions are made.
A critical requirement was not understood at the beginning of the project, and the team was under pressure to handle it during development (in this case, a decision to replace underlying technology after the project was already into implementation).	Upfront requirements analysis needs to be thoroughly reviewed by all parties on the team. An architect would have detected this specific example, whereas a project manager or the lead software engineer on the project may not have.

HABIT 6—TAKING TOO LONG TO NEGOTIATE FEATURE SETS AND SCHEDULES

For the sake of not inventing any more fictitious figures (or are they real?), I'll expand on the example presented in "Habit 3—Making Every Decision a Consensus Decision." Tim, the project manager, and Jody, the product manager, had together just finished successfully leading the delivery of a key project to market. The team was exhausted.

> A *postmortem* is analogous to an autopsy. Although the opportunity to learn from your mistakes is one of the purposes of a postmortem, sometimes there is simply no interest by the team to participate, can be easily mismanaged, and is viewed as "too little information, too late."
>
> What's worse is if the notes from a postmortem meeting are just stored away and never reviewed again.

Tim finished a postmortem meeting with the team by saying, "I'll summarize today's meeting, and then we should meet again and prioritize these requests into a project plan." The meeting disbanded, and Tim was the only one feeling good about the outcome. Tim tried to tackle getting the team to decide on feature sets for the next project release.

Tim decided to postpone further discussions on feature sets at that meeting. On the way out of the meeting, Jeff, in QA, told Sam, in Support, "This is going to take weeks if not months to get closure to define what we're going to do next." Because Tim had other priorities, meeting notes didn't circulate until two weeks later. By this time, the engineers were getting antsy and were looking for direction. Upper management was getting a little concerned as to how long these feature discussions were taking because each project had historically taken between nine and 12 months to release.

Several weeks later. . . Tim and Jody planned for another meeting with the team. This time, the feature set was identified based on both market demand and competitive offerings. What was missing was the development team's perspective of technical feasibility and the amount of effort it would take to document and test all of the requested features.

The information was well received by the team except that there had been no preparation to estimate the amount of effort it would take to accomplish these tasks. Both Tim and Jody were under considerable upper-management pressure to come up with schedules and costs. As an example, the engineers stated that they'd evaluate the information and come up with schedule estimates (time and resources). The list of feature requests was long, and Tim pleaded with the team: "You've got to size every feature so that I can estimate what we should plan for." (Tim was really thinking, "I don't trust them. I'll need to double or triple their estimates.")

Several weeks later. . . At the next meeting, the engineers came up with estimates for each of the features in the list. At that point, Jody picked which features she'd like, while Tim started adding up the level of effort with a calculator, as if the total effort was a simple matter of addition.

"Whoa, wait a moment," stated Howard, the lead engineer. "You can't just select from the list as if this is a buffet. If you had selected the first two features, you'd get the third for practically free. Since you wanted the first and third feature, the third is going to take about three times longer without the second feature. And that's just one example."

Jody was getting quite frustrated, "Okay, then we'll select the items, and you'll need to come back with the best level of effort and schedule."

"More analysis? Why don't you just tell me what you really want? What's more important—the schedule or the features?"

Jody and Tim piped out together, "Both."

Several more weeks later. . . After several meetings reminiscent of open warfare, the team finally decided on the schedule and feature set for their project. They lost three months of valuable time.

The product manager told the team, "I lost a lot." Howard, speaking for the rest of the team, boldly retorted, "Why weren't you reasonable to begin with? If you had been, we'd have had the schedule agreed to three weeks ago."

Table 1.8 summarizes what went wrong with this particular habit and what should have happened.

Table 1.8 Habit 6—Lessons Learned

What Went Wrong	What Should Have Happened
There was an unnecessary gap between the completion of a project and the start of the next one.	It is always a good idea to minimize down time by planning the next project before the previous project has been delivered. An agile-style software development places great importance on the planning phases of a project. By working in parallel, highly iterative techniques can reduce gaps of unproductive time, reduce project costs, and improve employee morale.
The staff needed work to do while management decided how to plan for the next project version.	In an *InDesign Magazine* interview, the senior product manager of the Adobe CS3 team stated they were so successful because work commenced on baseline feature requests and must-fix defects, while management was negotiating major new feature sets with the team. This approach shows continual forward motion and maximizes the effectiveness of the team.
The clash between project and product management with the rest of the team resulted in anger and distrust.	Rather than take months to negotiate project plans, make the effort collaborative and a well-understood number-one priority to address. In other words, lock everyone up together to get the next major project upgrade feature set and schedule defined. Let's simply get it done—you have too many stakeholders waiting for project commencement to take place.

HABIT 7—IGNORING A PROCESS IN ORDER TO RELEASE QUICKLY

The never-ending battle between development and product management can become really heated when you enter into a project development cycle. Whereas developers may be looking at attaining the next interim milestone, a product manager can only be thinking, "I know using a process is important, but we have no time for it. Process just gets in the way and introduces too much bureaucracy. We need to be nimble."

Somewhere in the industry journals, Robert, one of the company's most experienced product managers, remembered reading about self-managed teams who had released early because they bypassed all standard process. "Say, isn't that what agile methodology is all about?" claimed Robert with some degree of authority.

"Nope," Katie, the engineering lead on Robert's project, responded. You see, Katie had been leading development teams for some time, so she knew exactly how to begin every response to anyone in product management (with a negative—in fact, she had a list of negatives that she'd cycle through: "no," "nah," "are you kidding?," "nope," "over my dead body," and so on).

"You've got the terminology all wrong," Katie said. "What you really want is for us to ignore all planning and cross-checking in order to deliver this faster than planned. My experience assumes that working without process will result in a hodgepodge mess."

"I don't think so," claimed Robert. "My friend is VP of sales at an Oakland software startup. His company appears to be able to respond to the market with products faster than we do. They have no need for project management, and on one project, their engineering lead indicated it would take six months to complete. They decided to skip all process, and they apparently delivered it in four months. Everyone, including the development staff, was happy with the results. I've talked this over with our executive staff, and they're also supporting a change in how we deliver projects to market."

"Okay, I'll go along with it," Katie said. "Guess I have no choice in the matter."

So the project started out on good footing. To everyone's delight, there were no lengthy status meetings (yea!), but there were lots of e-mails flying back and forth between the teammates, since that was their chosen means of communication. Although it was difficult to determine the true status of exactly how complete the project was, progress seemed a lot better than in the past. Robert and the entire sales force were very pleased. How did sales know? Robert "accidentally" leaked a status e-mail to the sales team saying, "Without any process slowing us down, look what our guys can accomplish—we're right on track!"

Because there were few meetings and there was no regimented process, the team became very feature-driven. Katie knew to ask the question, "When are you all completing the quick analysis report? Can I see it?" Robert took the opportunity, by way of unplanned water cooler conversations, to ask for some additional features or modify ones that were being developed.

These special requests were making the product better, and the engineers were excited because they were building a killer application. Oftentimes, Katie would send an e-mail to the entire development team if there was a change to the original project scope. *But sometimes she forgot. . . .*

Sandra, recognized as the best QA tester on the team, complained to a senior executive who stopped her in the hall to ask how the project was going: "I don't know what to test, the specs keep on changing." Another engineer on the team overheard the conversation and couldn't wait to put in his feedback: "We shoulda spent the time designing up front. Now, it seems like we're designing and redesigning on the fly."

A few weeks later. . . Due to the growing frustration among team members, Robert and Katie got the team together to discuss the situation. The technique of "winging it" had become a disaster. There were fundamental performance issues, quality was in shambles, and with all the new features introduced during development, no one had planned for any form of a migration plan for existing customers.

"Argggh, we've got to reset expectations and start over," proclaimed Robert. "Perhaps *some* of the work can be salvaged."

Could this have been avoided? *Possibly.* . . Table 1.9 shows what went wrong and what should have taken place.

Table 1.9 Habit 7—Lessons Learned

What Went Wrong	What Should Have Happened
An overall perception is that a software company should be able torely on the brains of engineers, andthey'll somehow release cool and neat stuff.	There's an old adage that says, "An organization with a process (in fact, *any* process) will always run better than *without* one." Whenever you have more than one individual on a team, you have the opportunity to mis-communicate, which can result in a number of miscues.

BREAKING BAD HABITS

This concludes the seven deadly habits. These stories may appear fictional to some readers, but to most of us, these are all too real. The opportunity we, as software leaders, need to master is how to blend in just enough project management to work with creative teams that prefer to be less managed and more agile.

We as project managers need to understand how to use our process facilitation skills and tools to aid agile software development teams so that projects can be delivered on time with quality.

BIBILOGRAPHY

Yes, each chapter has its own bibliography! This one is rather small but here it is.

Blatner, David. "InPerson: Chad Siegel." *InDesign Magazine*, April–May 2007 (51–53).

2 Organizational Spring Cleaning

Welcome to your new nightmare—I mean *opportunity*! So, you're now in charge of a software development team—congratulations! Chances are you've earned the right to lead fellow software developers, build a new team, or have been placed in a position to turn around an existing team. Your boss has probably expressed confidence and high hopes for your success. No doubt you've walked into a situation that needs a major overhaul.

Unfortunately, your boss can't seem to find much time to help guide you. In addition, there isn't any notable training or courses available on software department turnaround techniques (let alone software leadership techniques). There's already the "show me what you've got" pressure building from upper management and the "prove you are better than the last guy" evil eyes from the developers themselves.

In fact, let's add fuel to the fire:

You have just 90 days to turn this organization around!

If you are taking over a new responsibility as a project manager (or software manager) *and* you don't have a lot of time to prove yourself, this chapter is definitely for you.

ACTION PLAN

There's nothing like a well-designed plan of action. You're committing considerable energy, expense, and time to build up a well-oiled software development machine, so you might as well diagram how you're going to do it (see Figure 2.1).

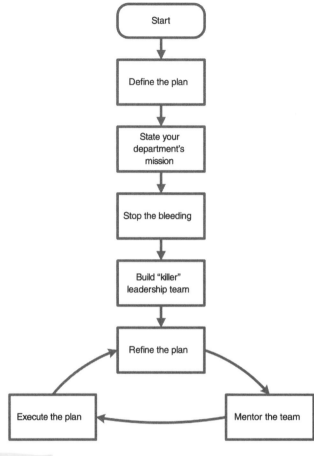

FIGURE 2.1
Steps in taking over a software organization.

Let's go through each step in the process:

- **Define the plan:** The first step is to lay out the plan that makes sense for your software organization.
- **State your department's mission:** To establish your role and help unify the organization, you'll need to agree to a department mission. This step is important because key decisions need to reinforce adherence to the mission.
- **Stop the bleeding:** Chances are your organization has been (and still is) in trouble—there's at least one major problem to solve. Examples of disastrous problems include product quality issues, employee attrition, or the handling of an unproductive (or ineffective) software team. You've got to address these issues fast.

■ **Build a "killer" leadership team:** There's nothing like surrounding yourself with an organizational structure and people who are trustworthy, dedicated, and can establish a track record of on-time project delivery. (Notice the use of the word "leadership" and not "management.")

Finally, you continuously cycle through a series of three substeps:

1. **Refine the plan:** Companies and organizations must build long-term value (sometimes referred to as "built to last") by creating plans and being flexible enough to recognize that change will occur. Over time, these plans will need to be refined and modified.
2. **Mentor the team:** Once you have assembled your "killer" leadership team, don't leave them unattended or the killer team becomes the "who's on first?" team. Coaching, mentoring, and most important, unifying the team are your most critical jobs.
3. **Execute the plan:** You'll need guideposts and a process to ensure that risks are minimized and that the schedule can be accomplished.

BEST PRACTICE To lead a successful action plan, you must prepare, prepare, and prepare.

It is not enough that everyone *understands* the plan—make sure everyone *buys into* the plan. The fastest way to fail with executing an accelerated action plan is to not put the time into *preparation*. You'll want to make sure that these steps flow easily but don't look like they are contrived.

You may have noticed the first Best Practice rule. This book is chock full of them because the goal of this book is to teach PMBOK best practice fundamentals to software practitioners.

DEFINE THE PLAN

> Make your plans attainable. Establish reasonable plans and get your team used to *committing* to a plan and *succeeding* on a plan.

You can help your team retain this plan by keeping it simple and visual. Detailed, wordy plans are simply not going to be read by everyone, and if it takes you 20 pages to describe the plan, the intent will most likely be lost in translation. The flow chart used in Figure 2.1 is an example of a simple visual graphic that communicates the plan.

FIGURE 2.2
Communicating the plan status.

Although it may appear repetitious, you should constantly reinforce this by communicating the plan and successes to date. Using the plan as an example, if you are currently in the State Your Department's Mission stage, make sure everyone knows that progress is being made. (For instance, the Define the Plan box in Figure 2.2 is checked off as completed.) Seeing progress, no matter how small, is motivating to your team and to organizations outside of development.

LEAD WITH A DEPARTMENT MISSION

It takes some effort to simplify any message regarding your organization's purpose—and your team needs a clear goal.

Let's first start with your company. There is some reason that your company is in business, right? There has got to be some value that separates it from all other competitors. Your department's mission should reinforce your company's goal and vision.

> Simply put, a mission statement should clearly indicate the organization's purpose, the business you're in, and the main objectives that will accomplish its mission. A mission concentrates on the *present*, a vision focuses on the *future*.

A mission should satisfy the following tests:

- Easy to recite
- Agreed upon by key constituents, including executives, employees, investors, and customers
- Long-lasting to withstand changing technology and customer needs
- Gives the customer a sense of comfort
- A motivator for employees

Take a moment and write down what your department's mission statement should be:

_____

_____

_____

Still not sure where to begin? If you've ever been involved with brainstorming sessions to come up with a mission statement, the result is invariably some long-winded, hyped up, multiple-paragraph mission statement that might make sense to the management team (who created it) but becomes useless to employees. Too often, mission statements have been

- A futile exercise without much reasoning other than possibly team-building.
- Too complicated and wordy.
- No follow-through with reinforcement of that mission.

Even though Wal-Mart isn't a software company, let's look at its corporate mission statement published on the web site, www.walmart.com. Wal-Mart's mission has always been based on three basic beliefs:

- Respect for the individual
- Service to our customers
- Strive for excellence

Does Wal-Mart's mission pass the mission test?

- **Easy to recite?** Yep, three simple concepts and simple to understand.
- **Agreed upon by key constituents, including executives, employees, investors, and customers?** Of course, hard to think that any of these folks would disagree.
- **Long-lasting to withstand changing technology and customer needs?** Sam Walton built Wal-Mart on these three revolutionary philosophies of excellence when he founded the company in 1962.
- **Gives the customer a sense of comfort?** Notice that the mission doesn't include anything about profits. Customers apparently feel great about doing business with Wal-Mart, since revenue growth has been nothing short of spectacular.
- **A motivator for employees?** There is no doubt that if you could see the Wal-Mart employees at company headquarters conducting business (I have!), you'd agree that this is one motivated bunch!

How has this mission helped Wal-Mart? Tremendous revenue growth—so much growth that it has even surpassed IBM in revenues. Customer retention? Unbelievable—if you haven't visited a Wal-Mart lately, please do. Racks filled with products and lots of customers down every aisle. Low prices have one thing to do with it, but K-Mart offered low prices, too (prior to their downfall in late 2001). Back in the 1990s, I was amazed at the then "catch phrase" posted everywhere: "What have you done for your customer lately?"

Powerful. Customer value, customer service, and a fun place to shop—all reinforced by Wal-Mart's employees who, by the way, are not exactly being paid competitive, top wages.

How is that possible? Do you get the same excitement walking throughout your company's building?

Hmmm. . . Does your company's mission statement pass the tests? Do you even know your company's mission statement?

*Oh, oh. . .*Okay, let's concentrate on creating your organization's mission statement with your team.

> Rather than use the services of corporate identity consultants, this is a fantastic team building exercise for you to lead as long as you don't let mission statement definition drag on for days and days.

Our department's mission is as follows:

_____

_____

_____

Validation:

1. Is it easy to recite? (Circle) Yes No
2. Is it agreed upon by key constituents? (Circle) Yes No
3. Will it last technically and service customer needs? (Circle) Yes No
4. Will the mission give your customers comfort? (Circle) Yes No
5. Will your staff interpret your mission as a motivator? (Circle) Yes No

Still struggling a little? Or is your staff not exactly cooperating? Creating a mission statement with your team can be a challenge. You can always count on a software department to be composed of strong-willed, opinionated developers who (A) like to argue, (B) distrust management (hey, that's *you!*), (C) are non-committal, and (D) believe that technology excellence usually has a higher importance than company business issues.

BEST PRACTICE Use a cross-functional team of managers and individual contributors to help you define your organization's mission statement.

Here's a decent mission statement:

Development's mission is to keep on the leading edge of technology in order to produce software products that our customers want.

The mission is certainly simple and easy to recite. However, the "leading edge of technology" part may not resonate with customers or your Sales organization. It is also too ambiguous. Here's another one:

Development's mission is to create an environment that fosters creativity and delivery of application software that satisfies market demands. In order to maximize our efforts, we'll be the leader in providing web services technology solutions.

The second example is not as simple nor is it easy to recite. Even though this goal could excite developers, it is not long lasting, especially in mentioning a specific technology like "web services." An example that most clearly communicates an immediate mission (goal) of a software development organization could be something like this:

Our department's mission is to deliver on-time, quality enterprise-wide software that provides a sustainable benefit to the healthcare industry.

Does your department's mission pass the test?

- **Easy to recite?** Sure, this statement would look good on a plaque.
- **Agreed upon by key constituents, including executives, employees, investors, and customers?** Your company's VP of Sales and CFO would be ecstatic with the "on-time" part, which usually implies an additional benefit: under budget. This mission could easily be printed in an annual report. Watch out—price could possibly rise with this kind of mission!
- **Long lasting to withstand changing technology and customer needs?** Even with your organization's delivery mechanism, changing from shrink-wrap to Internet and to web services—the same mission holds.
- **Gives the customer a sense of comfort?** Your customers would certainly appreciate the commitment to "quality," which means they will receive a product that works as expected.
- **Motivator to employees?** Couldn't get much simpler—your staff will probably test you to ensure that key decisions you make actually support this mission.

A mission provides the foundation that bonds the organization to a common purpose or objective.

There's another benefit you may not have considered. Having a clear goal can help in the hiring process, especially since a prospective new hire may be motivated to join a company that has a mission that implies the department (and the company) has a bright future.

STOP THE BLEEDING

It is time to go into immediate action.

BEST PRACTICE Never openly dismiss or discredit the prior leadership of the organization you've taken over.

Getting organized demonstrates to everyone that software development prefers to operate in a "controlled sense of urgency" mode rather than an "always late, random quality, and unorganized" mode of operation:

- **Listen to employees:** Your first action must be to meet with every employee (and possibly contractors). Take notes as you talk and don't make it appear that you're "fishin' for dirt" or have a hidden agenda. Get this done quickly! Listen and don't commit to specific actions you can't deliver on.
- **Listen to your peer organizations:** Don't forget to listen to leaders of other organizations you are dependent on or who are dependent on your organization. No doubt, they will have lots of opinions. Get their feedback on what is working well and what your department could improve on.
- **Communicate frequently:** Give a quick summary of the steps you are taking at staff meetings of your peers. Rather than have lots of meetings, why not consider producing a simple e-mail newsletter to distribute to your team weekly and meet with everyone in your department every other week?
- **Reorganize if required with a temporary organization:** If you find that your development's structure is simply not working, restructure the organization as a temporary measure.

One organization I joined had a tough situation where 60% of the staff were contractors. Three-quarters of the team reported to one manager, and some folks didn't really know who they reported to. No kidding!

Communicate that your time is available for impromptu feedback but that changes are going to happen quickly.

CREATING A SENSE OF URGENCY

Why should there be a sense of urgency? Chances are the dysfunctional nature of the organization you've inherited has evolved over a long time. You don't want to take the same amount of time to undo it. According to Hammer and Champy's book *Reengineering the Corporation*:

> . . . stretching it over a long time period extends the discomfort. People will become impatient, confused, and distracted. They will conclude that reengineering is another bogus program, and the effort will fall apart.

Time is critical—once you use it, there's no way to get it back. Since the majority of your waking hours are going to be tied up either *doing* your job or *thinking about* your job, take this simple quiz. How do you spend your time at work? Check one box per question: N is almost never (less than 10%), S is sometimes (between 10% and 50%), and F is frequently (greater than 50%).

> Don't check all Fs—this would imply that you spend the majority of your time on every activity, which isn't possible. If you averaged all four answers, they should be somewhere in the middle.

		N	S	F
1	In meetings			
2	Reacting to quality, schedule, or customer issues			
3	Technical, career, or performance coaching			
4	Planning (strategy, tactics, etc.)			

The following chart may be representative of your time allocation, especially if you are in a situation where there are considerable "fires" to put out:

		N	S	F
1	In meetings			✓
2	Reacting to quality, schedule, or customer issues			✓
3	Technical, career, or performance coaching	✓		
4	Planning (strategy, tactics, etc.)	✓		

If you want to promote a culture of nonstop meetings (with hardly any available time for work to be performed) then, by all means, spend 80% of the day in meetings. If you think that reacting to quality, schedule, and customer issues shows a real attention to what the company requires, then great!

Do you really want to be in catch-up mode forever? How would you like your time to be spent? Here's an example of what might be better:

		N	S	F
1	In meetings	✓		
2	Reacting to quality, schedule, or customer issues		✓	
3	Technical, career, or performance coaching			✓
4	Planning (strategy, tactics, etc.)		✓	

This shows a decent balance where coaching and mentoring take a good part of your time followed by planning and reacting to typical issues like quality, schedule, or customers. Lastly, meetings are least significant, which means you can make yourself available for the other three activities.

How do you get there? If you analyze how you are spending your time and what the gap is to get it to the right balance, you and your team will be happier. It is vital that you put your efforts on the most important stuff. Make sure that your boss and your team know what you are doing. If the company culture is too meeting-bound, chances are you are going to upset a few people when you don't accept meeting notices.

Making Time Management Everyone's Priority

Overall, time management is a huge issue, and your job is to ensure that you are optimizing everyone's time (and not just your own). We oftentimes inundate the team to perform unnecessary detailed analysis and reports, create a team culture consumed with e-mails, and invoke too many long-winded meetings.

NOTE

If there is *any* hint that the team wastes even one hour per day,[1] get the team together and collectively agree to eliminate these time wasters.

One of the most obvious improvements is to discuss the utter distraction of developers keeping their e-mail window in front of them all day. If you right now walk around your office, I bet you'll see that the majority of your staff have Microsoft Outlook (or some other equivalent e-mail application) up in full view. Why not set ground rules that e-mail should be checked only three or four times a day? And if there is an emergency, rather than send an e-mail, the best action is to get out of your chair and talk to the impacted individuals or even, heaven forbid, pick up the phone.

According to Jonathan Spira of Basex, Inc., *Time* magazine's study of office productivity, and those who make a living based on intellect and subject matter information rather than manual labor (also known as *knowledge workers*):

- Interrupts consume about 28%, or a little over two hours, of a knowledge worker's day.
- Knowledge workers spend only 11 minutes on any task before being interrupted.
- After an unscheduled interruption, it takes between 20 to 25 minutes to get back to what you are doing.
- In 2006, there was an estimated $588 billion of wasted productivity in the U.S. alone due to interruptions.
- Knowledge workers can be their own worst enemy: 55% said that they responded immediately to an e-mail (while only 35% said they responded when convenient).

> In Tom DeMarco and Tim Lister's excellent book *Peopleware*, their research found that if an interruption takes five minutes, then at least another 15 minutes is required to get "back into the work flow."

If you are interested in learning about a total program to handle everyday work flow, productivity, and managing interruptions, read David Allen's *Getting Things Done*.

BUILDING A KILLER LEADERSHIP TEAM

Next up is to create an effective software development organization! There's no better feeling than to have a team that you can rely on to deliver "the goods." First, you need to align your organizational structure to the company's goals and needs.

---

[1] For a team of five, one hour per day of wasted individual time is the same as 12 man-days per month of lost team productivity. Can you afford that?

STABILIZE YOUR ORGANIZATION

BEST PRACTICE Don't be tempted to reorganize for the sake of asserting or establishing control.

Various events can trigger an organization's need to redesign its structure:

- A new company or division has been started.
- Your organization needs to grow (or shrink).
- You have assumed a new role and, under evaluation, the organization needs to change to be effective.
- Strategy or company direction has changed.
- External factors dictate your organization must adjust accordingly.
- The organization hasn't delivered the expected performance.

Understanding your company's core strategy is fundamental to aligning your organization to support it. For example, *every* company believes that they are customer-centric, but if the organizations are not properly aligned to give customers the support they need, then management is only paying lip service. *And employees are the first to figure that out.*

BUILDING A TEAM OF "DOERS"

Put together a key list of attributes you expect your managers to have in order to demonstrate order and leadership:

- **Planning skills:** Ability to look for risks, good planner, great follow-through.
- **Process skills:** Belief and ability to enforce a common process life cycle (even when upper management and employees fight it).
- **People skills:** Ability to listen, facilitate, and communicate effectively.
- **Technical skills:** Knowledge of the craft they lead, such as software programming.
- **Domain expertise:** Over and above the other attributes, knowing the details of the industry and the product line can be critical when you need to make the right product decisions.

> These first three skills (planning, process, and people) will be a consistent theme throughout this book.

You'll need a methodology to come to terms with the caliber of the staff and, if there is any doubt, put yourself in an acting manager role until you properly assess the talent. This is a good time, however, to "flatten" the organization if it is too hierarchical with too many layers of management. This usually implies that it is time-consuming to get any decisions made. In simple terms, you can use a simple spreadsheet to help evaluate your staff's skills:

	U	N	M	E	O	Notes
People						
Planning						
Process						
Technical						
Domain						

Legend:
U—Unacceptable
N—Needs improvement
M—Meets expectations
E—Exceeds expectations
O—Outstanding (close to godliness)

Individuals who score high (at least an M) with solid people, planning, and process skills tend to make better managers, while those who score high on the technical and domain skills tend to make better individual contributors. The best you can hope for is to build a leadership team that consists of individuals who demonstrate strong technical *and* managerial skills.

Assessing Your Talent

Let's fill out an example. Jonathon, new to the company as of a year ago, is responsible for one of your most important projects. You've received positive feedback about his technical and managerial abilities. It doesn't hurt that his teammates uniformly respect him. This is how you'd evaluate his abilities:

Jonathon	U	N	M	E	O	Notes
People			✓			Listens, respected by staff
Planning		✓				Consistently thinks before doing
Process			✓			Runs teams with good methodology
Technical				✓		Excellent programming skills
Domain		✓				Knows his product line

Marta, unlike Jonathon, has been with the company from the beginning. She's been through countless organizational changes and knows the products inside out. She can be blunt (to a fault) and tends to rush to a solution without thinking it through. Some projects have gone well for her, but others have had mixed results. Marta is confident that without her, the organization would crumble. *Sound all too familiar?* This is your assessment of Marta:

Marta	U	N	M	E	O	Notes
People		✓				Struggles with managing her team
Planning		✓				Reacts to fires every day
Process		✓				Has little time for any process
Technical			✓			Appears to know her stuff
Domain				✓		Definite value to the team

Sometimes strong domain knowledge can be misinterpreted as having solid technical skills—that is not always the case. In the case where someone is a domain expert and not an effective manager (even if they think they are), you have a couple of choices:

- **Retain (or promote) that individual as one of your "killer" leaders:** This could risk alienating the entire team and impact the changes you need to make, especially if her managerial skills are less than satisfactory.
- **Place the expert into a designer/advisor role:** This doesn't diminish her importance, but readily takes advantage of her subject matter expertise, allowing you to go forward to create the leadership team that has the proper attributes you'll need to be successful.

In Marta's case, she clearly can provide much needed domain expertise, even though her management skills (the first three attributes) aren't her strengths.

> Individuals with high product domain expertise and strong customer-facing acumen can be very helpful in a troubleshooter or business analyst role that could provide critical benefits to your organization (and to the customer).

If, on the other hand, Marta's assessment has at least one unacceptable rating, her assessment could be slightly different:

Marta	U	N	M	E	O	Notes
People	✓					Too political, outwardly jaded
Planning		✓				Reacts to fires every day
Process		✓				Has little time for any process
Technical				✓		Appears to know her stuff
Domain					✓	Perceived value to the team

Unless Marta can dramatically improve her people skills (which anyone in a team-oriented leadership position has to have), you may need to ask yourself the following: *Is she the right individual to retain in your organization going forward?* One thing is for certain—you will be scrutinized with the personnel decisions you make and how you back up those decisions with the impacted individual, the team, and HR. Given Marta's original assessment, you may wish to sit down and talk with her about the skills needing improvement (shown in the U and N columns). Most important, don't forget to highlight where the employee excels.

Identifying and communicating the gaps (both positive and negative) provides an objective way to show the employee where he stands. In Marta's case, her basic management skills (people, planning, and process) are below par, whereas her domain skills are exemplary.

You might be pleasantly surprised at the outcome of a candid discussion. Marta won't like what you're telling her, but if you've performed an objective assessment, she will most likely appreciate the candid feedback.

Always have a plan of action following an assessment discussion with an employee—do not leave them hanging and wondering "now what?"

Bringing in Known Talent

We all have star players that we've worked with in the past, and we all have a tendency to want to overhaul an existing leadership team with trusted "friends and family."

Consider refraining from automatically bringing in your own stars—your team will most likely resent you (and the new hires) even if they have the right skills. Don't play favorites and definitely use an objective, fair hiring process to ensure that you are building your staff with the right people while getting buy-in with your existing staff.

Create a Discipline of Listening

Chances are you are inundated with decisions that are expected to be made quickly, and most likely you are being bombarded with opinions and suggestions. Your initial inclination may be to make quick, authoritative decisions—all of us have fallen victim to quick decision making (and sometimes that is absolutely necessary).

However, there is another approach, called "listening gray," popularized by Steven Sample, the president of USC, in his fascinating book entitled *The Contrarian's Guide to Leadership*:

> But contrarian leaders know it is better to listen first and talk later.

Sample goes on to explain his concept of *gray* (maintaining contradictory perspectives):

> The essence of thinking gray is this: Don't form an opinion about an important matter until you've heard all the relevant facts. F. Scott Fitzgerald once described something similar when he observed that the test of a first-rate mind is the ability to hold two opposing thoughts at the same time while still retaining the ability to function.

Remember Rowland's dialog with engineers in "Habit 5—Delegating Absolute Control to a Project Manager" from Chapter 1? In addition to asking the right questions, it was critical that he listened to all of their options before making a decision.

Consider the consequences of rushing into a decision prematurely:

- **You don't listen:** Software issues tend to be rather complicated in scope. Failure to understand *all* of the issues may result in the wrong decision being made. And if you get in the habit of making rash, uninformed decisions, you will quickly gain the reputation as a bull-headed, non-team player. Is this what you want?
- **Decisions don't rely on facts:** There's nothing like flip-flopping by reversing a decision after it has already been made because you learned the complete story after you made your decision. This doesn't raise anyone's confidence in your ability to make the correct decision—especially with software engineers.
- **You don't value teams:** Your team assumes that you are going to ask the right questions with the right audience. Jumping to a quick decision without the right level of buy-in may be perceived as your modus operandi (MO)—you don't want that.

Your Approach

How you approach your new role can impact the desired outcome (both positive or negative). Coming across too aggressively (like a lion) will most certainly alienate the organization, and coming across too cautiously (like a mouse) will rarely earn the respect of the organization or of your senior management. Whatever approach (or style) you choose, keep the following in mind:

1. Keep your approach simple—your job is already too complex as it is.
2. Make yourself visible, listen, constantly communicate, and ensure that you get key decisions bought into (hint: avoid lots of meetings).
3. Delegate and follow through with everything you said you would do.
4. Repeat the preceding steps (and *never* skip step 2).

As General James Longstreet recalled about General Robert E. Lee in the American Civil War:

> Lee was seen almost daily riding over his lines, making suggestions to working parties, and encouraging their efforts. . . . Above all, they soon began to look eagerly for his daily rides, his pleasing yet commanding presence, and the energy he displayed in speeding their labors.

Respect is not guaranteed by title alone. Anything you can do to gain that respect by balancing decision making and listening skills should go a long way toward building long-term respect with your managers and your teams. So, if nothing else, don't lock yourself up in your office—make yourself visible.

Keeping an Optimistic Outlook

As you are rebuilding the effectiveness of your organization, there are, most likely, product deliveries expected to be made. And, as long as there are customers wanting features, you'll face continual stress. To add to the pressure, it won't take long before your boss expects you to make significant inroads to drive the team as well as improving their morale and commitment.

One QA director told me that "I never get closure—as soon as we release something, there's always more requests and more projects needed. There's no time to ever feel good in this industry." *Yep.*

The same QA director was excited to perform a survey with everyone in the software development organization in order to get feedback on morale and quality issues that permeated the organization at that time. He was a trained auditor, and establishing a baseline was an important start toward eventual improvement. Possibly a good idea; however, it was like adding fuel to a smoldering fire. My response was, "Everyone already knows that morale is horrible, and the fact that we have to update customers weekly with emergency product updates is a clear signal that we've got significant quality issues. No, the team doesn't need to be reminded just how bad it is."

You'd be surprised how much more effective a smile is rather than a frown. A joke here or there can really ease the daily tension—and *everyone* on your team knows the stress you're put under to turn around current situations.

Dress for Success

Cliché, isn't it? You bet it is! Stepping up to a new opportunity where respect is an important ingredient of your success implies that you should dress as if you deserve that respect. According to *Dogbert*:

> Ask yourself if you would take advice on birth control from a guy wearing, let's say, a John Deere hat. I don't think so. Wear impressive clothes. This will be the primary source of your respect, if any, for the remainder of your career.

COMPLETING THE PLAN

Did you notice in Figure 2.1 that there is a Start but no End point? That's because your role is to continually look for ways to improve your department's operation. *Continuous improvement* is cyclical and never completes—by its very definition.

Each of these three steps must be carefully balanced, each with a different focus: planning, people, and process (see Figure 2.3).

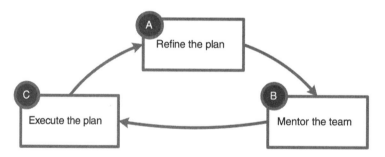

FIGURE 2.3
A. Planning focus, **B.** People focus, and **C.** Process focus.

- **Refine the plan:** Adjust the original plan as you learn more about the business, your teams, your products, and your customers. Not tweaking the plan will definitely be an alert to your staff that you are inflexible.
- **Mentor the team:** Take every opportunity to coach your staff at every level on how to make better, more timely, well-informed decisions, and on being decisive while getting buy-in (this *isn't* contradictory).

■   **Execute the plan:** The following is one of the most overused (and universally hated) of all phrases in PMBOK:

Plan the work, then *work* the plan.

There is, however, some merit to this catchy jingle. You need to establish credibility by being clear on what you and your team need to do. Then, just do it!

What may not be obvious is that one of the benefits of continuous improvement is the identification of what *not* to do. Some key habits should fall out naturally as you refine your plans, mentor your teams, and execute your plan (see Figure 2.4).

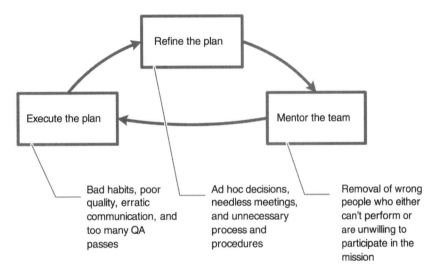

FIGURE 2.4
Removal of unwanted behavior and results with continuous improvement.

Clearly, this sequence of steps is designed to improve performance over time. This is a topic of many leadership books where the leadership team is never satisfied and is bent on continuous improvement.

These improvements can be created as goals for each software development leader and a key element of his annual review. As the outstanding *Built to Last* book states, "Nordstrom [a major U.S. retailer] created an environment where people can never stop trying to improve."

What else is interesting about this never-ending continuous improvement cycle? Anyone in a leadership role needs to master the balance between planning, people, and process—following project management procedures isn't nearly enough. (This balance is discussed in more detail in Chapter 3, "Relating PMBOK Best Practices to Software Development.")

There should be a point (and perhaps not quite a bell-ringing milestone) where the organization settles down under your leadership and facilitation. This "spring cleaning" action plan is designed to be temporary, and the continuous improvement steps outlined here should evolve into a more comprehensive, measurable program, which is a theme throughout the remainder of the book (especially in Chapter 8, "Deliver On-Time, Quality Products").

WARNING SIGNS THAT YOU'RE AT THE WRONG COMPANY

What if everything at your company isn't quite right? There may be instances out of your direct control where you must decide that you just can't win at your role:

- **"Ship it anyway!" attitude:** What if you and your team believe that a product isn't ready for general availability (GA), yet you're forced to ship? Once in a while, this added pressure can be expected. If this becomes a habit, you're in a no-win situation. What's worse, your customer loses every time because of quality issues that are more likely to appear due to shipping a product before it is ready.
- **Company prospects aren't what you were told:** Granted, the Internet dot-com crash in the early 2000s woke up everyone in the business to the fact that "just because you can build it doesn't mean that customers will come." Having the financial viability with enough cash to withstand tough times is a necessity for any company to be able to survive. Expecting that you'll be able to instantly turn ineffective teams into productive machines or inject quality into a company with no quality culture or quality infrastructure is a real warning sign. This is especially true if you are given a short amount of time to do it (like 90 days).

  With that information, you should be able to make a well-informed decision. When you interview at a company, ensure that you talk to a balanced set of interviewers from different departments—especially Sales and Finance. Better yet, is it possible for you to talk to a customer or a reseller? If there are only a few customers available to talk with, that speaks volumes. (In other words, the company may suffer from severe customer satisfaction issues, and you wouldn't know it just by interviewing with employees.) Regardless, use whatever means you can to ensure that the organization has a chance to succeed and that prospects are good.
- **Your boss micromanages you and your team:** Although typically an indication that your boss believes you and your staff are incompetent, your boss' inability to "let go" of the technical details and management decisions should be a huge signal that there's something wrong. In addition, a boss' meddling creates a company culture of distrust and frustration among the software development staff.

  As an aside, *Dogbert* gives horrid advice to the micromanagement boss on how to alienate your entire team: "Tell yourself that every one of your employees is dumber than a Yugo full of anvils."

- **Your company is a sweat shop:** Any company needs to have a change of pace once in a while or serious burnout will occur. As Ed Yourdon so eloquently summarizes in *Death March*, if there is a constant requirement for development to "burn the midnight oil," chances are extremely high that your Sales and/or Marketing machine is in need of a major overhaul. What is the connection with Sales and Marketing? It is Ed's opinion that if their overcommitment far exceeds a development team's ability to deliver, the work culture will demand a constant push.

  Alternatively, the want ad for a senior software engineer at Alien Skin Software (yes, that's their name!) states their philosophy clearly: "We have a sane work/life balance. It is rare that we work over 40 hours per week." (This is also from the company whose motto is "We will never wear suits.")

> We've all seen situations where there is a push for long hours to develop something that results in few financial rewards (revenue) for the company. For example, it costs $25,000 worth of labor for what ends up being only $10,000 of added revenue.

- **Financial policies are too aggressive:** As exciting as it can be for engineers to work for a company where innovation and great projects rule, if the company's finances maximize short-term results while jeopardizing the future, look out. For example, defining technical feasibility *a day before* you deliver a project to market is a clear indication of a healthy company budget (this, under FAS 86 accounting rules as defined by the Financial Accounting Standards Board, represents how much development expense is capitalized). If, on the other hand, the majority of all developments are capitalized because technical feasibility is defined from the moment the product is conceptualized, there may be an underlying financial instability with the company.

  In a Georgia Institute of Technology survey conducted by Dr. Charles Mulford, only 61 companies (out of 207 surveyed) capitalized software development costs. Of those who did defer software costs, about one-third capitalized at a high rate, with the highest at 82%. This survey found that, depending on how aggressive the capitalization was, operating cash flow was adjusted as much as 159%!

  Much like a never-ending credit card, deferred expenses mount up year after year to the point that your future budgets are restricted to include actual costs (payroll, equipment, travel, and so on) *and* growing chunks of deferred development costs. *Extreme use of capitalization is definitely not a good sign of future company financial health!*

- **You find yourself in constant conflict with your boss or peers:** Face it—if you believe you are being set up to fail and you find yourself starting to record conflicts with management, it isn't healthy. Possessing these secret notes (that you might want to pull out one day) won't make much of a difference anyway (except perhaps make you appear to have an ax to grind).

According to articles like those found regularly in the *Wall Street Journal*, if any or all of the preceding points are a consistent theme for your company, and you have, after your best efforts, concluded that this is a demoralizing environment, then you should "shift into gear with an *aggressive* job hunt."

BIBLIOGRAPHY

Adams, Scott. *Dogbert's Top Secret Management Handbook*. New York: HarperCollins Publishers, 1996.

Allen, David. *Getting Things Done: The Art of Stress-Free Productivity*. New York: Penguin Group, 1991.

Collins, James and Jerry I. Porras. *Built to Last: Successful Habits of Visionary Companies*. New York: HarperCollins Publishers, 1997.

Demarco, Tom and Timothy Lister. *Peopleware: Productive Projects and Teams, 2nd Edition*. New York: Dorsett House, 1999.

Galbraith, Jay, Diane Downey, and Amy Kates. *Designing Dynamic Organizations: A Hands-on Guide for Leaders at All Levels*. New York: AMACON, 2001.

Hammer, Michael and James Champy. *Reengineering the Corporation: A Manifesto for Business Revolution*. New York: HarperCollins Publishers, 1993.

Mulford, Dr. Charles W. *Capitalization of Software Development Costs: A Survey of Accounting Practices in the Software Industry*. Atlanta, GA: Georgia Tech College of Management, 2006.

Kaltman, Al. *The Genius of Robert E. Lee*. Paramus, NJ: Prentice Hall, 2000.

Sample, Steven B. *The Contrarian's Guide to Leadership*. New York: Jossey-Bass, 2002.

Spira, Jonathan B. "The High Cost of Interruptions." *KMWorld*, Sept. 1, 2005 (www.kmworld.com/Articles/News/News-Analysis/The-high-cost-of-interruptions-14543.aspx).

3 Relating PMBOK Best Practices to Software Development

For those of you familiar with project management best practices, this chapter will be a refresher. However, for those who aren't practicing project managers, it is a good idea for every software development leader to become familiar with project management fundamentals. If you have purchased the PMBOK reference book (*Project Management Body of Knowledge*) and are wondering how this gigantic thing actually relates to modern-day software development . . . *join the club!*

So far, I've covered the seven habits (Chapter 1) and presented a CliffsNotes rendition of what to do when you take over a new organization or role (Chapter 2). This chapter establishes how the PMBOK guide provides the project management basis to lead and facilitate the horrors, excitement, and lunacy of dealing with software projects and teams.

MAKING SENSE OUT OF PMI AND PMBOK

The Project Management Institute (PMI) is a worldwide body of experts who have defined and continue to develop the professionalism of the project management craft. To belong to the PMI, you have to pay an application fee to get access to a wealth of project management information. The networking and educational opportunities are more than worth the annual fee. PMI provides local support, and if you are located near a PMI chapter, you should consider joining that, too. More information can be viewed at www.pmi.org. To maintain PMI membership, you are required to pay renewal membership fees once a year. So, don't let your PMI membership lapse!

You've probably seen project managers with "PMP" after their name. PMI provides distinguished credentials, such as the ever-popular Project Management Professional certification. All of PMI's credentials require that you have the necessary background, based on a combination of educational and real-world project management experience.

> Don't despair if you don't have a project manager title when you apply for the PMP certification. Software management background should count as project management experience.

The PMP, for instance, requires you to apply and be totally familiar with the PMBOK, which is updated every four years and is now in its fourth revision. (I'll cover key topics primarily in the Fourth Edition and reference differences with the Third Edition where it makes sense.) As a prerequisite, you'll have to attend a week-long intensive PMBOK training class presented by an accredited PMI Registered Education Provider (REP). You'll also have to pass a comprehensive test with PMI.

How do you maintain PMP status? If you are going to spend the time, energy (you'll need lots of Red Bull), and money to become PMP certified, consider what you'll have to do to *retain* your PMP credentials. PMI has minimum requirements defined through the PMI Continuing Certification Requirements (CCR) program:

- PMP renewal is required every three years. In 2008, PMI changed the renewal date from the end of the calendar year to the anniversary date you earned your PMP certification. (This should make it easier for PMI to handle the renewals throughout the year instead of all at once.)
- You must complete a certification renewal application.
- You must accrue a minimum of 60 Professional Development Units (PDUs), where one PDU is equivalent to one hour of approved project management–related class instruction.
- Reaffirm that you'll abide by PMI's Code of Professional Conduct. (You must take this seriously, by the way.)

For those of you who have attended PMBOK-intensive training classes and received your PMP certification, congratulations! *Not an easy thing to do!*

BEST PRACTICE Every software manager and project manager should be PMP certified.

Becoming PMP certified implies that you have a solid understanding of the PMBOK, which is somewhat analogous to an accountant becoming a CPA (but probably not as difficult). When you review the material, you may come to the conclusion that the material within the PMBOK is only applicable for building an airplane on a multi-year project and that it doesn't appear to have anything remotely to do with software. *I'm going to prove that wrong.*

DEFINING PROJECTS, PROGRAMS, AND PRODUCTS

Most of us use the terms *projects*, *programs*, and *products* interchangeably. PMBOK treats them as distinct things (and so should you).

PROJECTS AND PROJECT MANAGEMENT

What is a *project*? A project has the following characteristics:

- It has a specific purpose and creates a unique product, service, or specific result.
- It has a definite start and finish, thus it is temporary (and temporary can be days or months).
- It can be progressively elaborated—this is where, contrary to the ugly impact of scope creep, the work is developed in steps and adjusts as more is learned. Does this remind you of agile methodology?

> *Agile (iterative) development* methodology "timeboxes" iterative development, encouraging rapid and flexible response to change.

The project team seldom outlives the project. Once the project completes, the team is typically disbanded and the team members reassigned. A project can optionally be divided into components (or *subprojects*) if necessary, as shown in Figure 3.1.

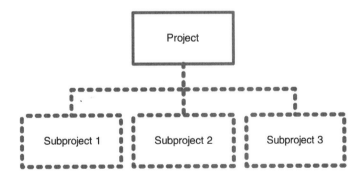

FIGURE 3.1
Projects can consist of optional subprojects.

An example of a project is an enterprise workflow software application that provides the overall user experience, and a subproject (to that project) may be an outsourced "workflow engine" being developed offshore. Another subproject could be the documentation and internationalization for the entire project being performed in parallel (to the development of the workflow software application project and the workflow engine subproject) at a site in the hills of Austin, Texas (see Figure 3.2).

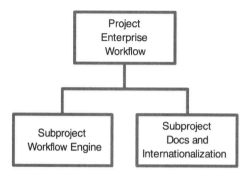

FIGURE 3.2
Project with two subprojects.

Subprojects can be unique based on a specific phase of the project, certain skills of the staff performing the work, specialized technology, or contracted to an external enterprise.

Project management is the application of knowledge, skills, tools, and techniques to project activities to meet project requirements. Alternatively, project management is used to denote the organization comprised of project managers. Ultimately, the project manager is responsible overall for accomplishing project objectives.

> A *project management system* is the set of tools, techniques, methodologies, resources, and procedures used to manage a project.

PROGRAMS

A *program* is a collection of related projects that are managed in a coordinated way (see Figure 3.3).

Managing projects as a program should result in much better benefits than if you managed projects separately. *Program management* provides more centralized management to achieve a program's strategic objectives and benefits. Adobe, a major software developer, most likely set up Adobe Creative Suite as a program composed of projects (for example, Photoshop, Illustrator, and InDesign) to be released together from geographically distributed software development teams.

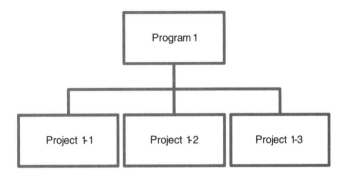

FIGURE 3.3
Program consisting of three related projects.

PRODUCTS

The term *product* was just mentioned. A product is different than a project or a program since it refers to the service or deliverable that is created as a result of a project.

> Adobe's FrameMaker software application is a product, and FrameMaker 8 is a project.

PUTTING IT ALL TOGETHER—THE PORTFOLIO

There is one more term that relates to projects, programs, and products: the *portfolio*. A portfolio is a collection of programs or projects that may or may not be related to each other but support an overall company vision (see Figure 3.4).

> A portfolio should support a three to five year strategic business objective of the company or business unit.

A portfolio typically has defined criteria that determine which programs or projects are to be included. Using the example of Adobe again, a product portfolio may include the entire line of graphical projects (with the Adobe CS4 family of projects being one of Adobe's many programs). Although a new sketch application product might fit in the CS4 portfolio, an object-oriented database product might not fit at all.

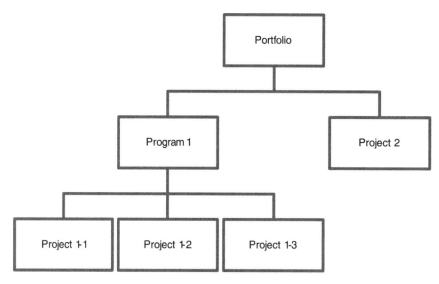

FIGURE 3.4
Portfolio management.

Portfolio management is the application of systematic management over projects and programs. Due to the importance of managing an entire portfolio of products or services, senior management generally takes on the responsibility for overall portfolio management.

STAKEHOLDERS

Every project has *stakeholders*, no matter how small or large the project is. Stakeholders are individuals who

- are actively involved with the project.
- have interests that may be impacted by the project.
- may exert influence over the project.

A project manager must know who the stakeholders are: the project manager (you!), program managers, portfolio managers, executive staff, customers, functional managers, the team performing the work, sponsors (who provide financial resources), and influencers.

Stakeholders generally want to be in the communications loop. For that very reason, the project manager should be aware of stakeholder influence on organizational culture and project outcomes. *Positive stakeholders* are those who benefit by ensuring that a project succeeds. *Negative stakeholders*, on the other hand, are often overlooked and can bring a project to an unsuccessful close.

BEST PRACTICE Keep stakeholders informed with the level of detail that makes sense and in the appropriate form they'll understand.

An example of a positive stakeholder is a customer who benefits by providing beta feedback and will eventually see the results of a successful software project's outcome (since they will most likely use the product or service). An example of a negative stakeholder would be a team member whose position is being transitioned offshore. If not properly managed, that individual could cause immeasurable delays by not cooperating in the transfer of knowledge to the outsourcing company.

The burden of communication and setting proper stakeholder expectations belongs to you (as if you didn't need *more* to think about). How you communicate project status with stakeholders is almost as important as the information itself. If you communicate to an investor every detail about the project, you've probably lost their interest. If you communicate superficial information to a QA manager, it will undoubtedly be interpreted as "suspiciously" insufficient.

In addition, a stakeholder's influence and role may change during the course of the project's life cycle. For example, a project sponsor from the finance department (the folks with the loot) may only be involved at project initiation (for example, "Here's the funds and the authority to assign resources to kick this project off—spend it wisely") and at project closure (for example, "WHAT did it cost?").

A power struggle could result in project failure if stakeholders have differing goals. Using Habit 1 in Chapter 1 as an example, the team doing the work (key stakeholders) believes it is most important to release a quality product, whereas the executive staff (another key stakeholder) believe that shipping in *any* state by a certain schedule (whether it is ready or not) should be the goal.

The project manager should always stick to the facts when communicating to stakeholders—too much optimism or pessimism doesn't help anyone. This will be covered in more detail in Chapter 8, "Deliver On-Time, Quality Products."

THE LIFE CYCLE

The term *life cycle* describes the duration of time from the point when a project is conceived with a business plan to the time of eventual release or termination. A life cycle has special meaning in project management and exists on several levels.

DEFINING LIFE CYCLES

A *product life cycle* refers to the overall life of the product from initiation (typically with a business plan) to when it is eventually mothballed (or, more appropriately, taken out of service). The *project life cycle* refers to the process of completing the work for a specific project. In Figure 3.5, there are four project life cycles (within the overall product life cycle).

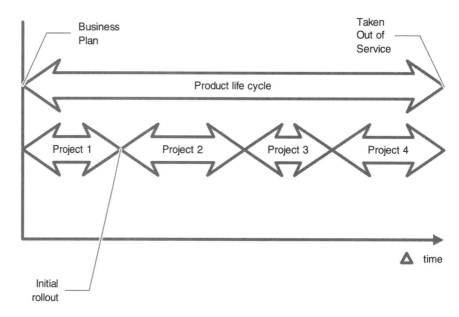

FIGURE 3.5
Product and project life cycles.

INTRODUCTION TO PROCESS GROUPS

The *project management life cycle* refers to the application of five process groups (Initiating, Planning, Executing, Monitoring and Controlling, and Closing) throughout the entire project. Each of these groups is stock full of processes:

- **Initiating:** Defines and authorizes the project or a project phase. (See the following Note for an explanation of what a project phase is.) The Project Charter and Project Scope documents are key deliverables.
- **Planning:** Defines objectives and plans necessary to achieve project (or project phase) objectives. Among other outputs, a Project Management Plan is the document that describes how the plan of the project will be implemented and monitored. (In case you were wondering, this used to be called the Project Plan in earlier versions of PMBOK.)
- **Executing:** Integrates people and other resources to carry out the plans defined in the Planning process group for the project or project phase. This is when software code is flyin', and the Executing processes create work results.
- **Monitoring and Controlling:** In order to meet project (or project phase) objectives, measure and monitor progress. This is necessary to identify gaps from the plan defined in the Planning process group. Quality control and all forms of change management represent the team's focus. If the Executing process group part was done well, this should be a breeze! Otherwise, Monitoring and Controlling results in corrective actions.

- **Closing:** Formally accept the product, service, or result—bring the project or project phase to an orderly end. If successful, this is the time for a big release celebration!

> The project manager must determine with the team what processes are appropriate in order to meet the project goals.

The diagram in Figure 3.6 starts with the Initiating process group and proceeds clockwise in a cycle. Once the results are met, exit with the Closing process group.

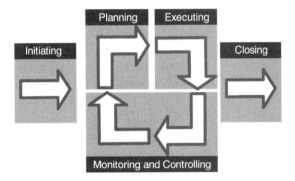

FIGURE 3.6
Process groups.

Process groups have specific dependencies on each other that assume processes within each group are executed in sequence even though they can, and most usually do, overlap in actual practice.

A project phase is simply a large project subdivided into multiple phases. The creation of a software prototype would be a good example of a project phase. If that prototype is successful, then the project would enter into the next project phase (for example, the build phase).

All of the appropriate process groups are expected to take place for each project phase. The same holds true for subprojects of a project (refer to Figure 3.1).

The project manager is responsible for ensuring that logical decision making and best practices rule in determining which processes are applicable to a project (even if it means not strictly adhering to PMBOK).

PLAN, DO, <SOMETHING>, AND ACT

That's an odd heading. Project management processes are usually regarded as well-defined *inputs* and *outputs* (collectively called *interfaces* throughout the PMBOK). In actuality, these processes usually overlap and interact in ways that aren't easily documented. An underlying concept behind the project management processes is the Plan-Do-Check-Act (PDCA) cycle popularized by W. Edwards Deming (see Figure 3.7).

The Third and Fourth Editions of PMBOK barely mention the PDCA concept, even though it is highly regarded as an important continuous process improvement model. To complicate matters, PDCA has been changed to PDSA (S for Study). This topic is revisited in Chapters 7 and 8.

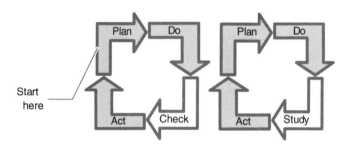

FIGURE 3.7
Plan-Do-Check-Act (PDCA) and Plan-Do-Study-Act (PDSA).

PMBOK makes an ill-fated visual attempt to show how either PDCA or PDSA relates to process groups. Figure 3.8 shows how it is really supposed to be visualized.

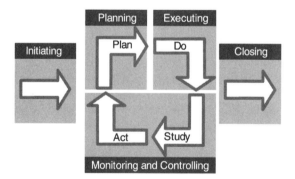

FIGURE 3.8
PDSA and PMBOK process groups.

Table 3.1 summarizes how similar PDSA is to PMBOK process groups. You'll notice that the Initiating and Closing process groups aren't explicitly defined in PDSA.

Table 3.1 How PDSA Relates to PMBOK Process Groups

PDCA	Process Group	Common Definition
	Initiating	Starts the process cycles
Plan	Planning	Establishes objectives and processes
Do	Executing	Implements processes (does the work)
Status	Monitoring and Controlling	Tracks and applies improvements prior to beginning of the next implementation
Act	Monitoring and Controlling	
	Closing	Ends the process cycles

One final important note: The Monitoring and Controlling process group, as you'll learn later, defines processes that can span all of the processes (not just Check and Act), as shown in Figure 3.9. You would think that Study and Act tasks would correspond just to processes that monitor and control. That is not strictly the case because just about everything you do from the very beginning to the end of a project has some sort of monitor and control activity.

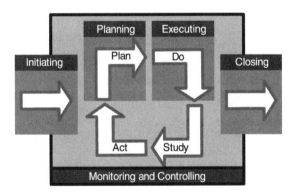

FIGURE 3.9
The Monitoring & Controlling processes can touch everything.

Organizing for Success

How your software development organization is structured has a direct impact on how effectively the team operates.

ORGANIZATIONAL STRUCTURE

> Isn't *development* the same thing as *engineering*? Throughout this book, development represents the cross-functional team that includes engineering, testing, and documentation. Engineering is part of development and consists of software programmers who design and create the software products.

PMBOK classifies all sorts of organizational structures based on how project management functions are handled with the team. You may choose not to use any of them in your organization, but it is worth understanding the definition of each structure (along with their pros and cons).

Organizations are an interesting, generally troubling, phenomenon, *especially* in the software world. Most of us don't really care about them and oftentimes see the negative in any structure imposed by management. Some organizations never really change their structure, while others seem to thrive on continual reorganizations in hopes that a new structure will act as a catalyst that will "magically" produce different results.

An organizational structure should reinforce and make it easy for project work to be accomplished. Alternatively, an ill-conceived, non-functional organizational structure can have a negative benefit by impeding project work from getting accomplished.

Organizational structure dynamics are getting more complicated as businesses adjust to a rapidly changing world economy that is demanding more efficiency with less staff. The book *Designing Dynamic Organizations* illustrates the impact of organizational structure on a company. For example, a survey of the 441 fastest growing U.S. businesses in 2000 found that 32% of CEOs believed that their inability to manage or reorganize their business would be an impediment to growth. That was a drastic change from 10% with the same survey just seven years earlier in 1993 (see Figure 3.10).

Would you expect the trend to continue into the future? There is no single positive organizational structure, since the choice of a supportive organizational structure depends on a number of factors that are unique to your organizational culture:

- Shared values, beliefs, standards, and expectations (typically exemplified in the company's code of ethics)
- Policies and procedures
- Authority relationships (who has the power to make key project decisions?)
- Work ethic (are you running a sweat shop?)

BEST PRACTICE Select the organizational structure that supports successful project outcomes.

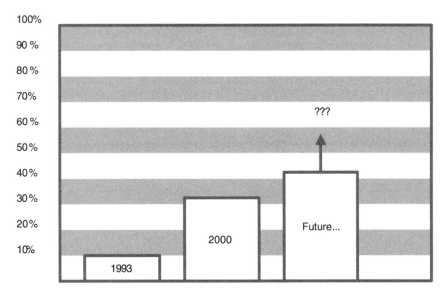

FIGURE 3.10
CEOs who believe that poor organizational structure impacts growth.

Knowing your company's culture and goals will help determine the organizational structure necessary for a specific project to be successful. You could assume that as long as you hire the right people, they'll figure it all out by themselves. *Wishful thinking.* As a leader, your responsibility is to structure the relationships so that your teams find it easy to collaborate, innovate, and achieve.

NOTE

Does your organization thrive on risk taking? A team proposing entrepreneur-like, aggressive projects will require a similar supporting organizational structure and thrive with equally aggressive stakeholders. This may require you, as a project manager, to be more of an agile facilitator than a rigid enforcer of project authority and control.

Within Amazon, for example, engineering teams thrive on self-empowered, small teams that derive assistance from other organizations that support delivery of their project to market. According to Amazon, if you can't feed the whole team with two pizzas, the team is too big. The project manager in this culture must be an excellent communicator and able to facilitate and influence within a dynamic, ever-changing organizational structure. (This gets especially complicated if other organizations don't see the need to cooperate in a timely manner.) So now you know where the term *two-pizza teams* came from!

According to the PMBOK, there are three types of organizational structures:

- **Functional:** Hierarchical structure based on specialty, with each employee typically reporting to a single boss.
- **Projectized:** Project-based structure where cross-functional skill sets are brought together for a project, with the team reporting to a project manager.
- **Matrix:** A blend between functional and projectized structures designed to be flexible to implement projects, resulting in individuals typically reporting to multiple bosses. PMBOK defines three variations to a matrix organizational structure.

> Run, don't walk, from those managers who mandate that teams must be an exact number of developers (usually an odd number like 5 or 7) in order to be successful.

Each structure has varying levels of project management control (see Figure 3.11).

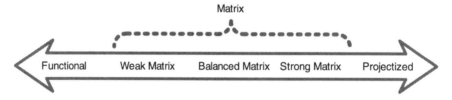

FIGURE 3.11
Project manager's authority based on organizational structures.

FUNCTIONAL ORGANIZATIONS

Functional organizations are derived from a more traditional, operational mindset where the organizational hierarchy presides over a specific project. Individuals are aligned together and managed by a single boss with typically the same skill set. For example, all technical writers would report to a single functional technical publications manager, while all software engineers would report to a software engineering manager.

Figure 3.12 shows how a functional organization could be structured with a cross-functional team of four developers (in light-shaded boxes) assigned to the project.

The functional managers (dark gray boxes) lead each of their respective organizations. Although this organizational chart shows a project manager (surrounded by dotted lines) assigned to the project, there may be no designated project manager, resulting in project management duties shared among functional managers. Functional organizations do not generally lend themselves to the needs of project management (see Table 3.2).

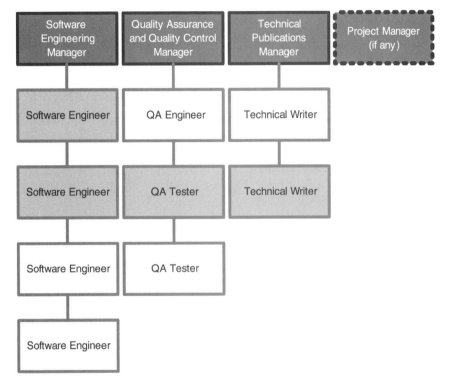

FIGURE 3.12
Project manager's authority in a functional organization structure.

Table 3.2 Strengths and Weaknesses of a Functional Organization

Strengths	Weaknesses
Simple reporting structure to grasp—only one boss to deal with.	Project manager has least amount of authority (refer to Figure 3.11), which is usually shared among projects on a part-time basis.
Organizational reporting structure remains intact even after completion of a project.	Difficult to focus resources on the project (resources are not always available).
	Not the most effective for agile projects—teams have more of an allegiance to their functional departments than to the project.

PROJECTIZED ORGANIZATIONS

Now to the other extreme. A projectized organization is often collocated and effectively works only for the project manager for the duration of the project. This structure effectively removes the specialized silos found in both functional and matrix organizations. A projectized organizational structure could be organized as shown in Figure 3.13.

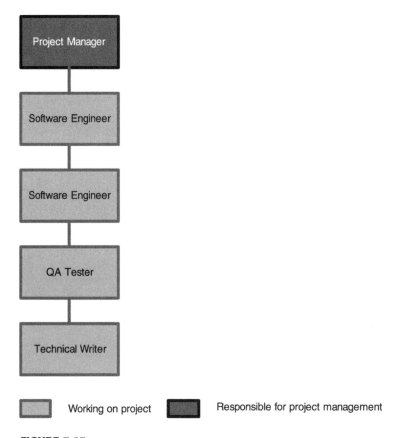

☐ Working on project   ■ Responsible for project management

FIGURE 3.13
Project manager's authority in a projectized organization structure.

Since the organization's resources are focused on project work, project managers usually enjoy a great deal of independence, control, and authority in order to make decisions quickly. Projectized organizations, as the name implies, lend themselves to the needs of project management (see Table 3.3).

Table 3.3 Strengths and Weaknesses of a Projectized Organization

Strengths	Weaknesses
Project manager has the most authority (refer to Figure 3.11) and is usually dedicated to the project.	At the end of a project, team members may not have positions to return to (or to go to).
Easiest to focus resources on the project (resources are readily available).	Resources can't be easily shared with other projects.
Teams consist of a variety of skills (good cross-functional mix).	
Best suited for agile projects—the team becomes a "family" for the duration of the project.	

MATRIX ORGANIZATIONS

Matrix organizations are a blend between functional and projectized structures where the team's leadership is shared between the project manager and the functional managers. PMBOK recognizes three types of matrix structures:

- Weak matrix
- Balanced matrix
- Strong matrix

The beauty behind matrix organizations is that they provide good cross-functional checks and balances between functional organizations and the project.

Weak Matrix Organization

A *project coordinator* can make some team decisions without getting the functional manager's approval. A *project expeditor* keeps track of the project status but has virtually no decision-making authority.

A weak matrix is basically a functional organization with the project manager acting as the project coordinator (or expeditor) instead of a project manager (see Figure 3.14).

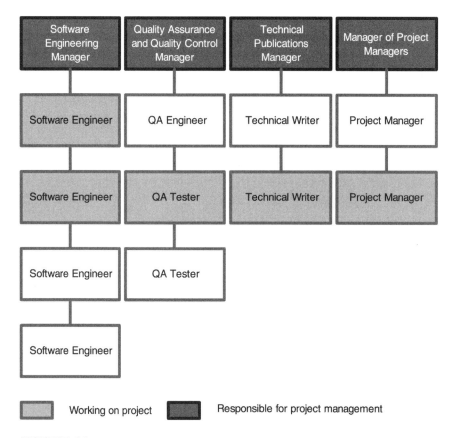

FIGURE 3.14
Project manager's authority in a weak matrix organization structure.

From the project manager's point of view, a weak matrix offers somewhat more benefit than a functional organizational structure (see Table 3.4).

Table 3.4 Strengths and Weaknesses of a Weak Matrix Organization

Strengths	Weaknesses
Simple reporting structure to grasp.	Project manager has minimal amount of authority whose time is usually shared among projects (part-time).
Organizational reporting structure remains intact even after completion of a project.	It is difficult to focus resources on the project, since resources are not always available.
Somewhat more effective for agile projects (where the team typically self-manages), the project manager coordinates team activities and expedites team needs.	

Balanced Matrix Organization

A balanced matrix is a weak matrix with a slight twist: a project manager runs team decisions past the functional managers (and vice versa). In this structure (see Figure 3.15), a project manager is recognized as an important part of a team's success while reporting into another functional organization (which could very well be another engineering department).

From the project manager's point of view, a balanced matrix offers more benefits than a weak matrix organizational structure (see Table 3.5).

Table 3.5 Strengths and Weaknesses of a Balanced Matrix Organization

Strengths	Weaknesses
Project manager shares authority with functional managers.	Project manager has some amount of authority and is usually full time to the project.
Can be effective for agile projects where the team self-manages while depending on leadership from both the project manager and functional managers.	Dual bosses can be confusing, so roles need to be clearly laid out for this structure to be successful—can be complicated at performance review time.
	Requires considerable amount of communication with the team and with functional managers.

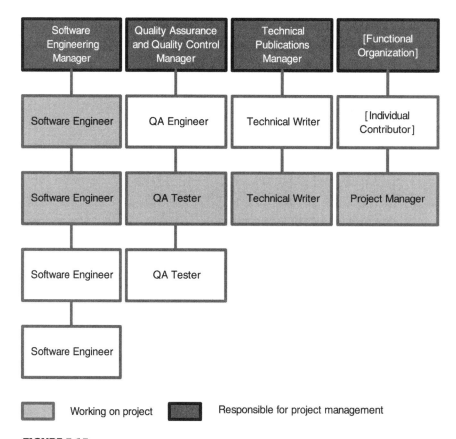

Working on project   Responsible for project management

FIGURE 3.15

Project manager's authority in a balanced matrix organization structure.

Strong Matrix Organization

A strong matrix has many of the same characteristics as a projectized organization where the project manager reports to a project management functional organization. Project management, however, has full access to resources in order to lead a project (see Figure 3.16).

The staff members still enjoy the benefit of being aligned to functional organizations (and so does the project manager). Since all members are somewhat dedicated to the project, a strong matrix organization lends itself more to agile methodology than the other matrix options (see Table 3.6).

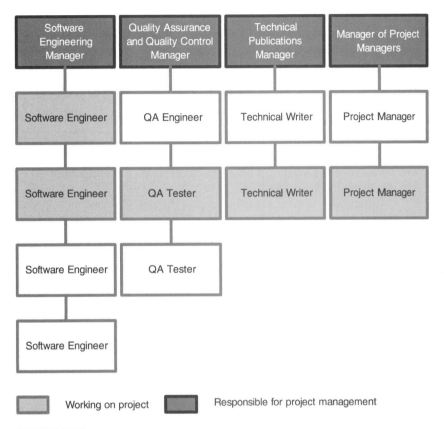

Working on project   Responsible for project management

FIGURE 3.16
Project manager's authority in a strong matrix organization structure.

Table 3.6 Strengths and Weaknesses of a Strong Matrix Organization

Strengths	Weaknesses
Project manager has more authority than functional managers (even though the team still reports to their own management).	Some difficulty to focus resources on the project (resources are assumed to be generally available).
The focus on the project is the most important activity.	This requires extensive communication with the team and with functional managers.
Organizational reporting structure remains intact even after completion of a project.	
Good compromise structure for an agile project.	

PMBOK recognizes two additional variations to these organizations: *projectized* (where project managers have a great deal of independence and authority) and *composite* (functional organizations with matrixed project management).

INTRODUCING THE FOUR PS (4PS)

As shown in Figure 3.17, the key ingredients of software development leadership success can be represented as a balance of *planning, process,* and *people* leadership in order to produce quality *products* (the fourth "P").

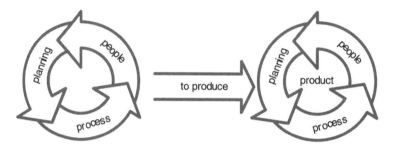

FIGURE 3.17
Balancing planning, process, and people to produce products (the Four Ps, or 4Ps).

In practice, each of these will blend into each other. For example, planning activities also involve both people and process. By balancing planning, process, and people, your organization should enjoy a long-term advantage, resulting in your department's goal being met (to produce quality products on time and under budget).

BEST PRACTICE Lead by carefully balancing planning, process, and people needs.

Using the sample mission in the section "Lead with a Department Mission" from Chapter 2 as a software organization matures, a software department's mission should be adjusted to stress the importance of this balance:

> By balancing planning, people, and process, we can achieve our mission to deliver quality healthcare software products on time and on budget.

BALANCING PLANNING NEEDS

Common planning activities you can perform are these:

- Creating project plans
- Working (and usually reworking) budgets
- Writing the "required" status reports

Planning usually implies meetings, and spending any amount of time in meetings should pay back in better planning. There are some potential negatives if planning is taken to extremes, especially if you spend most of your time behind closed doors in meetings:

- **Lack of credibility:** You could be viewed as a manager who develops great plans, but the sad truth is that few of your products reach the market on time.
- **Limited availability:** You may appear to be out of touch with your own development team! Does the comment "my manager is ALWAYS in meetings" sound familiar?

You may find that planning efforts you want to perform take a back seat to urgent people and process issues. When you do get around to plan, it may be too little, too late. On the other hand, if you spend the majority of your time on planning, you run the risk of having a great future mapped out, with little credibility established to get there.

BALANCING PROCESS NEEDS

Some common process activities you can perform include the following:

- Defining, monitoring, and controlling project processes
- Ensuring that quality is being designed in with everything the department does
- Tracking metrics to improve the efficiency of the development organization

As a leader, it is not enough to manage the process. As you become more of a manager of individuals and teams, there is less time available to keep your technical skills up to par. When asked to help us hire a director of engineering for our team, the recruiter responded to our job description, "How can you expect a software manager to still be technical?"

Yikes! The recruiter had a point, but unless the manager wants to be viewed as just an administrator, anyone leading or facilitating software developers has to be proficient in software development. Here are some hints that you've taken process to extremes:

- **Gestapo techniques:** Useless process monitoring can get in the way of crisp, cross-functional communications. An example is when your engineering leads are being interrogated twice a day for project status updates by an over-zealous project manager.
- **Software life cycle not being used:** The process life cycle is too cumbersome to administer, not comprehensible, or not consistent with what is really taking place. It isn't unusual when a software organization states that they have a software development process, but the teams aren't following it.

■ **Missing the big picture:** Spending too much effort on process-related mechanics (task attainment by a specific schedule) could result in missing obvious and not so obvious technical risks.

BALANCING PEOPLE NEEDS

Most managers want to be sure that their teams are satisfied with the operation of the department. Since there are only so many hours in the day, you may find that planning and process activities take a back seat to the constant stream of people-related issues.
Some key people activities are as follows:

■ Make sure that developers get the best assignments and that they are satisfied with their positions, work, and future prospects.
■ Efficiently use creative techniques to find and hire the best talent.
■ Frequently communicate both company and department information without burdening everyone's time with endless meetings and documentation.
■ Ensure that decisions have the buy-in of the team (and this *doesn't necessarily* mean consensus!).

Although these actions appear to be extremely positive, there are also some potential negatives if taken to an extreme:

■ **Decision indecision:** You are unable to make tough decisions that are necessary based on a concern that team morale will suffer.
■ **Contradictory perspectives:** Schedule attainment ("you need to release by a specific date") becomes de-emphasized within development ("don't worry what management is expecting, I know you guys are trying").
■ **Hiring based on fit and not skills:** Hiring of developers is generally based primarily on "culture fit" rather than "skills fit." (Remember "Habit 2—Hiring Someone Who Is Not Quite Qualified (but Who Everyone Likes)" in Chapter 1?)

BIBLIOGRAPHY

Deming, W. Edwards. *Out of the Crisis.* Cambridge, MA: MIT Press, 2000.

Galbraith, Jay, Diane Downey, and Amy Kates. *Designing Dynamic Organizations: A Hands-On Guide for Leaders at All Levels.* New York: AMACOM, 2001.

Greene, Jennifer and Andrew Stellman. *Head First PMP: A Brain-Friendly Guide to Passing the Project Management Professional Exam.* Sebastopol, CA: O'Reilly Media, 2007.

Johnson, Tony. *PMP Exam Success Series: Certification Exam Manual.* Carrollton, TX: Crosswind Project Management, 2006.

Larman, Craig. *Agile and Iterative Development: A Manager's Guide.* Boston: Pearson Education, 2004.

Project Management Institute, Inc. *A Guide to the Project Management Body of Knowledge: PMBOK Guide, 3rd Edition.* Newton Square, PA: Project Management Institute, 2004.

Project Management Institute, Inc. *A Guide to the Project Management Body of Knowledge: PMBOK Guide, 4th Edition.* Newton Square, PA: Project Management Institute, 2008.

Scott, Tom. "Two Pizza Teams." 20 Feb 2007 (http://derivadow.com/2007/02/20/two-pizza-teams).

Part 2 Planning

art 2 is focused on the planning part of your job. Not surprisingly, failure to put in the effort to plan usually ends up with results you didn't plan for—typically negative.

- **Chapter 4, "Run Development as a Business":** Running the software organization as a business requires leadership of overall project integration and controlling risks.
- **Chapter 5, "Partner with Product Management":** The importance of successfully partnering with product management.
- **Chapter 6, "Become Effective and Competitive":** Becoming effective (and competitive) by controlling costs and procurement (in other words, keeping to budget).

Out of PMBOK's five process groups, the Planning process group has by far the most numerous defined activities. Part 2, however, will not cover every one of those planning processes—they will be covered in their respective chapters throughout the book.

Planning is critical for any project. In addition to the obvious benefit of proper preparation, Planning process group processes are preventive in nature. The more time you spend anticipating issues, the more likely your project will be successful. Here's a key definition that will become a theme in the remaining chapters of this book:

> The jus' e'nuff process (a famous southern phrase) means efficient, plenty complete, useful, practical, non-redundant proactive stuff—perfect for agile software projects.

Don't laugh—this is serious! Many PMBOK concepts can be very confusing to the casual project management practitioner. So I'll focus on the "jus' e'nuff process," and if you need *more* than e'nuff, you can always resort to more process best practices found in the complete PMBOK reference.

4 Run Development as a Business

It is not typical to imagine the software development organization as an integral part of the operating business dynamics of a company. The common thought is that the other organizations are more concerned about the business: finance, sales, and marketing. Engineers are there to produce the product, but they are not exactly excited about their company's business dynamics. In fact, aren't they a little cynical?

Nothing could be further from the truth. The software development organization provides the fuel for your business to thrive, and for that reason, your role is to change the perception and your team's train of thought that software developers are different and want to be entertained rather than participate in any form of business planning. This chapter covers the following business-related planning activities:

- Integration planning that covers all phases of the overall project life cycle
- How to effectively manage risks throughout the project life cycle

WHY IS AGILE METHODOLOGY SO IMPORTANT?

We have a real conflict! PMI's PMBOK is the definitive project management reference guide. Digesting the details of the Third and Fourth Editions sure paints a picture of a thought-out structured set of rules. If you're in a leadership role, equipped with PMP certification (which implies that you know the ins and outs of PMBOK), and all around you there are projects and software developers that represent the antithesis of structure and control, what are *you* to do?

> The concepts of agile (and iterative) software development methodology will be covered in more detail in Part 3, "Process."

Since the commitment of this book is to apply PMBOK *practical* best practices to software development, and since software development has migrated rapidly to a more agile (iterative) methodology, is this really a "marriage of unlikely partners"?

- PMBOK provides the framework to successfully *project manage* teams and life cycle processes.
- Agile software development is the *methodology* that is used to develop software products.

According to the Agile Alliance's *Manifesto for Agile Software Development* (otherwise known as *The Agile Manifesto*), there are definitely biases as to what is important in order to successfully develop software (in fact, you could call it the art of software development):

- Individuals and interactions *over* processes and tools
- Working software *over* comprehensive documentation
- Customer collaboration *over* contract negotiation
- Responding to change *over* following a plan

Yet these preferred values appear to contradict the very teachings of PMBOK! *Or do they?* Before the discussion of how to apply PMBOK planning best practices with agile software development, a brief recap of the PMBOK process groups and knowledge areas is in order.

HOW PMBOK PROCESSES ARE ORGANIZED

There are five PMBOK process groups that should be used in every project (revisit the definitions in Chapter 3 if you need a refresher):

- **Initiating:** Define and authorize project to start.
- **Planning:** Define the project scope, objectives, and plan of action to ensure the project successfully meets a set of objectives.
- **Executing:** Perform the work.
- **Monitoring and Controlling:** Regularly measure, monitor, and regulate the progress of the work by identifying variances so that corrective action can take place.
- **Closing:** Formally finalize all activities so that the project comes to an orderly conclusion.

Each of these process groups has a distinct role in a project's life cycle, and since there are so many processes that can take place, PMBOK has grouped them into nine distinct categories called *knowledge areas*:

- **Integration:** Processes that unify all of the other knowledge areas across all process groups (starting at project initiation until project closure).
- **Scope:** Processes that ensure that the requirements, and only those requirements, are completed.
- **Time:** Processes necessary to complete all tasks in a timely manner.
- **Cost:** Processes for estimating, budgeting, and controlling all expenses so that the project can be completed within the approved budget.
- **Quality:** Processes that determine quality policies, objectives, and roles so that the project will satisfy customer expectations.
- **Human Resource:** Processes that organize, manage, and lead the project team individuals.
- **Communications:** Processes required to ensure timely and accurate gathering, publication, and communication of project information and actionable status.
- **Risk:** Processes that are designed to improve the possibility and impact of a positive project completion.
- **Procurement:** Processes that are used to purchase or acquire products or services from other sources outside the project team in order to complete the work.

IDENTIFYING PROCESSES BY KNOWLEDGE AREA

For all of the process groups, there are specific processes that take place in each knowledge area. In the Quality knowledge area, for example, there are typically no Initiating or Closing processes performed. And then there is the Integration knowledge area where processes are defined in every process group. (In fact, Integration is the *only* knowledge area that spans all process groups.) PMBOK expects that every project manager knows how each process works in every knowledge area.

By the way, this book uses lots of tables. A table is useful for keeping all of the many processes in some kind of order. Pages and pages of text simply don't register with most people. (This is also excellent advice for any project documentation you prepare to communicate to stakeholders.)

BEST PRACTICE One manager's advice I never forgot was, "if you ever want to present a complicated subject, use a table or diagram."

Processes in the Fourth PMBOK Edition

All of the PMBOK processes can be summarized as shown in Table 4.1.

Table 4.1 Processes in Each Knowledge Area (PMBOK 4th Edition)

	Project Management Process Groups				
		Implementation			
Knowledge Area	**Initiating**	**Planning**	**Executing**	**Monitoring & Controlling**	**Closing**
Project Integration Management	Develop Project Charter	Develop Project Management Plan	Direct and Manage Project Execution	Monitor and Control Project Work Perform Integrated Change Control	Close Project or Phase
Project Scope Management		Collect Requirements Define Scope Create WBS		Verify Scope Control Scope	
Project Time Management		Define Activities Sequence Activities Esimate Activity Resources Estimate Activity Durations Develop Schedule		Control Schedule	
Project Cost Management		Estimate Costs Determine Budget		Control Costs	
Project Quality Management		Plan Quality	Perform Quality Assurance	Perform Quality Control	
Project Human Resource Management		Develop Human Resource Plan	Acquire Project Team Develop Project Team Manage Project Team		

(continued)

Knowledge Area	Initiating	**Implementation**			
	Initiating	Planning	Executing	Monitoring & Controlling	Closing
Project Communications Management	Identify Stakeholders	Plan Communications	Distribute Information Manage Stakeholders Expectations	Report Performance	
Project Risk Management		Plan Risk Management Identify Risks Perform Qualitative Risk Analysis Perform Quantitative Risk Analysis Plan Risk Responses		Monitor and Control Risks	
Project Procurement Management		Plan Procurements	Conduct Procurements	Administer Procurements	Close Procurements

Even though this book concentrates on the most recent Fourth Edition, there are plenty of references to Third Edition material. This book is not a restatement of PMBOK. Instead, only the best practices and modifications of PMBOK that provide significant guidance for software development are documented. Not just *any* software development—*agile* (iterative) software development!

THE IMPORTANCE OF THE IMPLEMENTATION CYCLE

You may have noticed that there was a non-PMBOK term *Implementation* in the table column heading in Table 4.1. This *super* process basically encompasses the Planning, Execution, and Monitoring & Controlling processes first introduced in Chapter 3 in the section "Introduction to Process Groups."

After you initiate a project, the next step is to define the base foundation in the Planning process group. Once the overall plans are in place, you would perform the Execution and

Monitoring & Controlling processes, only to return again to update the Planning process group as you learn more (see Figure 4.1).

This "continual learning" approach is the cornerstone of agile and iterative software development.

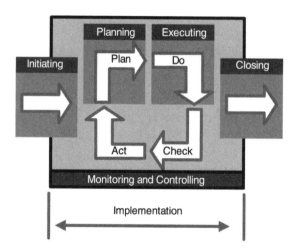

FIGURE 4.1
Overall implementation cycle.

This cycle is called *progressive elaboration*, and it continues until you enter the Closing process group's processes.

How Much Process Is Enough?

An over-zealous project manager might want to put the team through every process that PMBOK defines—whether the process is needed or not. I'll subscribe to a more practical approach—yep, you guessed it: the jus' e'nuff process approach. (See the introduction to Part 2, "Planning" for more information on this ridiculous but sensible concept.) In reality, you rarely need all of PMBOK's defined processes.

BEST PRACTICE Don't invest in a specific process when there is no use for that process.

Let's start with a simple exercise. Write down the basic processes or milestones you use on a typical project, along with who benefits (don't worry if it isn't an official PMBOK process):

Who Benefits?	Process (or Milestone)

Given a typical project, the project manager takes pride in putting together a very detailed weekly status report to distribute to stakeholders. In fact, this is a critical component of the Distribute Information process in the Project Communications Management knowledge area:

Who Benefits?	Process (or Milestone)
. . .	. . .
No one!	Distribute weekly status updates
. . .	. . .

And just as typical, nobody reads them!

Rather than stop communications all together, this lack of attention by your project's stakeholders may be due to a number of factors:

- The status report has too much information.
- The presentation style is not easily understandable.
- The status report has too little (and sometimes inaccurate) information.
- Weekly distribution is either too often or too infrequent to make it actionable by the team.
- The content may be missing the point, especially if your audience prefers to receive the highlights as an e-mail message and you submit Word novels.

If a process has no real significance to your stakeholders, it is better to modify how you're handling the process rather than put the team through unnecessary processes. You wouldn't put the team through detailed Project Human Resource Management processes for a simple software defect update project, would you? Of course not.

SUCCESS THROUGH INTEGRATION

The Project Integration Management knowledge area as defined by PMBOK acts as the glue that connects all the knowledge areas together.

OVERVIEW OF THE INTEGRATION KNOWLEDGE AREA

Integration processes are unique among the PMBOK knowledge areas because they span all five process groups, as shown in Table 4.2.

Table 4.2 Integration Management Knowledge Area Processes (PMBOK 4th Edition)

Project Management Process Groups				
	Implementation			
Initiating	**Planning**	**Executing**	**Monitoring & Controlling**	**Closing**
Develop Project Charter	Develop Project Management Plan	Direct and Manage Project Execution	Monitor and Control Project Work	Close Project or Phase
			Perform Integrated Change Control	

Integration ensures that the project has defined objectives and that these objectives are accomplished throughout a project's life cycle:

- Define and analyze the project's scope and requirements. (In other words, what is the project supposed to accomplish?)
- Transform project needs into a plan using structured approaches. (These approaches apply equally well to agile software projects!)
- Measure and monitor project status.
- Deliver a complete project that meets the original requirements.

So what is really going on during the overall Project Integration Management processes? Figure 4.2 summarizes it all.

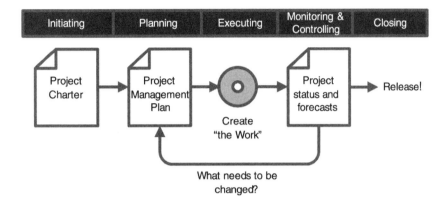

FIGURE 4.2
Overall Project Integration Management life cycle.

During a project life cycle, your integration role includes the following:

1. Create a clear and well-defined Project Charter.
2. Create a clear and well-defined Project Management Plan (usually composed of plans from other knowledge areas).
3. Lead the team that creates the product and/or services (the work).
4. Report and monitor project status and handle *when* (not *if*) changes occur in an organized fashion.
5. Iterate through step 2 and step 4 as needed, resulting in the release of the product and/or service offering.

> By the way, this set of steps represents the Implementation process cycle shown in Figure 4.1, which is a foundation of agile methodology.

Throughout this project management stuff, *expert judgment* may be the most important technique you can apply to ensure that all of the right inputs are considered in order to produce the right outputs. (You'll learn more about expert judgment throughout the rest of this chapter and the rest of this book.)

The impact of unclear project definition and lack of direction introduces significant project risk if Integration processes are not successfully performed.

Here's an example. Project code-named Jason ("no matter how hard you try to kill it, you can't!") was originally assumed to be designed for 32-bit targets. One of the engineers decided that 64-bit targets was just as important because his own development machine was running 64-bit Linux. Too bad QA didn't know about this decision, since their test machines were all configured for 32-bit Vista and XP. This misfire (or error in judgment) caused missed milestones and lots of angst within the team. This would be true in the Executing process as software engineers scramble to resolve unforeseen 64-bit anomalies throughout the source code.

Good idea in a perfect world? Yes. Ensuring source code is constructed in a way that isn't dependent on a specific data width (32-bit, 64-bit, and so on) represents good coding practice.

Bad idea in a practical world? Yes. It is still a 32-bit world! (This, of course, will change as the industry hungers for more and more computing power.) At the time, no customers were asking for 64-bit support. This phenomenon is called *gold plating*, where you give something more than what was expected, and it wasn't necessary or even needed.

BEST PRACTICE Avoid gold plating (and feature creep) at all costs.

INTEGRATION MANAGEMENT IN THE INITIATING PROCESS GROUP

There are two distinct processes to be performed during the Initiating phase.

- **Develop Project Charter:** The document that is used to formally authorize a project (or project phase) to commence.
- **Develop Preliminary Project Scope Statement:** The document that defines the characteristics and the boundaries of the project or project phase (Third PMBOK Edition only).

> From this point forward, a "project" refers to either a specific project or a "project phase" (a subproject within an overall project).

Develop the Project Charter

The Project Charter document clarifies the business need, project justification, and market (or customer) requirements, and describes the product and services to be delivered. There are many influences that can initiate a project, including the following:

- **Market demand:** The market you serve requires a new set of features (for example, all retailers have identified a standard XSLT to be used in processing B2B invoices between all retailers and their suppliers).
- **Business need:** There is a new revenue opportunity (for example, even though your company creates great products, your resellers need advanced technical training, implying that an instructional design project needs to be kicked off).
- **Technology advance:** A new technology innovation allows your company to leapfrog the competition (for example, the migration from fixed disk to NAND

flash memory has provided huge opportunities to downscale software solutions from PCs to handheld devices).

- **Legal requirement:** A legal or industry standard becomes a requirement to do business (for example, Sarbanes-Oxley, or SOX, requirements for financial reporting).
- **Social need:** Software provides real value by automating manual tasks that can have a huge impact on society. (For example, software can assist in the control and monitoring of technologies that combat global warming.) Who could have imagined the change in the publishing industry where Aldus, Adobe, and Apple Computer all but obliterated the manual typeface placement and paste up days in use just 15 years ago?

BEST PRACTICE According to PMI, there is no project if there is no Project Charter.

The Project Charter depends on expert judgment and project selection methods (no longer specified in the PMBOK Fourth Edition). The inputs to develop the Project Charter come from several sources:

- **Statement of Work (SOW):** Often called by its acronym, a SOW is a documented response to a customer's request, usually in the form of a request for proposal, request for information, request for bid, or even part of a contract. A SOW should include information summarizing the business need, product/service scope, and how it fits into the overall strategic plan. In many cases, a SOW estimates the amount of work required, terms and conditions, an estimated schedule, and even the cost to the customer.

> A SOW should remain an overview designed to initiate project approval by an executive who doesn't have the time to read more than a couple of pages.

- **Contract:** If the work is being performed by an outside party, a contract is written by the customer with your organization agreeing to perform the requirements of that contract. A business case may need to be periodically re-evaluated to ensure that the business needs still justify proceeding with a project.
- **Business case:** A business case provides the necessary information to justify if the project is needed. This is usually a task for a product manager and isn't necessarily a project manager's responsibility (nor a software manager's responsibility), but *you* may be asked to provide one. The business case has the single goal of proving that the project makes business sense with a *cost benefit analysis*.
- **Enterprise environment factors:** When new regulations require or mandate compliance, the official regulation itself can serve as the reason to embark on a software project. For example, if your organization provides Geographical Information Systems (GIS) software services for public utilities, regulations from the Federal Energy Regulatory

Commission (FERC) may impose that your software provides activity tracking to ensure that the information being processed by your software is of sufficient quality and secure. Complying with FERC can provide an overall benefit to Homeland Security initiatives initiated since 9/11. Another example is in the medical records and medical services software industry, where the Health Insurance Portability and Accountability Act of 1996, HIPAA, provides significant guidance to safeguard access to patient information. In both of these cases, the role of project management is critical in order to ensure structure and compliance.

Other factors outside of regulation that can have an influence on the success of a project include organizational culture and structure, skills of existing and available talent, marketplace conditions, stakeholder's tolerance of risk, and Project Management Information Systems (which provide the tools for scheduling, tracking, and collecting of project information).

- **Organizational process assets:** The primary benefit of these assets is a project knowledge base maintained from past projects, standardized guidelines and templates, defect tracking databases, change control procedures and corresponding systems, procedures for approving purchases, procedures for authorizing work to be performed, and expected methods of project status communication.

Expert judgment is used to assess the inputs needed in the development of the Project Charter document. This includes using experts from finance, stakeholders (including the customer or sponsor), professional and technical associations, industry groups, and the vast experience of a Project Management Office (PMO). A PMO is nothing more than a bunch of project managers working as a cohesive unit managing a portfolio of projects, usually across an entire company or division. The closest organizational structure supporting the PMO concept is shown in the "Strong Matrix Organization" section in Chapter 3.

When a management committee needs to decide on which projects to fund, there are two types of selection techniques that can be used:

- **Mathematical models:** Also called *constrained optimization*, this selection technique is based on mathematical calculations in an attempt to predict the future outcome. No one expects you to become a statistical or financial wizard; however, you should become familiar with basic calculations that are well recognized in finance circles that help determine whether a project is viable or not. These calculations are summarized in Chapter 6, "Become Effective and Competitive."
- **Scoring model:** This technique (also called *benefit measurement model* or *comparative approach*) takes into account a number of economics, market conditions, resource availability, benefits, and other factors.

Alternatively, some companies use *murder boards*, where a group of peers ask a barrage of difficult questions to try to "murder" the project. This forces hard thought by the team (and especially those who want the project to be approved), and it ensures that they are thinking through those issues that would cause the project to be unsuccessful.

The final output of this process is the creation of the Project Charter itself. The Project Charter contains "jus' e'nuff" information to initiate the project based on the input provided along with the application of expert judgment to lay the foundation for a successful outcome. The Project Charter should define the "what."(If you find yourself including the "why" or the "how" stuff, chances are you are making the Project Charter too detailed.)

According to Kliem and Ludin's book *Project Management Practitioner's Handbook*, your job is to include the project's vision in the Project Charter and to make sure that the team has a clear understanding of how the project will support this vision:

> "The vision is essentially an idea of some desired end state, expressed in a form that everyone understands, can relate to, and can feel a sense of commitment to."

If you get the vision right, you are one step closer to ensuring that through proper leadership, the team will be motivated to deliver on that vision. The Project Charter documentation should include the purpose, justification, measurable objectives, success criteria, basic requirements, project description and characteristics, identification of key project participants, and an estimated budget and schedule.

> Don't forget to take advantage of historical project information as a valuable source for creating the Project Charter.

There are two "watchdog project elements" that are vital to document in the Project Charter:

- **Assumptions:** Best guesses of critical elements for the project to succeed that are likely to be true. (If they turn out to not be true, other key planning documents like the Project Scope Statement may have to be changed.) For example, let's say that your software company supports patient record submittals, and a proposed year-long project will be based on the use of the UB92 medical claims format. What would happen to your project if, due to regulations outside your control, UB92 format is no longer going to be accepted (in lieu of another, more comprehensive format)? The dependency on UB92 is an important assumption you should document (especially if the medical industry has a habit of updating formats regularly).

   Another example of an assumption that is near and dear to this book's development was during the writing process. About a quarter of the way through the development of this manuscript, PMI delivered early review copies of the PMBOK Fourth Edition, which had an immediate impact on the final content of *Principles of Software Development Leadership*. Do we go ahead publish the book based on the Third Edition, or do we instead finish the book, accept the schedule "hit," and be one of the first books referencing the Fourth Edition? We chose the latter.

   Another clever word for assumption is *dependency*—ask yourself at the beginning of your project, "What does the project *depend* on?"

■   **Constraints:** Alternatively, constraints represent known limitations (usually cost, level of effort, or window of opportunity) that could impact project delivery. If your company produces tax software, a constraint would be that your projects are required to be released prior to the end of the calendar year (otherwise, it serves no purpose to your customer base).

Since the creation of the Project Charter effectively gives a project a start, what should you do to christen the start of the project? You are responsible to get the team together once the Project Charter is approved with a *kickoff meeting.* This is an important event because the project has been deemed officially approved, and this particular meeting gives you the opportunity to get the team organized in order to review the content of the Project Charter. It also gives you the chance to lay out the plan of action for the project.

At this point, according to *The Team Handbook* by Peter R. Scholtes, the kickoff meeting and getting the right stakeholders and project stakeholders together and coordinated is a critical role toward a project's success. In fact, the identification of a *sponsor* or *guidance team* is important to ensure that you and your team get the right amount of support and assistance, especially for requests or decisions that are outside of your control. *And who approves exiting this process?* The project sponsor or initiator authorizes the project to commence by approving the Project Charter.

Develop the Preliminary Project Scope Statement

The Preliminary Project Scope Statement includes many of the same inputs used in the creation of the Project Charter:

■   Project objectives
■   Product (or services) requirements and characteristics
■   Project constraints, risks, and assumptions
■   Initial project organization
■   Initial Work Breakdown Structure (WBS)
■   Order of magnitude (rough estimate) of schedule and cost
■   The Project Charter itself

PMI, in developing the PMBOK Fourth Edition, probably realized that this process overlapped and was redundant with the creation of the Project Scope Statement (in the Project Scope Management knowledge area). Since time is valuable for you and the recipients of any project management–created document, I'll focus on fewer, non-redundant processes and leave the Preliminary Project Scope Statement "in the dust."

Integration Management in the Planning Process Group

The Project Management Plan (and its associated planning documents) is the document that explains the *how* of the project.

Develop Project Management Plan

The Project Management Plan is the key document that provides the overall planning for the project. It takes information from a variety of inputs and applies primarily expert judgment to create the overall planning document. The inputs that are used to create the Project Management Plan are as follows:

- **Preliminary Project Scope Statement:** This document is usually only created for large, complex projects and is designed as an initial draft to the Project Scope Statement created a little bit later in the project life cycle.
- **Project Charter:** The overall project information from the Project Charter should provide the basis of the Project Management Plan.

> The plan is a living document in that it (and its associated other documents) will be constantly updated until entry into the project (or project phase) is closed.

- **Outputs from other planning processes:** The Project Management Plan includes the following information from other planning documents that are initially developed in draft form and progressively elaborated upon during the rest of the project:
    - Processes that the project management team will use to track progress (for example, the team will use an agile, Scrum methodology).
    - The description of tools and techniques used to accomplish these processes (for example, since the application being developed must work on Windows, Mac OS, and Linux, the team must use the cross-platform REALbasic language instead of C# used in the last version).
    - How work will be managed and executed (for example, work will be checked in daily so that a nightly build and test can be automatically run).
    - How changes will be monitored and controlled (for example, through the Perform Integrated Change Control process, public bloodletting, or whatever).
    - How configuration management will be performed (for example, this can be a collection of formally documented procedures that define how deliverables and documentation are controlled, updated, and approved).
    - How performance measurement baselines will be used. (In other words, how will *you* know if the team is on track?)
    - How information will be communicated with stakeholders (for example, weekly status reports will be published to all stakeholders).
    - Determine which project phases will be used (for example, the next product release will be a major upgrade, requiring a majority of the PMBOK processes).
- **Enterprise environmental factors:** This indicates how your company does business, which can have an influence on the success of a project. The factors include governmental standards, industry standards, organizational culture and structure, skills of existing and available talent, marketplace conditions, stakeholder's tolerance of risk,

and Project Management Information Systems. An example is a company's Work Authorization System—the procedures and automated system that keep track of a company's most valuable asset: its people and the work they perform.

■ **Organizational process assets:** You should take advantage of using a historical knowledge base from past projects (in other words, lessons learned), standardized guidelines and templates, defect tracking systems, change control procedures, procedures for approving purchases, work authorization procedures, and expected methods of project status communication. An example is documented lessons learned, which would include postmortem notes summarized by the project manager on prior completed projects.

Expert judgment is used to create the final Project Management Plan with the following activities:

■ Adjust the processes to be used to fit the project.
■ Decide on the depth of technical and management details to be included in the plan. (Remember, keep it simple!)
■ Determine the resources and skills required to get the job done.
■ Determine how much configuration management to use on the project.
■ Determine how much change control process to use on the project (how formal, what method to define changes, and most important, who approves the changes especially if the schedule is impacted).

NOTE

PMBOK's project management methodology defines the approach you should use to manage a project. If your company has an active PMO, chances are there is already a well-defined methodology. Otherwise, I'd suggest reverting back to expert judgment.

Whether you use Microsoft SharePoint, a collection of Word documents, a custom database, or a sophisticated project management system, it is a good idea to use an organized, shareable automated methodology to define, maintain, and communicate project information: According to PMBOK, this is known as a Project Management Information System.

What is the output of this process? The Project Management Plan is created as the sole output of the Develop Project Management Plan process. Rather than the plan being a huge document, it is usually a master document that references other planning documents defined in other PMBOK knowledge areas (see Figure 4.3).

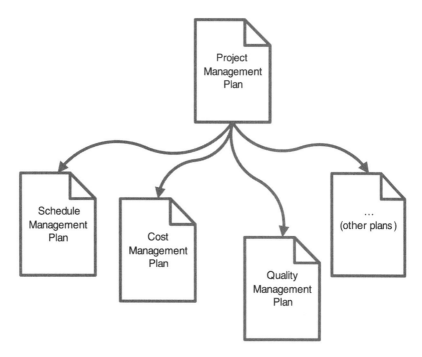

FIGURE 4.3
The Project Management Plan references other knowledge area plans.

Remember how the Project Charter focused on the *what* the project was about? The Project Management Plan focuses on how the project is to be planned. It provides the baseline for the project against which future project progress will be measured (similar to actual versus forecast methodology performed by your Finance department throughout your company's fiscal year).

Change will take place during a project's life cycle, so it is critical to keep all documents updated as change is introduced. Make sure that you have the team's buy-in when updating changes to any project plans—otherwise, why bother creating the plans to begin with?

BEST PRACTICE The Project Management Plan is NOT the schedule.

To properly ensure that there is a complete set of plans in place, a checklist in the Project Management Plan should be created that references the planning documents you use on your project:

Completed	Planning Document
	* Schedule Management Plan
	* Cost Management Plan
	* Quality Management Plan
	* Process Improvement Plan
	* Human Resource Plan
	* Communications Management Plan
	* Risk Management Plan
	* Procurement Management Plan
	* Project baselines that also include the following:
	* Schedule baseline
	* Cost Performance baseline
	* Scope baseline
	* Quality baseline

As more project information is learned, additional planning may be required, thus causing processes to be revisited. This progressive detailing of the Project Management Plan is called *rolling wave planning*. The Project Management Plan acts as the integrator for all of the other subsidiary project plans. That is why the Project Management Plan is key to the overall Project Integration Management knowledge area.

> This iterative learning style lends itself to agile software projects.

This feedback and refinement process, however, cannot continue indefinitely, and if implementation impacts the constraints identified in the Project Charter (like expense or schedule), the team may have to reconsider if the project will even be completed.

The results of these iterations and changes must be documented as updates to the Project Management Plan (along with other project planning documents). Once the baselines are established, the Perform Integrated Change Control process kicks in (discussed later in this chapter).

INTEGRATION MANAGEMENT IN THE EXECUTING PROCESS GROUP

The Direct and Manage Project Execution process is where all of the work is performed.

Direct and Manage Project Execution

Here are some sample activities that normally take place in this process:

- Perform activities (the work) to accomplish project objectives—without this you don't have much of a project at all.
- Staff, train, and manage the project team members assigned to perform the work.
- Obtain quotations, bids, offers, or proposals from among the vendors, and then select the best ones. (But don't wait until the last minute!)
- Implement the planned methods and standards identified in the Project Management Plan.
- Manage risks, and if a risk comes true, mitigate it immediately.
- Manage suppliers as if they were your own staff. This can be a lot of work, especially if you are dependent on their work to be performed at the same time your core team is performing their work.
- Adapt approved changes in the project's scope, plans, and environment. (Hopefully, these changes are kept to a minimum.)
- Collect and communicate project status information that can help in forecasting (usually includes costs, schedules, progress, and so on).
- Last, but not least, keep track of lessons learned and process improvements that can be applied in future projects.

There are many outputs produced from this process, which is quite understandable, since these outputs represent the totality of the work being produced. But, let's start with the key inputs (enterprise environment factors and organizational process assets were covered earlier in the "Develop Project Management Plan" section):

- **Project Management Plan:** This plan provides the integrated project summary so that the team knows what to do and how to do it.
- **Approved change requests:** If any aspect of the project has an approved change, you need to consider the impact on the team that is executing the work. The impact can be an addition or a reduction to key project elements such as the following:
  1. Features (the "scope"—more on this topic later)
  2. Costs and budgets (usually associated with resources)
  3. Schedule
  4. The Project Management Plan (the "how we're going to do it" plan)

  You'll need to consider handling actions and repairs that are a part of change requests:
  - **Approved corrective actions:** Directions that bring project elements into conformance with the Project Management Plan. An example would be if the engineers built a product for the English language only, and the Project Management Plan plainly indicated that support for five European languages was required.

- **Approved preventive actions:** Directions that reduce the probability of expected negative risks. An example would be where a software application needs to insert source code to properly handle out-of-bounds conditions (like an input text field that needs to restrict a social security number to a fixed number of digits).
- **Approved defect repairs:** When defects are encountered during development, each needs to be properly validated (can it be reproduced?) and categorized. If the defect needs to be corrected, the defect is fixed and the team subsequently notified. Most software organizations maintain a *defect tracking system* that tracks the state of each defect encountered.

One input identified in the Third Edition of PMBOK (and absent from the Fourth Edition) is the Administrative Closure procedure. This procedure is used to close a project whenever the project ends. The reason it would be important in this phase of a project's life cycle is if the project needs to be prematurely terminated. This may be due to market conditions, unexpected competition, failure of the team, or other reasons and may require that the overall integration direction use these procedures as a guide for project closure.

> Don't forget to utilize advice from experts during project execution (for example, stakeholders, other software professionals, your chief architect, and so on).

What about the key tools and techniques used to create the output to this process?

- **Expert judgment:** A departure from prior PMBOK editions, the Fourth Edition places expert judgment as the key method to assess the inputs needed to direct and manage project execution in many processes. You'll also need to ensure that the team's execution complies with the Project Management Plan.

  No longer explicitly stated in the Fourth Edition of PMBOK, the project management methodology represents the best practices and procedures that aid a project team in executing the Project Management Plan.
- **Project management information system:** This automated system used by project managers should help maintain information necessary to track the execution of work.

And what about the outputs expected? Well—there are lots of them:

- **Deliverables:** The key output of this process is of course the work. Simply stated, deliverables represent the completion of predefined project work that supports the Project Charter.

- **Work performance information:** These are the reported results you maintain to show the positive and negative variations to the Project Management Plan. Here are some sample performance indicators that you should consider tracking:
  1. Schedule attainment. (Are you hitting milestones?)
  2. Deliverables completed (and those that haven't been completed).
  3. Quality metrics. (Are incoming defects far exceeding the fix rate?)
  4. Costs authorized versus those actually incurred. (Is the project still under budget?)
  5. Resource utilization. (One of my personal favorites—are you using resources as you expected?)
- **Change requests:** Called *requested changes* prior to PMBOK Fourth Edition, change requests expand or contract project scope, policies, or other project elements. Oftentimes, change requests come from outside sources (like product management). There needs to be a *feedback loop* relationship between the original request (A) and the implementation of the request (B), as shown in Figure 4.4.

Resources aren't just people. Resources can be equipment, server utilization, and other things that need to be scheduled or acquired.

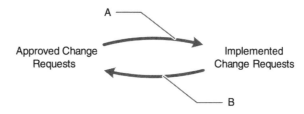

FIGURE 4.4
Relationship between approved change requests and their implementation.

If a change request is approved, it becomes part of the project deliverables. Once implemented, use whatever Project Management Information System you have to validate and document that the change request was properly implemented (hence, the "feedback loop").

There are other feedback loops in this specific process. The normal course of software development causes corrective, preventive, and defect repair actions to take place. For those that are approved for rework, the work commences generally as quickly as possible. The team should ensure that each original action is checked off once its counterpart has been completed and verified (see Figure 4.5).

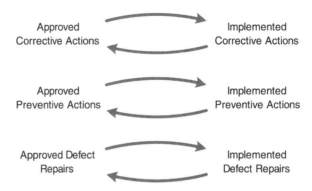

FIGURE 4.5
Relationship between approved actions and defect
repairs with implementation.

- **Project Management Plan updates:** Updates need to be carefully considered if folded into the Project Management Plan (which could be any of the planning documents in the other knowledge areas specified in the planning document checklist). Be especially careful if these updates continually move out the overall project schedule. If, for example, the schedule is in a constant state of change (usually indicating a *runaway project*), it is very likely that the project was not originally planned very well and may need a massive reset!
- **Project document updates:** You may have to update documents that are actively used throughout the project. This output is somewhat generic and applies to documents like the following:
    - Requirements
    - Project logs that keep track of issues, requests, assumptions, and so on

How can you influence the overall execution of this critical process? Your leadership and communication style can directly influence how well the team responds to your direction. Although this is covered in more detail in Part 4, "People," your approach toward leading and motivating the team will have a huge impact on the results. If, for example, your style is to control every aspect of project execution (lots of meetings, status reports, and so on) and your team prefers a looser, agile management involvement, your team might lose confidence in how the project execution activities are being lead.

Failure to do enough planning will probably bring up issues as your team is in this Direct and Manage Project Execution process, which could slow down progress as decisions need to be addressed at a time when completion of the work should be the main focus.

BEST PRACTICE If planning is done right, execution should be a breeze.

How do you know when you can exit this process? The project manager directs the work to be performed, and as the work gets accomplished, the status should be maintained in the performance reporting process. Once the work is deemed largely completed, the team (under your direction) makes the determination to exit this process.

Have you ever witnessed a situation where the effort spent on project management activities far exceeded the actual work being performed? Let's look at an example.

Over a 30-day time period, there are mandatory team meetings every other day, as well as weekly status reports, and yet the actual level of effort on the project is as simple as 10 to 20 lines of additional source code for a software update. If you see this situation taking place on your project, blow the whistle—chances are your team has become far too process-driven for its own good! Besides, who is reading all of those project management documents and worksheets anyway? (It might only be *you*!)

INTEGRATION MANAGEMENT IN THE MONITORING & CONTROLLING PROCESS GROUP

The Monitoring & Controlling process group provides for the overall tracking, reviewing, and regulating of project progress. Processes within this group act as traffic cops to ensure that performance objectives in the Project Management Plan are being met by the project being developed.

> Don't think of the term "performance" as "speed of execution." In PMBOK-land, *performance* means "how well the processes from each knowledge area are being accomplished."

The key purpose of the Monitoring & Controlling process group is "managing change" (and every project has to deal with change, whether planned or not). There are two key Integration Management processes in the Monitoring & Controlling process group:

- Monitor and Control Project Work
- Perform Integrated Change Control

You may wish to visualize the Monitoring & Controlling process group taking place after the Execution process group—but it can have a more expansive role throughout the entire life cycle of a project. The Monitoring & Controlling process group provides processes that can oversee the Initiating, Planning, Executing, and Closing processes of a project. For more on this topic, see the section "The Importance of the Implementation Cycle" earlier in this chapter.

Monitor and Control Project Work

As a key component of the Project Integration Management knowledge area, the Monitor and Control Project Work process provides project performance information and anticipates (or reacts to) change. Using non-scientific terms, the baseline (the Project Management Plan) minus the work actually completed (Work Performance Data) produces change requests (see Figure 4.6).

BEST PRACTICE You must proactively handle change if the project is to be successful.

Project Management Plan (the current baseline) **–** Work Performance Data (actual completed work) **=** Change Requests

FIGURE 4.6
A simplistic way to view how change requests are made.

Key activities in this process include (but are not limited to) the following:

- Compares actual project performance versus what is in the Project Management Plan (and all of its associated subsidiary documents).
- Assesses the overall progress (team performance) that determines whether corrective or preventive actions need to be taken.
- Evaluates critical project risks and that appropriate risk response plans are taken.
- Maintains an accurate information base concerning the project's products and services until project completion.
- Provides information that supports overall project status to stakeholders.
- Provides information that supports cost and schedule forecasts.
- Monitors and handles the critical changes based on approved change requests.

Key inputs to this process are as follows:

- **Project Management Plan:** This document or set of documents is your baseline set of plans to measure against.
- **Performance reports and forecasts:** Key status, accomplishments, scheduled activities, and issues that need attention provide information that you'll need to compare where the project stands versus where it should be. Predicting future outcomes (the forecasts) are also critical, especially since all of the stakeholders need to know the estimates for project completion (costs, schedule, resources, and so on).

You primarily use the following tools and techniques to make decisions:

■ **Expert judgment:** What? This again? Your experience and access to experts (within the team and those outside the team) are without a doubt the best tools in your tool belt to help you make the right decisions.

■ **Earned Value Management:** Although removed from this process in the PMBOK Fourth Edition, this is still important. There are some fancy calculations that can help your stakeholders get an objective evaluation as to just how well the project is proceeding. The Earned Value Technique (EVT) basically measures the amount of completion of a Work Breakdown Structure (WBS) or project. I'll get into this (with all of the other calculations you should know) in Chapter 6, "Become Effective and Competitive."

The outputs should look pretty familiar by now:

■ **Change requests:** As a result of comparing the planned results versus actual results, change requests are issued.

■ **Project Management Plan updates:** The Project Management Plan and any of other knowledge area plans are updated as necessary.

■ **Project document updates:** How many of your projects finish with documentation that isn't kept up to date with the changes? Close to 50%? Perhaps most of your projects? Change is inevitable and, thankfully, PMBOK recognizes that fact and encourages adoption of processes that deal directly with change.

BEST PRACTICE Keep project documents updated to match product changes.

Perform Integrated Change Control

The key inputs to this process are as follows:

■ **Change requests:** These requests can come from generally any source and should be handled as one of three general classifications:
  1. Corrective actions
  2. Preventive actions
  3. Defect repairs

■ **Work performance information:** Information collected during the project life cycle, including status, schedule, and costs.

■ **Organizational process assets:** These items can influence the integrated Change Control process:
  1. *Change control procedures*—The rules that indicate how changes will be submitted, approved, and validated.

2. *Process measurement database*—The change tracking system (new in the PMBOK Fourth Edition) that can be used to keep historical information, such as how many change requests take place weekly.
3. *Project files*—Project status reports, project calendars, risk registers, and so on.
4. *Configuration management knowledge base*—Contains the versions of company standards, policies, and procedures that can serve as a baseline (for this project and all other projects).

The tools and techniques used are as follows:

- **Expert judgment:** Stakeholders, in addition to your experience and judgment, should be in a position to make decisions on all change requests in a timely manner.
- **Change control meetings:** With the help of a decisive Change Control Board (CCB), all stakeholders agree that this cross-functional team has the responsibility to make decisions on change requests. It is always good to have a CCB that has a broad level of responsibility, ranging from sales to quality assurance, and should include at least one member of the executive staff.

A *change control system* applies to the set of procedures and tools used that enable changes to be handled in an organized way. It is more than a computer system, but you should use some automated mechanism that tracks the requests and identifies the procedures or workflow to ensure that a change request's impact considers all of the knowledge areas. Change requests must, for example, have an owner and should be formally documented in order to be considered.

How are decisions made? You and the CCB use expert judgment to determine the importance of each change request. If the CCB agrees that a change should be acted upon, the change request is approved. Otherwise, it is rejected (see Figure 4.7).

> Notice how happy the CCB folks are in Figure 4.7? They can make a positive difference to any project by making well-informed, timely decisions.

Delay tactics could occur due to a number of factors, but generally the phrase most often heard is "we need more information." If this happens, the folks who submitted the change request should have included enough information for the CCB to make a proper decision.

BEST PRACTICE The absolute worst thing the CCB team can do is put off a key change request decision.

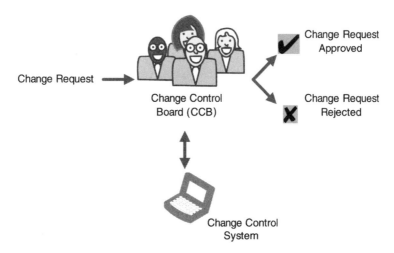

FIGURE 4.7
How the Change Control Board works.

In an agile environment, decisions need to be made with *all* of the pertinent information available, made once (not over and over again), and made with consideration of the Project Management Plan baseline. What are the outputs to the Perform Integrated Change Control process?

- **Change request status updates:** The status is processed by you or your designee (for example, a project coordinator).
- **Project Management Plan updates:** Although not always necessary, if the Project Management Plan (or any of the subsidiary plans in the other knowledge areas) needs to be updated, then get it done. You do not want to arbitrarily change your baseline planning documents without making changes "official" with CCB approval. This avoids the comment down the road, "So when did we decide THAT?" (Please keep in mind that "update" implies your project's baseline changes.)
- **Project document updates:** Any documents that are subject to the formal Change Control process (like status reports) may also have to be updated.

The Perform Integrated Change Control process is a sequence of mini-cycles among process groups (see Figure 4.8).

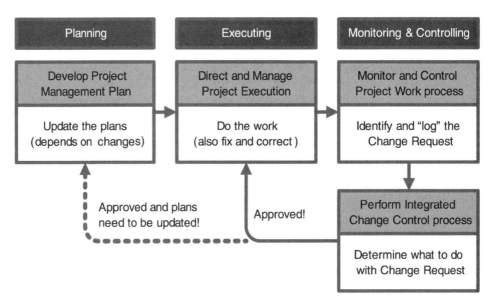

FIGURE 4.8
The Integrated Change Control approval cycle.

The Perform Integrated Change Control process determines what to do with submitted change requests. A change request is simply a request (or part of a wish list) that offers no guarantee of approval. No action is to be taken until the change request has been approved by the CCB. Of course, a change request can be rejected, which results in no action being taken.

Generally, change requests are prioritized based on an impact to the customer or to the project's current schedule. It is not a good idea to reject a change request that should be immediately corrected due to schedule impact. You might have to remake the decision at a later time (at which point the schedule impact could be far worse).

If approved and no change is required in the Project Management Plan, the fix (or correction) is performed by the Direct and Manage Project Execution process. Otherwise, if the change request is approved and the Project Management Plan needs to be updated, you make those changes back in the Develop Project Management Plan process and make the fix or correction in the Direct and Manage Project Execution process.

INTEGRATION MANAGEMENT IN THE CLOSING PROCESS GROUP

There is a single process in the Closing process group: the Close Project or Phase process.

Close Project or Phase

If there was ever a need to be organized and to validate all of the loose ends that can occur during a project life cycle, your role in the Closing Project process group is where it counts.

This is where most project teams get to the 90% complete mark and assume that everything has been "packaged up" when, in reality, it hasn't. And don't buy that "we are done since we're 90% there—all we need is the weekend to make *one more* change."

Simply put, the Close Project or Phase process is where all activities (in all knowledge areas and all Project Management process groups) are formally closed. Activities include the following:

- Confirmation that all deliverables have been completed, provided, and accepted.
- Pass all project deliverables and activities on to the next phase or to production (on media) or operations (for customer download).
- Collection of all records, status (whether or not they are successful), and lessons learned. Hopefully there is a Project Management Information System to save this information.

In case you haven't guessed, this process can be a huge coordination and validation effort among the entire team. In addition, your role is to ensure that the sponsor (or customer) accepts that the project has been completed to everyone's satisfaction.

The key inputs are as follows:

- **Project Management Plan:** This plan provides the integrated project summary so that the team knows what to do and how to do it.
- **Accepted deliverables:** The deliverables are those accepted through the Verify Scope process (see Chapter 5, "Partner with Product Management") and accepted by the Integrated Change Control process.
- **Organizational process assets:** This specifies how your organization has defined project closure guidelines or requirements as well as how lessons learned and other documents are cataloged in your Project Management Information System.

> In addition, you may need a contract document (which specifies what must be met prior to project close) or work performance information (which identifies what has been completed and not completed).

The key tools and techniques are as follows:

- **Expert judgment:** Use your team, product management, and other experts in your PMO to ensure that you've performed what is necessary to successfully close the project (or project phase).

  Don't forget to validate if the assets (software source, build procedures, documentation, and so on) are required to be packaged up for key customers' escrow accounts. These are usually contractual obligations that give the customer assurances that they can access the software assets for the products they have purchased or licensed in case your company goes out of business (or can't service their product needs any longer).

Previous editions of PMBOK specified both Project Management Methodology and a corresponding Project Management Information System to be important techniques for this process.

The key outputs are as follows:

- **Final product, service, or result transition:** This is the final handoff of the completed product or service that the project was authorized to produce. In most web-centric software companies, this is usually a notice to the IT department that "product XYZ can now be deployed for customer download."

  In the case of a SOW initially defined for a specific customer, acceptance should include a formal document that specifies the terms of the contract have been met. If your company allows celebrations, this is the point to bring out the bubbly—if your company has strict rules against alcoholic beverages of any sort, then sneak it in anyway. Celebrate!

  Though no longer explicitly stated as a key output in the latest edition of PMBOK, the Close Procurement process must be performed. There is probably some formalized process that your organization expects you to follow in order for contracts to be officially closed (for example, the customer is expected to sign an acceptance document).

- **Organizational process assets updates:** To provide information that can help with maintaining a historical project management database, the following assets should be saved in the Project Management Information System:
    - *Formal acceptance*—The sponsor (or customer) has formally accepted the project's product or service with this document.
    - *Project files*—The collection of all documents that have been tracked during the project (or project phase) from all of the knowledge areas.
    - *Historical information*—The lessons learned information should be saved to be reviewed for later projects.
    - *Project closure documents*—Basically, the signoff documents that indicate completion of the project along with the transfer of the deliverables to either the next phase or to Operations. If the project was prematurely terminated prior to planned closure, you are responsible to collect and create the documentation summarizing why the project was not properly closed. Failures can be just as important as successes, since the idea is to learn from past mistakes so that bad results aren't repeated.

I know of one major commercial software company that attempted to do a "100% agile" project, and unfortunately it failed. As a result, they lost valuable time to market, and the majority of their development staff on that project was terminated.

There can be many other formal project closure procedures and documents. In fact, there is the Administrative Closure Procedure process specified in the Third Edition of PMBOK (but no longer emphasized in the Fourth Edition).

A critical activity that you mustn't forget in closing out a project is the handling of lessons learned information. According to Paul Tedesco in *Common Sense in Project Management*, this must be a learning exercise and not a punishment exercise.

As outlined in Scott Seningen's white paper entitled "Learn the Value of Lessons-Learned," you need to ensure that the same mistakes are not repeated over and over again. The worst impacts of not learning from projects have a direct impact to cost due to project delay, budget overruns, and ultimately customer dissatisfaction. According to Seningen, the best opportunity to make sure that lessons learned information is tracked is to maintain a knowledge base (which would be a part of the Project Management Information System). This would allow lessons learned information to be recorded during the project and, more important, make it accessible to other project managers instantly.

> See the section "Habit 6—Taking Too Long to Negotiate Feature Sets and Schedules" in Chapter 1.

Granted, if you haven't taken notes on lessons learned along the way, your chances for meaningful feedback at the close of a project (when everyone is exhausted and thinking of their next assignment) is pretty much nil. That is why a lessons learned meeting is often-times called a postmortem (even the name doesn't sound like a positive experience at all).

In *Project Planning, Scheduling, and Control*, there are a couple of key points that James Lewis makes:

- Lessons learned should be shared with other project staff so that they can avoid mistakes made on your project.
- A lessons learned report should be standardized, and the more straightforward the report template the better. This will allow best (and worst) practices to be easily compared between a wide variety of projects.

BEST PRACTICE Keep a lessons learned database active throughout the entire project's life cycle.

Probably one of the most frustrating activities that you'll have as a project manager in the Close Project or Phase process will be getting lessons learned feedback and interest level from the team. More techniques to effectively lead lessons learned communications are covered in Chapter 10, "Create a Winning Workplace."

RISK MANAGEMENT—PREPARING FOR THE UNEXPECTED

Even the most carefully planned project can run into serious trouble, and it is your job to plan for those situations. The Project Risk Management knowledge area is centered around the area that frightens most of us: planning and handling uncertainty. PMBOK defines a bunch of processes (almost all in the Planning process group) that all focus on risk mitigation (see Table 4.3).

Table 4.3 Risk Management Knowledge Area Processes (PMBOK 4th Edition)

	Project Management Process Groups				
		Implementation			
Initiating	**Planning**	**Execution**	**Monitoring & Controlling**	**Closing**	
	Plan Risk Management	Distribute Information	Monitor and Control Risks		
	Identify Risks				
	Perform Qualitative Risk Analysis				
	Perform Quantitative Risk Analysis				
	Plan Risk Responses				

WHAT IS A RISK?

The definition of a *risk* is generally an event with some degree of uncertainty. The objective of the Project Risk Management knowledge area is to increase the probability of positive events (opportunities) and decrease the probability of negative events (threats) on a project. Let's look at some notable risk characteristics:

- Risk processes interact with each other and with other processes in other knowledge areas.
- Risk processes tend to overlap in ways that are hard to predict.
- On the topic of prediction, risks are always regarded as future events (none occur in the past).
- You may have heard that the probability of a specific risk occurring is close to 100%—that's not possible. If a risk is 100% certain, then it isn't a *risk* any longer—it is a *fact*!

BEST PRACTICE A 100% risk is no longer a risk but a certainty.

Risk events have at least one cause followed by one or more impacts (see Figure 4.9).

FIGURE 4.9
Project Risk Management of multiple causes and possible multiple effects.

Your role, given the tools available in the Project Risk Management knowledge area, is to plan (*anticipate* may be a better word) for risks and to handle them appropriately. The catalyst that usually makes a risk occur is called a *trigger*—and it is this event that, if you've planned accordingly, should initiate the proper risk remediation procedures.

BEST PRACTICE Risk Management and Quality Management processes are tightly related.

According to John Smith's *Troubled IT Projects*, one of the five leading root causes of troubled projects identified by KPMG and the Public Accounts Committee is "poor risk management and contingency planning." Let's look at an example with multiple causes that could create negative effects.

The software project named Alucard ("Dracula" spelled backwards) needs two additional software engineers to do the work. To top that off, the talent already in place on the team is relatively inexperienced. Failure to identify, analyze, and ultimately address both causes previously mentioned could result in the project not being delivered on time (*schedule impact*) and the project not being implemented correctly (*quality impact*).

Anticipating and recognizing risks are probably the most important activities that you can do early in the planning stages of a project. Figure 4.10 shows an example of what you could do after planning, identifying, analyzing, and then mitigating risks:

1. Assign an experienced mentor, like a software architect, to the team.
2. Commence looking for two contract software engineers who have experience in your product sector.

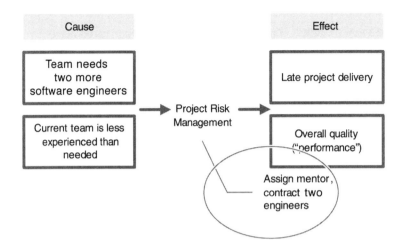

FIGURE 4.10
Mitigating causes through risk management.

BEST PRACTICE Anticipate and recognize risks early in the project life cycle.

THE INFAMOUS TRIPLE CONSTRAINT

Risks have the unique characteristic of impacting three constraints at the same time. Also referred as the Project Management Triangle, the traditional Triple Constraint diagram is used to show the relationship that risk has to scope, cost, and time (see Figure 4.11).

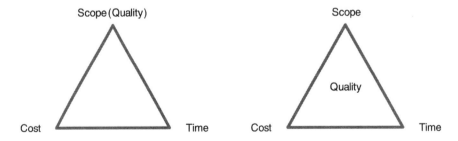

FIGURE 4.11
Triple Constraint used in risk management (two variations).

A fourth constraint, quality, is sometimes shown in the center of the triangle or as an extension to scope. The impact of change among any of the other constraints has a direct impact of additional work (or less, depending on the risk) required to perform quality validation of the project's work. Quality should remain a constant "must have" regardless of the change of any of the other constraints. (Throughout the duration of a project, quality can have a significant impact on time and cost.)

> Constraints are important to identify up front in the Project Charter.

If you impact one constraint (for example, time), there is equal impact to the other two (scope and cost). As an example, if you expand the feature set of a project (the scope), the project's expense (the cost) and required time to complete it (the time) are directly impacted and also expanded (as shown in Figure 4.12).

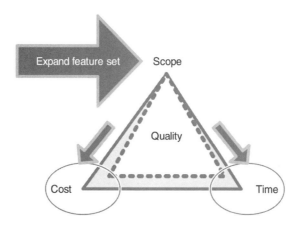

FIGURE 4.12
The impact to cost and time when scope is expanded.

Why not add more resources? Based on feedback from executives at your company, you've probably heard statements like "we can spend more money if we have to—just get this project completed at all costs!" But is the luxury of adding more resources really going to help? In Fred Brook's insightful book *The Mythical Man-Month*, assigning more programmers to a project running behind schedule will make it even later:

> "When schedule slippage is recognized, the natural (and traditional) response is to add manpower. Like dousing a fire with gasoline, this makes matters worse, much worse."

According to Ed Yourdon's excellent *Death March*, risk management techniques should be used when changing the team's focus to produce scope (the project's feature set) in less time. When under schedule pressure, the tendency is to divert common sense best practices into "ad hoc emotions and instinct, which should be avoided at all costs." This could, according to Yourdon, add even more risk to project completion, especially as entirely unanticipated challenges are introduced as a project progresses. Successful death marches (projects where process is abandoned and the teams are expected to work 24/7 to complete a project) are due to pure luck and never repeatable.

BEST PRACTICE Agile methodology abhors death marches.

A company that is prepared to risk its work-life balance philosophy by submitting its teams to endless all-nighters may not "achieve greatness" (even with temporary good results). When you and your team are exhausted, what progress are you really making anyway? This topic will be covered in more detail in Chapter 10, "Create a Winning Workplace."

Agile methodology takes a unique approach by turning the triangle in Figure 4.12 upside down, where the cost (budget) and time are constrained, resulting in variation with what is actually built (scope). This philosophy contradicts traditional software thought where features are usually expected, thus causing cost and time to contract or expand.

RISKS AREN'T ALWAYS NEGATIVE

BEST PRACTICE Your project may benefit from taking risks.

At this point, you may have come to the conclusion that you should never take any risks. According to author Michael Newell in *Preparing for the Project Management Professional (PMP) Certification Exam*, risks can be justified because they tend to have benefits, too: If you play it safe, projects could take twice as long and use twice the resources. Mention the word "risk" to anyone working on a project, and they'll automatically assume that something could possible go wrong. Yet a risk doesn't always have to be negative (see Table 4.4).

Table 4.4 Good and Bad Types of Risks

Bad Risk (Threat)	Good Risk (Opportunity)
A third-party software provider of sales tax calculation logic is working on a major update (and is consistently late in project delivery).	Add more quality assurance resources in order to accelerate a schedule (adding more engineers may be bad, but more testers may be a good thing).
Your key technical writer who is scheduled to author your project's user guide is on too many other projects at once.	Create more levels of technical support programs because the customer acceptance is greater than expected and willing to pay.

A *threat* is the occurrence of an event that has a negative consequence; a threat exploits a vulnerability, which is an exposure of a component. An *opportunity*, on the other hand, exploits an issue that can actually result in an improvement or benefit over a planned outcome.

Risks must be accepted by the team because there are consequences if the result isn't what you planned. Company culture can predict how risky projects are to be run. A company that thrives on overcoming risks with a consistent theme of long night "code fests" may *sometimes* achieve the impossible. In fact, there are three characteristics of how risk tolerant your work environment is:

1. **Risk averse:** Risks tend to be avoided, and the team gravitates toward tackling only low-hanging fruit (easy choices).
2. **Risk seeker:** Early adopters and startup folks hunting for the big win typically results in "all or nothing" impacts to the project.
3. **Risk neutral:** Risks are handled on a case-by-case basis with the overall result of middle-of-the-road decisions.

Let's go through a simple exercise. Check off what you believe the risk tolerance is between you, your team, and your company (management):

Risk Averse	Risk Seeker	Risk Neutral
You?		
Your Team?		
Your Company?		

If all three line up (meaning that all three constituents are consistently risk averse, for example), then that definitely defines your company's degree of risk tolerance. There could be a real breakdown in getting closure if the three groups operate with a different degree of risk tolerance. For example, risk management decisions could be difficult to achieve if you are risk neutral, your team is risk averse (as many software engineers are), and your management team clearly identifies itself (and the company) as a ruthless startup, competitive, and generally operates in a risk seeker mode. There's no easy answer to this situation, but recognizing the differences may facilitate better understanding for how best to manage risk situations.

YOUR ROLE MANAGING RISKS

Your roles, according to PMBOK, regarding risk management are as follows:

- **Consistency:** The manner by which risks are handled should be in a logical, thoughtful, and consistent manner. If on one hand you accept certain risks, and yet in other situations you dismiss certain risks, the team may lose faith in the decision-making process.
- **Proactivity:** Letting risks linger unattended, especially in a fast-moving agile software project, is a recipe for ultimate project failure (in other words, a negative risk becomes a reality).
- **Decisiveness:** Much of the Project Risk Management processes include an analysis of the risk, and there can be a tendency for software engineers to over-evaluate every risk when a team's product manager simply wants to make a decision and "get on with it." Hopefully, with expert judgment, you (and your team) will be able to make decisive and timely decisions.

The times when companies have re-invented themselves (for example, Oracle Corporation transitioned from providing generic database systems to providing vertical industry solutions) must have been viewed as a huge risk by management who believed that the company needed to remain strictly focused to its core database competency.

BEST PRACTICE Taking calculated risks is often necessary in order to grow your business.

Back in the "What Is a Risk?" section of this chapter, the phrase "planning, identifying, analyzing, and then mitigating risks" was used. This entire sequence of activities requires clear, transparent, and direct communication as you are handling risks. *This is really what all risk management is about.*

RISK MANAGEMENT IN THE PLANNING PROCESS GROUP

Plan Risk Management

The inputs to the Plan Risk Management process are as follows:

- **Project Scope Statement:** Document that clearly describes what the project is all about.
- **Cost Management Plan:** Describes how expenses will be tracked and reported. (This is especially important if you are in a start-up or a cash-strapped company where your finance team needs to watch every penny.) Wait a minute! What company isn't struggling a little these days?
- **Schedule Management Plan:** Shows how schedule contingencies will be reported and assessed.
- **Communication Management Plan:** Defines how all aspects of project activities are to be communicated (meetings, e-mails, status reports, and so on).
- **Enterprise environmental factors and organizational process assets:** The old trustworthy duo again—these define how risk tolerant the organization is and shows templates, risk definitions, authority levels, and even lessons learned information that will help you make the right risk management decisions. *You* might be willing to take a risk (for example, extend your expense budget by 20%, but your Finance department, another key stakeholder, might have safeguards that could "demonize you and your team" if you go over budget without their approval).

What tools and techniques are used? In order to prepare the Risk Management Plan, you should hold risk planning meetings (preferably one meeting and not a series of meetings—so prepare well). By using the templates and other assets just mentioned under organizational process assets, this is a golden opportunity to plan, organize, and clarify the types of risks that could occur in your project with key stakeholders.

Who gets involved? The following stakeholders should be included in this process of defining how risk management should be planned:

- You (the software manager or project manager)
- Select team members (especially the product manager and someone representing QA)
- Select stakeholders (perhaps someone from the IT/Operations side of the business, in case your software project relies on IT's server capacity in order to perform according to the requirements)

BEST PRACTICE The Risk Management Plan cannot be a "catch all" for any possible risk but should target key risks that impact the Triple Constraint.

What is actually created? The Risk Management Plan is created and includes the following topics:

- Methodology
- Roles and responsibilities
- Budgeting
- Timing
- Risk categories including the RBS
- Risk Probability and Impact Matrix
- How risks will be tracked

If you remember back to the creation of the Project Management Plan checklist, the Risk Management Plan is one of the most important of its subsidiary plans to complete during the planning process. The following topics should be included in the Risk Management Plan:

1. **Methodology:** How will risks be handled? An obvious technique is that, from an agreed-upon checklist of possible risks on a project, risks will be evaluated by the team on a weekly basis in the regular team meeting.
2. **Roles and responsibilities:** Break down the risks by category and by who is responsible for each. An example would be to identify owners for technical, personnel, and business risks.
3. **Budgeting:** Specify constraints as to how expenses are tracked and risks handled. It could be as simple as "expenses will be summarized weekly and, if expenses are within 10% over the expected target, then the finance stakeholders and the project manager will immediately meet to agree on an action plan."
4. **Timing:** To ensure that risks aren't just dreamed up during the Planning processes of a project and then ignored until a risk trigger occurs, the project team will, as part of the weekly team meeting, review ongoing risks and should meet monthly to go over risks with finance stakeholders.
5. **Risk categories and the RBS:** Since risks can "attack" from almost anywhere at any time, it is always a good idea to organize them based on the following categories:
   - Technical risks
   - External risks
   - Organization risks
   - Project management risks

You would next categorize the risks into a Risk Breakdown Structure (RBS), as shown in Figure 4.13. You aren't trying to solve the risks by creating an RBS—instead, you are categorizing the risks that could trip up (or accelerate) your project. As a result, reviewing the RBS diagram should become an agenda item for every team planning meeting.

FIGURE 4.13
Sample RBS diagram.

Think of the RBS as a WBS for risks. Figure 4.13 shows two levels of risks (the dark boxes represent the first level)—you can create the diagram several levels deep if you want.

Figure 4.14 is a sample three-level detail RBS based on the diagram in Figure 4.13. Notice that the first column contains categories: Technical, External, and Organization. The next column lists specific risk topics. Finally, each risk is summarized with a unique risk number and a one-sentence description. An RBS can be easily created with a spreadsheet or database (to be imported later into a Word document).

Category	Risk Topic	#	Risk
Technical	Requirements	1	New "core engine" may be too complicated to create in this version
	Performance	2	The project's overall throughout must be 20% better than before
	Quality	3	No blocking, crashing, or major defects are allowed in order to release
External	Market	4	The general market may not support our cost and distribution model
	Contractors	5	Our subcontractor is new and untested, there is some concern over their cash flow
	Regulatory	6	Rumors of new regulatory requirements (yet unknown) later on this year
Organization	Resources	7	Attrition on our team could impact delivery
	Funding	8	The schedule assumes a certain funding level, if exceeds 110% of funding, notify Finance and Executives immediately

FIGURE 4.14
Sample RBS detailed checklist.

Creators of Disaster Recovery Plans (popular with IT shops) most likely use an RBS for risk mitigation.

Risk Probability and Impact Matrix

Risks will need to be prioritized according to their potential impact on a project's outcome. When you need to handle a risk, you'd typically use some sort of a look-up table to evaluate just how to define where a risk "fits." This is similar to how sales organizations take a prospective lead and assign some sort of value that represents the following:

1. How likely is it that this prospect is an opportunity?
2. When is a deal likely to close?

Similarly, you need an objective mechanism to place a value for each risk. A risk value is ultimately placed on a chart based on two dimensions:

- Probability of the risk occurring (low, medium, or high).
- Impact to the Triple Constraint (cost, time, and scope).

Your team should assign values to a Definition of Probability and Impact chart like the one shown in Table 4.5. If you have an established PMO at your company, a chart is probably already predefined for your use.

Table 4.5 Definition of Risk Impact and Probability to Project Objectives (Triple Constraint)

Impact (I)

Project Objective	Low (L)	Medium (M)	High (H)
Scope	Minimal scope affected	Major feature changes affected	Scope reduction unacceptable
Time	Minimal time increase	Moderate time increase (<20%)	Significant delay
Cost	Minimal cost increase	Moderate cost increase	Significant cost increase
Quality (optional)	Minimal quality impact	Quality requires sponsor signoff	Product is effectively useless
Probability of Occurring (P)	**Low (L)**	**Medium (M)**	**High (H)**
	Not Likely (<33% chance)	Likely (>=33% <= 67%)	Most Likely (>67%)

These definition tables are used as a guideline for calculating the relative priority of the risk in the Perform Qualitative Risk Analysis process (discussed later in this chapter). It is vital that the team agrees on these definitions before you get into further risk processes.

Track Risks

Make a clear statement on how risks will be tracked. Tracking risk is critical during the life cycle of any project and should be placed in a knowledge base entry as lessons learned for future projects.

Identify Risks

After creating the Risk Management Plan, the next process is to identify risks, and, like other processes used in agile software development projects, this process is iterative, since risks will most likely be introduced as a project progresses through its life cycle.

BEST PRACTICE Keep risk planning processes as simple as possible.

By taking the Risk Management Plan, schedule and scope (feature) baselines, all pertinent planning documents, and project documents, you should have enough information to identify and characterize risks. Additionally, you can use the Stakeholder Register (which includes the information about the stakeholders that you'll use to decide who will help create the Risk Register) and enterprise environmental factors (and organizational process assets) that you'd expect to aid in identifying risks.

NOTE

There are some factors that can cause risks that are present on most every software project:

- **Team size:** Requiring more coordination and communication the larger the team is can increase the probability of risk.
- **Geographic distribution:** No doubt about it—remote development has its benefits, but it also contributes to the same issues associated with team size, compounded with time zone impact on timely availability.
- **Similar project history:** If the project is new to everyone, it is more risky than those that are similar to what the team has worked on before.
- **Staff expertise:** The more experienced and skilled the team is, the smaller the risk. There are certainly studies that have attempted to identify the difference in skill sets one software developer may have over another.
- **Management and company stability:** Management instability can have a disastrous impact on project teams who find themselves continually re-educating the "new guy(s)," all with a new philosophy toward project delivery and team efficiency.
- **Tasks on the critical path:** This concept will be discussed in Chapter 7, but the work with the most risk can usually be found with tasks that have little wiggle room for delays.
- **Availability of resources and time:** Time and people are key components of every project, and lack of either is a key risk contributor. For example, availability of staff in the middle or end of a project can be a huge risk if their other obligations haven't completed on time.

The tools and techniques used to prioritize and characterize risks include the following:

- **Expert judgment:** Although you need to be certain that the feedback is objective and relatively unbiased, you can't beat expert judgment in determining risks (especially if the experts you rely on have done this).
- **Diagramming techniques:** Some of us appreciate pictures and visual aids rather than reading long-winded documents. There are several visual diagramming techniques that are very helpful in identifying risks:
  - *Cause-and-effect (Root Cause Analysis) identification*—Also known as *Ishikawa* or *fishbone diagrams*, this technique visually represents the relationship between an effect and most of its causes. Figure 4.15 shows an example of a cause-and-effect diagram where the shape looks kind of like a fishbone. Starting with the effect (like employee attrition), the team brainstorms the possible causes of that effect (the risks) drawing each cause from right to left.

    Don't try to solve the risks at this point—you're just identifying risks and possible causes here! One downfall to fishbone diagrams is that, if the causes are not specific enough, you could create additional subcategories, each with a more detailed cause. This can overly complicate the diagram and make it unreadable.

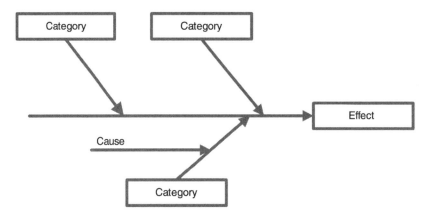

FIGURE 4.15
Creating a cause-and-effect (fishbone) diagram.

  - *Flowcharting*—Who in the world uses flowcharts anymore? Even though there's an obligation to mention flowcharting as a possible tool and technique, it can be quite handy to show how parts (and workflow) interact. Again, don't try to solve the issue here—you're just trying to identify and clarify risks!
  - *Strengths, Weaknesses, Opportunities, and Threats (SWOT) Analysis*—Although typically a technique used in preventive crisis management, SWOT Analysis has become a great decision tool for cross-functional stakeholders to identify risks

(see Figure 4.16). The team must agree on the goal of the SWOT Analysis and, in this case, to identify risks as either opportunities ("how can we take advantage of an opportunity?") or threats ("how can we defend against each threat?"). Note that strengths and weaknesses are not generally part of these discussions involving risks.

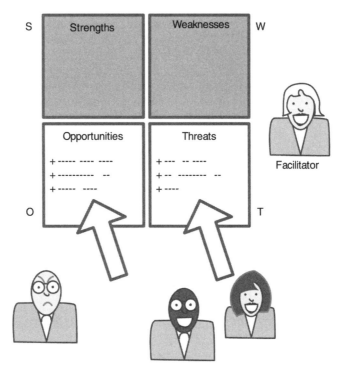

FIGURE 4.16
Using SWOT analysis to identify risks as opportunities or threats.

In order to have a productive SWOT brainstorming session, designate someone to be the facilitator. Should it be you?

Information Gathering and Analysis

Sometimes just gathering the right information can be a challenge. Once you get it, then how do you organize and analyze it?

■ **Brainstorming:** Usually requiring professional facilitation, brainstorming is one of the best ways to get risks out on the table. The facilitator (this is probably going to be you) should create an atmosphere where "no idea is a bad idea" and encourage a positive method of constructing a risk list. As the team brainstorms and writes down the possible risks on sticky notes, the facilitator then places them on a white board (or on the wall) under the appropriate categories and topics as defined by the group (see Figure 4.17).

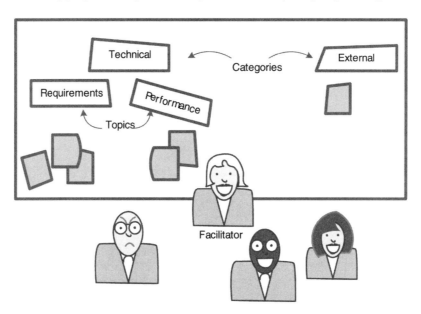

FIGURE 4.17
Brainstorming technique to identify risks.

- **Assumptions Analysis:** In the Project Charter, assumptions are identified that are used in project estimates. It is always a good idea to review those assumptions because, as a project progresses, assumptions that end up being false can become deadly risks.
- **Checklist Analysis:** Reviewing the lists of risks at key points throughout a project's life cycle can be a good exercise. If nothing else, it gets the team thinking in terms of risk management and can provide a good synopsis to keep as lessons learned for future projects.
- **The Delphi Technique:** This is a method to reach consensus where the team of experts' input is anonymous. Although originally designed as a forecasting tool during the Cold War, it is an interesting approach to creating unbiased agreement among experts.

    This is how it works: 1) A questionnaire is created and distributed to the experts. 2) Each expert comments about risks, anonymously giving honest feedback. 3) The feedback is summarized by the facilitator and recirculated anonymously for further feedback. The process continues until a consensus emerges (or until the team "runs out of gas").

    This technique limits any one individual from dominating the discussions, and it encourages feedback by all parties on major risks (and not just their own submitted risks). This also has the distinct advantage of providing a level playing field so that ideas from a more senior expert won't influence those more junior.

■ **Interviews:** Interviewing key stakeholders (especially those outside of the immediate project team) can be a very helpful technique to identify risks. Whereas a software engineer on the team may be concerned about the implementation of complex algorithms as a key risk, the product manager may be more concerned with the delivery timeline, even if it requires "dumbing down" the more complicated algorithms and feature sets. Bringing risks like these to the forefront early in a project may bond the team, in this case, to implement a simplified set of algorithms for the first version of this product in order to release on the expected timeline.

What is actually created with the Identify Risks process? *The Risk Register is created—that's what!*

BEST PRACTICE Risks can be threats (bad) or opportunities (good).

Using all of the tools and techniques at your disposal, a Risk Register is used to document information about each identified risk. Each risk has an entry that includes the following information:

■ The risk's description.
■ The risk category, risk topic, and a risk number.
■ Potential responses, or initial ideas for options that can possibly mitigate the risk. (It's okay if you don't know any responses yet!)
■ Root causes, or the underlying reason(s) derived from Root Cause Analysis that could cause the risk to occur—be very aware that one root cause can result in *multiple* risks.

The fishbone diagram technique does a nice job of providing information for the Risk Register because it can be created as a team exercise for gathering information on risks (effects) and possible causes.

There are a few rules about the Risk Register to keep in mind:
  ■ Each entry in a Risk Register should correspond to a risk in the RBS.
  ■ As each risk management process occurs, the amount of information kept in the Risk Register expands to accommodate added risk characteristics.
  ■ Risk management processes are cyclical, and other corresponding documents like the Risk Management Plan may have to be updated based on the outcomes of handling risks.
  ■ Last, but not least, the risk management processes should cycle and iterate throughout a project's life cycle (like all agile software projects do).

The diagram in Figure 4.18 will help illustrate how the Risk Register is created and subsequently updated (shown by the dotted lines).

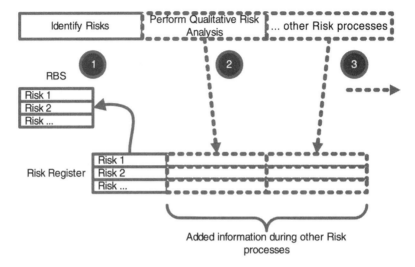

FIGURE 4.18
How the Risk Register is created and updated by other processes.

As a project advances through its paces, updating of the Risk Register is an ongoing activity.

The steps that take place are as follows:

1. In the Identify Risks process, the RBS and the Risk Register are created (each risk in the Risk Register references a risk in the RBS).
2. Additional information is appended to the Risk Register entry as a result of the Perform Qualitative Risk Analysis and other risk processes.
3. As other risk management processes occur, their results are updated in the Risk Register.

Perform Qualitative Risk Analysis

In order to determine which risks are the most critical to pursue, this process will provide the necessary tools and techniques to analyze and prioritize risks based on the impact (to the objectives of the project) and the probability of the risk occurring.

A qualitative approach toward risk management relies on a combination of expert judgments balanced by objective risk assessments and risk probability and impact tables. This process should be streamlined so that you and your team can take the key inputs and, sorry—this sounds like a broken record—objectively analyze both the impact and the probability of the risk taking place. These inputs include (but are not limited to) the following:

- **Risk Management Plan:** This includes the roles (for example, who makes risk decisions?), risk categories, definitions of probability and impact (refer to Table 4.5), and stakeholders' risk tolerances.
- **Risk Register:** Critical, since this table is what is going to be augmented by this process.
- **Project Scope Statement:** By evaluating the scope (in other words, the feature set definition of the project), you can determine whether much of the work is going to be new, complex, or more of the same.
- **Organizational process assets:** Risk Registers, knowledge bases, risk studies, and any information from similar past projects can be very helpful to qualify or to mitigate the risk.

The following tools and techniques are used:

- **Risk urgency and data quality assessment:** There needs to be information about the urgency of the issue and the quality of the data being analyzed. Urgency may carry incredible weight, especially in a time-driven project. If your project includes a tax preparation software component, certain risks are going to be very time sensitive so that ultimately your product will be deployed early in the calendar year in time for tax preparation. Equally important, if the quality of the data used for the analysis is suspicious, you may need to search further for better data. That outdated phrase "garbage-in, garbage-out" definitely applies to this issue.

> Once again, the favorite expert judgment will be used to add that necessary human touch to any evaluation of impact and probability analysis results.

- **Probability and Impact Matrix:** Although PMBOK recommends the use of the Probability and Impact Matrix, you rarely see it being used on software projects. So I'm going to introduce a variation called the JPIM.

> In case you were wondering what JPIM stands for, here are the choices for "J" (you decide): Jennifer (my daughter's name), Jethro (from the *Beverly Hillbillies*), or jus' e'nuff (a term I use throughout this book).

Referring to Table 4.5 as a model, you'll use the JPIM (Jus' e'nuff Probability and Impact Matrix) technique instead.

1. Select the project objective (from the Triple Constraint: scope, time, cost, and optionally, quality) that is most impacted by the risk. (As you learned before, impacting one of the Triple Constraints usually has equal effect on the others.)
2. Assign a low (L), medium (M), or high (H) value to the impact (I). In this case, let's assign a high (H) value to impact, since it is assumed that the risk could result in a significant schedule delay.
3. Do the same with the probability (P) of the risk occurring. In this case, I'll assign a medium (M) probability.
4. Apply an L, M, or H to urgency (U) of the risk. I'll assign an H.
5. Finally, identify the risk as a threat or an opportunity (T/O), and then use expert judgment (or, preferably, average the L, M, and H together) to agree to the overall priority. I'll assign an H to the risk's priority.

All of these additional fields *augment* the original Risk Register originally created in the Identify Risks process, as shown in Figure 4.19.

Identify Risks process		Perform Qualitative Risk Analysis				
#	Risk	T/O	P	I	U	Priority
1	New "core engine" may be too complicated to create in this version	T	M	H	H	H

FIGURE 4.19
Qualitative analysis updating of an example Risk Register item.

> There are many ways to derive a risk's priority. Some multiply probability (P) with impact (I) to derive a numerical value, while others work with specific percentages and complex lookup tables.

JPIM averages the P, I, and U qualitative values to derive the overall priority of the risk. In this example, it is high (H).

Let's look at another example where the risk is identified as follows: Possible attrition on your team could impact delivery. Your expert judgment and experience working with the team can play a large part in this analysis. In this particular example, the team has been working together for years, and not only is the team extremely talented, but they automatically operate as a strong, cohesive unit. Here's my qualitative analysis:

- The probability (P) is low (L). Currently, the team is a cohesive unit.
- Impact (I) is high (H). If the team begins to experience attrition, there is immediate impact to completing scope (the ability to develop the features).
- The urgency (U) of the risk is also low (L).
- The overall priority is therefore summarized to be somewhere between medium and low. Using expert judgment, go ahead and rate the overall priority as low (L). See Figure 4.20.

Identify Risks process		Perform Qualitative Risk Analysis				
#	Risk	T/O	P	I	U	Priority
6	Attrition on our team could impact delivery	O	L	H	L	L

FIGURE 4.20
Qualitative analysis second example.

Even though this risk has a low priority, you may wish to maintain a watch list, where low-risk items are monitored periodically. High-priority (and some medium-priority) risk items should be monitored more frequently. Another way to look at how to use the JPIM is with this simple (jus' e'nuff) formula:

```
Priority = Average(I, P, U)
```

Perform Quantitative Risk Analysis

This is what you've learned so far:

1. The Identify Risks process creates the list of risks.
2. The Perform Qualitative Risk Analysis process measures probability, impact, and overall priority for each risk.

The Perform Quantitative Risk Analysis process converts the qualitative measures to actual numerical weights and values so that decisions can be objectively made.

A quantitative approach of risk management is really one more step of detail that may be required after analyzing risks qualitatively. This technique relies on statistical calculations based on probability of occurrence and its impact on the project achieving its objectives. For that reason, you are placing an adjustment to a project's cost based on the *probability* that risks will occur. There are no guarantees, and coming up with costs associated if a risk happens can be suspicious at best (especially if you are just guessing what the cost would be).

Ultimately, this process adds quantitative information for every risk in the Risk Register. Inputs into this process include the Risk Management Plan (which specifies how risks are going to be managed), the Risk Register (which has been augmented with Qualitative Risk information), and Cost and Schedule Management Plans (which are critical, since they can provide the necessary background that goes into quantitative measurement). Additionally, organizational process assets can provide risk information from other projects and industry resources.

Tools and techniques used in Risk Quantitative Analysis are the following:

■ **Expert judgment:** First and foremost, you'll use subject-matter experts and quite possibly statistical experts to validate the data and techniques used in this process.

- **Data gathering and representation techniques:** Two techniques are typically used:
  - Interviewing
  - Probability distribution

By interviewing experts (you can get guidance from finance, historical information, and other leaders), you can provide a range of estimates for the overall project cost (see Table 4.6).

Table 4.6 Range of Project Costs Estimated by Interviewing

Work Unit	Low	Most Likely	High
Planning	$2M	$3M	$4M
Development up to technical feasibility	$1M	$1.5M	$2M
Development post-technical feasibility	$1M	$1.5M	$2M
Release	$.25M	$.35M	$.5M
Total project cost	$4.25M	$6.35M	$8.5M

What is this *technical feasibility* thing? I'll talk more about it in Chapter 10.

A set of costs based on low, most likely, and high estimates are often called *three-point estimates* that establish a budget range for the project. Why is this important? Having a cost range is invaluable during Quantitative Analysis. Even though the swing between the low and high estimates is large in this case, providing a range helps because the low becomes the best case, and the high is worst case. Your Finance department may wish to plan for somewhere between the most likely and the worst case. *You'll see why shortly. . . .*

Another technique that is mentioned in PMBOK is probability distribution, which takes time and cost into account. Now, with the augmented information in the Risk Register, along with cost data gathered, you can analyze the risks with Quantitative Risk Analysis techniques:

- **Sensibility Analysis:** If just one risk factor is uncertain and all others are fixed, then you can use something called a *tornado diagram* to visually show the magnitude of the one risk.
- **Monte Carlo Analysis:** Popular in cost estimating, this simulation technique allows you to predict outcomes based on the probability of the risk. This is a "mock up" that determines what kind of reserve should be planned.

- **Expected Monetary Value Analysis (EMV):** The most practical technique and the most used method to evaluate the cost of risks is the EMV. This method evaluates monetary outcome based on analysis predicting uncertainty.

But wait! Both the P and I are currently qualitative values (L, M, or H)! At this point, you augment the Risk Register again with three more fields of quantitative information, as shown in Figure 4.21.

Identify Risks process		Perform Qualitative Risk Analysis					Perform Quantitative Risk Analysis		
# Risk	T/O	P	I	U	Priority	P%	I$	EMV
1 New "core engine" may be too complicated to create in this version	T	M	H	H	H	50%	$125,000	–$62,500

FIGURE 4.21
An example of calculating the EMV.

The P% field represents the probability of the risk occurring as a percentage, and the I$ field represents the relative cost of developing, in this case, the "core engine" software module. The resultant EMV field is the multiplication of the two together. If the risk is viewed as an opportunity (a good thing to take advantage of), then the calculated EMV is positive; otherwise, the risk is a threat (a really bad thing) with a *negative* EMV. This can be shown in pseudo-code:

```
EMV = P% * I$
if T/O = T then
    EMV = - EMV
Endif
```

How does all of this go together then? You can add up all of the EMVs, or, preferably, you can add up only those that are critical and marked as high priority (H) that are going to be actively watched. The result becomes your EMV for the project, as shown in Table 4.7.

Table 4.7 Calculating a Project's EMV

Risk Register Items	P%	I$	EMV
New "core engine" may be too complicated to create in this version (a threat).	50%	$125K	–$62.5K
The product may not achieve 20% performance improvement (a threat).	50%	$60K	–$30K
There are 10 new features planned, and that may need to be scaled down (an opportunity).	20%	$200K	$40K
Total EMV for the project.			–$52.5K

The first two risks are threats, resulting in a negative cost to the project if they occur—and there is a 50% probability of that happening. The third risk may appear to be a threat, but the team believes that it is more important to release early with fewer new features. The opportunity to scale down scope could help the company before the competition can respond. So the benefit of doing fewer features (say, seven of the 10) is estimated to be a cost savings of $40K to the project.

The total EMV for these three prioritized risks is −$52.5K, which ultimately adjusts your overall project costs (remember Table 4.6). Table 4.8 shows a summary of how to look at the cost, including EMV.

Table 4.8 Range of Project Costs with EMV

Work Unit	Low	Most Likely	High
Total project cost	$4.25M	$6.35M	$8.5M
EMV total impact (reverse sign)	$.0525M	$.0525M	$.0525M
Total project cost with EMV	$4.303M	6.403M	$8.553M

Notice that EMV was originally calculated as an overall negative value, but when it is added to a total project budget, you'll need to reverse it. In other words, negative EMV threats should be added to the project cost, and calculated positive EMV opportunities should be subtracted from the project cost.

In Rita Mulcahy's *Risk Management*, she takes EMV calculations one step further. Instead of just quantifying risks as costs, why not do the same with level of effort (time)? Using the example in Table 4.7, you could augment the Risk Register with an additional risk value (called time) and calculate the Expected Value of Time (or EVT) from it (see Table 4.9).

Table 4.9 Calculating a Project's EVT

Risk Register (Excerpt)	P%	Time (Days)	EVT
New "core engine" may be too complicated to create in this version (a threat).	50%	10	−5
The product may not achieve 20% performance improvement (a threat).	50%	8	−4
There are 10 new features planned, and that may need to be scaled down (an opportunity).	20%	40	8
Total EVT for the project.			−1

Threats (the first two risks) are again treated as negative values, and opportunities (the third risk) are represented as positive values. In this case, the EVT results in a delay of one day. This technique may not be scientific nor discussed in PMBOK, but it is a practical way to plan for schedule impact should high-priority risks take place on a project.

Finally, there is Decision Tree Analysis! In the "real world" (if you call creating software "real"), quantifying project risks usually isn't quite as simple as adding a bunch of probable risk costs together. Armed with EMV information, you will usually have choices, and these choices are usually based on a combination of risks. Using a Decision Tree approach allows you to unravel all of the costs based on risks as a series of choices. The best way to work through Decision Trees is to break down the decision process into several steps.

Decision Trees start out with a decision, options, costs, and then choices based on probability and impact. With that information, you can calculate EMVs. The total cost is the summation of the options in the tree, as shown in Figure 4.22.

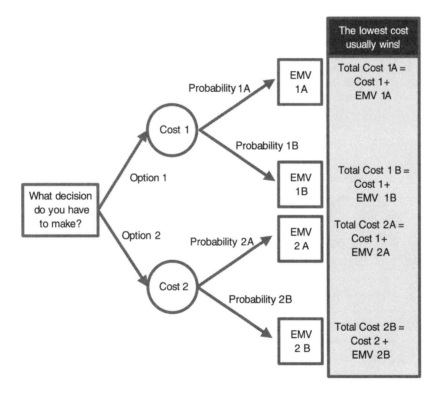

FIGURE 4.22
How Decision Trees work.

Decision Trees are a great way to validate outsourcing project work to a third-party software company in Bangalore, India, or to use available internal resources. The cost to build a core software module (the "engine") with internal resources is $350K and offshore is $200K. The quick assumption is that the least expensive course of action is to outsource the work.

But what is the risk with each choice? First, construct the Decision Tree with just the basic set of choices and costs, as shown in Figure 4.23.

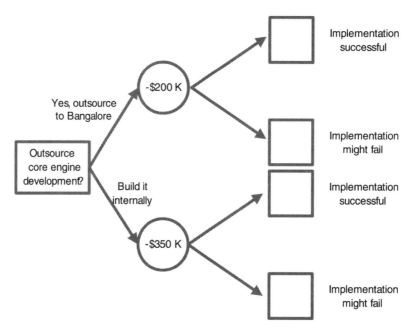

FIGURE 4.23
Setting up a Decision Tree to calculate EMVs.

Assuming that both teams are equally capable of doing the work, each of these options has two choices: The implementation succeeds or fails to get the work done on schedule. This is where expert judgment comes into play—you should put as much of an unbiased view with facts on forecasting the impact and probability of these choices (because chances are you'll have to justify them to your boss and the Finance department).

Next, the team needs to agree on the potential loss of revenue (impact to the project) should these events take place: $500K in this example. This particular outsource contractor is new and largely untested. So, the probability that its implementation might fail is 50%. Your internal staff is available and experienced; the probability that they might fail is estimated to be about 10%. The EMVs would be calculated as before, as shown in Figure 4.24.

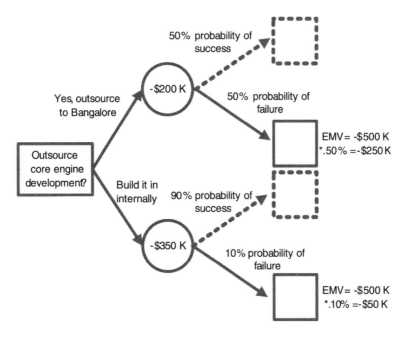

FIGURE 4.24
Calculating EMVs using a Decision Tree (simplified view).

When you estimate probabilities, they must add up to 100% for each decision. For example, to create the software with internal resources, there is either a 90% probability of success or a 10% probability of failure. The impacts may be dramatically different for each choice, and in fact one impact might be viewed as an opportunity and the other as a threat. The overall cost for each choice is the summation of the costs and EMVs for each branch (see Table 4.10).

Table 4.10 Summarizing Decision Tree Alternatives for Outsource Example

Decision: Outsource Core Engine	Cost	EMV	Total Cost
Outsourcing to Bangalore	−$200K	−$250K	−$450K
Creating software in-house	−$350K	−$50K	−$400K
Creating software internally is less costly by			$50K

Plan Risk Responses Process

The Plan Risk Responses process documents what you'll do if risks take place during a project's life cycle. So far, I've defined a project's set of risks, risk probabilities and impacts (both qualitative and quantitative), priorities to determine which risks are most important, and costs associated with each risk. The result will be to, once again, extend the Risk Register with additional risk-handling information and update any other planning, contract, and project documents to accommodate these risks. The inputs include the following:

■ **Risk Management Plan:** This document (or set of documents) defines how risks are to be prioritized, who is responsible for the project's overall risk management, and defines basic risk thresholds so that you know which risks should be attended to (and which ones simply fall below the line).

■ **Risk Register:** The table, spreadsheet, or database that identifies the risk, list of possible risk responses, Qualitative and Quantitative Risk Analysis, and costs (including EMV).

As always, the tools and techniques used to handle risks start with tried-and-true expert judgment. Strategies for threats and opportunities are a little more complicated. You may choose to handle the risk based on the techniques used in the prior two risk planning processes (Qualitative and Quantitative Analysis). If a risk is about to take place (where a third-party software supplier you are using is at the brink of reorganizing under Chapter 11 protection), you may wish to immediately calculate the EMV to help figure out what to do. Depending on the outcome, you may choose to either bail 'em out with a loan, choose another company, bring the work in-house, or even consider acquiring them.

The million-dollar question is, just what do you do when a threat needs to be handled? As shown in Table 4.11, PMBOK has identified several options (ordered from best to worst).

Table 4.11 Planning Strategies to Defend Against Threats

Ways to Handle Risks	Description
Avoid	Modify the plan so that the risk doesn't occur on your project. For example, if a risk is that your project is dependent on a third-party software vendor, make certain that you have an alternative third-party software vendor lined up just in case.
Transfer	Transfer the risk to another party. If your software project needs complicated algorithms to be implemented and your team doesn't quite have the experience to perform the work, subcontract the work to a contract software organization.

(continued)

Ways to Handle Risks	Description
Mitigate	Take action to limit the impact of the risk. Train a team inside the company to perform the work currently being performed by a third party on the next product upgrade. This could be more costly in the short term, but the company would benefit by having full control of the software knowledge internally.
Accept	Tolerate and deal with (in other words, "assume") the risk. This may be a far-fetched example, but if you are working with a distributed software development team and the World Wide Web "hits the dirt" for a period of time, how are you going to ensure that the project proceeds with your team dependent on Internet access? In April of 2008, this unthinkable situation occurred when an underwater cable break was discovered between Europe and northern Africa, thus disabling Internet connectivity for days in the Middle East.

What about positive risk opportunities? Although probably 99% of risks any project team deals with are negative threats, it is always nice to dream about positive risk outcomes if you have successfully planned for them (see Table 4.12).

Table 4.12 Planning Strategies to Take Advantage of Opportunities

Ways to Handle Risks	Description
Share	Spreading the ownership of the risk with another party who is qualified to realize the opportunity as a positive impact to the project (and, hopefully, to both parties). As an example, your project has a data reporting component, and your team can accomplish the work; if you partnered with a more experienced team of data reporting experts, the end result may not be a savings in cost but could benefit from a better implementation.
Exploit	Take all necessary steps to ensure that the risk is attained. A great example is where you have a choice to put your best software QA test engineer on your major maintenance upgrade project or on a next-generation project. Naturally, it would be the employee's desire to work on the other next-generation thing because it is new. However, if your project is a critical maintenance one, where existing customers are expecting a compatible, quality upgrade, you should be able to ensure an on-time, high-quality release using the best QA tester.

(continued)

Ways to Handle Risks	Description
Enhance	Increase the probability that positive impacts will occur. Not quite as guaranteed as exploiting a risk, but you can make the opportunity more probable. Rather than add more resources to bring in a schedule, you could ensure that your team is totally focused on the project by mandating a period of few meetings and minimal e-mail.
Accept	Tolerate and deal with (in other words, "assume") the risk. If your company's executive management team decided to unexpectedly allow you to hire a small software company from Ireland that had specific knowledge and experience that could help you reduce the schedule by one calendar month, accept it!

One other technique that is sure to be required is a Contingent Response Strategy. Any project (especially agile projects) will ebb and flow through a project's development life cycle, where some milestones will come in early and others a little bit later than the original project schedule assumed. Contingency plans are necessary to document in advance and to track continually. If an event triggers a risk and you need to execute some sort of contingency plan, then at least you have it identified beforehand.

If, for example, the risk has been identified and that if a specific third-party software contractor falls behind in its commitments to your project, your contingency agreed-upon plan may be to escalate to the third-party's managing director for resolution (this should be identified in a contract, by the way).

Another risk may be that the schedule assumes a certain level of funding, and as you track the remaining funds on a project, if the expenses exceed a certain threshold, you'll need to arrange for additional funding in order to complete the project.

> Remember the good ol' EMV that was calculated in the Perform Quantitative Risk Analysis process? Those estimated costs may justify the allocation of additional financial reserves for a project.

This brings up the topic of *reserves*. If you have set aside a pot of money for responding to risks, financial reserves should cover the high-priority Expected Monetary Value issues, which will undoubtedly occur (unless the risks are opportunities that could save you time and money). There are two types of reserves, shown in Table 4.13.

Table 4.13 Reserves Identified for Risk Responses

Reserve	Risks Awareness	Description
Contingency Reserve	Known-Unknowns	Risks that you anticipate might happen (for example, any in the Risk Register).
Management Reserve	Unknown-Unknowns	Risks that you don't know and are totally unexpected (for example, a hurricane hits St. Louis).

How do you calculate reserves? To calculate contingency reserves, add up all of the opportunity EMVs and subtract all of the threat EMVs. You could also calculate the schedule impact by multiplying your total time reserve by an average cost per day. To calculate management reserves, all you need to do is compute a percentage of the overall total project cost. If the total project cost is $6.4M and you believe that an overage of 10% is justified, the management reserve should set aside $640K.

NOTE Contingency reserves are not padding of any sort. If your planning effort is good, the contingency reserves should be very easy to document and support. To identify a project's management reserve, make sure that you have contingency reserves defined, too. Otherwise, a generic management reserve by itself can't really be justified, since it is based on unknowns.

The main output of the Plan Risk Responses process is an update to the Risk Register, as shown in Figure 4.25.

Identify Risks process		Perform Quantitative Risk Analysis				Plan Risk Responses	
#	Risk	P%	I$	EMV	Owner	Strategy	Responses
1	New "core engine" may be too complicated to create in this version	50%	$125,000	-$62,500	Joe	Mitigate	Assign a seasoned architect to the team

FIGURE 4.25
Updating risk responses to the Risk Register.

The owner is the "lucky" person who is responsible for handling any risk in case it occurs. (Don't forget: You are responsible for making sure that the risk is being monitored.) The strategies for both threats and opportunities are summarized in Table 4.14. Finally, you should include the planned primary and contingency responses that should be taken if the risk occurs.

The three threats are often referred to as ATM and opportunities as SEE.

Table 4.14 Possible Strategies for Handling a Risk

Defending Against Threats	Taking Advantage of Opportunities
Avoid	Share
Transfer	Exploit
Mitigate	Enhance
	Accept (Threat or Opportunity)

NOTE PMBOK gets a little verbose on the sheer number of items that can be tracked in the Risk Response Plan. I recommend keeping the Risk Register as simple as possible with jus' e'nuff actionable information.

Let's continue with the outputs, shall we?

- **Update Project Management Plan:** Depending on the nature of the risks, it is recommended to update the Project Management Plan (or its many subsidiary plans). For example, the Quality Management Plan may have to be changed to reflect the fact that an outsourced contractor's quality isn't performing to the plan, thus requiring a heightened QA activity by your team to ensure that quality project objectives are met.
- **Risk-related contract decisions:** Contracts may have to be adjusted or reconsidered if potential risks with partners, subcontractors, customers, or outside technologies are added in the Risk Register. If, for example, a third-party contracting company is perfect for the project (talented, experienced, easy to work with, low cost, and so on), yet there is a huge risk that they may not have the business acumen to remain in business for the long term. This risk could have a mitigate strategy where all source code is to be frequently placed in escrow.
- **Update project documents:** Project documentation, bug-tracking databases, end-user manuals, and other documentation may require updates based on the possibility of risks tracked in the Risk Register. As an example, if a core software engine's original design was too ambitious for a "version 1.0 product" and its algorithms are reduced in complexity as a result, this will have a direct bearing in technical documentation that may accompany the software. It could also impact internal project planning documentation (like the Project Scope Statement discussed in Chapter 5, "Partner with Product Management").

BEST PRACTICE All risks can't possibly be known at the beginning of a project. In planning risk responses, you might uncover new risks!

That's about it for the Risk Management knowledge area's planning processes! Here's a review of the risk planning steps by process, as shown in Figure 4.26 (labeled 1 through 5):

1. Initially, the Risk Management Plan is created along with a Risk Breakdown Structure (RBS) that categorizes risks (much like the way a WBS categorizes work).
2. In the Identify Risks process, a Risk Register describing all risks is created.
3. Each risk in the Risk Register undergoes Qualitative Analysis, which assigns a priority (low, medium, or high) based on the probability and impact of each risk.
4. In the Perform Quantitative Risk Analysis process, each potential risk in the Risk Register is designated as a threat or opportunity, assigned an impact cost and a probability percentage that the risk might occur, and a calculated Expected Monetary Value (EMV) of additional costs (if a threat) or cost reduction (if an opportunity).
5. Finally, the Risk Register is enhanced by the Plan Risk Responses process to include the risk owner, strategy as to how to handle the potential risk, and a brief description of the best risk response and contingency.

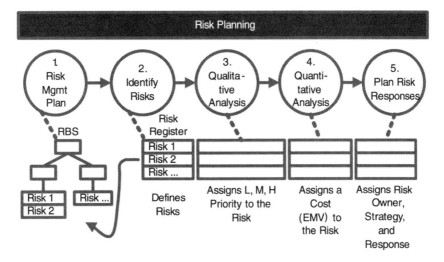

FIGURE 4.26
Summary of risk planning processes.

Risk Management in the Monitoring & Controlling Process Group

The Monitor and Control Risks process is highly dynamic, with the basic premise that risk management is treated similarly to change management.

Monitor and Control Risks

Key activities are the following:

- Validates that project assumptions still hold up.
- Risks need to be monitored with the lookout for major changes in trends. For example, if one of the risks is keeping to budget, and halfway through the project 75% of the funding has already been spent, this should set off a trigger that you might need to find additional loot.
- Risk management policies and procedures are not being followed by the team. (For example, an engineer, in order to accelerate delivery of a key software module, authorizes a contractor to help without getting the proper approval.)
- Contingency reserves are updated as the project proceeds and risks change. (The prospect of adding more reserves is one of the toughest pills to swallow by any Finance department.)

BEST PRACTICE Regularly monitor assumptions identified in the Project Charter.

NOTE

If assumptions start falling apart, you can bet that a potential risk is right around the corner. If, as an example, your Mac software project assumed a certain set of Power PC compiler/build tools, and in the early stages of your project development, Apple unexpectedly announces a major switch of tools and their underlying architecture to Intel's Core Duo (from Power PC), that change would have an immediate risk impact and require a risk response. (This situation, of course, really took place in early 2006.)

The negative threat you'd have to defend is that the cost of switching gears to a new architecture might cost you precious time, and yet, if you don't, it could alienate prospective customers who will automatically switch to the new machines and expect your software to run on it.

The positive opportunity would be to immediately switch to the new tools, take a schedule hit, and be the first application in your market to support the new Intel Mac architecture.

The Risk Management Plan and Risk Register are the primary inputs into the Monitor and Control Risks process. A variety of different performance reports are also valuable (but not always necessary) to track project history. With these reports you should be able to see trends that indicate the presence of risks that will need to be handled. These performance reports aren't your typical product performance things—these instead refer to status information objectively stating just how well your team is progressing with the project activities. Typical information you'd track is as follows:

- Progress on deliverables (for example, tasks)
- Progress on schedule (for example, milestone attainment)

- Costs to date and budget remaining
- Defect resolution (for example, comparing incoming and resolved rate of change)

All of the preceding should be tracked frequently, and these trends can be used for Variance and Trend Analysis. Comparing progress against baselines already established in project planning documents is an outstanding method to recognize potential for risks (for either threats or opportunities).

BEST PRACTICE Put risk reassessment and audits on the agenda of every project team meeting.

The team should frequently review existing risks for change of status (also known as *risk reassessment*), identification of new risks, and how effective risk responses have been to date (known as a *risk audit*). Contingency and management reserves need to be validated with something called a Reserve Analysis to ensure that the remaining reserves are adequate.

It almost seems silly to state this but, yes, regularly scheduled status meetings are very important to ensure that all the rest of these techniques used in monitoring and controlling risks are occurring on a frequent basis.

NOTE

How often is often enough to have status meetings? A good rule of thumb is to provide a forum in which the team can evaluate what has changed and what needs to take place in under an hour. Meetings that last longer than an hour and become a marathon are just that— a tiring experience.

And, as a project gets closer to final release, you may wish to have more frequent meetings just to be sure that there are no gaps being left on the table and no mishaps that cause the schedule to slip.

BEST PRACTICE Don't use the Risk Register as a defect (bug) tracking database!

There are several outputs to this process that are similar to the previous Plan Risk Responses, but this time a change *has* occurred and action is needed:

- **Update Risk Register:** The Risk Register will need to be updated if new risks have been identified or changes have occurred with risk responses or priority (maybe the risk becomes more or less important). The Risk Register is basically a live database that should keep potential risks on every team member's mind.

- **Update Project Management Plan:** If an approved change request has an impact on the Project Management Plan, you'll need to update the plan (and any of its subsidiary plans) accordingly. Any adjustments to the plan become the new plan baseline.
- **Change requests:** Typically a result of the team identifying a potential risk; handling the risk requires an official request so that risk mitigation occurs. These requests are usually submitted to the Perform Integrated Change Control process for approval (see "Perform Integrated Change Control" earlier in this chapter).
- **Update project documents:** Project documentation, bug tracking database entries, end-user manuals, and other documentation may require updates based on action taken to handle each risk.
- **Update organizational process assets:** You may wish to document and save risk-related project statuses that can spare embarrassment (or frustration) in future projects. This includes assets like lessons learned, the Risk Register, RBS, and project meeting notes.

Let's look at an example. Your team has a history of difficulty in resolving critical defects in a timely manner. A risk, already in the Risk Register, might be something like, "Resolve critical defects immediately upon detection." Its risk response might be, "Meet on the top-10 priority defects on a daily basis and to engage other engineers part time to aid in defect resolution."

> Pair programming and the use of "buddy systems" is a popular characteristic of agile software development.

Project trends for incoming defects (those found) and resolved defects (those fixed) are tracked as part of the Variance and Trend Analysis activity. In the project's Risk Management Plan, there is special mention that in order to release the product, incoming severe defects must be quickly resolved (the team's number-one priority). The department's goals state that in order to release a quality product, the rate by which defects are resolved should keep up with the rate of defects detected. In fact, the *closer* the project gets to completion, the *lower* the rate of detected defects should be. (By the way, a guiding principle of agile software development is to *test early* and *test often* to avoid this situation.) Figure 4.27 shows the project's latest historical defects chart and defect trends.

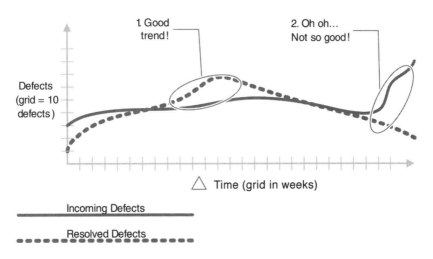

FIGURE 4.27
How Variance and Trend Analysis can help spot risks.

Here's a look at the two trends:

1. Several weeks back (point 1 in the chart), incoming defects were fairly constant, and defect resolution was keeping up with incoming detected defects. After that, incoming defects started to drop off—a great sign that there was light at the end of the tunnel.
2. At point 2, the rate of incoming defects shot up, and the resolved defects rate actually dipped, causing the need to execute the Risk Response Plan. In this particular case, a change request was immediately formalized to add an expert software engineer from another project who could "buddy up" with the team and had prior experience with this code on past projects.

BIBLIOGRAPHY

Agile Alliance. *Manifesto for Agile Software Development.* www.agilealliance.com.

Brooks, Fred. *The Mythical Man-Month: Essays on Software Engineering, Anniversary Edition.* Indianapolis, IN: Addison-Wesley Professional, 1995.

Greene, Jennifer and Andrew Stellman. *Head First PMP: A Brain-Friendly Guide to Passing the Project Management Professional Exam.* Sebastopol, CA: O'Reilly Media, 2007.

Hillson, David. "Use a Risk Breakdown Structure (RBS) to Understand Your Risks." Proceedings of the Project Management Institute Annual Seminars & Symposium (2002).

Johnson, Tony. *PMP Exam Success Series: Certification Exam Manual.* Carrollton, TX: Crosswind Project Management, 2006.

Kliem, Ralph L. and Irwin S. Ludin. *Project Management Practitioner's Handbook.* New York: AMACON, 1998.

Larman, Craig. *Agile & Iterative Development: A Manager's Guide.* Boston: Pearson Education, 2004.

Lewis, James P. *Project Planning, Scheduling, and Control, Fourth Edition.* New York: McGraw-Hill, 2005.

Mulcahy, Rita. *PM Crash Course.* Minneapolis: RMC Publications, 2006.

Mulcahy, Rita. *Risk Management: Tricks of the Trade for Project Managers.* Minneapolis: RMC Publications, 2003.

Newell, Michael. *Preparing for the Project Management Professional (PMP) Certification Exam, Third Edition.* New York: AMACON, 2005.

Project Management Institute, Inc. *A Guide to the Project Management Body of Knowledge: PMBOK Guide, Third Edition.* Newton Square, PA: Project Management Institute, 2004.

Project Management Institute, Inc. *A Guide to the Project Management Body of Knowledge: PMBOK Guide, Fourth Edition.* Newton Square, PA: Project Management Institute, 2008.

Scholtes, Peter R., Brian L. Joiner, and Barbara J. Streibel. *The Team Handbook, Third Edition.* Madison, WI: Oriel, 2003.

Seningen, Scott. "Learn the Value of Lessons-Learned" (www.projectperfect.com.au/downloads/Info/info_lessons_learned.pdf).

Smith, John L. *Troubled IT Projects: Prevention and Turnaround.* London: The Institute of Electrical Engineers, 2001.

Tedesco, Paul A. *Common Sense in Project Management.* Course Technology PTR, 2006.

Yourdon, Ed. *Death March.* Upper Saddle River, New Jersey: Prentice Hall PTR, 1997.

Vanderbilt University. "Ishikawa Diagram." *Quality Library* (http://mot.vuse.vanderbilt.edu/mt322/Ishikawa.htm).

5 Partner with Product Management

Your responsibility is to facilitate and lead software teams to release quality products to market. You have a partner that you may not even think much about—product management (aka marketing to some of you). Not only are they participants in the overall project life cycle, they are depending on you to deliver the project to market on time and on budget. So, in many ways, decisions that you make are made with the product manager as the project's business owner and partner.

This chapter includes the following topics, critical to ensuring that the project leadership team (you and the product manager) are working together:

■ Unquestionably, your role is as a leader. (Should your title be project leader and not project manager?)
■ Tips and techniques for keeping software development and product management aligned.
■ Planning and controlling the project's features (PMBOK uses the term *scope*) according to Project Scope Management best practices.

WHAT IS MEANT BY LEADERSHIP?

The next few sections represent leadership areas that we all can improve on, and it starts with making sure your role and that of product management work well together (and for the same cause).

KEEPING DEVELOPMENT AND PRODUCT MANAGEMENT ALIGNED

KEY ROLES AND RESPONSIBILITIES

The success of a project team requires a close relationship between the following leaders, shown in Figure 5.1.

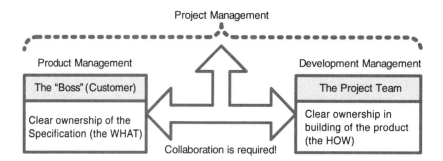

FIGURE 5.1
Relationship between the management leaders.

For software development projects, there tend to be three distinct roles:

- **Product manager:** Owns the overall success of the project, empowered to ensure that it succeeds once it is delivered to the market, and that the customer's best interest is served. The product manager sets the overall roadmap and vision for the product line and how it relates to the overall company mission. Starting with the beginning of a project, a product manager usually is concerned about "the what" that is being built.
- **Development manager:** Even though there may be a host of different managers from different departments (Engineering, QA, Technical Publications, IT, and so on) involved with a project, there needs to be a single manager acting as the one responsible for getting the work done. (Engineering management is normally concerned just with the design and programming.)
- **Project manager:** Facilitates the overall process so that the project is completed by planning, communicating status, watching and acting upon change, removing obstacles, and ensuring that all of the stakeholders work together to deliver on time. The project manager is the single-most critical point of contact that makes sure that the what and the how are getting done on time and to specifications. The project manager is the person to go to for information at any point during a project's life cycle.

The everyday interactions between these three roles assume the following:

1. Decisions will need to be made throughout a project.
2. There is a unified overall roadmap and vision that have been bought into, clearly communicated, and constantly reinforced.
3. Success is based on team collaboration, and roles will blend and cross boundaries sometimes (as shown with the multi-headed arrow in Figure 5.1).

INTRODUCING THE DECISION PYRAMID

Let's talk about how decisions need to be made. Projects have many stakeholders. For simplicity's sake, I've divided them into three groups (see Table 5.1), each of which is commonly known as a "decisionaker" (a combined word for *decision maker*—if it isn't a real word yet, it should be).

Table 5.1 Group Decision Makers

Decisionaker	Description
Company	This group represents those who are mostly concerned about the business—executive management, Sales and Finance, stockholders, and investors. These folks mostly see the benefit from the financial success (typically revenue) that the product generates.
Employee	The team on the project (you, software engineers, testers, writers, support, and so on)—those who mostly benefit from the development and creation of the product.
Customer	The users and resellers—those who mostly benefit from the product after it is released. This group should represent the market and not just a specific customer. (Product management usually takes the role of representing the customer in key decision making.)

There will be times when you'll need to make key product or project decisions throughout a project's life cycle. Let's say, for example, that a new set of features is to be introduced in a major product update. Collectively, there is a high probability (75%) of failure that all features will be implemented along with lightning-fast performance. Delivery of features and performance could give the company a real competitive advantage. Alternatively, there might be only a 25% probability of failure if two of the key features were implemented and "killer" performance wasn't expected (at least for the first version).

The team rightly decided to take the "all features with lightning-fast performance" route, and like any great agile project, the two most important key features were designed, prototyped, engineered, and tested first. This was an excellent test case to see how the new features would function and perform.

Well, it didn't quite work out that way! Although the two key implemented features functioned as expected, the performance was not blazingly fast, and management was concerned that, unless time was spent on improving performance, there would be significant risk trying to get all of the features to operate at the expected level of performance. The team, however, was convinced that they should "do the right thing" by fixing the performance issues and completing the rest of the features, even if there was schedule impact! "The customers would want this," was the overwhelming team war cry. However, the customers only knew about the key features—they hadn't expressed the need or commitment for anything more than that. (But if they got more features than expected, they'd certainly be pleased!) Finance, of course, wanted the product released as soon as possible.

Most of us have been in this situation multiple times: A key decision needs to be made, and yet the decisionakers representing the employee (the team), company (Finance), and the customer (product management) have different biases as to what is most important.

A Decision Pyramid is used to clarify how key decisions are made based on satisfying the needs of the most important decisionaker (see Figure 5.2).

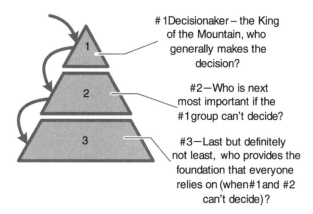

#1Decisionaker – the King of the Mountain, who generally makes the decision?

#2–Who is next most important if the #1group can't decide?

#3–Last but definitely not least, who provides the foundation that everyone relies on (when#1 and #2 can't decide)?

FIGURE 5.2
Defining the Decision Pyramid.

BEST PRACTICE Use the Decision Pyramid to provide a consistent priority for tough project and product decisions.

The Decision Pyramid places the most important decision-making process to the decisionaker at the top pinnacle of the pyramid (marked as #1). Given the project example, if the topmost decisionaker is represented by the company, the decision between going ahead with implementing all of the features and improving the product's performance becomes the right decision if the financial rewards are better than the alternative of completing the two key features.

The second Decision Pyramid decisionaker (#2 directly below the pinnacle) should be used as the basis for a decision if the choices can't easily be made by the first, topmost level decisionaker's viewpoint. In this same example, if the product choices are determined to return the same financial benefits to the company, then the next level of decisionaker is called upon to break the tie. And last but not least, if the top two decisionakers can't easily provide the necessary facts to make a decision, then it is up to the third-level decisionaker, #3 in the figure, to make the final call.

The lowest level in the Decision Pyramid shouldn't be regarded as the least important decision maker of the three—instead, view it as the foundation (or tie-breaker) in case the other two levels can't make a final decision.

So what does your company's Decision Pyramid look like? In Figure 5.3, I've constructed a sample Decision Pyramid where the employee is the first decisionaker, followed by the customer, and then the company. That ordering works when the philosophy assumes that the employees have the first and final say toward key decisions. If the employee (again, representing the team) can't decide, then it becomes the role of the needs of the customer to make the decision. Finally, if a decision can't be made, it becomes a company (or, typically, financial) decision. There have been a number of companies that practice this decision process—especially those that tend to believe they should "let the employees make cool stuff and the customers will come, which ultimately benefits the company!" It can also backfire if employees make decisions on products based on whiz-bang features that customers aren't necessarily willing to purchase. *Oops!*

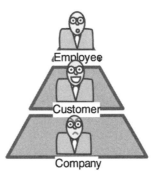

FIGURE 5.3
Assigning decisionakers to
the Decision Pyramid.

A sample Decision Pyramid that can be regarded as poised for long-term growth is shown in Figure 5.4. In this example, key decisions are made based on the needs of the customer first. If customer needs are equal in importance (for example, some customers want all features implemented regardless of performance and others want fewer features that have blazing performance), then you make the decisions based on the needs of the business. For example, Finance may determine that the customer base is willing to pay more for fewer features with blazing performance than those who want all features implemented with no performance improvements. And finally, if a decision still can't be made easily among the customer and company decisionakers, the employees (the team) should decide.

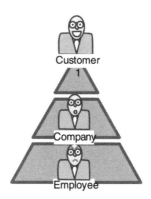

FIGURE 5.4
Decision Pyramid based on
customer need first (#1).

The result of making decisions based on the Decision Pyramid can have an equally profound impact on making the right decisions. If the customers are satisfied, they will reward the company with revenue. With the company doing well, the employee should be satisfied knowing that customers are happy and their company is successful (in other words, profitable). Oh yeah—there are a couple of rules in defining your Decision Pyramid:

1. Keep your decision criteria as simple and intuitive as possible. If making decisions takes lots of e-mails, meetings, and conversations, then you've definitely made it way too difficult.
2. Apply the Decision Pyramid methodology in a consistent way. Despite the pressure, don't make a customer-company-employee decision one day (in order to please technical support), and then an employee-customer-company decision the next day (to please an engineer who refuses to work on an important feature that is boring work).

Once the team gets in the swing as to how key decisions are made, everyone pitches in! Questions like this can be heard at a project team meeting:

Okay—we have this so-called serious bug. It is going to take about one week to resolve it, and the software engineers say that they don't have time. Since we need to make key decisions based on the customer first, what impact would not correcting this defect have on our #1 decisionaker, the customer?

In summary, the cross-functional project leadership team should get in the habit of making key, critical decisions in a consistent manner. The Decision Pyramid can be a useful tool for that purpose.

MANAGING BY OBJECTIVES

Having a project roadmap and an overall vision can become very critical. You don't hear much lately about the old-style Management by Objectives (MBO) anymore, but I'm going to bring it out again—even with the advent and acceptance of agile methodology. In order to create a project, there needs to be a rationale and a purpose. Any and all projects being considered should not only play a vital role in a project but should also reinforce the company's product vision.

A pivotal scene in *Miller's Crossing* is when Tom, played by Gabriel Byrne, is asked to "whack" someone, but he is reluctant to do the assignment even though it is expected of him: "What's the reason? I've got to have a reason."

A more applicable example might be the case where the project you are leading is terminated or "put on the backburner." Management always has to make those tough decisions if a project no longer aligns with the company's vision or when a product has outlived its usefulness. This is especially true if the cost of maintenance far exceeds any derived financial benefit. Once a project commences, however, it is your job to make sure the team understands how it fits in to your company's overall plan. This is where managing to objectives can make a huge difference to the successful delivery of a project. The simple explanation of adhering to MBO is relevant for anyone leading a project:

- Setting attainable goals (both tactical and strategic)
- Monitoring for variance
- Adjusting as necessary (but still keeping objectives in mind)

Let's talk about strategic goal setting for a moment and make sure that you are working with product management to construct a "reason" that shows product direction and helps the team understand how the project fits into the grander company picture. When your teams work on projects, naturally there is a project schedule posted somewhere, right??? Well, let's assume there is! If you asked anyone on the team how their project relates to the overall product roadmap, and you get a "sure, I know" response—then wonderful! You may as well skip right on over to the next section in this chapter! If you get a blank stare, just think of all the times you've discussed and presented schedule information to the team and they haven't known or cared. Publishing bunches of Microsoft Project schedules and detailed status reports are not going to give the teams the overall perspective they'll need in order to make informed decisions. Figure 5.5 should give you an idea of a product roadmap that the collaborative set of managers (development, project/program, and product) should all agree to.

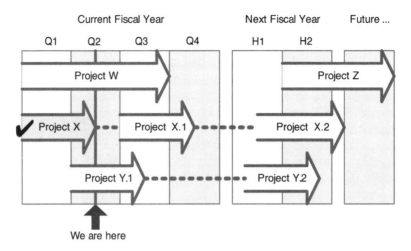

FIGURE 5.5
Sample project roadmap.

Remember the United Way campaigns? A big thermometer visually showed how far contributions had progressed over time. It is a great way to make goals visible and to show just how far you have to go (and, very importantly, how much time you have left). A simple progress diagram, like the United Way barometer or the project roadmap in Figure 5.5, shows the development teams a number of things:

- A three-year project outlook (seven projects are currently defined).
- Range of estimated schedules for projects (the further out, the less specific).
- Which projects have been completed (the one with the checkmark).
- Clarity of product lines (there are four of them labeled W, X, Y, and Z) and which ones are updates. (There are four of them planned: X.1, X.2, Y.1, and Y.2.)
- Where their project fits into the grand company vision and product roadmap.

In Tony Johnson's book *PMP Exam Success Series: Certification Exam Manual,* he reinforces the importance of keeping MBOs in everyone's mind: If your project doesn't align properly to the overall goals, vision, and roadmap, you could find your favorite project de-prioritized or even cancelled.

INTRODUCING THE AGILE PRODUCT MANAGER

Does your partner in product management also need to think in terms of being agile? According to the product management training firm, Pragmatic Marketing, Steve Johnson and Luke Hohmann make a couple of key assertions in an article entitled "Living in an Agile World: The Strategic Role of Product Management When Development Goes Agile":

1. Most software development approaches put their teams through a life cycle to create a specialized project and not as a product. This is wrong. Decisions must be made for the good of the overall market rather than for a one-off customer (unless your business is strictly professional services). Your delivery life cycle will be elongated, and chances are that your company won't scale because you missed overall market needs. (Of course, if there are unlimited resources available, you could attempt to satisfy the needs of the market and those of select customers *if* there is enough time and budget!)

2. The role of the product manager is that of the customer (or, more appropriately, the customer base you serve). Agile projects depend on "the boss" (the customer) to be central in product decisions. The reality is that the customer is not always readily available to interact with the team. This requires someone to stand in for the customer, and that is the product manager. (That's a big responsibility, and no wonder they are sometimes cranky.)

ENSURING PROJECTS STAY ON SCOPE

It isn't just project management or software development that needs to think and act agile—so does product management.

OVERVIEW OF THE PROJECT SCOPE MANAGEMENT KNOWLEDGE AREA

Software development, product management, and project management will team up to drive the definition of what is being built (in other words, the scope) for a product with a specific project. There are three Planning processes and two Monitoring & Controlling processes, as shown in Table 5.2.

Table 5.2 Scope Management Knowledge Area Processes (PMBOK 4th Edition)

	Process Groups			
	Implementation			
Initiating	Planning	Executing	Monitoring & Controlling	Closing
	Collect Requirements		Verify Scope	
	Define Scope		Control Scope	
	Create WBS			

As with most PMBOK definitions, there are some basic characteristics for Project Scope Management:

■ These processes interact with each other and oftentimes overlap.
■ These processes interact with other knowledge area processes (especially the overall Project Integration Management processes covered in Chapter 4).
■ Each process occurs at least once in every project (definitely more than once in agile projects).
■ Each process occurs in a project phase, if the project is divided into project phases.
■ There needs to be team flexibility for these processes to be distinct, combined, not used, or even behave differently than defined in PMBOK.

There are basically two types of scope:

■ **Product scope:** Features and functions that characterize a product (or service).
■ **Project scope:** The actual work that needs to be accomplished to deliver a product (or service).

Scope Management is centered on a single document that serves as the baseline definition of the project: the Work Breakdown Structure (WBS).

> The WBS serves as the initial baseline definition of the project, and once created and agreed upon, the scope is continually monitored and controlled throughout a project's life cycle.

SCOPE MANAGEMENT IN THE PLANNING PROCESS GROUP

The planning activities, once again, are the most critical tasks in defining a project's scope. The three Scope Planning processes defined in the Scope Management knowledge area are as follows:

■ Collecting the requirements
■ Defining the scope
■ Creating the WBS

Collect Requirements

This initial planning process has been dramatically changed (perhaps the better word is "enhanced") in the PMBOK Fourth Edition to take full advantage of information-gathering techniques.

A project's success is directly impacted by how well all stakeholders are aligned with gathering the right, complete set of requirements. Most of us have seen the situation where halfway through a project the team becomes disoriented in attempting to accommodate scope creep. Or what about the situation where the team is focused on one set of project objectives ("we're adding 10 major new features") while product management was really focused on an implied additional set? ("Well, it *has* to outperform the competitors by 10%, take advantage of the video graphics GPU, and run on less memory, too!")

According to Barry Boehm, research conducted some 25 years ago found that correcting a requirement after a product was put into users' hands cost as much as 68 times more than if it had been defined correctly during the early requirements-gathering stages of a product life cycle. *Just what is a requirement anyway?* Although there are many definitions, for software development, probably the most sane description is this:

> A feature/function definition that satisfies a customer need (and that you intend to build).

According to the IEEE, a requirement is as follows:

> "A condition or capability needed by a user to solve a problem or achieve an objective."

And, last but not least, according to PMBOK, a requirement is defined as the following:

> "The project and product features and functions needed to fulfill stakeholders' needs and expectations."

As defined by Alan Davis in his book *Software Requirements: Objects, Functions, and States*, characteristics of a great requirement are defined in Table 5.3.

Table 5.3 Characteristics of Great Requirements

Requirement Characteristic	Description
Complete	Fully describes the functionality to be delivered.
Correct	By reducing the speculation of what a customer expects—make sure that it is accurate.
Feasible	Not a bad idea to have both engineering and product management work together—it doesn't make much sense to dream. It's better to deliver.
Necessary	Trace back to the customer's real need; gold plating doesn't help anyone.
Prioritized	All feature requests can't be the highest priority; there should be a ranking and a must have/need to have determination.
Traceable	You may want to consider numbering each one to make sure that as it gets referenced, validated, and updated and that the history is maintained.
Unambiguous	By analysis and inspection, stakeholders should walk away with exactly the same understanding.
Verifiable	QA will want to be sure that there is a test case associated with each requirement. (If they can't test it, how will you know whether it will perform as expected?)

BEST PRACTICE Use a checklist to make sure that each requirement passes the "great requirements" test.

The key activities for this critical process result in producing the Requirements Management Plan by gathering the requirements from the Project Charter document and stakeholders. The inputs for this planning process are as follows:

- **Project Charter:** This document provides the *what* for scope planning. It contains an overview (not detailed!) of project and product requirements.
- **Stakeholder Register:** This document (or database) describes who will be involved with scope planning. This Register identifies those stakeholders who can provide the information about project and product requirements.

Requirements-Gathering Techniques

You know where to get the basic information and who to get it from. *Now what?* This is where the fun begins, and this is where, in an agile software project, you'll need to figure out the best way to gather the project and product requirements with enough detail to start building. But, on the other hand, you'll need to retain enough flexibility to adjust scope as the discovery process takes place during the project life cycle. There are many tools and techniques used to collect the requirements.

Please keep in mind that requirements gathering should result in a *minimum* amount of paper. Creating simple visual aids, tables, charts, and one-page documents is the best way to remain effective and to capture the team's attention span.

Although PMBOK distinguishes individual from group requirements-gathering methods, I'm introducing them all as a single set.

- **Interviews:** Often in a one-on-one setting, stakeholders are asked questions to identify and define the features of the desired project deliverables. This technique can work well in a group setting so long as you don't let a subset of individuals dominate the feedback from others less inclined to speak up.

> Although ad hoc interview techniques are preferred, it is always a good idea to have a set of prepared questions to ask stakeholders.

- **Facilitated workshops:** Usually requiring a professional facilitator, a workshop that encourages requirements gathering can be very successful. These Joint Application Development (commonly called JAD) sessions are very popular in software organizations. If you are working in a cost-conscious startup, be aware that the budget commitment can be prohibitive. These sessions typically result in well-organized lists that can easily fit into a WBS (more on this later).
- **Brainstorming:** A fast-paced technique where ideas are encouraged in a rapid fire group setting. Brainstorming helps bring the experience of all team members into play during requirements gathering. There are many variations to brainstorming (Nominal Group Technique, Idea/Mind Mapping, and so on) that you may wish to consider, but until you get really good at it, simple brainstorming and recording of all ideas (no requirement is a bad requirement, okay?) is the best way to go.

> Brainstorming is also a key technique when identifying risks (see the section "Identify Risks" in Chapter 4).

- **The Delphi Technique:** This is the method where you lead a team through several rounds of unsolicited feedback. This technique, also used to identify risks, is especially useful if your staff shows particular distain toward management, doesn't get along, or are combative and difficult to handle. (Yet they could be the most valuable, talented team on the planet!) This takes some practice in order to work the facilitation process well.
- **Questionnaires:** The age-old technique of getting feedback with questionnaires and surveys can be a very easy way to collect requirements. This is useful as long as your intention is to mold the feedback to conform to a preset group of options. Although this is typically performed in a non-group setting, it is always a good idea to present the results in a group (or webcast) setting to summarize the results (most of us forget to do this part).
- **Group Decision-Making Technique:** Generally a secondary stage of requirements gathering (after the other techniques have been used), this method encourages group consensus (or voting) in order to categorize project and product requirements (see Table 5.4).

Table 5.4 Group Decision-Making Techniques

Technique	Description
Unanimity	Everyone agrees or it isn't prioritized.
Majority Rule	At least 50% agree (basically this is a vote, a democracy).
Consensus	Majority agrees, and the minority agrees to support it.
Dictatorship	One individual makes the final decision (not my favorite!).

Regardless of which technique is used, there needs to be a way to work with the team to determine if requirements are in scope for a specific project. As you and your team identify requirements, do yourself a favor and decide if those requirements are *really* essential for the project. For traceability reasons, each requirement should be numbered or uniquely identified and placed into one of three "buckets" (see Figure 5.6):

- **In scope:** There is a need for these requirements in this project.
- **Out of scope:** There is not a pressing demand for these requirements in this project. (These features could be prioritized in a subsequent project, however.)
- **Possibly in scope:** The team is not sure whether these features should be included in this project.

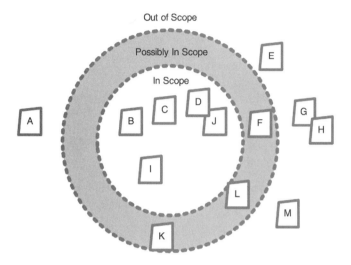

FIGURE 5.6
Deciding which requirements should be in scope for a project.

In the example shown in Figure 5.6, requirements labeled B, C, D, I, and J are in scope, and requirements A, E, G, H, and M are out of scope. Requirements F, K, and L are possibly in scope. Before the team advances too far into the project life cycle, each one of these possible requests should be moved to either the in scope or out of scope category. Furthermore, the team needs to take the suggested in scope requirements one step further and decide which features must be accomplished and which ones it would be nice to accomplish (see Figure 5.7).

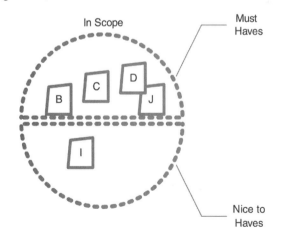

FIGURE 5.7
Deciding which in scope requirements must be performed.

Other than a question of wills, use objective criteria to select which requirements must be in the project. Here are a few examples:

- Conformance to your company's overall Decision Pyramid (presented earlier in this chapter).
- Features are required to gain competitive parity or competitive advantage.
- The software source code foundation needs to be rebuilt primarily due to software becoming unmaintainable over time. (It may be difficult to convince the product manager because there may not be any visible customer benefit to restructuring or redesigning the underlying software.)

BEST PRACTICE Gathering requirements should be a positive team-building experience.

Table 5.5 outlines a summary of the techniques for collecting requirements and when best to use them.

Table 5.5 Group Requirements-Gathering Techniques

Use This Technique	For This Situation
Interviews	Individuals who are very knowledgeable but don't enjoy group settings. (If you are new in this leadership position, this is a great way to demonstrate your listening skills to stakeholders who don't know you very well yet.)
Facilitated workshop	You have the money and time to build up a strong case for requirements. Works best if customers are prime stakeholders and professional handling of feedback is required.
Brainstorming	Stakeholders gel as a team and naturally enjoy throwing out ideas in a group setting. This is the fastest way to gather requirements.
The Delphi Technique	When stakeholders struggle working in a collaborative team setting, yet individually their ideas are spectacular.
Questionnaires	When the options for requirements are understood and you need a way for stakeholders to prioritize them without the need for group interaction. This is a great technique for stakeholders who are remote or not integrated with the development team (like customers).
Group decision-making technique	Stakeholders easily come up with a laundry list of requirements but need a forum to prioritize them (usually comes to a vote).

Prototyping and Observation

Prototyping and observation represent another set of requirements-collecting techniques that are very popular, especially if the software being developed requires a good amount of human interaction.

Observation is also called *job shadowing*—observing how users interact with a product's features can be illuminating, especially if some stakeholders have a difficult time with other requirements-gathering techniques. Another technique for gathering requirements is to *prototype* (or "mock up") possible implementations so that the stakeholders can give feedback after a "test drive." Most teams face the dilemma of deciding whether to modify the actual software product to be used as a prototype or to use a throw-away prototyping software tool (usually very fast to construct).

These techniques can work together and are not necessarily mutually exclusive. You could easily perform observations first and progressively elaborate with working prototypes during the actual development of the software (which is the very core of agile software development).

NOTE

Collecting requirements is largely based on effective communications. Software developers can become absorbed with attempting to define every detail, and product managers tend to leave out most detail while focusing on the user experience.

If a requirement is not fully understood, according to James Lewis in *Project Planning, Scheduling, and Control*, use *analogies* (a similar yet unrelated, easier-to-understand example for comparison) and *metaphors* (using a word or phrase out of context but with the term you're describing). These can add a little bit of humor to long requirements-gathering sessions as well as ease the tension.

Imagine your project being a major upgrade to a workflow software product that will introduce a hierarchical message queuing mechanism. (Previous product versions only had a single queue.) Instead of Engineering describing the requirement in terms of queuing theory, why not present it as lots of people ("messages") being directed ("queued") into a Busch Gardens theme park with different payment lines for cash, credit card, or VIP customers ("hierarchical message queues")? Analogies are great techniques when other attempts fail; and in the case of techniques like brainstorming, Lewis states, "metaphors can stimulate creative thinking."

Using the message queuing example, Busch Gardens was used as an analogy, whereas a metaphor could be something like "a queue is a straw with a funnel on top." It's a silly concept, but it works.

Outputs for the Collect Requirements process are what you'd expect, as discussed in the following sections.

Requirements Management Plan

This document explains *how* requirements will be analyzed, documented, reported, and managed throughout the project life cycle. This document acts as a "shell" that plans out *how* the team will

- Define the scope
- Prioritize requirements
- Define, organize, and develop the WBS
- Track a project's performance through the use of metrics
- Verify and control the scope

If your company has established a standard for a Requirements Management Plan template, you should be able to reuse it over and over again.

Stakeholder Requirements Documentation

This document explains the results of the stakeholder requirements-gathering activities. This document may also include an executive summary, but most important, it has information from each stakeholder's point of view, including

- Business problem to be solved (opportunity to be seized)
- Functional (for example, features) and non-functional requirements (for example, compliance or customer service levels)
- Quality requirements
- Impacts to other organizations (support and training, for example)
- Requirements assumptions and, of course, constraints

Requirements Traceability Matrix

This is a table, spreadsheet, database, or document that, for each of the requirements prioritized for the project, the following is linked together in one place:

- Description of the requirement
- Acceptance criteria
- Associated WBS deliverables
- How it supports the overall project objectives
- How to validate (test) that the requirement is truly satisfied
- Where detailed requirements information is located
- Status of the requirement (active, cancelled, deferred, added, or approved)
- Finally, the date the requirement was completed

If you do keep track of a Requirements Traceability Matrix, it is a good idea to provide some sort of tracking mechanism that provides a link from the requirement to the work package (which I'll be presenting soon). In fact, Activity 10 of the Software Product

Engineering key process part of Level 3 of the Capability Maturity Model and the Software Engineering Institute (otherwise known as CMM/SEI) states the following:

"Consistency is maintained across software work products, including the software plans, process descriptions, allocated requirements, software requirements, software design, code, test plans, and test procedures."

What If Requirements Aren't Done Right?

Because risk management was a hot topic in the previous chapter, it begs the following question: Are there risks associated with not defining the requirements correctly? *You bet!* Table 5.6 shows some real risks that can be introduced during a software development project's life cycle if requirements aren't done well.

Table 5.6 Risks Associated with Inadequate Requirements

Inadequate Requirements	Leads to
Insufficent user (and stakeholder) involvement	Products not accepted by the customer.
Creeping user requirements	Project overruns, poor product quality, team morale issues.
Ambiguous requirements	Rework, team confusion, time waster, and quality becomes an "open sore." (How do you test something that isn't well defined?)
Gold plating	*Yeow!*—project overruns, unnecessary features, and so on.
Minimal (or incomplete) specifications	Gaps in key requirements. (Don't worry—these gaps will eventually be discovered when it is *way too late* in the project life cycle!)

MRDs and Use Cases

Product managers typically create a Marketing Requirements Document (MRD), which details each feature and function from the product management point of view. Interestingly, MRDs aren't even mentioned in PMBOK or in most agile software engineering books.

So what do you do if the requirements can't easily be described with words? Incorporating alternative visualization techniques can provide a user-centric (and hopefully non-technical) way of describing how the software should work prior to committing to any code. There is a benefit to describing a product's scope by making it easy for all key stakeholders to agree on how the software should interact with the user.

Emerging from the object-oriented programming world in the 1980s, *use-case analysis* has proved an effective way to present requirements from the view of the customer. The use case presented in Figure 5.8 shows the *goal* (benefits) to use a *system* (the software being described) from the needs of an *actor* (the user or system).

There is a wealth of use-case information available on Jason Gorman's web site, aptly named www.parlezuml.com.

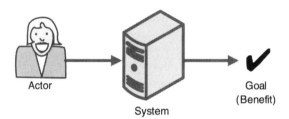

FIGURE 5.8
The three basic components of a use case.

Use cases provide a great way to show flow and relationships (between components) but are primarily used during design and not during requirements. More detailed explanations of use cases are covered in Chapter 8 in the section "Use Cases—Why They Are Important for Quality."

Define Scope

Now that you have gathered the requirements (list of project and product features), you need to rally the team to create a Project Scope Statement. Building upon the project's master framework document, the Project Charter, and a summary of stakeholder needs in the stakeholder requirements documentation, you should have enough information to properly define the scope of the project. Using existing organizational process assets can help with the creation of these documents by providing examples of past project scope documents, templates, and lessons learned. Expert judgment is by far the best tool at your disposal to define a project's scope because it is derived from past experience from many sources: you, your team, stakeholders, industry groups, and especially subject-matter experts. The more experienced and knowledgeable the experts are, the easier it is to translate raw requirements into a believable scope.

Do you remember the discussion of the Preliminary Project Scope Statement? If you created one, the Project Scope Statement becomes the final version of that document.

Finally, PMBOK calls the technique to identify different approaches to perform the work as *alternatives identification*. Rather than assume one way to get the job done, you owe it to all stakeholders (even those who aren't open to other creative ideas) to think through all options. Let's say you want a real distinctive look in your enterprise software application, which happens to be web based. The graphics and coloring can be real attention getters or a turnoff. One of the requirements from the Marketing department was to use the corporate look and feel (colors, icons, and so on) on the main screen. The least expensive choice might be to develop the graphics yourself. Not so fast! Alternatively, you and the team could examine other options, such as the following:

- Do the work yourself and apply the rules spelled out by the guidelines in Steve Krug's book *Don't Make Me Think*.
- Contract a professional design firm to lay out the look and feel of the artwork (could be expensive).
- Hire a graphic designer to augment your own work (perhaps a compromise, especially if you have worked before with someone you trust).

Now let's talk about what is produced. The overriding goal is to provide measurable (quantifiable) scope definitions for the project and the product. Aren't they the same? Nope! If you remember, one of the key benefits for the Design Scope process was to make sure that the "scope is quantified with measurable success criteria." Table 5.7 shows the relationship between product and project scope.

Table 5.7 Product versus Project Scope

	Product Scope	**Project Scope**
What It Is	Features and functions of the product	Work that must be done to deliver the product's scope.
Measured Against	Requirements documents	Documents created to describe the WBS, Project Scope Statement, and Project Management Plan.

NOTE

You might be getting a little confused between requirements and scope. The easiest way to keep their differences straight is to think of requirements as "features and functions" and *scope* as "the work necessary to deliver the requirements." In addition, each and every scope item should have measurable success criteria.

All of this sure sounds like a lot of paperwork. You may find that you're becoming consumed with the sheer volume of documentation that PMBOK suggests. The trick is to utilize the tools and techniques that make sense—at the beginning of the project, the Project Management Plan identified what steps and what documentation a project would need.

BEST PRACTICE If the project documentation serves no useful purpose for stakeholders, don't bother creating it.

Simply put, one of the prevailing agile philosophies is as follows:

More time working on products and *less* time working on documents.

Documents like the Project Scope Statement can be as simple as a two-to-five page document providing a basic framework of the project. This is a project management guideline designed to keep the overall project's scope in check. If you put too much detail in it, not only will it not be read (boring), but it will easily become out of date during a project's life cycle and require constant rewriting and consequently more time by the stakeholders reviewing it.

As an example, you could document every milestone and find yourself re-evaluating the schedules weekly (if not more often) with a Microsoft Project schedule from hell! Or you can make it simple and guide the schedule expectations with the following:

1   Planning should be complete by Aug 1.

2   Checkpoints will be based on frequent Sprints.

3   Product release will be between Nov and Dec.

The foundational initial planning has a firm date (Aug 1), the way the product will be constructed will take advantage of rapid Sprints, and although the final delivery schedule hasn't been discovered quite yet, the realistic release schedule range is a 60-day period (from Nov to Dec). This is readable, simple to understand (even if you are in Sales!), and gives the stakeholders (and especially the team) overall guidance.

BEST PRACTICE The Project Scope Statement must be written down—there is no such thing as a verbal scope agreement.

The most critical output is the Project Scope Statement that should include the information shown in Table 5.8.

Table 5.8 Project Scope Statement Topics

Topic	Description
Project overview	Name and simple project description.
Project objectives	Overall goals, each with measurable success criteria (should be associated with the Triple Constraint).
Product scope description	Overall definition and characteristics of the software product features.
Project requirements	Limited to the key project (not product!) requirements; provide enough detail so that the scope planning efforts are successful.
Project boundaries	Usually includes the work (project and product) that is not included in this release.
Deliverables	Product and project results of work being performed.
Product acceptance criteria	Overview of how you'll know that stakeholders' requirements have been validated.
Project constraints	Identify key known limitations that typically impact the overall scope of the project (the Triple Constraint again).
Project assumptions	Identify what you think are "givens" (truths and those that aren't).
Initial project organization	List the key resources used to build this product or service.
Identified risks	Although not to the level of the Risk Management Plan, identify a few key risks that can directly impact the project objectives.
Schedule milestones	Identify key milestones (most practically, these are ranges initially)—these usually are imposed by management or market conditions.
Cost estimate	Estimate the range of costs as well as any funding limitations. (Don't forget maintenance efforts after delivery!)
Project specifications	Identify specific project and product documents that will be developed for this project. (The project specification should reference the MRD if one was created.)
Approval requirements	Identification of approval authorities.

Finally, updates to the following documents may be required based on scope changes. (As with all of these processes, this is a cycle that will evolve and become less ambiguous over time.)

- **Stakeholder Register:** You may change which stakeholders provide scope input.
- **Requirements Traceability Matrix:** Produced from the Collect Requirements process, this provides all of the information of the raw requirements gathered from stakeholders.

Create WBS

What could be viewed as an "organization chart for project work," the WBS identifies the work to be performed. The overall dynamic of this process is to create the WBS from the outputs of the Collect Requirements and the Define Scope processes. Putting it plainly, a WBS is the hierarchical decomposition of the work to be executed by the project team in order to accomplish the project objectives and to create the required deliverables.

> PMBOK defines several hierarchical structures, including the Organizational Breakdown Structure, Bills of Material, Risk Breakdown Structure, and Resource Breakdown Structure.

The lowest level WBS component is called a *work package* that can subsequently be

- Scheduled
- Cost estimated
- Monitored
- Controlled

In order to create WBS work packages, you'll use the following outputs of other processes:

- **Project Scope Statement:** This document specifies the product and project scope, including the most important deliverables.
- **Stakeholder requirements documentation:** The set of documents is where all of the requirements are identified and prioritized from the requirements-gathering techniques discussed earlier in the chapter.
- **Organizational process assets:** Policies, WBS templates, and especially files from previous projects (including lessons learned) can save a lot of time so that you do not reinvent the wheel.

Taking that input, *decomposition* subdivides the project deliverables into smaller work packages. There is no hard-set rule for the number of levels, but you'll want to create a WBS that is in line with the complexity of the project. The *less* complex the project, the *fewer* the levels.

The *scope baseline* can be created in any number of formats, including documents, PowerPoint presentations, drawings, spreadsheets, or whatever media works best for you and your team (see Figure 5.9). The scope baseline is under the umbrella of the overall Project Management Plan.

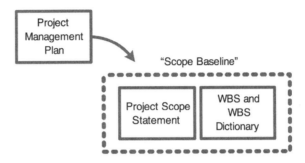

FIGURE 5.9
What the scope baseline includes.

BEST PRACTICE If a WBS exceeds more than four hierarchical levels, consider breaking the project into subprojects.

A WBS is represented as a hierarchy of work packages. The first level can be broken down in a number of ways (Figure 5.10):

- **By organization:** You may wish to break down the work based on department (Engineering, QA, Documentation, and so on). This is especially useful if you are outsourcing part of your project. However, there is a big negative to creating the WBS based on the organization. A WBS is a work chart, and structuring the work to fit how your team is organized may not yield the best breakdown of the work.
- **By phase:** This may work especially well when you define the work in terms of a stage in the project life cycle (like planning, design, and so forth).
- **By deliverables:** You could align work by subsystem of the software project (for example, communications, calculation engine, security and authentication, user interface, and so on).

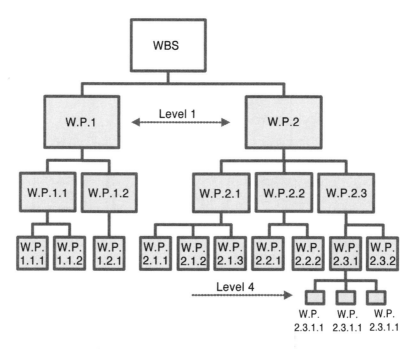

FIGURE 5.10
Basic WBS hierarchy.

The lowest level of the WBS diagram represents the actual work packages. The WBS is, for the most part, a "discovery" tool that allows you and your team to visually organize all of the work that needs to be performed. For example, suppose your project provides a Software as a Service (SaaS) offering for food processing companies that operate only within the state of California. The software automatically calculates California sales tax, which is added to every order. Most recently, the company has expanded its market to other states, thus requiring a more sophisticated sales tax calculation enhancement. A subset of this project's WBS is shown with shaded boxes in Figure 5.11. In this example, the "Build state tax software module" represents a work package.

BEST PRACTICE Use the creation of a WBS as a cross-functional team-building exercise.

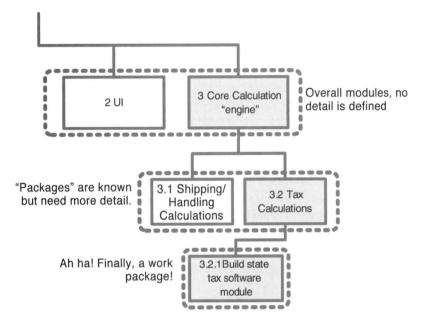

FIGURE 5.11
Sample work package.

According to Rita Mulcahy in her *PM Crash Course* book, building a WBS based on phases (and not by organization or deliverables) tends to works best due to the implicit relationship of one work package being dependent on the one before it. This also fits well into agile software projects, especially if each set of work packages goes together and is built upon short development cycles.

Through project discovery during a project's life cycle, some WBS work packages may not be known. Through the use of *rolling wave planning*, the project team postpones the definition of some work packages until they can be clarified. (This usually takes place after completion of other work packages.)

A WBS does not include specific project activities or schedules. A WBS should be useful on a project that is similar or going to be repeated.

Other than to keep you and your team organized, all but the lowest level work packages can be tossed or simply used as a frame of reference. The real power is in the definition of the work packages.

In order to provide an easy reference, each work package should be numbered (usually based on the hierarchical structure) in some sort of sequence (refer to Figures 5.10 and 5.11). For traceability purposes, you may also wish to use a unique identifier (usually a number) that cross-references the original requirements. (This is invaluable for making certain that quality assurance and quality control procedures test every work package.)

BEST PRACTICE If you use a WBS Dictionary, keep it simple with jus' e'nuff information necessary to monitor and control the work.

There is another output that can be equally important but not always necessary: the WBS Dictionary. This document (or, preferably, a spreadsheet) contains supporting detailed work information (see Table 5.9).

Table 5.9 WBS Dictionary Example Contents

WBS Dictionary Entry	Example
Identifier	3.2.1
Work package name	Build state tax software module.
Scope of work	To date, the only tax that needed to be charged was in-state; now all states must collect the appropriate sales tax. This work will provide that functionality.
Responsibility	Bill (U.S.) and Madhu (Bangalore).
Last updated	Date of last update (to the WBS Dictionary).
Billing/charge account	Engineering core team—Project X.
Required resources	Three engineers.
Schedule and costs	Estimated work period of 5–7 weeks, starting on Aug 1; estimated cost is $15,000–$20,000 USD.
Acceptance criteria	The U.S. team will perform final validation; however, engineering tests will be performed throughout the entire development life cycle.
Other vital information	This is a convenient location to identify assumptions, risks, and constraints.

You may be inclined to start detailed activity schedule planning for specific tasks. This will be discussed in Chapter 7, "Master the Art of Scheduling."

Depending on the experience level of the team, for fast-paced projects with a team that works very well together, the detail of the WBS Dictionary may be completely ignored—and like everything presented in this book, you don't *do* it unless you *use* it! (There other levels of detail that can also be produced: the Activity list and the Milestone list.)

What's the relationship between the WBS and the WBS Dictionary? If you remember back to the discussions of risk management in Chapter 4, the RBS (Risk Breakdown Structure) relates to individual entries in the Risk Register. Similarly, each entry in the WBS Dictionary relates back to a corresponding WBS work package (see Figure 5.12). In actual practice, the WBS serves as a great brainstorming and organizational tool; however, the value is actually in using the WBS Dictionary.

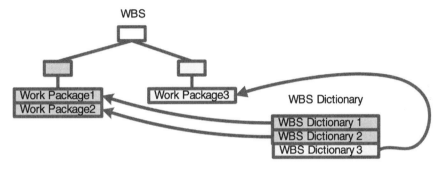

FIGURE 5.12
The WBS Dictionary is created from the WBS.

If the WBS isn't decomposed to the right level of detail or isn't complete, scope creep could become a real risk factor. Knowing what is in scope, along with having well-defined work packages, is critical to the success of any project.

This situation could result in a project that slips past its expected schedule, and according to the rule of the Triple Constraint, the impact to the schedule (time) will have a direct impact on project cost.

The success of planning out project work is directly related to the completeness and accuracy of the defined work packages. No project management magic is going to compensate for missing work packages. In fact, you could say that the total project work equals the sum of the work packages:

```
Project Work = sum(Work Package 1, Work Package 2, ...)
```

If you miss defining work packages, you'll definitely *miss* your schedule!

Scope Management in the Monitoring & Controlling Process Group

Has your team built what was originally planned?

Verify Scope Process

The Verify Scope process assumes that stakeholders will periodically meet to make sure that all the project work was really performed. In fact, this process continues throughout a project's life cycle. The Verify Scope process takes a number of inputs and, through the process of inspection, either accepts the deliverables or requests change (or corrective action).

- **Validated deliverables:** Project and product deliverables should have been developed and already passed quality control testing procedures.
- **Scope baseline:** Referring to Figure 5.9, the scope baseline includes the Project Scope Statement (the planning document that indicates a summary of the product and project scope), the WBS (hierarchical breakdown of work packages), and the WBS Dictionary (which has the details of each work package).
- **Stakeholder requirements documentation:** This is the list created in the Collect Requirements process that identifies requirements from each stakeholder.
- **Requirements Traceability Matrix:** A very important document used to keep a history of requirements.

> Scope verification concerns the *acceptance* of deliverables, while quality control is concerned with *meeting the quality requirements* of deliverables.

The key technique for validating scope is called *inspection*, which relies on verifying that the deliverable, as defined by the work package, executes as planned (see Chapter 8). According to PMBOK, there are three possible outcomes, as shown in Figure 5.13.

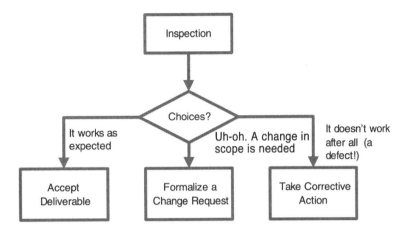

FIGURE 5.13
Inspection's possible outcomes.

Either the deliverables are accepted and signed off or more work has to be done requiring a decision by the CCB as part of the Perform Integrated Change Control process. This outcome could take place if the inspection process determines that what has been verified doesn't match at all what was intended in the scope baseline. Corrective action may be necessary in order to modify either the plan or the work being inspected. In other words, inspection found that when the deliverable was validated, the test results did not match the scope baseline. A good example is where a specific feature was tested as being functionally correct (perhaps it accessed the database information and returned the right results). The test log, however, showed that the content retrieval actually took 20% longer than before. The inspection process referred to the Project Scope Statement and found there was a clear expectation that *performance must not be any slower than the previous software version.* So the work needed additional tweaking before the deliverable could be formally accepted as complete.

Can the scope baseline change, or should it remain the same as originally intended? The simple answer is yes. Especially with agile software projects, the baseline always needs to accommodate that change happens. And when it happens, the baseline (which represents stakeholder expectations) needs to be adjusted to the most recent requirements and work definition. That adjusted document becomes the new baseline. Keeping a history of changes to a project's scope baseline is important for lessons learned purposes.

The Verify Scope process may not require the whole team's involvement during inspection, but the results certainly need team involvement to ensure that the deliverables are truly complete. Frequent team reviews are required for fast-paced, agile projects. This ensures that scope validation takes place nearly as fast as delivered work packages are being completed. Once all of the work packages have been formally accepted, YOU CAN SHIP THAT PIG!

Control Scope

Change is inevitable during a project's life cycle, and any change that has to do with scope needs to be handled using the Perform Integrated Change Control process with stakeholder knowledge and approval. This escalation avoids the inevitable frustration that we've all heard a time or two: "So, *who* authorized *that* feature?"

> The Perform Integrated Change Control process requires formal approval from some governing group, like the CCB, in order to authorize rework as a result of scope change.

How is *controlling* scope any different than *verifying* scope? Scope verification basically answers the following question: "Have we built what we were planning to build?" This occurs when a deliverable is believed to have been completed, tested, and ready for signoff. Controlling the scope, on the other hand, is all about constantly monitoring the state of project scope or product scope and controlling change. One process doesn't necessarily lead into the other—Verify Scope and Control Scope processes take place in parallel.

NOTE

A change of scope can come from many different sources. From anywhere! From you, a member of the team, outside market influences, a stakeholder, and so forth. As an example, if your team, building a mobile GIS tracking software product, learns that your key competitor has just added speed limits and real-time traffic information route planning features in their GIS software product, a change of scope may be required (especially if your software doesn't have those features).

More common, however, is when project scope needs to be enhanced because a feature doesn't fulfill a customer's needs, typically due to product management feedback. (It should have been caught at the initial planning, but with agile software projects, a customer may not have realized what was needed until they saw it work.)

Your role (and obligation) is to keep the team focused on getting the project delivered. The formalized Integrated Change Control process should ensure that trade-offs are presented to the governing stakeholders and the right decision is made.

You can't stop scope change, but you can ensure that it is handled with the least disruption to the team. If it has been your experience that the majority of change requests aren't approved by your CCB, key stakeholders, or managers, then you don't want to divert your team's attention to evaluate every change that comes up. If, on the other hand, you have too many change requests taking place throughout a project's life cycle, something may have been fundamentally wrong with how the original requirements were gathered in the first place. They may, in fact, have been incomplete to begin with.

The inputs to the Control Scope process are as follows:

■ **Scope baseline:** There are three planning documents that comprise the scope baseline: Project Scope Statement, WBS, and the WBS Dictionary (refer to Figure 5.9). As a reminder, the scope baseline is indirectly part of the overall Project Management Plan, and you may wish to examine its many other subordinate documents. The Project Management Plan should provide the necessary guidance that will help you determine how to handle change actions.

■ **Work performance information:** For each work package defined in the project, the following information is captured:

   ■ Which deliverables have started
   ■ Progress toward completion
   ■ Which deliverables have finished

■ **Stakeholder requirements documentation:** This is the list of requirements that may need to be adjusted and updated during a project's life cycle.

■ **Requirements Traceability Matrix:** The document (a spreadsheet or database is a better choice) that maintains the history of the project's requirements.

The tool/technique in the Control Scope process is primarily *variance analysis* (alternatively known as *gap analysis*), used to evaluate the cause of the variance to the baseline and what action you and the team need to take. If after the analysis it is determined that there is a gap, you'd normally take one of the steps outlined in Table 5.10.

BEST PRACTICE A project's scope baseline must be continually compared with actual results.

Table 5.10 Possible Actions to Take When the Scope Baseline Doesn't Match Actual Results

Action	Next Step
Change	Formally make a change request.
Corrective	Correct the scope issue.
Preventive	A scope change is on the horizon; keep it from happening.

Part of the cyclical, learning nature of projects is that the variance may require modifications to the "then current" scope baseline set of planning documents if the Scope Change is approved. This is what PMBOK refers to as *replanning*!

It is very important that a *configuration management system* is used to keep track of all of these changes. All project assets should be maintained so that a history of changes can be tracked, much like versions of source code are maintained throughout its life time. A system like this has two key benefits:

1. The team always has access to the very latest version of project documents.
2. The team can easily retrieve previous versions of project documents to review what took place earlier in the project.

As a result of handling scope change, the following outputs are produced:

■ **Change requests:** A change request may be created and then submitted for a decision, according to the Perform Integrated Change Control process.

> PMBOK Fourth Edition rightly expects that, as you monitor and control scope, progress is continually communicated to stakeholders (see Chapter 10).

■ **Work performance measurements:** Metrics are used to evaluate true progress. These metrics are used to track planned versus actual performance results toward completion. How do you know when you are finally done? That's what the scope verification process is all about! It is the *only* process where a project's scope (composed of work packages) is tested for completeness. When all of the work is verified, the project should be done!

■ **Scope baseline updates:** If approved change requests impact the current project or product scope, the scope baseline documents (the WBS Dictionary, WBS, Project Scope Statement, and the Project Management Plan) will most likely need modifications, too. As a result, the new updated documents become the new baseline.

■ **Organizational process assets updates:** It is always a good idea to keep track of lessons learned as they are encountered in a project. Lessons learned can help future projects make better decisions by identifying the cause of the variance and which corrective action was selected.

That just about covers managing scope!

BIBLIOGRAPHY

Boehm, Barry, J.R. Brown, and M. Lipow. "Quantitative Evaluation of Software Quality," *Second IEEE International Conference on Software Engineering*. Los Alamitos, CA: IEEE Computer Society Press, 1976.

Davis, Alan M. *Software Requirements: Objects, Functions, and States*. Englewood Cliffs, NJ: Prentice Hall PTR, 1993.

DeCarlo, Doug. *eXtreme Project Management: Using Leadership, Principles, and Tools to Deliver Value in the Face of Volatility*. San Francisco: Jossey-Bass, 2004.

Gorman, Jason. "Use Cases – An Introduction." 2006 (www.parlezuml.com/tutorials/usecases/usecases_intro.pdf).

Greene, Jennifer and Andrew Stellman. *Head First PMP: A Brain-Friendly Guide to Passing the Project Management Professional Exam.* Sebastopol, CA: O'Reilly Media, 2007.

IEEE. IEEE Std 830-1998: "IEEE Recommended Practice for Software Requirements Specifications." Los Alamitos, CA: IEEE Computer Society Press, 1998.

Johnson, Steve and Luke Hohmann. "Living in an Agile World: The Strategic Role of Product Management When Development Goes Agile." *The Pragmatic Marketer.* Vol.6(5) 2008 (www.pragmaticmarketing.com/publications/magazine/6/5/living-in-an-agile-world-the-strategic-role-of-product-management-when-development-goes-agile).

Johnson, Tony. *PMP Exam Success Series: Certification Exam Manual.* Carrollton, TX: Crosswind Project Management, 2006.

Krug, Steve. *Don't Make Me Think: A Common Sense Approach to Web Usability, Second Edition.* Berkeley, CA: New Riders Press, 2006.

Lewis, James P. *Project Planning, Scheduling, and Control, Third Edition.* New York: McGraw-Hill, 2001.

MindTools. "Brainstorming" (www.mindtools.com/brainstm.html).

Mulcahy, Rita. *PM Crash Course: Tricks of the Trade for Project Managers.* Minneapolis: RMC Publications, 2006.

Project Management Institute, Inc. *A Guide to the Project Management Body of Knowledge: PMBOK Guide, Third Edition.* Newton Square, PA: Project Management Institute, 2004.

Project Management Institute, Inc. *A Guide to the Project Management Body of Knowledge: PMBOK Guide, Fourth Edition.* Newton Square, PA: Project Management Institute, 2008.

6

Become Effective and Competitive

As the changing times require companies to make tough decisions, your role leading and facilitating software teams to be as effective as possible becomes even more important. This chapter focuses on two PMBOK knowledge areas.

- **Project Cost Management knowledge area:** Manage costs efficiently.
- **Project Procurement Management knowledge area:** Provide alternative sources to deliver the project.

Cost Management processes are very much aligned with Time Management processes (covered in Chapter 7, "Master the Art of Scheduling") since costs are based on scheduled events. This chapter also includes a great deal about the art and best practices of outsourcing. This is by far one of the most difficult PMBOK concepts to master, since the quality of your cost planning has a direct impact on how well you'll be able to control just how well your project keeps to budget.

CONTROLLING THE COST OF A PROJECT

You've probably heard about *earned value* and other cost and expense calculations that are used to evaluate if your project is on track. Needless to say, planning for how projects are to be budgeted and cost-controlled is a key element of your role. In fact, some management types only want to see the progress of a project in terms of costs. Perhaps a little short-sighted? Possibly, but it is a valid metric as long as you spend the necessary time up front to anticipate true project costs and *cost ranges*. (If cost planning is simply not planned, tracking financial metrics like earned value will be meaningless.)

OVERVIEW OF PROJECT COST MANAGEMENT

Value engineering refers to getting more out of a project without sacrificing scope. Examples include increasing the bottom line (profits), decreasing costs, shortening the schedule, and (hopefully) improving quality while you're at it.

179

That's exactly what Earned Value Management is all about! A project must be completed within budget, and according to PMBOK, project budgeting is simply the planning and controlling of the costs of resources needed to complete work activities. *Are costs to create a project the true costs for the project?* Nope. Don't forget to consider the overall *life cycle costing* that includes not only the cost of the initial project development but also the cost of maintaining and supporting the product once the project is completed.

BEST PRACTICE Controlling scope creep is the best way to control cost creep.

And who does the cost estimating anyway? If no official estimators are available (most of us have never even heard of software project cost estimators), it is up to the team to perform project cost estimating, which falls squarely on your shoulders. In fact, if you refer back to the Triple Constraint diagram (see "The Infamous Triple Constraint" in Chapter 4), your role is to constantly monitor and control cost against time, scope, and quality (see Figure 6.1).

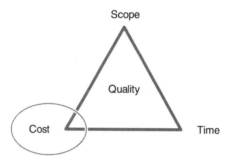

FIGURE 6.1
Monitor and controlling costs impacting
the Triple Constraint.

The Types of Project Costs

Before I dive into the cost planning elements of Project Management, let's first cover what the different types of costs are (see Table 6.1).

Table 6.1 Types of Costs

Cost Type	Description	Example
Direct	Exclusively for your project	Customized UI (user interface) code
Indirect	Shared among other projects	Development server systems

But wait! There's more. Direct or indirect costs need to be characterized based on how payment is made (in other words, usage), as shown in Table 6.2.

Table 6.2 Cost Usage

Cost Usage	Description	Example
Fixed	Pay for it once, use as much as you want.	Fixed price contract to develop product logo to be used for your project and future upgrades.
Variable	Pay only when you use it.	Contract testing that is required for as long as it takes for the project to be completed.

You could argue that full-time staff is a *variable cost*, although most of us think of full-time staff as *fixed*.

Thus indirect costs that are fixed might be office rent, since the costs are shared and the price is fixed regardless of what project you and your team are working on. An example of *direct variable cost* could be the cost of goods associated with producing DVDs of your demonstration software—the more you ship out to prospective customers, the *higher* the cost. *That's all you really need to know!*

OVERVIEW OF THE COST MANAGEMENT KNOWLEDGE AREA

There were three processes identified in the PMBOK's Third Edition, but cost processes have been modified slightly in the Fourth Edition of PMBOK with more action-oriented process names (see Table 6.3).

Table 6.3 Cost Management Knowledge Area Processes (PMBOK 4th Edition)

Process Groups				
	Implementation			
Initiating	Planning	Executing	Monitoring & Controlling	Closing
	Estimate Costs		Control Costs	
	Determine Budget			

Each of these processes takes place at least once, can overlap with each other, and may need to be updated as the project progresses (which is, of course, in line with agile software development).

Let's first understand how the cost processes work, and then summarize Cost Management best practices and cost calculations that provide jus' e'nuff control without enlisting an army of finance folks. (And, who wants that?)

NOTE The one thing you'll notice is that all of the Cost Management knowledge area processes have an abundance of inputs, tools, techniques, and outputs. The most important ones used in agile software project are discussed (but I won't cover those that have little benefit to software project management).

Cost Management in the Planning Process Group

A key component of the integrated Develop Project Management Plan process (see the section "Develop Project Management Plan" in Chapter 4) is the creation of the Cost Management Plan. In order to properly plan for costs, other knowledge area components must be well defined, particularly, project scope. The more accurate the planning documents, the more accurate will be the cost planning. There are two Project Cost planning processes:

■ Estimate the cost
■ Determine the budget

BEST PRACTICE For costs to be accurate, the project's scope must be well defined.

Estimate Costs

The first step is to estimate project costs. Although information comes from a wide variety of sources, cost calculations usually rely on a combination of both resources and time:

■ **Material cost:** The cost of goods or services
■ **Time and labor costs:** How much time work should take and clarification of the rate.

Although you may not consider cost estimating to be part of a cyclical software development process, it should be. You'll want to estimate initially with a Rough Order of Magnitude (ROM), and as the project progresses, the cost estimates become much tighter.

BEST PRACTICE Progressively narrow your project cost estimate by starting with a Rough Order of Magnitude.

PMBOK emphasizes the importance of ROM cost estimating by specifying a cost range table that indicates how the costs should be tracked from initiation of the Project Charter to the planning processes, and then refined as the project unfolds (see Figure 6.2).

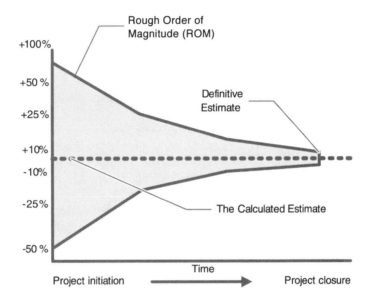

FIGURE 6.2
Rough Order of Magnitude cost progression.

> When you get an estimate around the +/–10% range, it is viewed as a *definitive estimate*.

At the very beginning of a project, a ROM estimate should range anywhere from –50% (best case) to as high as +100% (worst case). This first estimate is identified in the Project Charter and is what the project sponsor needs in order for the project to be funded.

With the cost planning tools and techniques discussed in this chapter, a more detailed cost estimate should be calculated (PMBOK likes the –10% to +25% range). As the project progresses and based on agile methodology that you "learn more as you go," the ROM becomes a more definitive estimate (typically in the –5% to +10% range).

The first step then is how do you arrive at an estimate? There are many sources of information and techniques that the Estimate Costs process has to consider in arriving at a sound project cost estimate. The key sources to be used for cost estimating are as follows:

■ **Scope baseline:** Using Figure 5.9 from Chapter 5 as a guide, the Project Scope Statement (the planning document that indicates a summary of the product and project scope), the WBS (hierarchical breakdown of work packages), and the WBS Dictionary (which has the details of each of those work packages) are necessary to estimate a project's cost.

■ **Project Scope Statement:** Although it describes the business need and other project overview information, this provides an overview list of deliverables and acceptance criteria that all factor into a project cost estimate.

■ **WBS Dictionary:** This provides the detailed summary of work packages that will be used for the cost estimates. (If you don't have a WBS Dictionary for your project, then the Project Scope Statement will have to be good enough—and in an agile software project, it might just be all you need!)

■ **Project schedule:** The Estimate Activity Resources process, presented in Chapter 7, specifies the availability of resources (people and other things), a sequence of when the work should be accomplished, and the time that work activities will take. (This includes the Activity Resources, Activity lists, and Estimate Activity Durations that I'll also cover in Chapter 7.)

■ **Human Resource Plan:** Part of the Project Management Plan (see "Develop Project Management Plan" in Chapter 4) that identifies information about the staffing sources, personnel rates (for example, hourly charges), skill set, and other information that may influence cost estimating. For example, an experienced QA architect will more likely have a higher billing rate than an associate QA tester fresh out of college.

■ **Risk Register:** The Risk Register includes a complete summary of each risk, including risk description, threat or opportunity, root cause, and even risk responses. Understanding the impact of the most important, high-priority risks is important in setting the cost range, since negative risks (threats) can have a corresponding negative impact on the overall schedule, level of effort, and ultimately, cost. The opposite might be true for opportunities. (But be very conservative if you hope for cost relief by taking on an opportunity—well-chosen opportunities might actually just keep your costs in line!)

■ **Enterprise environmental factors:** More than other knowledge areas, the overall work ecosystem can have a direct impact on costs. This includes market conditions (for example, tight job market) and commercial rates (for example, leasing of servers or prevailing contracting rates).

■ **Organizational process assets:** Why reinvent the wheel with the result of upsetting your Finance department? See Table 6.4 for a few of the resources that will help you produce standard cost estimates that everyone will appreciate.

Table 6.4 Organizational Process Assets to Be Used for Cost Planning

Resource (Asset)	Description
Cost estimating policies	Policies and procedures usually mandated from Finance. If you don't know about them, ask!
Cost estimating templates	When you ask for the policies and procedures, you'll probably be given some templates (usually in the form of a spreadsheet).
Historical information (or lessons learned)	Remember the knowledge base I've been talking about providing? If you have one, access it—there's nothing like not making the "same mistake twice." An example would be looking at the estimates for certain common subsystems that were updated for another project.
Project team knowledge	Using the project team (or even ex-project team members) for their suggestions is very valuable.
Resource cost rates	There may be standard cost rates used by your company, especially when it comes to contracting. Also bear in mind that offshore development may incur other fees or special budgetary treatment that only your Finance department will know for sure.
Cost assumptions	Using Tables 6.1 and 6.2 as guides, describe costs in those terms, since inaccurate cost allocations across shared projects can be interpreted as a "bargain" or "too costly." Your Finance organization should be able to help you allocate these cost parameters correctly.

That's it for the inputs to the process—what about tools and techniques used to develop a cost estimate? These are discussed in the following sections.

BEST PRACTICE It is perfectly acceptable to mix estimating techniques to derive an overall project cost estimate.

Estimating Techniques

There are three estimating techniques that PMBOK has established as credible to create valid project cost estimates:

- **Analogous estimating:** As its name implies, this technique takes the actual costs of a previous, similar project and applies some sort of adjustment factor based on the perceived complexity of the project and level of effort you are estimating.

  Let's take an example where a prior project was an update of an existing product, and it took a staff of three software developers three months to develop. The actual cost was $200,000. Now, your current project is estimated to be the same level of complexity and should take the same length of time, but instead will take four software developers to complete it. Assuming that each software developer's cost is averaged out to be roughly the same, the cost estimate would be the addition of another software developer for that length of time, which would calculate to $267K. Easy—but probably the least exact of all of the cost-estimating techniques!

- **Parametric estimating:** Using a combination of historical data and other parameters, produce a statistical model that will result in a cost estimate for the project. A great example of a parametric technique that PMBOK recommends is the ill-fated "lines of source code" thing. To come up with a qualified model for this technique, you'll need to experiment with a combination of parameters, including assigning a scale based on software engineer skill level. There is the 10x factor where some of your best engineers may be as much as ten times more skilled than another engineer. If you can come up with algorithms that are consistently "in the ballpark," this may be the most satisfying technique that would appeal to your engineering sense!

- **Bottom-up estimating:** This technique takes each component of work and a cost estimate assigned to the work through a variety of analysis techniques. The overall project cost estimate then is derived from the aggregation of the work component's estimates. Whew—this could take quite a long time just for an estimate but is probably the best technique to arrive at a qualified cost estimate!

Reserve Analysis

Also called *contingency allowances*, cost estimates may plan for additional costs that give you the discretion to deal with anticipated but not exactly known events that inevitably occur during any project life cycle. Reserve Analysis essentially gives you budget relief for those *known-unknowns*! (Lessons learned documentation may also help keep this in check.) Reserving no "pad" can put the schedule at budgetary risk, whereas too much padding bloats the project's cost structure, making it unrealistically more expensive than it really should be (also known as "sand bagging").

BEST PRACTICE Always proactively work with Finance in preparation for project reserves in the project cost estimate.

Your Finance department should be willing to help you and your team achieve a realistic reserve amount. If you don't get their early buy-in, you'll most likely receive their scorn in a management review when you are trying to defend your cost estimates and Finance doesn't believe how you arrived at it. Avoid that situation at all costs!

Project Management Estimating Software

Probably the best two reasons to use estimating software is that it is usually more accurate, and it will definitely save you time. Most software projects (except for the very big ones) rarely need sophisticated estimating software. In fact, using the project cost feature of Microsoft Project is usually jus' e'nuff!

Vendor Bid Analysis

When you work with contractors (see "Project Procurement Best Practices" later in this chapter), you'll review and analyze what you believe a project should cost from bids you've collected from qualified (and not so qualified) vendors. Keep in mind that there's always a risk working with vendors and outside contractors.

BEST PRACTICE The lowest vendor bid may not be best choice, despite company guidelines that "best prices must prevail."

Not surprising to most of you with experience with cost estimating (and not specified by PMBOK), expert judgment and combined team experience are probably the best techniques to arrive at a decent project estimate. Team experience can be a critical factor, since the longer a team has been together, the easier it is to justify the overall level of effort, which translates into cost.

I've spent quite a bit of time with inputs and technique; let's get into what is produced by this very important process. The Project Management Plan should include a Cost Management Plan. This establishes the standards and guidelines to be used in the project, including the following:

- **Level of accuracy:** How are costs recorded (in terms of precision)? An example is "all costs are expressed and rounded in $1,000 increments."
- **Units of measure:** Specify how different cost types are recorded (specific dollar amounts, hourly, and so on).
- **Organizational procedures links:** Although this term is not very obvious, the Cost Management Plan is the perfect place to uniquely identify cost items to be linked back to the Finance organization's accounting system. There are a couple ways to do that, as shown in Table 6.5.

Table 6.5 Linking the Cost Estimates with the WBS and the WBS Dictionary

Unique Identifier	More Information
Work package identifier in the WBS	Refer to Figure 5.11
Billing/charge account in the WBS Dictionary	Refer to Table 5.9

- **Control thresholds:** You better get straight at the very beginning of the project what level of cost overrun you'll be able to handle without escalation.
- **Rules of performance measurement:** Although I haven't covered Earned Value Management (EVM) quite yet, this identifies which parts of the WBS will be measured for costs, which earned value metrics will be used, and how earned value will be calculated.

> In PMBOK Third Edition, this was called earned value rules.

- **Reporting formats:** Specify the types of reports and how often you will distribute them. The more frequent the better, the simpler the message the better, and indicate in bold print if a cost issue is ready to take place (or has taken place).
- **Process descriptions:** Briefly summarize the Cost Management processes used on the project. This is used as a simple reminder for those stakeholders who are more concerned about project results than the costs (until it is too late!).

Cost Management Plan

Let's talk about the outputs in cost estimating. This document or set of documents answers the basic question, "How will I plan project costs, manage the project's cost performance baseline, and handle cost variances?" This is basically your guidebook for managing the project's budget.

The most important output of the Estimate Costs process is to create activity cost estimates. This document (or spreadsheet) provides the overall quantitative assessment of the costs by activity (see Figure 6.3).

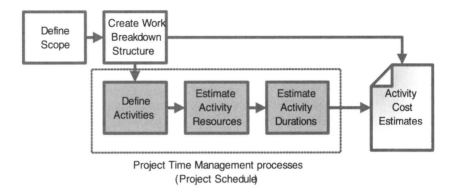

Project Time Management processes
(Project Schedule)

FIGURE 6.3
Processes that assist in creating activity cost estimates.

The shaded scheduling processes are described in the section "Time Management Fundamentals" in Chapter 7.

The overall cost estimate should be a range following the Rough Order of Magnitude methodology that was discussed earlier in this chapter. Figure 6.4 shows an example of a relatively small project lasting approximately three calendar months with a number of activities. The activity and WBS information are actually referenced by number for easy lookup in an activity list and the WBS (and WBS Dictionary). Contingency reserve and shared costs (IT services, in this sample) are also shown—although there are no corresponding activity list or WBS entries for them.

| Activity Information | | | | | Cost Estimate | |
Activity	Cost Type	Description	Activity	WBS	Min Cost	Max Cost
Engineering Module 1	Direct, variable	Build UI	3.1.1	3.1	$15,000	$24,000
Engineering Module 2	Direct, variable	Build core engine	3.2.1	3.2	$10,000	$16,000
Engineering Module 3	Direct, variable	Build communications module	3.3.1	3.3	$12,000	$20,000
QA Testing Module 1	Direct, variable	Test UI	3.1.1	3.1	$6,400	$11,200
QA Testing Module 2	Direct, variable	Test core engine	3.2.1	3.2	$3,600	$6,000
QA Testing Module 3	Direct, variable	Test communications module	3.3.1	3.3	$4,800	$7,040
Tech Pubs Module 1	Direct, variable	Document UI changes	3.1.1	3.1	$3,000	$5,000
Contract Engineer	Direct, fixed	Checksum and security extensions	3.2.1	3.2	$48,000	$48,000
Contingencies Reserve	Direct, variable	New contractor working remote, new feature unknown			$8,000	$12,000
IT Services	Indirect, variable	Development servers, facilities, beta program, ...			$30,000	$35,000

FIGURE 6.4
Sample activity cost estimates (total not shown).

In PMBOK Third Edition, the basis of estimates was called activity cost estimate supporting detail.

But the estimates aren't enough—you'll need some background, and that is what the Basis of Estimates is for, which describes the following information:

- How the estimate was developed (for example, Parametric Estimating technique)
- Assumptions
- Constraints
- Possible range of estimate (for example, –5% and +10% estimate range)
- Degree of confidence in the cost estimate (high, low, "tentative—will know within the first month," and so on)

NOTE

Let's keep documents created in this process as simple as possible—it is a good idea to combine the basis of estimates information with the activity cost estimates.

To ensure that the activity cost estimates are accepted by upper management, take the time to get feedback and acceptance from your Finance department before you present your estimate. (It is a great idea to always maintain a two-way, transparent relationship with your Finance department.)

Like all processes in an agile software project, cost estimates can continue to be refined throughout the project life cycle.

Finally, any of the documents identified as an input can be updated (PMBOK labels this as project document updates) due to approval feedback or adjustments due to change requests taking place throughout the project, and so on. It is likely that the Cost Management Plan, the Project Management Plan, and the Risk Register will be updated. The Risk Register is specifically vulnerable to cost estimates because of the cost impact associated if a risk takes place. (See the "Identify Risks" section of Chapter 4 to review the components of the Risk Register.)

Justifying a Project's Cost

PMBOK places almost as much credibility in costing as it does in project delivery. In other words, to be successful, your team must deliver not only on time with quality, but a key measurement requires that the costs are in line with expectation. There are several budgetary planning guidelines that you should keep in mind during the Estimate Costs process. In fact, depending on the results of these calculations, you may find that a project needs to be reconsidered (of even terminated). See Table 6.6.

Table 6.6 Project Cost Calculations

Justification	Acronym	Definition	Selection Criteria
Return on Investment	*ROI*	The amount of income, not revenue, divided by the investment. (Benefit – Cost) / Cost	Biggest number or percentage (for example, if a project earns $300K of revenue the first year and it costs $200K to develop, the ROI is $100K, or 50%).
Internal Rate of Return	*IRR*	Similar to a bank's interest rate on a savings account, this represents the amount of money a project will return versus the cost of development and support.	Biggest percentage is best.
Present Value	*PV*	Assuming that a dollar *today* is worth more than a dollar *tomorrow*, evaluate the value of a project based on today's dollars.	Bigger value is best. If a project expects revenue of $100K for five years, in today's dollars, the value is less than what you'd expect of a $500K project.
Net Present Value	*NPV*	Taking a project's Present Value, calculate the cost to determine the net profit in today's dollars.	Biggest number is better. As revenue loses its value in future years, costs may have a larger impact in subsequent years (one reason would be the increasing cost of labor).
Benefit Cost Ratio	*BCR*	Subtract the total cost of doing the project from how much revenue the project will take in.	Biggest rev:cost ratio (for example, 2:1).
Opportunity Cost		The money you would have made because you did not choose the project. Also known as "what you left on the table."	Smaller number (because it made less money than the project you selected).

(continued)

Justification	Acronym	Definition	Selection Criteria
Payback Period		The amount of time it takes for you to recoup the cost of a project's development.	Shortest time is always better. If Project A has 10 months payback versus Project B of five months, Project B is better.
Sunk Costs		Costs that have already been spent on a project.	When making project selection decisions, if you have already spent $50K on the product, do not consider this cost as to whether or not to continue with the project.

Two other project selection factors that should be considered are as follows:

- **Depreciation:** As most software projects take a larger expense up front in order to create a product, associated revenue can't be expected until the project releases. For this reason, your Finance organization may wish to spread the cost of a project over the likely expected product lifetime. To compound the calculations, a product (especially in the software world) can lose value over time.

  You may lose revenue by an expected price reduction over time (as the competition heats up), and you may wish to plan for that by reducing development and maintenance with off-shoring the development after the second release. This has significance with FAS 86 general accounting recommendations already mentioned in Chapter 2. Work closely with Finance before your project goes too far down the road because how costs are depreciated can get quite involved:

  1. *Straight Line Depreciation* is where costs are evenly distributed over the expected lifetime of the software product.
  2. *Accelerated Depreciation* is where costs are spread on a non-linear basis, utilizing techniques like Double Declining Balances or Sum of the Years' Digits. (This technique is a little odd but some Finance folks swear *by* it— I prefer swearing *at* it.)

- **Life cycle costing:** Take into account the overall revenue less the cost of development and maintenance throughout a project's forecasted history. For example, planning for increased competition may impact profitability in the third year of production (unless expenses are reduced).

Determine Budget

In the last Planning process, all activity costs were estimated. In order to manage these costs so that they all don't occur at the beginning or the end of a project, you'll need to "map" these costs into a time-based budget that hopefully corresponds when the work is performed.

BEST PRACTICE For small projects, both Cost Planning processes may be combined into one.

The cost baseline will, like all agile software projects, be adjusted (perhaps "refined" is a better term) as a project progresses through its life cycle. There is, however, a major constraint—when you got your project funded, there should have been an expectation set with the Finance department that a certain amount of money would be spent.

> Why can't software companies be like construction companies? They mastered cost baseline budgeting years ago!

Small companies, in particular, have to plan out expenditures to match incoming revenue, investor cash infusion, and overall company cash flow. These specific constraints should have been identified up front in the Cash Management portion of the Project Management Plan. *Let's look at how this fits into the sequence of events.*

If you remember how the previous Estimate Costs (produces activity cost estimates) process was calculated (refer to Figure 6.3), the Determine Budget process takes cost planning one step further by producing the cost performance baseline (see Figure 6.5).

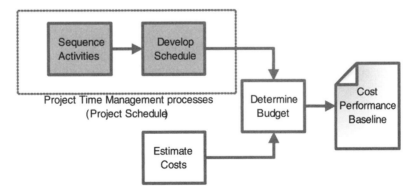

FIGURE 6.5
Processes used to determine budget.

The combination of the schedule of activities and the cost estimate of activities are the key drivers in creating the budget. Since a lot of factors are involved with budgeting, the Determine Budget process, like in the previous Estimate Costs process, has a fair amount of inputs, tools, and techniques to produce the cost performance baseline. Inputs into this process that produces a budget are as follows:

- **Cost Management Plan:** Although not explicitly stated in PMBOK, the Cost Management Plan (created in the previous Estimate Costs process) provides guidance and standards for your project budget.
- **Activity cost estimates:** Ah ha! Activity cost estimates are the most critical input to directly produce a budget (which becomes the authorized cost baseline).
- **Scope baseline:** The key elements that describe what is being developed. The applicable documents include WBS, WBS Dictionary, Project Scope Statement, and optionally the Project Management Plan. Having this information helps identify background information for work that has been time-proven, is brand new, or has other factors that may influence budget preparation.
- **Project schedule:** This includes planned activities start and end dates, key milestones, and information about work packages and control accounts (helpful for the Finance department). Without this information, you'll find it difficult to sum up costs over time as costs are going to be incurred.
- **Resource calendars and contacts:** Availability of resources during the project and contact information. This has a real cost impact if, for example, an independent contractor is only available for a limited time period that, if missed, could lead to schedule impact or even penalty costs to re-engage the contractor.
- **Organizational process assets:** Undoubtedly, your company has many resources at its disposal that can help minimize your efforts to invent schemes to formally prepare and report budgets.

Tools and techniques for the Determine Budget process are as follows:

- **Cost aggregation:** Using a bottom-up approach, isolate each work package's activities. (There are three of them in the example shown in Figure 6.6.) If the cost of all three activities is $5,000 each, the total cost for the work package is $15,000. *However, activity costs don't represent the entire story!* You'll need to identify the schedule duration, when the activity is to be performed, and the cost. Aggregated costs are typically magically summed up with project management software. (There are usually different ways to aggregate these costs based on the WBS structure, department level, project phase, and so on.)

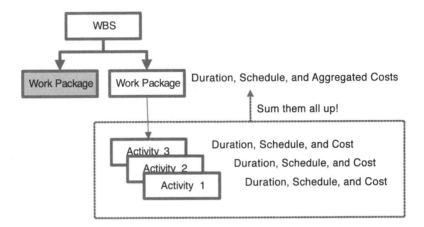

FIGURE 6.6
Aggregating work package costs.

You may also want to roll costs up for the WBS hierarchy rather than work exclusively with work package budgets.

Although tracking costs at the work package level is probably the most practical approach, you're expected to manage and control aggregated costs throughout the project. Hopefully, you enjoy assigning project performance metrics based on cost budgeting; otherwise, the task of cost aggregation can quickly become "cost aggravation." Your team doesn't want that!

Rita Mulcahy presents a logical way to construct the overall project budget:

1. Create the project costs by adding up the cost of the activities for each work package. If there are two work packages, each with three activities costing $1,000, the project cost is $6,000.
2. Add the contingency reserve to the project costs. In this case, a percentage of 10% is used, representing $600. The total project cost is now $6,600.
3. Then add the management reserve to the project cost. Using this same example, $1,000 is estimated to be good enough, resulting in a total project cost of $7,600.

■ **Expert judgment:** Consistent with many of the processes in all knowledge areas, use the expert advice of other stakeholders, your team, and your own experience to determine the overall project cost baseline.

■ **Reserve Analysis:** Contingency reserves are available to help buffer those unplanned changes to the project's scope and cost (all based on managing risks). You can over-inflate the use of reserves, so some rules are in order:

1. Contingency reserves are usually not part of the project cost baseline.
2. To use contingency reserves, you'll most likely need upper management and Finance approval.
3. There are different techniques that can be used (percentage of costs, specific amounts, and so on) to calculate reserves.
4. It is not unusual to employ a mix of reserve techniques on a single project (based on the type of expense).

> Managers who subscribe to "cost per line of code" cost estimating are not being realistic.

■ **Historical relationships:** Once you and your teams have developed a track record of successful project deliveries, you may have identified some sort of model that provides a way to predict what a cost baseline should be. According to PMBOK, there are some rules that you need to consider in using historical relationships:

1. Information to develop the model(s) should be accurate and time-proven.
2. The parameters you use (like "number of features") should be somewhat quantifiable and defendable.
3. The model should be scalable (up and down), since no project is going to be exactly like another.

NOTE   Using historical facts to determine costs is a valued technique. As an example, let's pretend that your company focus is creating embedded software products that target specific mobile processors. You've hosted your software for PalmOS, Brew, and WinCE, and now you need to support Android. Chances are the cost baselines developed for the first three operation system environments provide a great working model for Android.

■ **Funding limit reconciliation:** Funding usually occurs in increments. Any excess is usually taken care of with reserves. It isn't unusual that, for a company to carefully control funds, limits have been allocated for the project; if the workload isn't aligned with those allocations, work may have to be adjusted. (This is not necessarily a good thing!) Since companies need to report financials on some regimented schedule (quarterly, annually, and so on), it is important that project costs are in line with Finance's expectations. This is especially true for public companies.

And what about the outputs of the Determine Budget process?

■ **Cost performance baseline:** This is the budget that is a time-based summation of project expenses. Since the cost performance baseline indicates *how much* will be spent and *when* it will be spent, you may wish to present this baseline in a variety of forms: by department, by phase (or milestone), or even according to WBS level (for example, by module). Cumulative expense planning can be shown based on costs to be accumulated over time with a chart something like the one illustrated in Figure 6.7.

This used to be called Cost Baseline in the PMBOK Third Edition.

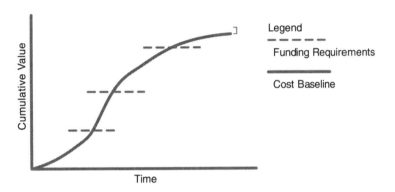

FIGURE 6.7
Cumulative expense planning (the infamous S-Curve).

The planned expenditures are shown ramping up slowly at first (early in the life cycle), ramping up when most of the engineering and testing activity is taking place, and then finally slowing down as the project gets to the end (the Closing process group). This report provides the basis for earned value reporting that is going to be covered in the next section.

The cumulative expense planning chart shows the costs added for every time period (usually weekly) and often looks strangely like an elongated "S." Perhaps that is why this chart is often called the S-Curve. Although not explicitly stated in PMBOK, a budget spreadsheet can be submitted to Finance. With that information, Finance will transform your spreadsheet into their accounting system and will expect updated budget information from you during the Control Costs process.

■ **Project funding requirements:** At certain points along a project's planning life cycle, funds should be released (shown with horizontal bars along the curve). A document describing how funds will be released throughout the project's life cycle should be created. This same chart will be used to track earned value in the Control Costs process. Depending on the need, you may wish to add some portion of the contingency reserve.

Next, the S-Curve graph (from Figure 6.7) can be extended even further to show how long funding should last in the project's time line (the accumulated stair step "to heaven"). See Figure 6.8. This will show you two important expense items:

1. The management reserve is set up to be a pre-planned monetary buffer, just in case you need a little bit more funding during the project's life cycle.
2. By graphing the funding requirements along the time axis, you can plan for the amount of accumulated cash flow.

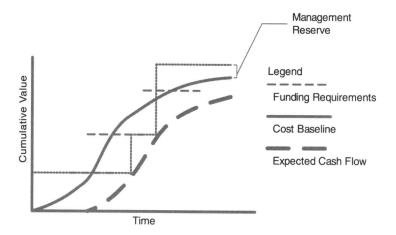

FIGURE 6.8
The S-Curve can show expected cash flow and management reserve.

■ **Project document updates:** What documents would need to be updated? Any project document impacted by cost planning adjustments, such as the project schedule (if the project has slipped and is going to cost more), Risk Register (if a risk is determined to be a threat or an opportunity, there is probably a cost impact), and so on.

COST MANAGEMENT IN THE MONITORING & CONTROLLING PROCESS GROUP

Now you get into the fun part—might as well shock you with a best practice that will surely get your attention!

BEST PRACTICE Mishandling costs usually creates project risk.

Let's pretend (this is make believe, you know) that your team is halfway through a project with a $200,000 budget. Unfortunately, $190,000 has already been spent. Knowing the budget isn't quite enough—you need to know both spent costs *and* value. This effectively compares your project's performance against the current baseline.

NOTE

It makes sense to evaluate project expenses in terms of currency (monies planned and monies spent), but tracking project performance is usually reported in a non-monetary basis—in other words, as progress on a schedule.

By transforming schedule and project progress into monetary values, you can show expenses and project progress in one cost-based chart. This will be explained in "Calculating Project Cost Performance Metrics" later in this chapter.

> Variances will be minimal if everything on your project is progressing well (on budget and on schedule).

Costs can be monitored and controlled by proactively looking for *variances* (the difference between what should be accomplished and how the project is performing) throughout the project's life cycle. The steps you'll most likely take in controlling costs are as follows:

1. Determine the cause of a variance from the current baseline.
2. Analyze the magnitude of the variance.
3. Decide if the variance requires corrective action.
4. Update the baseline if required.

The steps, as any process in an agile software project, repeat until the project is released. Said another way, Earned Value Management (EVM) is a set of techniques that provides an integrated way to report and control the very heartbeat of a project: the Triple Constraint (scope, time, cost, and optionally quality). See the section entitled "The Infamous Triple Constraint" in Chapter 4.

Control Costs

You can track how a project is performing in relation to spending (cost), activity completion (time), with an understood feature/function set (scope). Needless to say, the Control Costs process is *the* key component of the Integrated Change Control process!

The Control Costs process includes the following cost control tracking activities (and there's a lot):

- First and foremost, ensure that cost expenditures don't exceed what was authorized to spend on the project.
- Monitor cost performance variances (actual versus planned).
- Manage actual changes—this includes making sure that change requests are handled in a timely manner. (In fact, not handling changes quickly usually results in a negative impact to project costs.)
- Manage that non-approved changes aren't snuck into the project (gold plating).
- Proactively inform key stakeholders of all approved changes and costs (especially earned value).

The key inputs for the Control Costs process are the outputs of the Determine Budget process:

■ **Cost performance baseline and project funding requirements:** The cost baseline and funding requirements define the planned costs and funding required throughout the project's life cycle.

■ **Work performance information:** Required for controlling project costs, you'll need to track *what* work activities (the deliverables) have been completed, *when* they were completed, and *how much* expense (cost) has been incurred. This requires that the team agrees to what work has been completed. (You'll want to avoid the unfortunate situation where the Engineering manager says that certain work has been completed and the QA manager doesn't agree.)

■ **Organizational process assets:** Again? Does this input have to show up in almost every PMBOK process??? Cost Management, in general, is a touchy subject with Finance and upper management, so keeping in mind that there are formal policies, procedures, and guidelines, along with Finance-required tools and methodology, should keep you out of Finance's "dog house."

Tools and techniques used in the Control Costs process include the following:

■ **Earned value measurement:** The primary measurement technique is the Earned Value Technique (EVT) that integrates project scope, cost, and time into cost measures to be used to determine if the project is on track or not. The next section, "Calculating Project Cost Performance Metrics," will summarize the key cost performance measurements you'll need to track.

> Earned value measurement tends to focus on progress to date (the present), while forecasting tends to focus on progress to come (the future).

■ **Forecasting:** Based on completion of work, you and your team should be able to project estimates for project completion. The benefit of forecasting is that you can supply the team, finance, and upper management with early warning (usually based on project experience to date).

■ **Variance analysis:** As a key part of the Project Management Plan, the Cost Management Plan describes how cost variances will be handled if costs exceed the allowable percentage of deviation allowed at a particular stage of the project's life cycle. Like all agile software projects, the allowable cost range will be a larger percentage early in the project and will decrease as the project nears its completion. This is expected because, prior to achieving technical feasibility on a project, your team will still be learning what is possible (and what isn't). It's the effort to deliver on those components that will impact project costs as risks are removed and the project completes. Regardless, you'll need to adjust the cost performance baseline to accurately reflect anticipated costs going forward.

■ **Project status performance reviews:** In order to get the team involved in cost performance, there should be regular meetings set to review the following key project activities. Although it might be obvious, these reviews gather information and report status with the team that directly relates with the other tools and techniques used in this process, which include the following:

1. Completion of work packages (what work is done)
2. Variance analysis (cost metric differences)
3. Trend analysis (plot out what has changed)
4. Earned value performance (compare the baseline versus progress to date)

■ **Project management software:** The use of software tools to help monitor the EVM dimensions, to track trends, perform "what if" analysis, and to prepare reports is a necessary tool (otherwise, you'll be maintaining all of this in your own database or spreadsheet).

The outputs to the Control Costs process include the following:

> Work performance measurements and forecasted completion outputs use calculations that are presented in the next section.

■ **Work performance measurements:** The results of a project's overall progress to date can be expressed as costs—typically shown as variances and as index values (and there are a bunch of them) .

■ **Forecasted completion:** You can forecast a likely project completion date by estimating the costs that will most likely be required to complete the project.

■ **Change requests:** The analysis of cost measurements can result in project change requests that could either increase or decrease the budget. These requests, like all other change requests, should be formally presented to the Integrated Change Control process for approval. As part of the overall change request procedures, there are usually recommended corrective actions to bring future performance project work in line with the current Project Management Plan. This plan will most likely be adjusted during the project life cycle.

■ **Project document updates:** A number of documents may be updated, including but not limited to the Cost Management Plan, organizational project assets (like lessons learned), and the cost performance baseline. If you find that the cost performance baseline is changing at a brisk rate, chances are the project was not originally cost estimated very well.

CALCULATING PROJECT COST PERFORMANCE METRICS

There are so many cost performance calculations summarized in PMBOK that I'll step you through the most important ones in a sane, logical manner. (I'll also point out those that are most and least important.)

The Earned Value Measurement Dimensions

Earned Value Technique (EVT) directly monitors three variables that will help you determine if your project is on track (see Figure 6.9).

PMBOK refers to variables as *dimensions*.

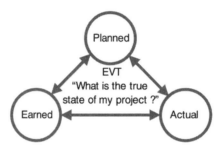

FIGURE 6.9
EVT compares planned, earned, and actual costs.

All three values are expressed in monetary terms, and all relate to each other (see Table 6.7).

Table 6.7 Earned Value Dimensions

Value	Also Known As	Description
Planned (PV)	*Budgeted Cost of Work Scheduled (BCWS)*	The budgeted (or estimated) cost of work being planned.
Earned (EV)	*Budgeted Cost of Work Performed (BCWP)*	The budgeted cost of work that has been performed (or accomplished).
Actual (AC)	*Actual Cost of Work Performed (ACWP)*	The actual cost of work that has been performed (includes all costs, even if more than expected).

Let's use an example of a small software project where the project is a well-contained maintenance update that will take a couple of software engineers and a QA tester a few days to complete. For the sake of simplicity, let's say that the overall project costs $2,500 per day and that the project is assumed to be completed in four days (total cost $10,000). Also for simplicity's sake, the planned schedule assumes the following:

- There are four activities.
- Each activity follows the other in sequence. (You don't start an activity until you finish the previous activity.)
- Because this is an agile project, the entire team designs, creates, builds, and tests each activity in a brisk daily cycle (see Figure 6.10).

FIGURE 6.10
The PDSA cycle.

Figure 6.11 shows what was originally planned to be completed and what has actually been performed by the end of the third day of the four-day project.

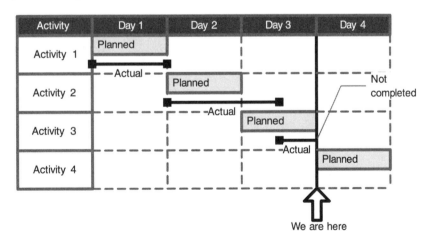

FIGURE 6.11
Sample project to demonstrate EVT.

Activity 1 and activity 2 have been completed, and the team is still working on activity 3. Activity 4 has yet to commence. Table 6.8 summarizes what was planned and what has actually occurred in terms of costs.

Table 6.8 Planned and Current State of Activities and Costs

Activity	% Complete	Planned Time	Planned Cost	Actual Time	Actual Cost
1	100%	1 day	$2,500	1 day	$2,500
2	100%	1 day	$2,500	1.5 days	$3,750
3	50%	1 day	$2,500	.5 day	$1,500
4	0%	1 day	$2,500		
Total	62.5%	4 days	$10,000	3 days	$7,750

Activity 2 took 50% more time than expected; activity 3 is only 50% complete and cost $250 more than expected (to try to catch up). *But cost summaries don't tell the entire story . . . .*

Calculating True Project Status with Earned Value

Continuing with the same example, there are four calculations you need to look for in Earned Value Management (see Table 6.9).

Table 6.9 Calculating Earned Value Management Basic "Dimensions"

Earned Value	Result	How Calculated	Description
BAC (Budget at Completion)	$10,000	BAC = sum(planned activity costs) $2,500 (activity 1) + $2,500 (activity 2) + $2,500 (activity 3) + $2,500 (activity 4)	Aggregate all planned activities (in other words, add all of the planned costs up to derive the total project budget!).
PV (Planned Value)	$7,500	PV = BAC * planned % of completed activities 75% of 10,000 or $2,500 (activity 1) + $2,500 (activity 2) + $2500 (activity 3)	The planned work that should have been performed up to now (three full days of work or 75% of the total project budget).

(continued)

Earned Value	Result	How Calculated	Description
EV (Earned Value)	$6,250	EV = BAC * actual % activities completed 62.5% * 10,000 or $2,500 (activity 1) + $2,500 (activity 2) + $1,250 (half of activity 3)	How much work was actually earned (two and a half days of planned work or 62.5%).
AC (Actual Cost)	$7,750	AC = sum(actual activity costs to date) $2,500 (activity 1) + $3,750 (activity 2) + $1,500 (activity 3)	The actual cost spent so far. On the third day, the team did half the work but brought on a contractor to help out, which cost $250 more for the day (total of $1,500 instead of $1,250).

What does all of this mean? The project is behind. The PV (planned value) is $7,500, and at this point, the actual value earned (EV) is only $6,250. The actual cost so far is $250 more than expected.

As if I haven't shown enough ways to show progress, there's yet another way with the standard S-Curve introduced in the Determine Budget process. The chart in Figure 6.12 shows a time-based cumulative performance value using the three value dimensions: planned value (PV), earned value (EV), and actual cost (AC).

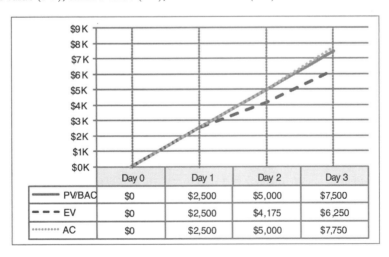

	Day 0	Day 1	Day 2	Day 3
—— PV/BAC	$0	$2,500	$5,000	$7,500
– – – EV	$0	$2,500	$4,175	$6,250
·········· AC	$0	$2,500	$5,000	$7,750

FIGURE 6.12
S-Curve showing cumulative Earned Value Management.

From these three dimensions (PV, EV, and AC), you can objectively calculate the health of your project.

After three days of work, PV is the same as the Budget at Completion (BAC). At the end of day 2, the actual cost was kept close to the budget with some additional costs to try to make up for lost time ($250). But just because you are successfully *controlling* costs doesn't mean your project is *on track*—that's what EV determines. Starting on day 2, EV starts to dip, since activity 2 was only 67% complete (instead of 100% as it was originally planned). In addition, activity 2 took half of day 3 to complete, which pushed into the time allotted for activity 3, resulting in only 50% of the work completed.

Hey, wait a minute! If Figure 6.12 is supposed to represent an S-Curve, why does it look so flat? Typically, you start out with very few cost variances, then as the project builds up steam, costs also grow, diverge, and then gradually slow down at the end of a project's life cycle. This particular example is somewhat linear (for example, one activity for every day with each activity performed one after the other). Not exactly the real world!

The values in Figure 6.12 track percentages of activities performed by day. In the case of AC, you may have to go back and recalculate prior days' AC values once an activity's work is completed.

For example, upon completion of day 3, activity 3 is just 50% complete—but what happens if it takes three days to complete activity 3? Your total AC for activity 3 took three times what you expected. Yikes!

Calculating If Your Project Is on Schedule

Using the previous project as an example, you can always remember which of these EVTs is concerned with schedule: They both start with an "S" (see Table 6.10).

Table 6.10 Earned Value Management Showing Whether Your Project Is on Schedule

Earned Value	Result	How Calculated	Description
SV (Schedule Variance)	–$1250	SV = EV – PV $6250 (EV) – $7500 (PV)	If negative, your project is behind; if greater than or equal to 0, the project is in good shape. The larger the variance, the bigger the gap versus the plan. (In this example, the project is quite a bit behind!)

(continued)

Earned Value	Result	How Calculated	Description
SPI (Schedule Performance Index)	.83	SPI = EV / PV (with the result being a ratio and not a dollar figure) $6250 (EV)/$7500 (PV)	An index indicator, in PMBOK terms, basically compares schedule attainment to 1 (or 100%). This is basically the ratio of earned value versus planned value. (This project is behind schedule and progressing at 83% of the planned rate.)

If the SPI is less than 1, that means the earned value is less than planned value, so your project is behind. The smaller the resultant SPI value, the more in trouble the project is. If the SPI is greater than 1, that means the earned value is greater than the planned value, so your project is ahead of schedule. The larger the SPI, the more ahead you are in actual work. If your SPI is equal to 1, your project is right on schedule (but it certainly won't remain exactly at 1 for very long). Figure 6.13 shows this relationship between earned and planned values (EV and PV).

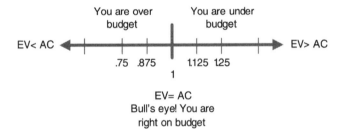

FIGURE 6.13
Calculating if your project is behind or ahead of schedule.

When communicating to stakeholders, SV puts a dollar value on how far ahead or behind your project is, while the SPI indicates whether the project has delivered value as originally planned.

Calculating If Your Project Is on Budget

You can always remember which of these EVTs is concerned with costs: They both start with a "C" (see Table 6.11).

Table 6.11 Earned Value Management Showing Whether Costs Are on Track

Earned Value	Result	How Calculated	Description
CV (Cost Variance)	-$1,500	CV = EV − AC $6,250 (EV) − $7750 (AC)	If negative, the project is over budget; if 0 or positive, the project is on budget or under budget. (In the example, even though the costs to date are only $250 over, the actual cost variance for the overall project is $1,500 over budget.)
CPI (Cost Performance Index)	.81	CPI = EV / AC $6,250 (EV)/$7,750 (AC) (with the result being a ratio and not a dollar figure)	An index indicator that compares cost performance to the value of 1 (or, more accurately, 100%). (If negative, earned value is less than the actual value achieved to date. In this example, the project is way over budget with an index of .81.)

The greater the distance from the center point (1, or 100%), the wider the budget gap. A CPI of .75 is worse than .875, and a CPI of 1.25 is better than 1.125 (see Figure 6.14).

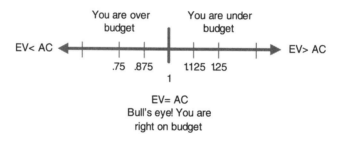

FIGURE 6.14
Calculating if your project is over or under budget.

Forecasting Future Project Performance

Since you know the CPI (Cost Performance Index), you can predict what your project should cost to complete based on performance so far. Table 6.12 references the same example used for all of the prior budgetary calculations.

Table 6.12 Forecasting Future Project Performance

Earned Value	Result	How Calculated	Description
EAC (Estimate at Completion)	$12,345	EAC = BAC / CPI $10,000 / .81	Assuming that the CPI to date is an indication of future efficiency, this can predict the overall costs for the remainder of the project work. If CPI is less than 1, the EAC will be larger than your current budget (which isn't good). If your CPI is at or greater than 1, the project is on track to finish on (or under) budget. (The EAC will always be a positive budgetary value and hopefully will be close to the BAC.)
ETC (Estimate to Complete)	$4,650	ETC = EAC − AC $12,345 − $7,750	The estimated budgetary cost to finish the project. Hopefully, the amount is less than the remaining budget; in this case, the estimate is $2,250 more than remaining budget.
VAC (Variance at Completion)	−$2,345	VAC = BAC − EAC $10,000 − $12,345	The forecasted dollar variance at project close based on the EAC project close based on the EAC calculation. If the result is negative, the remaining budget is going to cost more than expected ($2,345 in this example). If positive, the project should cost less than originally planned.

As soon as you know that your project's VAC is way off the mark, it may be time to set up an appointment with the Finance department and upper management in order to reset expectations. (Don't forget to smile a lot and come prepared with mitigation alternatives.)

> PMBOK acknowledges several ways to predict future performance, including disrupting the team to re-estimate remaining work.

One final note: Even though there are no Cost Management processes defined by PMBOK for the Closing process group, make sure that any pertinent cost history is recorded for future lessons learned.

PROJECT PROCUREMENT BEST PRACTICES

UNDERSTANDING PROJECT PROCUREMENT MANAGEMENT

Project Procurement processes have been somewhat redefined in the Fourth Edition of PMBOK, with more action-oriented process names and two fewer processes than the Third Edition (see Table 6.13).

Table 6.13 Procurement Management Knowledge Area Processes (PMBOK 4th Edition)

	Process Groups			
	Implementation			
Initiating	**Planning**	**Executing**	**Monitoring & Controlling**	**Closing**
	Plan Procurements	Conduct Procurements	Administer Procurements	Close Procurements

Project Procurement Management defines the processes required to purchase (or acquire) product or services needed to complete the work. Your role includes the following key activities:

- Contract management and administration
- Responsible for change control processes as a result of the product or services being performed

> These processes appear to be distinct, but in actual practice, they tend to overlap in a highly iterative, cyclical nature after a seller has been selected.

Figure 6.15 illustrates a clear set of definitions for the two organizations involved. There is always a *buyer* (the organization that needs the products or services) and a *seller* (the organization that provides the products or services).

FIGURE 6.15
The buyer and seller relationship.

To clearly define the terms of the relationship, a contract of some form is needed between the buyer and the seller. A contract is an agreement with the following characteristics:

- Legal document that represents a mutually binding agreement.
- Obligates the seller to provide the specified product or service.
- Obligates the buyer to provide agreed-upon payment or terms as a result of receiving the product or service.
- A schedule for delivery and quality (or warranty) expectation.
- Adheres to both organization's procurement policies and procedures.
- Has designated authorities who can sign and administer the agreement on behalf of both organizations.
- In case of a dispute, the contract should provide enough clarity and definition for resolution. (If it is too ambiguous, both parties suffer.)
- There are usually terms and conditions that identify the contract's life cycle (for example, royalty payments expected for a period of five years following delivery).
- Agreement is written and approved by both organizations (never accept a verbal agreement) before work officially commences.

It is your responsibility (or your designee) to help tailor the contract to the project needs. Most procurement activities answer the age-old "make versus buy" decision. It is important that you make the right decision that ultimately benefits the customer (see "Keeping Development and Product Management Aligned" in Chapter 5), the buyer (you), and the seller.

BEST PRACTICE By crafting a fair and practical contract, some project risks can be avoided or mitigated.

The overall workflow to manage the entire procurement process (once a seller is selected) is as follows:

1. Identify sellers.
2. The buyer issues the Statement of Work (and possibly a purchase order) to the seller.
3. Select the seller and start the work.
4. The cycle commences with the seller issuing invoices and the buyer issuing payments until the work is done.
5. Finally, the procurement process is closed.

> **The Statement of Work more commonly uses the acronym SOW.**

After the seller is selected, the purchase order (along with a Statement of Work) is created and agreed upon by the seller. (There may also be other documents, such as license agreements, among other things.) If applicable, the buyer submits invoices, and the seller, upon accepting the work, authorizes payment for the invoices based on the Procurement Management Plan and the terms of the agreement. Finally, the work is formally approved in writing and the procurement closed. At this point, there is usually a maintenance or warranty period, but for all intents and purposes, the work is completed.

NOTE

If quality work completion doesn't occur, PMBOK has put a lot of thought into identifying a superb set of management processes that should effectively help minimize negative risks from taking place between a buyer and seller. Procurement processes in PMBOK tend to present material to the reader from the view of the seller—but that may not be your situation. In fact, you might be the buyer providing the products or services to a seller. In any case, the following pages should be equally helpful to you.

If the decision is to obtain products or services from outside of your company's resources, PMBOK recommends a set of procurement processes to be performed (see Figure 6.16).

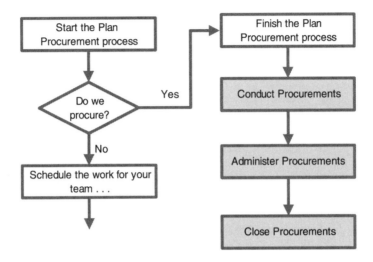

FIGURE 6.16
Do you procure outside products or services?

PROCUREMENT MANAGEMENT IN THE PLANNING PROCESS GROUP

The planning stage of the procurement set of processes is critical in order to analyze your project's procurement and outsourcing needs.

Plan Procurement

During the Plan Procurement process, if you decide not to procure products or services, then schedule the work for your own teams to do the work. Otherwise, you should follow the processes outlined in this chapter to line up the right source, and then schedule the work to be performed.

The inputs to the Plan Procurement process are as follows:

- **Scope baseline:** As you may remember, the scope baseline (see Figure 5.9 in Chapter 5) defines the work and incorporates the Project Scope Statement, the WBS, and the WBS Dictionary. Part (or all) of the work may be better suited to be acquired from an outside source so that your project team can focus on the most important, core components of the project.
- **Stakeholder requirements documentation:** A perfect example might be that any products outsourced to a third party for development to your specifications should not require any additional end-user licensing obligations. (In other words, you have the right to distribute the product incorporating a third party's code without additional payment to that third party.)

- **Teaming agreement:** In order to reduce the risk of a buyer and seller not understanding their respective business relationships, PMBOK Fourth Edition has introduced the concept of a teaming agreement to provide benefits that include the following:
  - Establishes a contractual arrangement between both entities (the buyer and the seller).
  - Defines rules of engagement, who points of contact are, dispute clauses, and so on.
  - Reduces the time needed to agree on specific work, since the teaming agreement provides the framework for multiple work assignments.

  In many respects, think of a teaming agreement as a temporary "master agreement." When the benefits of the business relationship end, so ends the teaming agreement.
- **Outputs of the Project Management Plan:** Mentioned a little earlier in conjunction with the scope baseline, the Project Management Plan provides the basis of a set of plans, as well as a number of outputs related to that plan, that may be needed for the Plan Procurement process, including the Risk Register, project schedule, activity resource requirements, activity cost estimates, and the cost performance baseline.
- **Organizational process assets and enterprise environment factors:** There are several company assets that should be used in the Plan Procurement process, including formal procurement policies, procedures, and guidelines. If your organization doesn't have those, work with Finance to properly plan for work to be performed by a seller. Also, other assets include using an established supplier system or prequalified sellers (possibly with pre-established billing rates). In addition, when the software market was booming, you could expect to pay premium rates for work—with the downturn of the software industry (post-Internet bust), rates became a lot more reasonable and competitive.

Tools and techniques used for the Plan Procurements process are as follows:

- **Make or buy analysis:** This is a management technique where you need to make a decision whether to do work in-house or out-house. (I love that term even though it has other meanings.) There are many considerations for make versus buy, oftentimes based on the industry your company serves. In some industries, for example, you may wish to rent equipment before actually having to decide when to purchase it.

> Remember the Decision Tree Analysis example in the section "Perform Quantitative Risk Analysis" in Chapter 4, where you examined the cost and risk of outsourcing work?

In the software world, however, you typically have to make decisions whether or not you build something with your own teams or acquire it from a third-party source. As a rule of thumb, use the following criteria to help you decide between using a seller's services or your team's (the buyer) services: skill (who has the skill and expertise to perform the work), capacity (who has the ability to deliver in the timeframe desired), cost (who can deliver in the most cost-effective manner), and risk (who can deliver with the least amount of risk).

If it is overwhelming that the buyer can provide these services or if it is a toss up, it is highly recommended that you do the work with your own teams (and don't engage with a seller). Otherwise, if the seller can accommodate the majority of these criteria, it may be wise to buy.

There are other costs (especially with offshore outsourcing) that need to be considered in a make versus buy situation. If the plan is to simply delegate all of the work to a third-party vendor, their work may get done but may fail upon integration back into your project if you don't consider the some key roles and additional work on your team's part (which would increase the overall cost). These indirect considerations apply particularly to offshore work and are presented in "Making the Most with Outsourcing" later on in this chapter.

BEST PRACTICE In a make versus buy decision, don't forget the indirect costs in your analysis.

- **Expert Judgment:** Using experience and expert judgment with key stakeholders (Legal, Finance, yourself, and your team) may prove to be the best selection process rather than just being a pure monetary decision.
- **Contract types:** A contract establishes a formal agreement between two parties, and each contract should have the components outlined in Table 6.14.

Table 6.14 The Basic Components of a Contract

Component	Definition
Capacity	The name and the abilities of the seller.
Consideration	The clear identification of the item that is going to change possession from the seller to the buyer.
Offer	This represents basically the form of payment for the consideration (money, barter, no cost, and so on).
Legal Purpose	The reason that the contract is being performed.
Schedule	When is the deliverable due?
Acceptance	Two-fold: How the item that is going to change hands is going to be accepted and approval signatures from both the seller and the buyer. (Without this, you should never start the work or transfer the item.)

Who takes over project management control of the execution of the work as per the contract usually depends on the completeness of the offering (the *consideration*). For example, if the contract item is going to have to be developed, usually the seller manages and controls the overall work; otherwise, if the contract item delivered is done and just needs to be integrated into the buyer's solution, usually the buyer will take control and manage the final integration (with the seller's help, of course).

> You may also wish to combine specific features into a contract from a variety of different contract types.

There are four logical contract categories (even though the PMBOK Third Edition states that there are three categories, and the Fourth Edition combines them all into two categories):

- **Fixed-Price contracts:** Products or services that have a specific cost. (These tend to benefit the buyer.)
- **Cost-Reimbursable contracts:** Products or services that are paid as costs are incurred plus usually an extra handling fee that provides the seller with an extra margin for profit.
- **Time and Materials contracts:** You pay only for the work performed. (These tend to benefit the seller.)
- **Purchase Order contracts:** These are neutral to both parties (and are sometimes lumped into the Fixed-Price category).

Let's go over Fixed-Price contracts first (by the name, these projects are paid a specific amount of money). See Table 6.15.

Table 6.15 Types of Fixed-Price Contracts

Contract (and Acronym)	Benefits	Definition
Fixed-Price (also known as *Lump Sum*; *FP*)	Buyer	The seller assumes all responsibility to deliver exactly what is specified at a fixed cost. If the work gets done on or ahead of schedule, the seller earns at least the expected amount of profit. (Obviously, the opposite can happen, which is disastrous to the seller if the work incurs more expense than planned.)

Contract (and Acronym)	Benefits	Definition
Fixed-Price Incentive Fee (FPIF)	Buyer	The seller assumes the responsibility to deliver exactly what is specified at a fixed cost with one hitch: If the delivery takes place sooner than expected, the seller receives some sort of benefit (usually additional fees). This contract type is usually based on a critical market need that should be met sooner than the seller is willing to commit. This is risky to the buyer if the seller "cuts corners" in order to beat the schedule! (Work submitted using FPIF requires extra-careful validation.)
Fixed-Price Economic Price Adjustment (FP-EPA)	Buyer	When the seller's work is part of a multi-year agreement, you may wish to tie an increase to an annual fee based on some independent economic metric (like Wall Street Journal Prime Rate, Consumer Price Index, or others).

NOTE

The FPIF (Fixed-Price Incentive Fee) contract poses a real obstacle for the seller if the work isn't delivered on time and there remains no opportunity to earn any of the incentives.

In addition, I'll introduce you to a term you may not have heard of before: the Point of Total Assumption (PTA). The PTA occurs when a seller assumes responsibility for all additional costs.

There are three different cost variables you need to monitor:

- Target cost: The seller's estimated costs (hopefully less than the target price).
- Ceiling price: The buyer sets the "cap" to protect against serious cost overrun.
- Target price: The buyer's target that it would like the seller to achieve.

The formula is as follows:

PTA = target cost + [(ceiling price - target price) / buyer's % share of cost overrun]
As an example, let's assume that the buyer's share is 3:1 (or 75%) and:
Target cost = $71K
Ceiling price = $84K
Target price = $75K

Then:

PTA = $71K + ($84K - $75K) / .75 equals $83K

At the point in the contract where the buyer has paid $83K, the seller will have to absorb any costs over that amount out of their own pocket, and the buyer is limited to a maximum of $84K payout.

There are three Cost-Reimbursable types of contracts (see Table 6.16).

Table 6.16 Types of Cost-Reimbursable Contracts

Contract (and Acronym)	Benefits	Definition
Cost Plus Fee (also known as **Cost Plus Percentage of Costs**) (**CPF** or **CPPC**)	Seller	Covers the seller's costs for delivery of product or service and pays a percentage of that cost as a fee. The more the seller spends, the higher the fees (since the fees are a percentage). There must be complete trust for a seller to enter into a Cost Plus contract. These costs are usually treated like a handling fee.
Cost Plus Fixed Fee (**CPFF**)	Seller (and possibly the buyer)	Although less negative to the buyer than a Cost Plus Fee contract, the buyer generally knows what it wants the seller to deliver. The fee is agreed to as a specific monetary value or as a percentage of the initial estimated total project cost and is usually paid at project completion. This technique is useful for agile software projects if the technical details are not initially known but will be learned along the way as the team learns what is needed.
Cost Plus Incentive Fee (**CPIF**)	Seller and buyer	Similar to a Cost Plus Fixed Fee contract, this contract is also based on work that is only generally detailed up front. Because there is a market (or customer) urgent need, an incentive fee schedule is identified to motivate the seller to complete the work sooner than the scheduled completion date. This places a burden on both the seller and the buyer: The "learned as you go" details could easily result in a contract dispute if the seller tries to beat the scheduled date and misses because the buyer's needs were misunderstood and never clarified.

Like all contracts, even Cost-Reimbursable contracts should have a scheduled completion date.

Time and materials contracts are a hybrid between Cost-Reimbursable and Fixed-Price contracts (see Table 6.17).

Table 6.17 Time and Materials Contract

Contract (and Acronym)	Benefits	Definition
Time and Materials (*T&M*)	Seller and buyer	The requirements of the work are defined up front, and the expense is paid out based on the ongoing level of effort needed. This is one of the only contract types where this approach benefits both the seller and the buyer, can usually be terminated by either party at any time, doesn't have a specific end date (although there may be an estimated completion schedule range), and has costs that are simple to calculate (since there are no special incentives).

Finally, even though there is no specific mention of this in PMBOK, there is a simple Purchase Order contract category (see Table 6.18).

Table 6.18 Purchase Order Contract

Contract (and Acronym)	Benefits	Definition
Purchase Order (*PO*)	No special benefit to seller or buyer	A purchase order is a special contract type for a predefined price and for a predetermined, off-the-shelf product. When you purchase a software tool from Provantage, for example, the PO represents the contract. (You, the buyer, issue a purchase order, and the seller delivers the product to you.) If there is a warranty or guarantee, the manufacturer honors resolution of product issues or defects.

Now that I've covered the inputs, tools, and techniques for the Planned Procurements process, let's examine what is produced (outputs).

■ **Procurement Management Plan:** A subsidiary document of the Project Management Plan, this includes guidance for procurements in the form of the following:
   ■ Types of contracts
   ■ Standardized procurement documents or other templates

- If the procurement is shared with other projects (very important for software if some product or service will be used by multiple project teams)
- How to manage multiple suppliers
- Constraints and assumptions
- Handling the make or buy decision and how the decision will be used in Project Time Management processes
- The schedule for deliverables and how this procured product or service will be integrated with your project's processes
- If the sellers are expected to develop and maintain their WBS
- Identifying prequalified sellers to be used
- Metrics to be used to manage contracts and evaluate sellers (probably more pronounced a process than how eBay customers rank sellers)
- Determine the process by which sellers will submit invoices and how payments will be handled according to payment terms

> Even though there may be a single Procurement Management Plan, there can be individual SOWs for each acquired product or service.

- **Procurement Statement of Work:** The Procurement SOW specifies what is to be included in a particular contract. It has the following characteristics:
    - Description in sufficient detail so that the prospective sellers can determine if they possess the skill or are capable of providing the product or service.
    - Includes whatever information is necessary for the prospective sellers to respond with a proposal: quantity, performance, work location, and requirements. For example, if your team needs a contract tester, then the Procurement SOW might indicate how many testers, for how long, what location, and what background would be required.
    - Written in a clear, complete, concise, and informative format so that the prospective sellers can produce an informed response.

Like agile software methodology itself, the SOW can be revised and refined as it moves through the procurement processes until a signed contract is awarded. If the procurement SOW, however, goes through many iterations, you may burn out the sellers who are constantly asking questions or resubmitting proposals.

- **Make or buy decisions:** This is the document that lists the work items that went through the make versus buy decision process, and it indicates the following:

Work	The work, work activity, or technology description
Decision	Make or buy?
Notes	Any explanation or background that would help in a lessons learned

Although not discussed in PMBOK, you may wish to incorporate a Certificate of Originality (CoO) as part of its Close Project or Phase process. Regardless if you make or buy technology, this document clearly identifies what your company built and what you incorporated from any third party. In the future, if there is a legal ownership or licensing concern, you'll have it covered.

> A CoO may be important for your business in order to respond to a customer's request to prove your product's technology origin.

Change requests: The Plan Procurement process may illuminate changes that need to be incorporated in the Project Management Plan or any of its subsidiary planning documents. The update of planning documents suggests the flexibility that PMBOK acknowledges will take place during a project's life cycle.

■ **Procurement document packages and source selection criteria:** In order to standardize procurements, a procurement document package may be used as a standard template, which includes everything that prospective sellers will be able to respond to in order to earn the right to be awarded the business. The buyer uses a procurement document package of some sort in order to make sure that all of the information is fairly distributed to each prospective seller. Table 6.19 outlines the four key package types.

Table 6.19 Procurement Document Packages

Procurement Document	Acronym	Favors Contracts That Are
Request for Quote	*RFQ*	Smaller monetary deal or a commodity item (such as a volume purchase of a software tool).
Request for Information	*RFI*	To learn more about a seller that could eventually provide a service to the buyer.
Request for Proposal	*RFP*	Requests an approach, cost, level of effort (this may have a direct bearing on the schedule), and associated detail that justifies the seller response.
Invitation for Bid	*IFB*	Basically, the same as an RFP (common in the aerospace or government markets).

BEST PRACTICE If it is not in the contract, then it must not be a requirement!

Before you go out for a competitive bid, follow your company's procurement best practices. The last thing you'll want is to be challenged that you played favorites after a selection is made. Even if all of the details are not quite fleshed out, it is wise to specifically mention where there is a lack of detail in the procurement document package. This way, it doesn't look like last-minute requirements are being added (or verbally mentioned) that may favor one prospective seller over another.

The source selection criteria are a critical creation of the Plan Procurement process because it clearly defines how a make or buy decision is going to be made. It may be as simple as a list of justifications that will be used or as complex as a risk/reward decision matrix. It generally includes items like those shown in Table 6.20.

Table 6.20 Source Selection Criteria

Selection Criteria	Explanation
Understanding of need	How well does the seller's proposal address the Procurement Statement of Work?
Overall life cycle cost	Are the long-term costs (including future maintenance) in line with your project's goals?
Technical capability	Does the seller have the necessary skills to perform the work?
Risk mitigation	Has the seller thought through the risk in the proposal, and are there documented mitigation strategies?
Technical approach	Do the seller's technical methodology and approach meet (or even exceed) the contract requirements?
Warranty	Does the proposed support after delivery meet the project's needs?
Financial capacity	Does the seller have enough financial resources and a sufficient track record to carry through on the delivery and warranty?
Strategic partner	After this project has been completed, does the seller have other resources, ideas, and the capacity to provide more services?
Past performance and reference accounts	What has been the past performance of the seller with similar business opportunities? What do the references say? (Warning: You are taking a huge risk if the seller has very few, if any, suitable references!)
Intellectual property (IP) rights	Does the seller specify or imply IP that may be used for the work may your project's ability to use their work in this or future impact versions? (Remember the Certificate of Originality mentioned earlier? Insist on a list of IP the seller will use for the work!)

You'll most likely use expert judgment to rate the seller's responses and to make the final selection (especially if there isn't a clear winner based on selection criteria scores).

To properly score selection criteria, I suggest using Excel rather than Word because you can calculate a rating (say, from 1 to 5, with 5 being highest) along with a priority (high, medium, or low). You initially set up the priority, and then fill in the rating for every seller that responds with a proposal (see Figure 6.17). Through the magic of Excel's formulas, you can produce a weighted score!

Selection Criteria	Rating	Priority	Score	Explanation
Understanding of need	5	M	10	This Seller addresses the Procurement SOW as
Overall life cycle cost	1	H	11	Costs long-term are within expectations, proposal addresses maintenance
Technical capability	4	M	9	Very good staff experience, has a background in
Risk Mitigation	5	M	10	Proposal has identified known risks and

FIGURE 6.17
Sample source selection criteria.

PROCUREMENT MANAGEMENT IN THE EXECUTION PROCESS GROUP

PMI has done a marvelous service combining the PMBOK Third Edition's Request Seller Responses and Select Sellers processes into a single Conduct Procurements process in the Fourth Edition. As its name implies, this is the set of steps where you and your team obtain seller responses, select a seller, and award a contract.

Conduct Procurements

There are several factors that go into evaluating which seller to select:

- **Price:** This is usually the prime criteria for selection (even though the lowest price may not produce the best possible product).
- **Technical (approach) and business (cost):** By separating the responses into these two buckets, the selection process should be more objective and easier to make.
- **Decision to use multiple (not a single) sellers:** Based on your organization's risk tolerance (see "Risks Aren't Always Negative" in Chapter 4), you may wish to divide the work among third parties or even select competing solutions (although this is highly unusual).

There are several inputs (primarily from the Plan Procurements process) that are used in the Conduct Procurements process:

- **Procurement Management Plan:** This document explains how procurements are to be performed.

- **Make or buy decisions:** Created as a result of the Plan Procurement process, this list identifies which components need to be made internally or acquired. The latter is used in the Conduct Procurements process.

- **Procurement document packages and source selection criteria:** These two key document sets specify a buyer's formal request to obtain a seller's response along with selection criteria that will be used in analyzing those responses. Both sets of documents are usually made available to prospective sellers. The most important piece of the Procurement Document Package is the Procurement SOW. The source selection criteria can set the level playing field among prospective sellers by clarifying what evaluation criteria will be used for an award.

- **Qualified seller list and seller proposals:** Depending on the sophistication of the work, you may need to use a qualified seller list that can be derived from a variety of sources, including (but not limited to) the Internet, a list of qualified vendors, referrals, and sellers you've used before. In addition, you can't conduct any procurements without receiving proposals from sellers. Seller proposals represent a formal response to the procurement document package (that includes an RFP).

- **Teaming agreement:** A teaming agreement provides a mechanism for the buyer and seller to actually work together to prepare a Procurement Statement of Work with the goal that this collaboration will produce a result that benefits both parties. According to Onvia (a Seattle-based sales and marketing contracting firm), a teaming agreement provides a way for a seller to parcel out the proposed work among a set of subcontractors. This can be viewed as a negative to the sellers but can also be a positive risk mitigation technique.

- **Organizational process assets:** What? This again? There may be a list of sellers that have been contracted before and are recommended by other teams or are qualified according to company guidelines. Also, lessons learned can go a long way, especially if past projects had unsuccessful outcomes with some of the sellers.

> Keep in mind that a bad experience with a specific seller years ago may change for the better under new management (and vice versa).

Given the many inputs I've just discussed, there are some key tools and techniques used in the Conduct Procurements process that will produce the outputs you want. These include the following:

- **Bidders conference:** Also known as a vendor conference, this is where the buyer meets with prospective sellers prior to obtaining proposals. This interactive session (whether face to face or over web conferencing) allows the seller to ask questions pertinent to clarifying the requirements. To make this process flow smoothly, prepare an FAQs (frequently asked questions) list for all sellers.

Maintaining a level playing field is critical, and it is the buyer's responsibility to indicate the ground rules among sellers. The buyer must ensure that information gathered from one seller does not "find its way" to another seller, thus compromising the integrity of disclosure. This is *not* a forum to gain competitive advantage. Although organizing and executing a bidders conference is probably not justified for most third-party needs, if you do have a competitive situation where you have plenty of choices among sellers, this is a valuable technique to use.

NOTE

A bidders conference has the added benefit of giving you first-hand knowledge of what it is like dealing with a seller's team. Negative signs are overcommitting, ruthlessness, know-it-alls, and so on. Positive signs include lots of listening, cooperation, logical skills in how questions are formulated and probed, and so on.

- **Proposal evaluation techniques:** Taking the source selection criteria, expert judgment, and seller proposals (also known as *seller responses*), a formal evaluation process should be used to determine which seller to select (see Figure 6.18). The evaluation committee's selection will then be approved by management (executive management, Finance, and so on) prior to contract award to the lucky seller (or sellers).

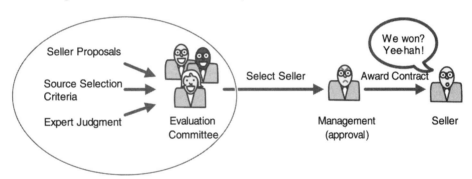

FIGURE 6.18
The proposal evaluation techniques workflow.

Most startups can make this decision with a technical lead, project manager, and someone from Finance. It does *not* have to be complicated or bureaucratic.

- **Independent estimates:** If you want to stage a baseline, utilize an independent resource to prepare an estimate using the Procurement SOW as the source. If the proposed seller's responses are dramatically different, chances are that the Procurement SOW did not provide clear and complete information. Should this happen, you'll need to figure out the best way to quickly get all of the sellers on the same page. For planning purposes, it might be a good idea for you and your team to estimate an expected procurement cost baseline. You don't always have to rely on an outside independent professional estimator.

■ **Procurement negotiations:** Whatever process it takes to negotiate a final agreement needs to be performed to both parties' mutual consent. No verbal warranties or agreements are allowed—all terms and conditions need to be written. The final negotiated agreement should include items like the following:

- Roles, responsibilities, and authorities
- Approaches to take (both business and technical)
- Proprietary rights (for example, the seller does the work but passes all ownership rights to the buyer)
- Schedule payments and ultimately the overall price for the work or service (also include financing, if that applies)
- Terms, compliance, and governing law (if applicable)

■ **Expert judgment:** Probably the most important ingredient in the Conduct Procurements process is, once again, Expert Judgment. A cross-functional team needs to use its collective wisdom to help decide which seller to select. This review committee can help provide a well-rounded tactical and strategic decision.

You don't want to make a procurement decision over and over again if you have the wrong team assembled. It goes without saying that there are industry cases where a project's scope, as stated in the Procurement SOW, mysteriously changed in favor of one seller over the others (who thought everyone was playing by the same set of expectations).

> In 2008, Boeing successfully challenged the Air Force Super Tanker contract award to a competitor, asserting that, among other things, the scope changed at the last moment without Boeing's knowledge.

There are a couple of other tools that can be used that are worth mentioning:

■ **Advertising:** You can solicit sellers by advertising that you are looking for a special expertise (typically for government software contracts). This is also a good way to find potential sellers if you focus your efforts on industry-specific periodicals or events. For example, if your company provides GIS software solutions, making your needs known to GIS industry magazines and tradeshows might be an outstanding technique.

■ **Internet search:** The Internet provides incredible search facilities that help find possible sellers in most any industry imaginable.

The result of using the tools and techniques defined in the Conduct Procurements process is to select and formally award the procurement to a seller.

- **Selected sellers:** This is the final set of sellers who are in the running for the final contract award due to the fact that their responses met the objectives of the Procurement SOW and pricing.
- **Procurement award:** This is what you've all been waiting for! The procurement award is usually issued in the form of a purchase order along with the negotiated contractual agreement (discussed in the procurement negotiations). After selection, a purchase order is drawn up by the buyer (for the seller) along with a mutually agreed-upon contract, as shown in Figure 6.19.

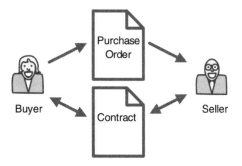

FIGURE 6.19
Contract award includes a purchase
order and contract.

Whereas a purchase order is pretty cut and dry, a contract may take a little bit of negotiation back and forth between the buyer and the seller (hence the double-headed arrow). The contract is a legally binding agreement that obligates the seller to provide the specified product or services to the buyer. A contract obligates the buyer to compensate the seller (hence, the purchase order) based on the terms and conditions of the contract.

BEST PRACTICE For a contract award to be successful, it should be a win-win for both the buyer and the seller.

As change will inevitably occur during a project's lifetime, and if the contract needs to be amended, the best solution is to amend the original contract with an appendix or exhibit outlining the changes. Starting over from scratch with a new contract and new paperwork is not a good idea (besides being expensive).

The contract itself may contain redundant information found in other project documents, but keep in mind that the contract is traditionally viewed as the single source of information. In case of any dispute, the contract will be used to sort out any issues or misunderstandings. Table 6.21 shows some of the highlights of what should be in a contract.

Table 6.21 Key Topics to Include in a Contract Agreement

Contract Topics	Examples of Contract Contents
Statement of Work (SOW)	Deliverables
Schedule and availability of resources	Performance reporting
Roles, responsibilities, and authorities	Pricing, pricing terms, penalties, and incentives
Acceptance criteria	Warranty and support
Insurance and performance bonds	Termination and dispute mechanisms
Limitation of liability	Change request handling

- **Resource calendars:** Although usually a component of a seller's response, a calendar of available resources for the awarded seller will help with scheduling work (see "Estimate Activity Resources" in Chapter 7).
- **Change requests:** As a result of the Conduct Procurement process, changes might be requested that impact the project schedule or the Procurement Management Plan. Any change request should be reviewed and authorized through the Perform Integrated Change Control process ("Perform Integrated Change Control" in Chapter 4). What change could occur with procurement? Plenty! For example, a change may be requested if the selection of a specific seller impacts the project's schedule because the seller can't start the work for another three months (and you were hoping they could start immediately).
- **Update documents:** Finally, project documents may have to be updated (especially if the procurement negotiations made numerous trade-offs that required project changes). These include the following:
    - Stakeholder requirements. (You may wish to add the seller to the list of stakeholders or require modified roles of a stakeholder based on the selection of a specific seller on the project.)
    - Requirements Traceability Matrix.
    - Risk Register (hopefully using a qualified third party should reduce initially planned risks).

The most important thing to remember about this process is that you should have successfully awarded a contract to a seller (or multiple contracts to sellers).

PROCUREMENT MANAGEMENT IN THE MONITORING & CONTROLLING PROCESS GROUP

By now, you've selected the seller. Both parties, the seller and the buyer, are typically responsible for monitoring that a contract is being performed as expected.

Administer Procurements

The focus of the Administer Procurements process depends on the seller's need to frequently monitor progress, and if changes are needed, they are handled through the Integrated Change Control process. It is rarely one party's fault if issues occur, since the seller can have dependencies on the buyer's technology in order to complete their work.

> If a seller gets off track and progress is not regularly monitored, the impact can be devastating (both in time and possibly cost). Remember the infamous Triple Constraint?

Doing the seller a favor by not handling the situation when unexpected results occur will most likely result in a contract dispute later on in the project life cycle. The sooner an issue is handled, the better. (That's what change requests are all about!)

BEST PRACTICE It is in the seller's and buyer's best interest to identify and handle immediately any gap in work execution.

In order to administer procurements, there are several inputs to this process you'll need to have available:

- **Procurement Management Plan:** This explains how procurements are to be performed.
- **Procurement document packages:** This set of documents includes buyer's information necessary to guide the seller with what is required for the project.
- **Performance summaries:** This includes two types of performance information:
    - *Performance reports*—Ongoing performance-related documentation, such as seller technical documentation, deliverable information, and seller performance reports that indicate the current state of completed (and uncompleted) work.
    - *Work performance information*—Although easily confused with performance reports, PMBOK identifies actual work execution data (in other words, facts) that include quality standards that are being satisfied, costs incurred, and seller invoices that have been paid.
- **Approved change requests:** Any change requests that include adjustments in the contract by either the seller or the buyer need to be administered during this process. Changes from the list below need to be formally requested and formally approved:
    - Terms and conditions

- Procurement SOW (that describes the work to be performed)
- Pricing

The Administer Procurements process defines several tools and techniques that should be very helpful in your role of keeping procurements running smoothly (see Figure 6.20).

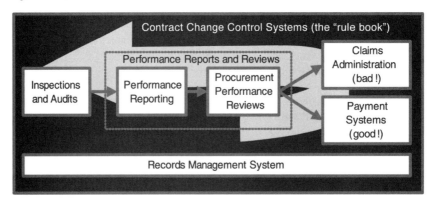

FIGURE 6.20
Relationship of Administer Procurements process tools and techniques.

As you can see in Figure 6.20, the cycle repeats itself (the big curved arrow in the background) throughout the project's life cycle until the Close Procurements process. In fact, each action leads into the other:

1. Perform inspections and audits of the seller.
2. Document and communicate the results.
3. Perform performance reviews (otherwise known as "inquisitions").
4. If all is going well, pay the seller (according to the contract terms and conditions); otherwise, enter into claims administration proceedings in case of a dispute or seller non-performance.

All of these actions are performed using established guidelines from your company's contract change control systems (informally known as the "rule book"). In addition, all of the activities are recorded in some form of a records management system. If these steps are foreign to you, sit down with your Finance organization and make sure that you agree to procedures to handle a seller's non-performance and someplace where you can keep chronological records of events. (The same may be equally true for a seller to keep track of similar activity with the buyer.)

You'll need the assistance of upper management, Legal, Contracts, or Finance if a procurement contract needs to be changed.

- **Contract change control systems:** Recognized as a part of the Integrated Change Control process, the system that defines procurement policies and procedures should define what to do in order to modify a procurement. This includes key systems and processes like the following:
    - Dispute resolution procedures. (Probably number one in the list, right?)
    - Approve rules of engagement for authorizing changes. (You'll probably need some more signatures, since a procurement change will impact one or more of the Triple Constraints: time, scope, or cost.)
    - Contractor tracking systems.
- **Inspections and audits:** In order to ensure that the work is being performed, the buyer typically obligates the seller (in the contract) to support compliance-verification inspections and audits. (Often, this requires that the seller provide documentation and resources to assist the buyer in this information gathering.)
- **Performance reports and reviews:** The techniques to verify how well the contractor is performing. PMBOK breaks this into two categories:
    - *Performance reporting*—Used to report and communicate just how effectively the seller is achieving contractual obligations according to the Procurement SOW.
    - *Procurement performance reviews*—Buyer and seller formal status reviews to ensure that the work is being performed as expected (according to the Procurement SOW) and, if not, to decide on a collective course of action.

The contract change control systems provide the tools to track and manage the work being performed by the seller, and the performance reviews and reports are the techniques used to make sure the seller is fulfilling the needs of the project.

Procurement performance reviews are expected to take place at regular intervals based on information prepared for performance reporting.

- **Payment systems and claims administration:** Payments to a seller are typically handled by the buyer's Accounts Payable (AP) department. Upon the terms and conditions of the contract and your authorization, the seller is paid. It is always a good idea to organize payments based on intervals (milestones) rather than one big glob at the end of the contract. Frequent payments help manage cash flow, establish focus between both parties, and are a motivator and constant reminder to the seller of how important their work is to the buyer's project.
- **Records management system:** There should be a set of processes, control functions, and automation tools that are a part of the project management information system (first described in Chapter 4's "Integration Management in the Initiating Process Group" section). This records management system provides tools for you to keep track of all the contract and procurement documentation and records for the project. In addition, this information can prove invaluable for lessons learned feedback for other projects that have similar scope or wish to use the same seller on their project.

Outputs of the Administer Procurements process are as follows:

■ **Procurement documentation:** This includes a number of documents that describe the original intent of the work and the current status of the work (see Table 6.22). There's a lot to keeping contract obligations in check besides all of the initial work in selecting a seller with the Plan Procurements and Conduct Procurements processes. You may wish to consider assigning a contract monitoring activity to another project manager, especially if you are working with multiple sellers at the same time. Although oftentimes overlooked in the planning stages, there is always a management burden and cost to the buyer to monitor and control sellers.

> Procurement documentation is not the same thing as procurement document packages (described in the "Conduct Procurements" section of this chapter).

Table 6.22 Procurement Documentation

Procurement Document	When Created
Procurement contract (including SOW)	At award
Current contract schedule	Ongoing
Unapproved and approved change requests	Ongoing
Seller-developed documentation	Ongoing
Seller performance reports and inspections	Ongoing
Seller warranties	At award
Financial documents (invoices, payments, and so on)	Ongoing

■ **Change requests:** Change requests to the Project Management Plan (and any of its subsidiary planning documents) may need to be escalated as part of the Integrated Change Control process.

■ **Project Management Plan updates:** Other documents that may need to be adjusted are as follows:

   ■ *Procurement Management Plan*—Update if changes have impacted the Triple Constraint (time, cost, scope) as a result of adjustments requested by either party (the seller or the buyer).

   ■ *Schedule baseline*—The schedule document (spreadsheet, Microsoft Project document, or project management system) may need to be updated due to schedule slippage or schedule acceleration.

- Organizational process asset updates—This represents the documentation (usually in the form of e-mails) that keep a record of key buyer and seller actions, including those that should have been documented in the Procurement Document Packages and in the contract itself. These include:
    1. Correspondence between buyer and seller
    2. Payment schedules and associated invoices
    3. Seller performance and status
    4. Meeting agendas and key status results

PROCUREMENT MANAGEMENT IN THE CLOSING PROCESS GROUP

Close Procurements

This is the point in a project where you need to be sure that everything is *really* closed and not just 80% (or the traditional statement of 99%) completed.

> The Close Procurements process is closed prior to the Close Project or Phase process (see Chapter 4, "Run Development as a Business").

The Close Procurements inputs are as follows:

- **Procurement Management Plan:** This explains how procurements are to be performed.
- **Procurement documentation:** Created in the previous Administer Procurements process, this set of documentation describes the state of the work (as well as the original planned work to be performed).

Tools and techniques for the Close Procurements process are the following:

- **Procurement audits:** An audit, similar to summarizing information for lessons learned, is a team-driven, buyer/seller review of the successes and failures during all of the procurement processes leading up to the Close Procurements process.
- **Negotiated settlements:** This is the goal at the close of a contract to settle all outstanding issues, claims, and disputes. If there are absolutely no issues—then great! Otherwise, there are three levels of negotiated settlements from best case to worst case (see Figure 6.21). If there are gaps in performance, both parties should want to negotiate an *equitable settlement* without involving other legal routes. If that proves unsuccessful, the next choice is to enter into alternative disputes resolution (also known as ADR). This is where *mediation* (or *arbitration*) is useful (through the use of some sort of rational, independent go-between) to assist the buyer and seller to agree on a compromise. Finally, if the other

two techniques fail, your last recourse is *litigation* in court. This is very expensive and non-productive, and most likely will damage the long-term relationship between the buyer and the seller.

FIGURE 6.21
Levels of negotiated settlements.

Notice that in these explanations there is an underlying assumption that the work is completed or that the buyer and seller are responsible to close out the contractual arrangement. That may be the case if the work completes successfully. But what if it doesn't?

Based upon termination clauses in any agreement, the buyer may have the right to terminate the contract due to outcomes like "failure to perform" on the part of the seller.

Regardless of the reason for termination of a contract, the buyer may have to compensate the seller for most expenses incurred up to the point of termination.

Outputs of the Close Procurements process are as follows:

- **Closed procedures:** The buyer formally communicates to the seller that the contract has been completed. As part of the Procurement Management Plan, the requirements for formal closure are also typically defined in the terms and conditions section of the contract.
- **Organizational process assets updates:** You'll want to update and store assets in the following places:
    - *Procurement file*—Complete set of contract documentation.
    - *Formal acceptance*—Don't forget this one! This single document should be copied, converted to a computer format like PDF, locked up, and so forth.
    - *Lessons learned*—Document anything to do with the entire Contract Procurement processes that may help future projects work better with the procurement process.

MAKING THE MOST WITH OUTSOURCING

Since this chapter is aimed at tips and techniques to help your organization become more effective and competitive, one of the best opportunities in both the Cost Management and Procurement Management knowledge areas is outsourcing. *And not just outsourcing in general—offshore outsourcing.*

A HISTORY LESSON IN REDUCING COSTS

According to Ed Yourdon's thought-provoking *Outsource* book, a Cutler Consortium survey presented in 2004 showed that an overwhelming 64% of companies interested in offshore technology outsourcing were motivated by cost savings benefit. Sixty-four percent! The next highest objectives, productivity improvement and faster turnaround, were a far distant 7.5% and 2.9%, respectively.

Table 6.23 shows some other striking information concerning salaries (not including average benefits and general and administrative costs that need to be considered) that Yourdon found in his many trips overseas.

Table 6.23 Estimated Annual Salaries

Year	USA Minimum Wage	Entry Programmer USA	India
1990	$7K	$25K	$4K
Early 2000s	$10K	$56K	$6K

In 1990, Chinese programmers were making about half of what an Indian programmer was making annually ($2.1K), and Russian programmers were making even less at $1.5K.

Salaries have definitely slowed down in the USA, and overseas salaries have risen much more rapidly; but take note that Indian salaries do not represent what is actually being charged to American companies. In 2008, for seasoned Indian software engineers, the annual contracted charge was in the range of $50K (at $25/hr), whereas the American senior software engineer earned about $100K on average. As a result, be prepared to reduce your costs to about half for pure software labor with outsourcing to India. You'll save a little more if outsourcing to Russia, Eastern Europe, Mexico, or China.

According to a 2003 Cutter Consortium survey of 240 software companies participating in outsourcing, only a little more than 50% believed that they'd have moderate success in achieving cost-reduction objectives (see Figure 6.22).

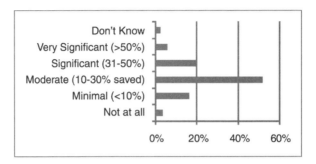

FIGURE 6.22
Likely success in achieving cost-reduction objectives.

According to *Business Week*, as the U.S. dollar declines in value, offshore outsourcing may make less sense. For example, the value of the dollar has declined 16% between 2003 and 2008, making the benefit of outsourcing to certain countries less attractive.

Certain *nearsourcing* countries, like Argentina, Brazil, and Mexico, have invested in building up software talent, and even though their costs are more than those of India and China, they are still far less than the USA. As an example, companies like Avantica (www.avantica.net) offer a strong U.S. presence with staff in nearby Costa Rica and Peru. In a 2007 salary survey report by Alsbridge, an outsourcing consulting firm, if India's software engineers are paid in the $8K range, Argentina software engineers are paid $9.5K, Brazil $13K, and Mexico is close to $18K. But Indian salaries are increasing rapidly, and with the benefit of Latin America being in the same time zone as the USA, we'll see more and more work being displaced from the USA and India to "south of the border."

OUTSOURCING LOGISTICS AND OTHER BENEFITS

As communications technology continues to improve due to the ubiquitous Internet and skilled talent becomes more available, the cost differential becomes even more beneficial to outsource or nearsource alternatives. (In 2003, according to Yourdon, only 1 million out of 1 billion Eastern Indians had access to the Internet. Contrast this to the United States, where over 50% of the population had Internet access. Technology access is increasing, however, and at some point Internet access will be as pervasive as owning a television or a telephone.

BEST PRACTICE For outsourcing to succeed, you'll need assigned project managers for both the buyer and the seller.

There are some rules of thumb that will help outsourcing succeed:

- **Project management presence with both parties:** Nothing could be worse than to simply let software engineers work undirected (especially when language, culture, and time zone issues automatically put outsourcing at a disadvantage). Table 6.24 shows several possible arrangements where your company has (or doesn't have) project management versus an outsourced team with (and without) a project manager. Without at least one project manager engaged between the seller (outsource team) and the buyer (your team), your chances of project success are minimal. With a single project manager, your chances are better but still not risk free. With a project manager engaged for both the seller and the buyer, you dramatically reduce the project risk. Regardless, it is important to identify single-point contacts who are entrusted to make key decisions for the seller and the buyer.

Table 6.24 Chances for Success with (and without) Project Management

Your Team	Outsource Team	Chances for Success
No Project Manager	No Project Manager	✗
Project Manager	No Project Manager	✗ or ✓
No Project Manager	Project Manager	✗ or ✓
Project Manager	Project Manager	✓

- **Regular status checkups:** Make sure that teams are communicating actual status (as often as both parties agree). Note that the amount of time that goes without a status checkup is about the amount of time you should be willing to lose if the project goes awry.
- **Integration and configuration management system:** If the seller's work is going to be further integrated into the buyer's software building environment, versioning, build scripts, automatic bug tracking mechanisms, installation scripts, and so on are necessary to accommodate the seller's work. Also, a well-documented mechanism to exchange files other than e-mail must be set up (for example, FTP, VPN, and so on). And don't forget security—exposing public mechanisms to private data should be set up and communicated so that there is no risk that the work taking place can get into a competitor's (or hacker's) hands.
- **Quality and productivity:** Okay, you're saving lots of money by outsourcing! As Yourdon says it so well, "The lower cost of labor in developing countries doesn't matter unless you also take into account productivity and quality." It won't help productive use of resources if you have to spend considerable time and effort double-checking all of the outsourced work or redoing the work.

When outsourcing, everyone hopes that the project completed work can be validated upon delivery to the buyer and doesn't enter into numerous unplanned QA test cycles. On the other hand, multiple QA passes (especially if the outsourcing seller is 12.5 hours away) can be a huge issue when attempting rapid turnaround. Continuing with Cutler's 2004 survey of software executives, only 21% believe that quality will be at least significantly better than expected (see Figure 6.23). Put another way, a little under 50% believe that they will have less than moderate expected quality goals met.

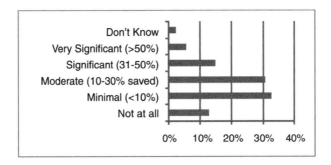

FIGURE 6.23
Likely success in achieving quality objectives.

According to *SD Times*, the best way to ensure that outsourcing will succeed is to have a "trust, but verify" approach. This means that a quality audit plan is required such that, according to Insight Venture Partners, the buyer makes sure the seller has the ability to deliver quality results. Insight has defined this as five distinct phases in the audit:

1. **Pre-assessment planning:** Involving key stakeholders, the buyer gets management approval and creates the quality audit plan.
2. **Data gathering:** Develop interview questions and surveys, and retrieve all quality documentation from the seller (for example, bug reports, test plans, test cases, and so on).
3. **Assessment:** Interviews are conducted with key buyer and seller team members in addition to assessments of data gathered in step 2. The more non-confrontational and confidential the interviews are, the better.
4. **Post audit:** After the assessment, the summary and action steps are prioritized.
5. **Presentation of findings:** The audit analysis is presented to the appropriate stakeholders with the understanding that quality metrics need to be met.

Productivity can be difficult to measure, but if you look simply at "adhering to the schedule," some foreign-born seller executives of American software companies have found that their USA counterparts are four to six times more productive than their native country's software talent base.

BEST PRACTICE You may wish to rethink outsourcing software development if the costs, quality, and productivity benefits are not significant.

According to Cutler's 2004 survey of software/IT executives, more than 75% believe that there will be no better than moderate productivity improvements due to outsourcing (see Figure 6.24).

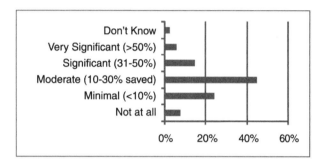

FIGURE 6.24
Likely success in achieving productivity improvement objectives.

Let's continue with our best practices for outsourcing:

- **Availability of talent:** With a declining enrollment of computer science majors in American universities and a growing number of computer science graduates of offshore talents (many of whom come to America for their education), it is no wonder that there is more available talent outside the USA. When you consider how much effort it takes to find available talent for new job openings, there will be increasing pressure to find talent where the talent is located. Companies like Intel, IBM, Adobe, HP, and Microsoft continue to invest in growing staff across continents for that very reason. In fact, some software product lines (like Adobe's excellent FrameMaker) have quietly shifted from development in America to Indian-based development without apparent loss of momentum or quality. But that didn't happen overnight!
- **Technical support:** The seller will certainly have technical questions of the buyer throughout the contract and being very clear as to how the buyer will support the seller's activities is important from the outset of the project.
- **Improvements in the overall international software ecosystem:** There is an Indian organization called National Association of Software and Service Companies (NASS-COM) that performed a study called "The Impact of Offshore IT Software Services

Outsourcing." Their results indicated that outsourcing was a benefit to the seller's country due to the following factors:

1. Increased total employment
2. Lowered inflation
3. Increased demand for U.S. exports

■ **Political and economic instability:** Although there are no guarantees, developing software offshore can yield issues if anti-American sentiments take place or even inflation takes hold where non-U.S. seller's cost benefits become less attractive. The more system-related process and procedures you have in place to avoid loss of intellectual property, the better. This means you need to have systems to ensure up-to-date storage of the following:

1. Frequent backups of software content
2. Up-to-date specifications that truly match the theory behind a seller's implementation
3. Cross-training of buyer's staff by the seller

What About the Other Benefits of Outsourcing?

If you haven't read Thomas Friedman's *The World Is Flat*, you need to. According to Friedman, there have been a number of compelling technological events that have allowed the best work forces to provide value-added benefits regardless of location. As a result, governments are getting serious about investing in education. In 2004, India sent over 80,000 to attend college in the United States. But that's not all—China sent over 60,000, and South Korea sent over 50,000!

Besides costs, are there benefits? *Absolutely!* Once again using the Cutter survey of software executives, each evaluated the following benefits to their own domestic software staff based on outsourcing (see Figure 6.25).

You could view some of these results (like the 14% that believed there were improved relations between the software/IT department and business units) as a signal to non-developers that there is a desire to find alternatives for timely software delivery. About 50% believed that outsourcing redirected maintenance and more mundane activities from their own staff. This benefit, above all, enables your core staff to focus on more strategic tasks and the offshore partner on more tactical tasks. In this case, everybody wins!

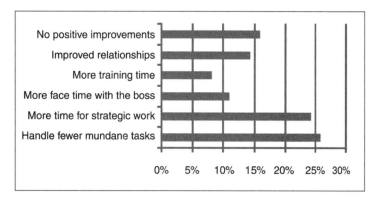

FIGURE 6.25
Outsourcing benefits to the buyer's staff.

If your plan is to outsource work, present this to the staff as a strategic plan and not as a secret out of fear that the "engineers will feel threatened." Also, pay very close attention to presenting the benefits this gives to the three components of the Decision Pyramid based on the customer (faster turnaround of work and extended hourly coverage), company (cost benefits), and the employee (who can focus on next-generation stuff).

Symbio's "Introduction to Successful Outsourcing to China" identifies some additional benefits:

- Globalizing your product—this can be a great starter project.
- Provide other sales opportunities with local country presence.

Mercury Interactive (now a part of HP) has identified other impressive benefits:

- Outsourcing can enable the buyer to become more of a proactive player (rather than reactive, with a "fire drill" mode of operation) based on additional staff assisting with work that constantly derails core engineering from their roadmap or core roles.
- Outsourcing companies can also influence and improve a buyer's capabilities by introducing best practices.
- Regardless of the time of day (not including holidays and weekends, of course), work can proceed, especially if the outsourcing partners are located in other parts of the world.
- Lastly, and not surprisingly, planning for successful outsourcing may actually help get the buyer's own "house in order." This includes formalizing developer change and configuration management, escalation policies, metrics, technical documentation, training material, and best practices in general. In other words, preparing to outsource might uncover inadequacies in your own policies and procedures that need to be improved.

Qualifying the Outsourcing Vendor

Although a key part of the Procurement Management processes, there are some specific steps you can take to be sure that an outsource vendor (in other words, the seller) is qualified:

■ Review the seller's attrition rates, education levels, and depth of engineering experience. (Is there any bench strength in case the seller needs to replace or augment the team with another software developer?)

■ Interview the seller's key staff members—make sure that the company cultures won't clash and that the type of work is in keeping with what the seller is *able* to do and *wants* to do.

> A case in point is where the buyer wants the seller to perform routine maintenance work, but the seller is really expecting to work on next-generation new stuff.

■ Evaluate the maturity of the project management experience, systems, and depth. It won't help if the buyer expects a certain amount of control that the seller cannot (or is unwilling to) provide. If there is a mismatch, you (the buyer) will have to pitch in and absorb some of that seller internal coordination that the seller should be performing.

■ References, references, and *more* references—check 'em all! No company is perfect, but you really want to know if another buyer would engage with the specific seller again for future work (or recommend them to others). If they hesitate wanting to use the vendor, then you can bet there's a problem with the vendor!

Tips and Techniques for Successful Outsourcing

There are a few key tips and techniques to determine if outsourcing is right for you and your company:

■ You need to train them—invest in a train-the-trainer (either at your site or overseas) education program by initially training the vendor's core developers and let them train others in their own organization. This can be very effective for everybody (seller and buyer)!

■ Be patient—establishing partnerships, as well as working through communications and cultural issues, are just the highlights of obstacles you'll need to overcome with outsourcing development. No matter how much time you think it will take to assimilate outsourcing, count on it taking more time.

> According to Thomsett in his book *Radical Project Management*, he claims there is a 20% performance penalty for outsourcing without regular face-to-face communication.

- Plan on lots of communication (written and verbal). Periodically meeting together in a single location does wonders to improve confidence and trust. Keep the meetings focused with clear agendas and action items. (Remember, you are typically dealing with cultural and language issues!)
- Swap project managers—with so much going on, why not periodically swap the buyer's project manager with the seller's project manager? In other words, for a couple of weeks in every project, have the seller's project manager work from the buyer's location. It will do wonders for both parties to appreciate the complexities of each other's business dynamics.

NOTE

Depending on the seller's local intellectual property (IP) protection laws, you may wish to stay clear, especially if you run the risk of losing rights for software being developed outside of your country.

According to Karl Wiegers' white paper "See You in Court," he presents some valuable advice to keep in mind with vendor procurement and outsourcing:

1. Document requirements thoroughly.
2. Negotiate costs that are reasonable and fair for both parties.
3. Define quality, constraints, performance, and scope thoroughly (and minimize any ambiguity).
4. Define a mutually acceptable Change Control process that includes how issues will be handled (because change will take place during the life cycle).
5. Identify single points of contact between buyer and seller. It is also a good idea to identify who the key decision makers are.
6. Agree on significant milestones, establish key deliverables, and manage risks throughout the project *aggressively*.
7. Track status frequently and accurately—re-plan if milestones are slipped or the scope changes.
8. Last, but not least, define how the product will be accepted and establish the exit procedures. Ensuring that there are clear expectations as to how the project will close as well as insisting on a complete transfer of knowledge is vital.

BIBLIOGRAPHY

Austin, Robert D. "Strategies for Sourcing: In, Out, and Offshore." *Cutter Benchmark Review*, June 1, 2004. Cutter Consortium (www.cutter.com/benchmark/fulltext/2004/06/index.html).

Beharvesh, Nariman and Lawrence Klein. "The Impact of Offshore IT Software Services Outsourcing." IHS Global Insight (www.nasscom.org/artdisplay.asp?Art_id=2524).

Correia, Edward J. "Offshoring Strategy—Trust, but Verify." *SD Times*, November 20, 2007 (www.sdtimes.com/SearchResult/31377).

Crowe, Andy. *The PMP Exam: How to Pass On Your First Try, 3rd Edition*. Kennesaw, GA: Velociteach, 2008.

Friedman, Thomas L. *The World Is Flat*. New York: Farrar, Straus, and Giroux, 2006.

King, Rachael. "The New Economics of Outsourcing." *BusinessWeek*. April 7, 2008 (www.businessweek.com/technology/content/apr2008/tc2008043_531737.htm).

Mercury Interactive Cooperation. "How to Manage the Outsourcing Relationship for Maximum Business Value." Feb 2005 (http://whitepapers.techrepublic.com.com/abstract.aspx?docid=124428).

Mulcahy, Rita. *PM Crash Course*. Minneapolis: RMC Publications, 2006.

Newell, Michael. *Preparing for the Project Management Professional (PMP) Certification Exam, Third Edition*. New York: AMACON, 2005.

Onvia. "Teaming Agreement: The Role of the Prime Contractor." Posted January 17, 2006 (http://government.onvia.com/?p=24).

PriceWaterhouseCoopers, LLP. *10th Annual Global CEO Survey* (www.pwc.com/extweb/pwcpublications.nsf/docid/76730ce269229b908025726b004d8cf7).

Project Management Institute, Inc. *A Guide to the Project Management Body of Knowledge: PMBOK Guide, Third Edition*. Newton Square, PA: Project Management Institute, 2004.

Project Management Institute, Inc. *A Guide to the Project Management Body of Knowledge: PMBOK Guide, Fourth Edition*. Newton Square, PA: Project Management Institute, 2008.

The Symbio Group. "Introduction to Successful Outsourcing in China" (www.symbio-group.com/knowledge/).

Thomsett, Rob. *Radical Project Management*. Upper Saddle River, NJ: Prentice Hall PTR, 2002.

Wiegers, Karl E. "See You in Court" (www.processimpact.com/articles/court.pdf).

Yourdon, Edward. *Outsource: Competing in the Global Productivity Race*. Upper Saddle River, NJ: Pearson Education, 2005.

Part

3 Process

Most of what we, as leaders and managers, spend a great deal of time on is schedule adherence and processes. Upper management wants to know the schedule, and your teams want to be sure that the process is being followed. Much of PMBOK is geared toward providing tools and techniques for you to effectively project manage these in light of these knowledge areas:

■ **Chapter 7,** "Master the Art of Scheduling": Agile software methodology is described, along with project scheduling best practices that support agile, iterative product development.
■ **Chapter 8,** "Deliver On-Time, Quality Products": The delivery of software that meets quality expectations is required. This chapter explores quality assurance and quality control best practices in depth. Agile methodology assumes that you build in quality from the start.

7 Master the Art of Scheduling

Much time and effort is spent handling the unrelenting pressure of time. When you deliver a project status to the management team, the highlight of those meetings is usually dependent on how you answer the question, "Where are you on the schedule?" It is absolutely vital that you, as a software leader, develop the ability to predict the amount of time as a sequence of key tasks that a project should take. And yet we all work with software developers who hate the pressure of committing to a schedule because to complete work usually takes "as long as it takes." But you can't effectively run a business without the confidence to work toward a schedule. (Not to mention the fact that your company could have limited success if you drag your feet too long and miss the available "market window.")

PMBOK has defined scheduling as a formal set of Time Management processes, and yet the validity of any schedule is directly impacted by the software processes you and your management team follow. And in order to please two key sets of stakeholders (the team and upper management), the last thing you'll want to do is redefine the process to fit the schedule.

This chapter presents best practices for the following:

- Working in an agile software development environment
- Scheduling the software development process that conforms to agile software development

AGILE SOFTWARE DEVELOPMENT METHODOLOGY

Some say that the *process* used on a software development project makes all the difference to its outcome.

INTRODUCTION TO SOFTWARE DEVELOPMENT PROCESS

Given equal development talent, equal attention to requirements and/or specifications, and equal leadership—is there something that distinguishes one team's success versus another?

Is There a Problem?

Is there really a problem to solve? According to The Standish Group's CHAOS annual survey, there is (see Figure 7.1)! Although somewhat subjective, of the companies surveyed, less than 30% said that their projects were successful, while 18% said their projects failed. Interestingly, over 50% weren't exactly sure and reported that it was unclear if their projects were successful or not (the challenged category).

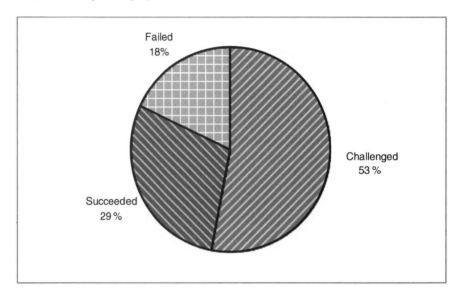

FIGURE 7.1
CHAOS 2004 project resolution survey results.

Back in 2000, the CHAOS survey indicated that in large companies (those with greater than $500M in annual revenue), only 9% of their projects were successful. That same year, 61% of all large company projects were challenged. Not surprisingly, small companies fared better with 28% of their projects successfully completed.

These results are all part of the annual CHAOS surveys performed by The Standish Group.

What are some of the key causes of project failure (or, more appropriately, lack of success)?

- **Restarts:** For every 100 projects that start, there were 94 restarts.
- **Cost overruns:** Almost a third of those companies surveyed reported cost overruns in the neighborhood of between 150 and 200%.

■ **Time overruns:** Remembering the Triple Constraint concept, if you've experienced an impact to project cost, you'll impact the schedule (time). Over one-third of the companies surveyed overran their original schedule estimates at an average of 200 to 300%. Yikes!

No wonder project management is so critical to a project's success! Not that large companies or well-funded projects have better luck—look at the results in Table 7.1 based on a CHAOS survey published in 1999.

Table 7.1 Project Duration and Team Size Impact a Project's Success

Project Size	People	Time (Months)	Success Rate
< $750K	6	6	55%
$750K to $1.5M	12	9	33%
$1.5M to $3M	25	12	25%
$3M to $6M	40	18	15%
$6M to $10M	250	24	8%
> $10M	500	36	0%

It appears that a smaller project's success is a *little* better than big ones. There is also a prevailing theme that "smaller is better" (smaller company, dividing work into small iterations, smaller teams, and so on). What if there was a way to get success rates nearer the 100% mark?

Predictive versus Adaptive Projects

You can probably build a house once you have the blueprints and a couple of house-building projects under your belt. These types of projects are often viewed as *predictive*. Software projects, on the other hand, are usually inventing new features or even new concepts—having too much of a blueprint might result in a product that isn't what the customer is willing to pay for. Software projects are often viewed as being *adaptive* (or *iterative*):

■ **Predictive projects:** It would be silly not to take that same blueprint to build similar houses. You'd have a good handle on the dependencies, resources required, material to be used, costs, and an approximate schedule. Even though you can vary the work by performing some work in parallel, there is a specific sequence that you must follow. For example, you can't put on the roof before you have the house framed.

■ **Adaptive, iterative projects:** Up-front specifications are not really firm until the user sees it, complexity of implementation isn't always known when a project commences, and details emerge as the project unfolds, requiring the team to adjust and learn "by doing."

A Sample Case of What You'll Want to Aspire To

Consider what Geoff Perlman (founder and CEO of REAL Software in Austin, Texas) has done with his company. REAL Software is the maker of cross-platform REALbasic initially used for Mac software development that now supports Windows and Linux platforms. For some time, REAL Software has lived by the rule that innovation and quality are never compromised, but releases need to be regularly scheduled. REALbasic is updated quarterly, and each release includes a few key features plus other important enhancements and corrections. This has the benefit of defocusing the software development team to accommodate the inevitable need for interim, unplanned updates. In fact, REALbasic's versioning is generally predictable by including the year of release and release number (1 through 4) in it, as shown in Table 7.2.

Table 7.2 REALbasic Updates (as of August 2008)

REAL Software Releases	Major Feature Enhancement(s)
REALbasic 2008 R1	Introspection feature
REALbasic 2008 R2	Pair classes
REALbasic 2008 R3	Integrated profiler and Attributes feature

> Did you know there could be five quarters in a year? In 2007 and in 2008, a fifth update of REALbasic was released. Pretty awesome!

Look at their most recent press releases (www.RealSoftware.com), and you'll see a history of timely and regular product updates. According to REAL Software's web site:

> "The latest version is yet another delivery on the promise of continuous improvement made by the company."

It is the continuous improvement part that should interest all of us. It is one thing to define an agile software process, but it is another to direct the whole company to execute to it. This implies a commitment to the following:

- **Customer focus:** Most of us don't like to see frequent updates of software products. REAL software, on the other hand, makes their software effortless to update. It strives to remain backward-compatible and takes no more than a few moments to download and update.
- **Quality:** To release that often, you better have all facets of configuration management and test automation "nailed." If your teams are manually running through comprehensive tests, you won't have any time to build new features (let alone test

corrections to defects). In addition, manpower needed to execute manual tests can cost a fortune (in time and resources).

■ **No gold plating:** Strict adherence to the key new feature (or features) to fit the release timeline is imperative. Product Management may wish to squeeze in new features, but with a release scheduled again (another three months from the current update), a customer won't have to wait too long.

Simply put—REAL Software is one of those rare cases of a company built upon agile principles.

THE WATERFALL SOFTWARE METHODOLOGY

PMBOK desperately tries to tie down software development into a predictive set of processes. This style of software development is often called *waterfall software methodology*, which has the characteristics shown in Table 7.3.

Table 7.3 Waterfall Methodology Characteristics

Feature	Description
Specifications	Lots of them—requirements and specifications are well defined.
Schedules	Laid out, usually to a specific delivery date (precise).
Sequence of events	One process after another.
Adaptable to changes	Not at all—most any change implies a schedule slip.
Easy to understand	Yes, especially for non-technical stakeholders.
Useful to the team	Not really—management may wish projects to be developed using a waterfall approach, but in reality, software developers will probably argue that they don't build software that way!
Customer involvement	At the end (or near the end with a beta program).

The waterfall method takes steps one at a time in a sequence similar to that shown in Figure 7.2.

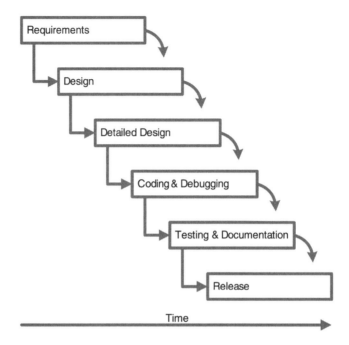

FIGURE 7.2
Waterfall software methodology flow.

Notice that the steps in Figure 7.2 have some overlap (in time). This presentation shows that each process flows from one to another like a "waterfall."

In his book *Agile and Iterative Development: A Manager's Guide*, Craig Larman outlines some key barriers that make the waterfall method unattractive to modern-day software development:

- The clients (users) aren't really sure what they want.
- Clients (users) have trouble specifying their needs.
- Details of what they want will come out during work.
- Forcing up-front specifications can be too complex.
- Once a client (user) sees it, he'll want to change it.

But there are reasons why waterfall techniques are rapidly falling out of favor for software development projects. One of the most important characteristics is the up-front level of effort spent with requirements definitions and analysis (refer to Table 7.3 and the "Collect Requirements" section in Chapter 5). There are a couple of statistics that might surprise you regarding the impact of requirements:

- According to Capers Jones in *Applied Software Measurement*, requirements change at least 25% of the time.
- According to a study presented by Jim Johnson of The Standish Group as a keynote at the XP 2002 conference, the projects surveyed showed that well over 50% of requested features were actually never (or barely) used (see Figure 7.3).

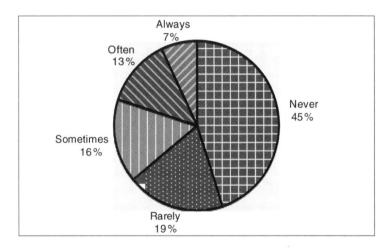

FIGURE 7.3
Frequency that requested features were actually used.

There's also the issue of risk. Projects managed using waterfall methodology depend on testing and final integration to occur after design and implementation. As a result, most of the risk builds up at the tail end of a project (the dotted curve in Figure 7.4). In fact, the more complex a project, the more risk is introduced, which can directly impact the overall schedule.

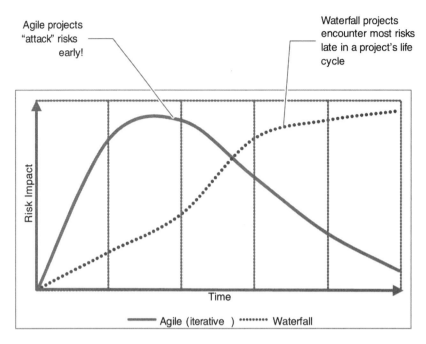

Agile projects "attack" risks early!

Waterfall projects encounter most risks late in a project's life cycle

Risk Impact

Time

———— Agile (iterative) ·········· Waterfall

FIGURE 7.4
Impact of risk over a project's life cycle.

For a refresher on managing risks, see "Risk Management—Preparing for the Unexpected" in Chapter 4.

If you compare this with an agile project, the idea is to always reduce the risks early in the cycle. In Figure 7.4, each horizontal axis represents an iteration (or phase); in this example, an agile project's risk starts its downward swing in the third iteration, while a waterfall project's risk dramatically climbs as the culmination of untested features grows. Subdividing a project into small feature-based components also reduces the risks accordingly. At the risk of stating the obvious, the more complex a project, the more risk is introduced, which can directly impact the overall schedule. *Just the opposite of the waterfall approach!*

BEST PRACTICE In agile projects, the most risky features are usually completed first.

Remember the phrase "plan the work, work the plan" mentioned under the heading "Completing the Plan" back in Chapter 2? For environments that have a fair degree of possible change, this structured approach (as used in waterfall projects) simply won't work.

As in agile-developed methodologies, there isn't just one type of waterfall. According to Steve McConnell (who most of us consider the guru of modern day software), there are a couple of modified waterfall techniques:

- **Sashimi waterfall:** This is where the waterfall steps overlap (refer to Figure 7.2) and take advantage of some form of concurrency (hopefully reducing the overall schedule). The negative to Sashimi? The overlap usually encourages steps to be started too early, and the definition of what it means for a step to complete is often confusing (especially to the team). Communication is also tough (on you), since it isn't clear how to inform the team status so that everyone knows exactly where they are.
- **Waterfall with subprojects:** You can break a large waterfall project into subprojects, where each has its own "little" waterfall (all usually being performed in parallel). The common thread is that the beginning steps (concept, requirements, and design) and the ending step (testing) are shared by all of the subprojects. The negative about this technique is that the interdependencies among subprojects may result in total chaos, or worse, one subproject has to stop and wait for another subproject to complete.

AGILE SOFTWARE METHODOLOGIES

I've used the term *agile methodology* throughout this book, and now it is finally the right time to dig into that subject.

A Gentle Introduction to Agile Development

Being "agile" in software development relies on a few basic concepts. (And what better way to show it than with yet another figure?) As a project's scope is broken down into iterations of development, customers should get happier and happier as the feature set becomes more complete (see Figure 7.5). This customer interaction and feedback is fundamental to agile software development.

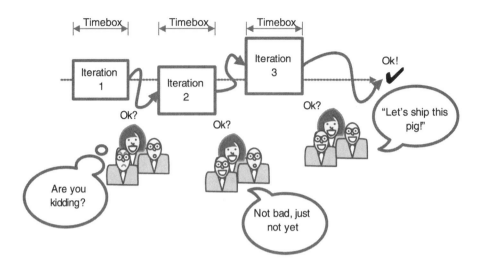

FIGURE 7.5
Customer involvement throughout iterations of agile development.

Agile methodology assumes the following:

■ **Iterations:** You can minimize risk by developing the software in short iterations (*timeboxes*). Each iteration passes though a full software development cycle. Each of these timeboxes is considered to be a fairly short amount of time (between two to four weeks). Each iteration passes though a mini-software development cycle in a fairly short amount of time (typically between two to four weeks). In Figure 7.5, there are three iterations, each executing the Plan-Do-Study-Act cycle.

> Remember the PDSA mini-cycle presented in Chapter 3? Agile pulls that concept together in the form of iterations!

■ **Open collaboration:** Also known as being *customer-centric*, you'll want to get feedback from the customer (your user community) and, based on their feedback, move forward with another iteration. At each completion of an iteration, the product under development should be ready to ship with few known defects. Because agile methodology relies on customer direction and feedback, customers should get progressively happier as the project progresses. (See their smiling faces in the figure?)

Agile projects emphasize face-to-face communication over written documents (who reads stuff anyway?), and the team is typically colocated to facilitate open yappin' and feedback. If possible, the customer should also reside in that work setting or at least be readily available for feedback and guidance.

BEST PRACTICE Every agile project must have a customer representative (even if it is *you*)!

■ **Process adaptability:** Change is embraced, and as long as change brings more customer value, it is incorporated into the planning of the next iteration. You may have noticed that in Figure 7.5 the boxes are not exactly on a straight road (the dotted line with an arrow at the end). That is expected—the steps in creating a great product oftentimes require an "off-road excursion from the highway" (a metaphor!), where some experimentation might yield a phenomenal, unique solution.

According to Doug DeCarlo in his book *eXtreme Project Management*, it is expected and wise to let a project fluctuate a little, as long as you place a lot of checkpoints along the way so that the project doesn't become a runaway. The overall idea is that eventually the project will complete and give customers the value they expect (and hopefully even more than they expect).

An iteration may not have enough value to release, but the goal of iterative (agile) development is to exit an iteration as if you were going to release! This technique effectively acts as a risk reducer as well as a team motivator, based on frequent team completions of work.

How many iterations should a project take? According to Craig Larman, the number of iterations depends on the scope of the project. His experience is that most projects take at least three iterations. Yet one project had 45 iterations. Whew—that's a lot!

Is there a definition for agile? One of the best is from Steven Goldman, who back in 1995, recognized that there was a need to introduce agility into the business world. His definition was as follows:

"Agility is dynamic, context-specific, aggressively change-embracing, and growth-oriented. It is not about improving efficiency, cutting costs, or battening down the business hatches to ride out fearsome competitive 'storms.' It is about succeeding and about winning: about succeeding in emerging competitive arenas, and about winning profits, market share, and customers in the very center of the competitive storms many companies now fear."

The Agile Manifesto

Back in 2001, a bunch of prominent proponents of agile methodology believed so much in ensuring that lightweight standards were agreed upon that they got together to form the Agile Alliance. This team created their version of a software "Bill of Rights," appropriately called the *Agile Manifesto*:

1. Satisfy the customer with early and continuous delivery.
2. Accept changing requirements for competitive value.

3. Deliver working software frequently.
4. Customers and developers work together daily.
5. Trust, support, and motivate the team.
6. Face-to-face communication is required.
7. Working software is the true measure of progress.
8. Agile processes promote sustainable development.
9. Sponsors, developers, and users could maintain the pace indefinitely.
10. Enhance agility with technical excellence and design.
11. Constant attention to maximizing simplicity.
12. The best results come from self-organized teams.
13. Regularly re-evaluate how to become more effective.

> Agile methodology insists on not working burnout hours and not changing the length of time for a timebox. It is better to reduce scope in order to keep to the timebox schedule. New requests can wait until the next iteration.

The "agile way" is quite a bit different than how typical software engineering processes and procedures were taught before, as shown in Table 7.4.

Table 7.4 Comparing the Agile Way versus the Traditional Way

The Agile Way		The Traditional Way
Individuals and interactions	*over*	processes and tools
Working software	*over*	comprehensive documentation
Customer collaboration	*over*	contract negotiation
Responding to change	*over*	following a plan

The PM Declaration of Interdependence

This same team knew that this agile (some call it "lean") approach toward software development would have a possible negative connotation to project management (where control and procedures are commonplace). This resulted in the yet another historical document entitled the *Declaration of Interdependence* (not Independence!). Six principles enable project managers to be effective with agile software development teams (see Table 7.5).

Table 7.5 Declaration of Interdependence

We Hereby Commit to	We'll Do It by
Increase return on investment (ROI)	Making continuous flow of value our focus—with each iteration, more customer value is produced.
Deliver reliable results	Engaging customers in frequent interactions and shared ownership.
Expect uncertainty	Managing for uncertainty through iterations, anticipation, and adaptation—the road may not be straight, but you'll eventually get there with a superior product offering.
Unleash creativity and innovation	Recognizing individuals as the source of value and creating an environment where they make a difference.
Boost performance	Group accountability for results and shared responsibility for the team's effectiveness.
Improve effectiveness and reliability	Embracing specific strategies and processes with a dynamic (not static or structured) approach based on the needs of the project and of the team.

BEST PRACTICE Agile projects depend on an interdependent focused team.

Stated plainly, your role changes from the typical "controlling things that go wrong" to "facilitating that things go right."

Comparing Agile Methodologies

You've probably heard the software methodology called XP (stands for *eXtreme Programming*); and even though most associate XP with agile, it is one of many specific agile technologies that appears to have emerged from Alistair Cockburn's original Crystal method (see Table 7.6).

Table 7.6 Leading Agile Software Methodologies

Methodology	Developed by	Emphasizes
Adaptive	Jim Highsmith	Collaboration and learning and less on telling team what to do.
Crystal	Alistair Cockburn	Different projects demand different approaches (small/large, complex/simple, and so on).
Extreme Programming (XP)	Kent Beck	Programmer accountability, testing during development, and other stringent agile practices (has been loosened up in the Second Edition of *Extreme Programming Explained*).
Feature Driven Development (FDD)	Jeff De Luca and Peter Coad	Interesting twist where there are two types of technologist on a team: the class owners who do most of the programming and chief programmers who coordinate the work.
Rational Unified Process (RUP)	Philippe Kuchten, Ivar Jacobson, and others	Unified Modeling Language (UML), RUP supports an iterative development process
Scrum	Ken Schwaber and Jeff Sutherland	30-day "sprints" without prescribed specific software development practices.

And these aren't all of them! The two I'm going to concentrate on are XP and Scrum.

Why XP Has Transformed the Agile World

Extreme programming, otherwise known as XP, has gotten a lot of press over the years as one of the most notable forms of agile, iterative software development. XP's "embracing change" philosophy is based on five key values, as outlined in *Extreme Programming Explained* (see Table 7.7).

Table 7.7 XP Methodology Characteristics

Value	Description	Benefit
Communication	Fosters questions, status, and knowledge with the team.	Sparks effective cooperation and builds "sense of team."
Simplicity	Elimination of wasteful and oftentimes not user-centric complexity.	Reduces unimportant explanations (simple is as simple does)! Everyone wins when there is a focus on keeping things simple.
Feedback	Get user, team, and system feedback as quickly and as early as possible.	Almost like creating a culture of "checks and balances," tests to verify code, users to review a product's UI, and flow, and so on.
Courage	Design and build a stellar product/service for today; if the future requires a new design, do that work then and not now. Refactoring (or "cleaning up") is one example of building a great product now. Courage also promotes full transparency of information among the team.	As in many software projects, some issues can be swept under the rug. In the case of XP, it takes courage to get in there and fix an issue now. The team benefits with an overriding "can do" attitude.
Respect	Introduced in the Second Edition of *Extreme Programming Explained*, the team must respect the project (and its needs) as well as other team members.	An XP project will most likely fail if each team member is not committed to the success of the project or doesn't trust other members of the team. Total trust can occur where the team becomes a family, each helping the other to achieve the project's goal. Everyone must "leave their ego at the door."

XP, originally conceived by Kent Beck back in 1996, has gone through a couple of evolutions, with the idea that taking best practices to an "extreme" will produce a more customer-centric focus, resulting in software of higher quality than traditional software development schemes. XP defines two roles: the team and the customer.

Funnily enough, there isn't much mention of management in XP. So you'll have to insert yourself into a facilitation role!

The Role of the Team

Nine times out of 10, this is the software engineer, but it also includes the quality assurance engineer or technical writer (in other words, any developer on the team). There is something rather unique about an XP team: *pair programming*. Designating personal time to programming is key for any software developer, and XP assumes that the best way to get things done is to pair with a buddy in front of a computer. This means that two developers are working with each other and communicating while programming is being performed.

BEST PRACTICE Your role when leading an XP team is to ensure that XP principles are being followed.

The benefit of this approach is that two heads are better than one, which encourages brainstorming, reduces frustration when stuck trying to solve a problem by yourself, clarifies ideas, and reduces the risk that only one developer understands how something is designed and implemented.

There are notable drawbacks, however: ego clashes, intimidation among developers ("I won't pair with that jerk!"), a developer's preference to work alone (ever seen a software engineer try to mingle at a company party? Whew—not a pretty sight!), and even annoying personal habits. On an overall project scale, development is normally accomplished with the team divided into pairs with an emphasis on the key activities shown in Figure 7.6.

FIGURE 7.6

Key activities that paired programmers should perform on a project.

As you can see in Figure 7.6, the emphasis on pair programming is based on frequent code integration (from each pair to the team's code repository), test-driven emphasis, and followed by instant code reviews and analysis (by your partner).

There have been several surveys on evaluating the effectiveness of pair programming. Here are a couple of results that might be of interest:

- According to *The Economist* article "Agility Counts" in 2001, not only are two programmers working together more productive than by themselves for a specific task, they produced 50% fewer defects (from 30% to 15%).
- Studies by Lui et al. and Arishom et al. shared similar results in that there was a reduction in defects (48% increase in correctness in the latter report), but there was a fairly substantial increase in effort (as much as 15% to 60%).

BEST PRACTICE XP pair programming may take a little more effort, but it can result in dramatically higher quality results.

NOTE

Overall, it appears that pair programming reduces the number of defects but can take more effort (perhaps due to the fact that the overall speed of the work is somewhat slowed down to the slowest member of the pair).

According to The Menlo Institute's "Paired Programming in the Software Factory" white paper, it is not the individual's productivity that is important—it is the team's productivity that benefits. They argue that pair programming is similar to a sports analogy where an individual's performance may shine, but it is the team that ultimately wins. In the case of software, perhaps the right question is, "How much customer value is created per dollar spent"?

Wait! What about work hours? While most agile methodologies hate the idea of working more than normal work hours, XP extends the concept that if you are motivated to put in some more hours and you can still remain productive, do it! Also, part-time staff members are a real no-no! Not having teammates that are 100% dedicated means that they have their minds on other projects and may not be as dedicated to produce insanely great customer value if they are fractured in focus. Overall, extensive additional hours spent on an XP project typically implies that the team is not productive. Long hours are discouraged.

The Role of the Customer

Usually the actual end-user who is the domain expert for the project is directly involved with ensuring that the software developers understand what is being requested. A suitable alias for this role can be a product manager. But there isn't much documentation to speak of on an XP project (see Table 7.8).

BEST PRACTICE XP eschews formal documentation and depends on oral communication, superb program code, and tests.

Table 7.8 XP Key Documentation

Document	Does What?	Benefit
Stories	Oral communication between the customer and the team that is put on a white board or on a sticky sheet planted firmly on a *vision board*. (You try to keep this as simple as possible.)	Contrary to requirements, a story can be a more realistic simple phrase describing what the customer wants. Initially, stories are used to plan for an initial estimated level of effort and approximate schedule.
Story cards	Described somewhat as a "learning trail of thoughts," each story has an associated detailed story card with additional information shared between the team and the customer, including level of effort and, most important, the priority from the customer's point of view. A story card should be simple enough to have a single priority and be able to be tested.	These simple explanations between the customer and the developer become the specifications (the implementation details are typically not documented). Story cards can serve as a great mechanism to summarize how the feature should be validated and accepted.

Figure 7.7 shows an example of a story card designed to add multiple levels of undo to a software application's user interface.

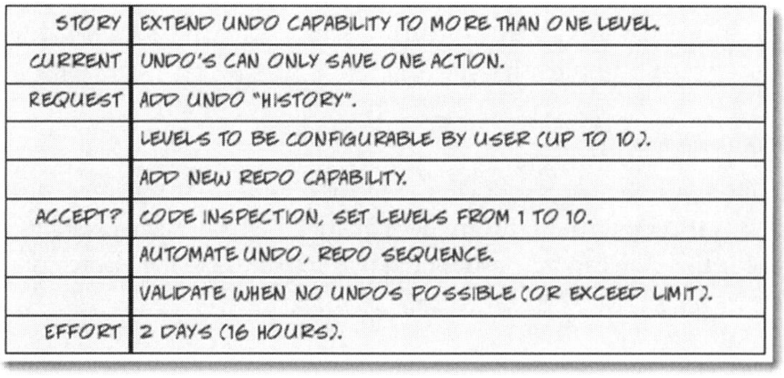

STORY	EXTEND UNDO CAPABILITY TO MORE THAN ONE LEVEL.
CURRENT	UNDO'S CAN ONLY SAVE ONE ACTION.
REQUEST	ADD UNDO "HISTORY".
	LEVELS TO BE CONFIGURABLE BY USER (UP TO 10).
	ADD NEW REDO CAPABILITY.
ACCEPT?	CODE INSPECTION, SET LEVELS FROM 1 TO 10.
	AUTOMATE UNDO, REDO SEQUENCE.
	VALIDATE WHEN NO UNDO'S POSSIBLE (OR EXCEED LIMIT).
EFFORT	2 DAYS (16 HOURS).

FIGURE 7.7
Sample XP story card.

Not unlike a visual project dashboard, it isn't too far fetched to use this concept on a wall where the state of story cards actually is an indication of the state of the project. By organizing the story cards into specific groups, the placement of story cards could easily represent project status and focus (in other words, forward momentum). Here are some sample groupings that could be used:

- **Done:** Story cards (activities) completed. (Where I grew up, we spell this d-u-n-n.)
- **For this release:** Story cards are actively being developed.
- **To be estimated:** Story cards not yet scoped or scheduled (although initial rough estimates have usually been performed).

XP places importance on testing as follows:

- Tests must be created before coding (not the other way around). This test-driven development philosophy is mandatory for XP. It further solidifies the bond between the customer and the team by ensuring the following:
    1. There are acceptance criteria (the test) that will prove that the story card has been successfully implemented.
    2. The feature has a higher probability of being a *quality* feature because of the emphasis on creating up-front tests.
- Tests must be automated (where possible) with the understanding that running the tests returns a pass (or fail) result that can be further evaluated as to what actually happened. This automation allows tests to be run every night with a simplified result summary awaiting the team when they start work in the morning.

The XP workflow is shown in Figure 7.8.

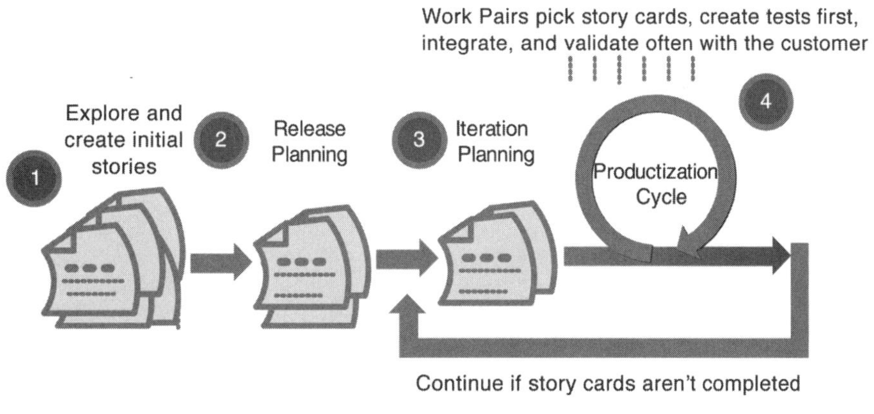

FIGURE 7.8
Extreme programming workflow.

BEST PRACTICE In XP, the customer prioritizes the content (stories), and the team decides its level of effort and how it should be implemented.

Each step is summarized in Table 7.9.

Table 7.9 XP Workflow Cycle

Step	Step in the Cycle	Key Roles	What Takes Place
1	Exploration	Customer and team	Stories are created, prioritized, and researched. In case there are any unknowns (for example, "I have no idea how to implement that!"), team members should create a throw-away prototype to reduce the risk of the unknown. (This quick prototype is known as a spike, according to Newkirk and Martin's book *Extreme Programming in Practice*.)
2	Release planning	Customer and team	Affectionately called the *release planning game*, the customer and the team completes the story cards and decides what to do in the next iteration.
3	Iteration planning	Customer and team	Assign activities to the paired programmers and divides story cards into tasks (as a reminder, PMBOK calls them activities). If the total estimated time is too much for the iteration, the customer influences the team as to which tasks are postponed until a later iteration.
4	Productization	Customer and team	Continuous integration, tests, and nightly builds takes place. Rather than wait for customer input later, the team works closely with the customer all along the way. When this step completes, the product should always be in a shippable state (as far as quality goes).
			Although not a specific step, if the release is not complete, the team continues with iteration planning (step 3). The cycle continues until the product is complete and the customer is satisfied.

In summary, the most notable XP characteristics are described below in Table 7.10.

Table 7.10 XP Highlights

Feature	Description
Requirements	Features are described as story cards.
Schedules	Assumes that a project will have a certain number of iterations.
Sequence of events	One iteration follows another.
Adaptable to changes	Yes—XP thrives on being adaptable due to the proximity of the customer with the team.
Easy to understand	Mixed; the rules of engagement are intuitive, but sometimes there are interpersonal pitfalls (for example, pair programming) that can cause dysfunction.
Useful to the team	Customer involvement helps focus the team; frequent iterations add to the feeling of success.
Customer involvement	Continuously throughout every step of the project.
Process	Cycles of Iteration Planning and Productization.
Meetings	Few—in the beginning and at the start of every iteration.
Team size	10 to 12 maximum.
Timeboxing	Typically one to three weeks maximum (one week is now the preference).
Team organization and structure	Colocated ("no walls") with an emphasis on pair programming.

Sprinting to Delivery with Scrum

Scrum has a lot of visibility in a number of industries but particularly in the software world. The overriding theme is best captured in Ken Schwaber's *Agile Project Management with Scrum*. He assumes that *every* software engineer who practices Scrum refers to this book on a regular basis. Well, he must sell a lot of books because Scrum is gaining popularity not only in software development but in other professional disciplines as well.

BEST PRACTICE Adapting Scrum requires the same agility by product and project managers (not just by the developers).

The heart of Scrum is to *adapt as you learn* through a rapid series of iterative steps (where each takes place one after the other). There are specific roles and responsibilities, all designed to ensure that the team is dedicated and focused. Part-time involvement *isn't* going to be very successful with Scrum. The roles in a Scrum project are shown in Table 7.11.

Table 7.11 Scrum Key Roles

Role	Does What?	Benefit
Product Owner	Represents the views of the customer; usually creates user stories or specifications that are placed in a Product Backlog.	Balances business and customer needs.
ScrumMaster	Facilitates by removing obstacles that would slow the team down; ensures that the team is following the Scrum process and best practices.	Keeps the project on track. (You can be expected to fulfill this role if there is no dedicated ScrumMaster assigned.)
Team	Develops and delivers the product or service (typically a small team).	The team's commitment produces the results (which depend on having an effective Product Owner and ScrumMaster).
Customer	Provides the customer input required for the product owner to properly represent them. Should be involved in iteration checkpoints.	Getting actual customer involvement is one of the hallmarks of Scrum that increases the probability of customer satisfaction and future acquisition of products and/or services.

By the way, there are other roles that contribute to the overall effectiveness of a Scrum project including stakeholders, management, and even Finance.

The documentation used on a Scrum project is minimal, as shown in Table 7.12.

Table 7.12 Scrum Key Documentation

Document	Does What?	Benefit
Product Backlog	The feature list (requirements) with estimated level of effort (usually in days).	The storehouse of feature requirements that drives the content to be developed in Scrum iterations.
Sprint Backlog	The details of the Product Backlog, estimated level of effort (usually in hours), and the plan for the next iteration (also known as a Sprint).	The team members rely on the Sprint Backlog as their "to-do list." Each member self-assigns his work from the Sprint Backlog.
Burndown Chart	Shows the number of tasks remaining for the current Sprint, along with the number of tasks remaining for the project.	Clearly shows what is left to do—benefits the team by keeping them focused.

BEST PRACTICE Working *more* hours doesn't mean that the team produces *more* output.

The cyclical workflow during the delivery processes can be highly intuitive and is typically very fast-paced without tons of long-winded meetings (see Figure 7.9).

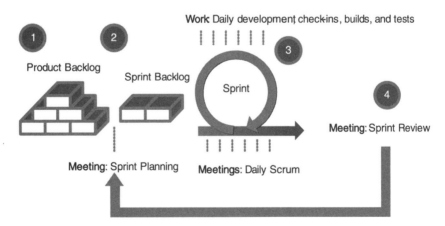

FIGURE 7.9
Scrum workflow.

Table 7.13 shows the steps of the Scrum workflow.

Table 7.13 Scrum Workflow Cycle

Step	Step in the Cycle	Key Roles	What Takes Place
1	Vision Planning	Product Owner	Formulates overall project plan, identifies features (with customers), and creates the Product Backlog, which should have the same information as the Burndown Chart.
2	Sprint Planning	Product Owner and the team	Two parts: First, remaining Product Backlog presented to the team who collectively decides on what to prioritize (the Sprint Backlog). Second, the team creates the collective Sprint plan. BAM—the Sprint kicks off!
3	The Sprint	Team and ScrumMaster	The work gets completed (and as the work is done, the Burndown Chart is updated). The key work activities include daily development, check-ins, builds, and tests. The team meets daily for no more than 15 minutes to go over (A) what was just completed, (B) what the team is doing next, and (C) identification of anything hindering work. A Sprint should never last more than 30 calendar days. (Research Sprints shouldn't last more than 15 calendar days.)
4	Sprint Review Meeting (also known as a Sprint retrospective)	Team, ScrumMaster, and Product Owner	The team presents to the Product Owner (and other interested parties) what has happened and re-evaluates how to adjust practices and roles in order to make continuous process improvement. Go to step 2 and continue the cycle.

NOTE

Does the role of the project manager support Scrum at all? You can view Scrum as a license to work in a chaotic manner destined for failure, or you can embrace it by applying those components of PMBOK that best fit the way the team chooses to operate.

The backlogs are really nothing more than simple-to-understand requirements and activity estimates. The Burndown Chart should not be used as a simple earned value calculation. Follow the guidelines in the "The PDSA cycle" section in Chapter 6.

Expert judgment is required to make sure that the right resource is assigned for a specific task, and a team member's self-assignment may yield disastrous results if not properly monitored.

Your role is to communicate often to the team, customers, and stakeholders—keep it simple. (Exhaustive charts and calculations may make the project manager in you feel good, but that level of detail may have little significance to most of your audience.)

With frequent intermediate deliveries, manage risks often and mitigate them (akin to the Monitor & Controlling process group activities). Lastly, you must inspire an environment of complete transparency where clear accountability rules and issues are never to be "swept under the rug."

The most notable characteristics are shown in Table 7.14.

It isn't unusual in a multi-iteration Scrum project to expect more QA (testing) effort in the final iteration. (The cycle for each iteration is very similar in concept to PDSA.)

Table 7.14 Scrum Highlights

Feature	Description
Specifications	Create an overall game plan; create a backlog of requests/needs and chisel away at the list with each iteration.
Schedules	Assume that a project will have a certain number of iterations (iterations must not be extended).
Sequence of events	One iteration follows another.
Adaptable to changes	Yes, each iteration is geared to handle change.
Easy to understand	Yes, especially for non-technical stakeholders (very few rules and techno-jargon).
Useful to the team	Exciting, early, and frequent successes.
Customer involvement	At the end of every iteration (the *Sprint review*).

(continued)

Feature	Description
Process	Iterations of planning, staging, development, and release.
Meetings	Daily, stand-up, affectionately called *The Daily Scrum*. (Hey, I didn't name it!)
Team size	No more than seven (preferred); if more, then divide into mini-teams.
Timeboxing	No more than 30 calendar days (15 days is rapidly becoming the norm).
Team organization and structure	Self-directed; mentored by the ScrumMaster, who protects the team, removes obstacles, attacks and removes project risks, and ensures that Scrum methodology is enforced. There is also a Product Owner identified who has the responsibility to re-prioritize the backlog to accommodate the timebox for a Sprint. Communication is key for Scrum to be successful.

TIME MANAGEMENT FUNDAMENTALS

Time management may appear to be an easy concept to understand, but it can be one of the most difficult knowledge areas to grasp. According to PMBOK, Time Management takes place in the Planning as well as in the Monitoring & Controlling process groups; however, it is not usually a part of the Initiating, Executing, or Closing process groups.

Let's look at how to interpret PMBOK Time Management best practices for software projects. While time (or schedule) is usually defined in terms of tracking tasks, PMBOK recommends the use of the term *activities* instead. An activity is a component of work to be performed during the course of a project. An activity typically has a resource assigned, an estimated cost, and expected duration of time to complete.

BEST PRACTICE Activities are derived from work packages—they are not one and the same!

A constant theme in the world of project management is to subdivide big items into smaller, more manageable items. In this case, you'd break down the work into a detailed set of activities.

This does not mean that just because you *defined* detailed activities that you always need to *communicate* detailed activities to your stakeholders. Project managers must remember to communicate the proper level of detail effectively.

The more you break down your project into activities and subactivities, the more accurate your time estimate will be for the overall project schedule. For example, a project could be as simple as three activities to be performed in sequence (see Figure 7.10).

FIGURE 7.10
A project with three sequential activities.

The interpretation of this project's activities is quite simple. After the project starts, activity 1 begins. Once activity 1 ends, activity 2 begins. And when activity 2 ends, activity 3 starts. Once activity 3 completes, the project ends. This is called a *network diagram*. The total estimate of time (in other words, the project schedule) should be the summation of the time taken for those three activities:

```
Project Schedule = A1 + A2 + A3
```

More realistically, however, a typical software project is actually composed of a complex, interconnected series of activities, as shown in Figure 7.11.

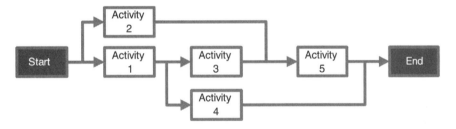

FIGURE 7.11
A project with a more complex set of activities.

In this case, when activity 1 starts, so does another activity (in this case, activity 2). Once activity 1 completes, activity 3 starts and so does activity 4. When activity 2 and activity 3 complete, activity 5 starts. The project doesn't end until activity 4 and activity 5 are both completed. So how can you effectively estimate the schedule for a project like this? Estimating the overall project schedule is never as simple as adding the time duration for all activities together:

```
Project schedule not= A1 + A2 + A3 + A4 + A5
```

What's worse, you can't assume the summation of only the key activities either (those activities leading to one another in Figure 7.11):

```
Project schedule not= A1 + A3 + A5
```

Mastering the fundamentals of time management will help you *plan* as well as *monitor and control* activity schedules. (Perhaps that's why Time Management processes are in the Planning and the Monitoring & Controlling process groups.)

Activity management is usually performed with a project management scheduling application (like Microsoft Project), but most of us work fine with a simple spreadsheet—it all depends on how complex the schedule is and how granular you want the scheduling to be. The beauty of agile software projects is that timeboxing activities is one of the best ways to complete a project on time with a self-imposed "sense of urgency."

The complication arises, however, when there are complex dependencies between these activities. (And the project depicted in Figure 7.11 is nowhere near the complexity of activity dependencies you'll encounter with your projects.) *So, let's head into the world of time management!*

Overview of the Time Management Knowledge Area

The Project Time Management knowledge area, as defined by PMBOK, you could argue is more of a planning process (most of the steps are in the Planning process group). However, how the schedule is planned and how work is determined are very much part of the overall software development process.

The PMBOK knowledge area processes have been simply renamed between the Third and Fourth Editions (see Table 7.15).

Table 7.15 Time Management Knowledge Area Processes (PMBOK 4th Edition)

	Process Groups			
	Implementation			
Initiating	Planning	Executing	Monitoring & Controlling	Closing
	Define Activities		Control Schedule	
	Sequence Activities			
	Estimate Activity Resources			
	Estimate Activity Durations			
	Develop Schedule			

TIME MANAGEMENT IN THE PLANNING PROCESS GROUP

There are five distinct processes in the Planning process group to be performed during schedule planning (and they are usually performed in the following order):

1. **Define activities:** Identify schedule activities to complete project deliverables.
2. **Sequence activities:** Plan dependencies among activities.
3. **Estimate activity resources:** Type and quantities of resources needed to perform each activity.
4. **Estimate activity durations:** Define the number of work periods to complete each activity.
5. **Develop schedule:** Create the project schedule using all of the above information.

> These steps can be performed as a single process or as overlapped processes, depending on a project's scope. As described in the earlier section "Agile Software Development Methodology," there is more than one way to derive activities for scheduling.

Although all of this stuff may look like busy work, each of these steps is important in breaking down a project into activities in order to produce the best possible schedule.

BEST PRACTICE You can always combine the five activity planning processes into one to save time!

Define Activities

To properly create a visual network diagram that can be used to estimate a project schedule (refer to Figures 7.10 and 7.11), you'll need to create an activity list and a milestone list first (see Figure 7.11). By focusing on what should be performed, the work identified by the WBS becomes the basis for further time planning processes. Inputs needed to define your project's set of activities are as follows:

- **Scope baseline:** This includes the Project Scope Statement (the planning document that indicates a summary of the product and project scope), the WBS (hierarchical breakdown of work packages), and the WBS Dictionary (which has the details of each of those work packages).
- **Enterprise environmental factors:** The use of a Project Management Information System (PMIS) can provide an integrated system that keeps track of all of the project information (rather than have individual documents).

- **Organizational process assets:** These artifacts hold lessons learned and the policies, procedures, and guidelines to be used in breaking down the work into activities.

The tools and techniques used are as follows:

- **Decomposition:** Subdivide the project work packages into smaller components by the team who will be doing the work, as shown in Figure 7.12. (As a reminder, these components are called activities.)

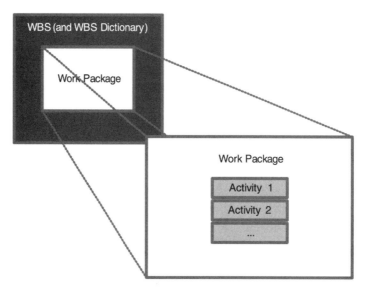

FIGURE 7.12
Creating activities from a work package.

To save time, you and the team may wish to perform the Activity Definition process in the Create WBS process (see "Create WBS" in Chapter 5).

- **Expert judgment:** Your experience creating activities is the most valuable technique of them all.
- **Rolling wave planning:** As a form of progressive elaboration (and a fundamental technique for agile methodology), detailed activity breakdown should occur *before* the work is being performed. (There is some risk involved if you or your team is inexperienced with the requirements of a project. This could result in miscalculation of the number or complexity of activities too late in the project development life cycle.)
- **Templates:** Industry or company standard templates can be used to ensure that information about activities and milestones is documented in a complete manner.

Outputs of this process are as follows:

■ **Activity list:** This is a document (spreadsheet, sticky notes, and so on) that includes all scheduled activities that are planned to be performed on the project. Given the example shown back in Figure 5.11 (in the "Create WBS" section of Chapter 5), the work package would have the following activities:

Activity	Scope of Work
3.2.1.1	Gather all (and possible future) state tax algorithms.
3.2.1.2	Design code changes required.
3.2.1.3	Implement and test state tax algorithms.

The sample work package was identified as "3.2.1 Build state tax software module."

■ **Activity attributes:** New in the Fourth Edition of PMBOK, some prework would be helpful when later scheduling activities. These include but are not limited to the following:
   ■ Activity number, WBS number, and any other identifier.
   ■ Predecessor activities, successor activities, logical activity relationships. (This may be important to show the dependencies activities might have with one another.)
   ■ Resources responsible, along with their location (or, in the case of outsourcing, the company they belong to).
   ■ Any level of effort (even if just a swag).

The reason that activity attributes are now an output is that since you (and your team) are creating the Activity list, you might as well gather other pertinent information at the same time rather than have to go back through the list later.

Throughout the rest of this chapter, the term *period* is used to signify a duration of time measured in hours, days, weeks, months, or quarters.

■ **Milestone list:** Identification of all milestones that may be imposed from outside influencers (stakeholders). This is critical to know up front because there may be, as in the tax software example, a fixed period of time that the project must be completed. Using the same example, there will have to be definite hard stops for tax software development year after year:

Milestone	Scope of Work
Sep 1	Functionally complete, early previews to partners.
Dec 1	Final validation complete, go to production.

To summarize, Figure 7.13 shows how you can combine the activity list and activity attributes into a single spreadsheet (although you'd probably want to use Microsoft Project for this).

Activity List		Activity Attributes				
Activity ID	Scope of Work	WBS ID	Predecessor ID	Successor ID	Resources	Est. Level of Effort
3.2.1.1	Gather all (and possible future) state tax algorithms.	3.2.1		3.2.1.2	In-house	2 Days
3.2.1.2	Design code changes required.	3.2.1	3.2.1.1	3.2.1.3	In-house	2 Days
3.2.1.3	Implement and test state tax algorithms.	3.2.1	3.2.1.2		In-house	5 Days

FIGURE 7.13
Sample Activity list and activity attributes definitions.

Sequence Activities

Okay, I've just defined the activities! That's a great start, but how do activities relate to one another? Here are a couple of tips you should consider in sequencing activities:

- Keep a mindful eye on ways to lay out activities as efficiently as possible. Overcomplicating the ordering and relationship of activities in a project can make a short project appear to be longer than it should be.
- Make sure that you always cross-check the sequence with the team before committing them to a schedule. What may be logical to you may be far from reality with the team members actually performing the work.

To create your project's network diagram, you'll take the defined activities from the previous process and use several tools and techniques to sequence them.

Inputs to the Sequence Activities process are as follows:

- **Activity list and activity attributes:** A list or database of a project's activities and their attributes (optional) that can assist in helping to sequence activities to create the schedule.
- **Milestone list:** Any defined due dates that should be considered in sequencing activities.
- **Scope baseline:** Both the Third and Fourth Editions of PMBOK presume that the Project Scope Statement is a key input. This is incomplete—the scope baseline is more appropriate because it refers to not only the Project Scope Statement but also the WBS and WBS Dictionary!
- **Organizational process assets:** Information from your company's project knowledge base that can assist in sequencing project activities (this includes templates, samples, and case studies).

Tools and techniques used in the Sequence Activities process are discussed in the following sections.

Precedence Diagramming Method (PDM)

Used in Critical Path Methodology (CPM) to create a visual network diagram, with each activity labeled using a simple identifier (in Figure 7.14, for example, A, B, C, D, and E). This technique is used to show the relationship between one activity and another. Activities A and B are completed right from the start of the project. Activity C starts after B completes, and Activity D starts when both Activities A and B are completed. Activity E (you should be getting the idea how this works by now) starts only when Activities D and C have been completed.

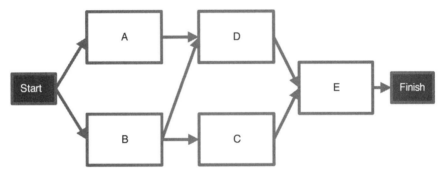

FIGURE 7.14
A network diagram produced using PDM.

PDM is also called Activity-On-Node (AON).

For this particular example, assume that each successor activity will only start when its predecessor activity completes. The type of predecessor-successor relationship you choose may significantly impact the overall schedule. Table 7.16 shows the relationships between activities that are recognized by PMBOK.

Table 7.16 Dependencies Between Predecessor and Successor Activities

Dependencies Between Predecessor and Successor Activities	
Finish-to-Start (FS)	An activity must finish before the successor can start. (Complete one activity before starting the next.)
Start-to-Start (SS)	An activity must start before the successor can start (implies parallel development of more than one activity at a time).
Finish-to-Finish (FF)	An activity must finish before the successor can finish. (For example, the application development must be finished before final documentation is finished.)
Start-to-Finish (SF)	An activity must start before the successor can finish. For example, the user's manual activity (successor) must be completed for printing before the indexing (predecessor) has been completed.

Dependency Determination

There are three types of dependencies that are used in sequencing activities:

- **Mandatory dependencies:** Also known as *hard logic*, the project team should ensure early on that the team is on board, with everyone knowing which activities must be performed before other activities. In the home construction industry, before you can build the house, you better put in a solid foundation. Likewise with software: Core engines and frameworks typically need to be built before the user interface logic. Typically, you'll want the team to build the mandatory activities first.
- **Discretionary dependencies:** Unlike mandatory dependencies, the project team should determine which activities are discretionary and have no strict dependence on other activities. Also known as *soft logic*, these types of activities can be performed usually most anywhere in a project life cycle, enabling you to plan for these when there are openings in the workload. Identifying these early certainly gives you more freedom when you are trying to best fit activities into a workable schedule.
- **External dependencies:** These are activities outside of a project that are needed by at least one of your project's activities. An example would be an activity that includes the purchase and setup of hardware purchased from a reseller. Another example is a software subsystem that is developed by a third party and is required to be licensed for use on your project.

Applying Leads and Lags

So far the predecessor-successor relationship for sequencing activities works pretty well for the majority of activities you'll need to schedule. However, without complicating the relationships of activities to one another, there are times when you'll want to indicate delays or opportunities to accelerate work.

> Always use leads and lags to represent early starts or delays rather than artificially adjusting the duration of activities. (Also, don't forget that work days and calendar days are not the same!)

PMBOK defines leads for opportunities to accelerate work and lags for delays. Let's apply leads and lags to an example where the duration of a predecessor activity A is two days and the duration of its successor activity B is also two days (see Figure 7.15).

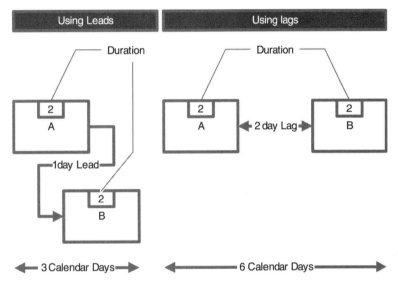

FIGURE 7.15
How lead and lags can accelerate (or delay) a project schedule.

- **Lead:** Use a lead when an activity can begin before its predecessor has completed, as shown in Figure 7.15. In this particular case, Activities A and B both take two days of effort (for a total of four man-days). Yet the calendar days both projects take can be reduced to three days—a savings of one day (which represents a 25% benefit than if you didn't start early).

  An example is where the team believes that Activity B (building the user interface) can start before Activity A (building the foundation modules that the user interface depends on) completes. Additional risk can be introduced by taking advantage of leads, so use expert judgment in your decision.

■   **Lag:** If your project has a mandatory delay between activities, you should schedule a lag. In Figure 7.15, there is a two-day lag between both of the planned activities. The work effort for the two activities is still four man-days of effort, but with the lag, there is a 50% increase in calendar time from four to six calendar days.

   The typical example is where a house is painted (Activity A) and you have to delay hanging the artwork (Activity B) while waiting for the paint to dry. A more appropriate example with software is when data has been collected and processed (Activity A), but it will take a delay period to migrate the data to a shared database repository before the application is updated to use that information (Activity B). (In high transaction count medical systems, it isn't unusual that migrating and deploying information to a data warehouse might take several days before it is usable.)

Schedule Network Templates

Why reinvent the wheel? If you can save effort by reusing project files or even a portion (subsystem) of a network file, then do it. This is analogous to reusing code by making it into a shareable subroutine (or subsystem) that is invoked from multiple sources. In this case, you can save time and reduce errors by reusing project templates as starting points.

   Outputs of the Schedule Activities process are as follows:

■   **Network diagrams:** Project schedule network diagrams are visual diagrams that show the relationships between a project's activities. Some sort of simple narrative is usually helpful to go along with the diagram (this is highly recommended by PMBOK). A network diagram built using a visualization tool, like Microsoft Visio, is a total waste of time. Visio diagrams may look great, but using a project management system, like Microsoft Project, maintains the activity information and can produce the network diagram as needed. If the scheduled activity sequences change, you simply generate a new network diagram—no manual redrawing would be required!

BEST PRACTICE The network diagram is by far the best visual way to present schedules.

■   **Project document updates:** Activity lists and activity attributes might be updated based on outcomes and adjustments made during this process.

Estimate Activity Resources

You've now defined and sequenced a project's activities. *Are you done yet?* Not so fast! You still need to determine all of the resources required: personnel, material (otherwise known as "stuff"), and equipment (or "great stuff").

This process (as well as other time processes) are used for the Estimate Costs process. Figure 6.3 in Chapter 6 depicts the close relationship between the Project Cost and Project Time knowledge areas.

In the Estimate Activity Resources process, you aren't doing anything more than identifying all of the resources required. Besides the obvious team members, some resources you may not have considered are the following:

- **Consultants:** You might need experts if your staff doesn't have the necessary experience to complete the project. These mentors, even if part-time, can really help move a project along rather than find itself stagnant due to a lack of knowledge.
- **Training:** Your team may be composed of talented programmers, but they may need to update their skills. I can't think of a better way to reduce project risk and motivate the team than investing in employee training. (Conversely, it can be a dramatic demotivator if you don't authorize training for your staff.)
- **Specialized equipment and tools:** Usually you think of equipment as being PCs, network gear, and servers. If, for example, your team is working on an important embedded software project, make sure there are enough embedded target boards for Engineering and the other departments, like QA, Technical Publications, and Technical Support.

What is the impact if the Estimate Activity Resources process isn't performed? Try these project risks on for size:

- There aren't enough resources to perform the work.
- Resources aren't allocated for enough time to complete the work and are to be reallocated to another project.
- Much-needed resources were accidentally not planned at all (and so you are scrambling at the last moment to get some talent).

Key inputs to the Estimate Activity Resources process are discussed in the following sections.

Activity List and Activity Attributes

The Activities list and the activity attributes are used together to identify all of the information for all of the activities. (Talk about obvious, eh?)

Surprisingly, PMBOK Fourth Edition dropped the Project Management Plan from the list of specific inputs to this process.

Resource Calendars

Identified as resource availability in the PMBOK Third Edition, resource calendars actually come from two sources in two different knowledge areas, as shown in Figure 7.16.

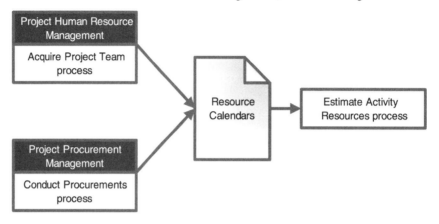

FIGURE 7.16
Sources used to create resource calendars.

The output in the Acquire Project Team process of the Project Human Resource Management knowledge area contains information about people resources (see Part 4, "People"). The resource calendars produced from the Conduct Procurements process in the Project Procurement Management knowledge area usually contain information about third parties contracted to do the work (see Chapter 6).

> Don't forget to consider resources other than people.

These resource calendars include valuable information:

- Personnel resources by name, experience level, and skills.
- Availability of the resource.
- Duration of the resource. (The resource won't do you much good if it isn't available for as long as the project requires it.)
- Geographic location of the resource.

Enterprise Environmental Factors

Probably worth repeating from before, these factors include items like marketplace conditions (if you need to contract, is it a seller's or buyer's market?), organizational infrastructure (is staff readily available?), or government or industry standards you must comply with (for example, bringing on expert auditors certified in Sarbanes-Oxley procedures and standards).

Organizational Process Assets

Look no further than your own company's warehouse of information that might save you time and effort with templates, policies and procedures, historical information, and lessons learned documents from other projects. Tools and techniques for the Estimate Activity Resources process include the following:

- **Expert judgment:** In addition to those who can bring resource planning and estimating assistance, rely on your experience and know-how to make the right resource estimates.
- **Alternatives analysis:** This analysis is new in PMBOK Fourth Edition. You should always make a point to evaluate alternatives to resources currently available. For example, if you planned for a senior software engineer to work on an activity, would you consider a junior engineer instead (if senior engineers are in short supply)? Instead of building a test suite from scratch, would you consider purchasing a test framework? The list goes on and on. . . .
- **Published estimating data:** There are plenty of online sources that can be used to validate standard costs for people, equipment, and any other resources you might need. Here in Seattle, we've had great luck identifying competitive pay scales using a combination of surveys from local professional human resources organizations and PayScale (www.payscale.com). (By the way, this data is a new tool introduced in the Fourth Edition of PMBOK.)
- **Bottom-up estimating:** If an activity is too complex to easily estimate, the activity should be broken down into smaller components where resource needs are estimated. The resources required should equal the sum of the resources for each of the components.
- **Project management software:** As you might expect, project management software can help with planning, organizing, and managing resources in order to develop resource estimates.

Outputs to the Estimate Activity Resources process are as follows:

- **Activity resource requirements:** This list (typically created in a spreadsheet, project management software, or document) includes a compilation of all of the resources required for each activity (spreadsheet version shown in Figure 7.17).

ResId	Description	Activity ID
1	Engineering design - David	3.2.1.1
2	Engineering implementation - Crazy Max	3.2.1.1
3	Shared server machine for product build and design	3.2.1.2

ResId	Dependent On	Needed By	Availability	Notes
1	3.2.1.2	Sprint 2	Anytime	David is already on the team
2	3.2.1.2	Sprint 2	Sep 10-20, 2008	Crazy Max only has a short window between projects available
3		Sprint 2	2 weeks	Buy Quad-Core server from Dell

FIGURE 7.17
Activity resource requirements (separated for readability).

NOTE

You may have wondered—if you're estimating activities resources, why are specific names (like David or Quad-Core server in the example) even mentioned in Figure 7.17?

The theoretical practice is to not use actual people or product names for activity estimating purposes. But how practical is that? You probably already know the individuals you want to use, the type of equipment you'll need, and so on. The rule is this: "If you know the best resource for the activity, go ahead and identify it!"

In addition, the availability (or unavailability) of key resources at certain projected times on a project may require a modification of how activities are to be sequenced. (Convincing other managers to make key resources available for your project may also take some negotiating, hopefully without any groveling.)

- **Resource Breakdown Structure:** Not to be confused with the RBS (Risk Breakdown Structure), the Resource Breakdown Structure is useful for identifying people resources in a hierarchical way, usually by organization (see Figure 7.18). A Resource Breakdown Structure provides the plan identifying who is doing what across the organization for a given project. Depending on the sophistication of your company's HR and financial systems software, you could also track costs by applying activity costs associated on a specific project for billing (or allocation) purposes.

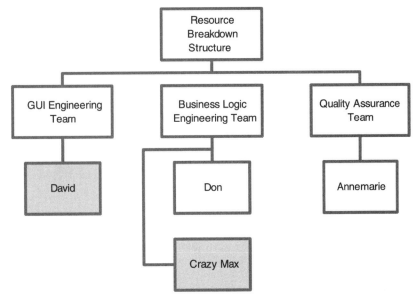

FIGURE 7.18
Sample Resource Breakdown Structure.

I'd recommend always using RBS to refer to the more popular Risk Breakdown Structure.

BEST PRACTICE To estimate resources, the activity resource requirements is typically more useful than a Resource Breakdown Structure.

■   **Project document updates:** The same project documents (activity list, activity attributes, and resource calendars) may have to be updated as a result of analysis performed. For example, the activity list may have to be expanded to accommodate the fact that multiple people resources could be required to perform parts of an activity.

Estimate Activity Durations

Schedule planning takes some time. You've identified activities, sequenced them, estimated all of the resources required, and now you need to set the durations for each activity. And, after this, the only remaining step is to develop the final schedule. But let's estimate the durations first.

Although universally regarded as a truism, Parkinson's Law specifies that "work will automatically expand to fill the time available." Do everything in your power to avoid this situation!

> The level of effort estimated when you created the Risk Register (see the "Identify Risks" section in Chapter 4) may come in real handy when estimating activity durations.

To properly define a project's activity durations, you'll have to draw on many sources of information. Brace yourself—there are a number of inputs to consider, as discussed in the following sections.

Activity List and Activity Attributes

The activity list and the activity attributes are used together to identify all information for the activities defined for the project.

Resource Calendars

Resource calendars specify the availability of resources and can be derived from two sources: the Acquire Project Team process and the Conduct Procurements process. Although equipment and material resources are usually important in resource calendars, the emphasis is usually on available people to perform the work. (See Figure 7.19 for an example of a consolidated resource calendar.) Information typically collected includes the following:

- When available to other projects.
- Length of time available.
- Percentage of time available (50% if half time).
- Constraints (contractual, legal, and so on).
- Skills and capabilities. (For example, you wouldn't want to put a zealous Linux programmer on Windows.)
- Seniority. (For example, a senior software developer should be able to multitask, whereas a junior developer is more suited to focus on a single, well-defined task.)
- Relevant performance data. It may be necessary for you to know how accomplished the development resource is toward completing tasks on time and with quality. This is especially true if you have a choice of resources to use on a project. (For example, a less successful software developer, for that very reason, may be more available than those who consistently demonstrate a history of project accomplishments.)

Figure 7.19 shows an example of a consolidated resource calendar.

ResId	Type	Name	ID	Availability	Perc	Senior?	Skills	Contraints
1	People	David	220	On Project X	100%	No	C	David is already on the team
2	People	Crazy Max	157	Sep 10-20, 2008	75%	Yes	C, C#, C++	Crazy Max only has a short window between projects available
3	Equipment	QA Test machine	SYS05	2 weeks at a time	100%			Buy Quad-Core server from Dell, schedule lead time two weeks out

FIGURE 7.19
Consolidated resource calendar example.

Activity Resource Requirements

Balancing a project's resource requirements against the actual resources available utilizing the resource calendars is sometimes a real trick. In fact, that is exactly your main task during this process. You'll need to make sure that you are planning for the best use of resources at the right time and for the right activities.

Scope Baseline

As part of the scope baseline, the Project Scope Statement, the associated WBS, and the Project Management Plan will need to be referenced to estimate activity durations. Examples that could be used include the following:

- Availability of information. (For example, a recommendation that a third-party software provider may provide the best solution for work to be performed.)
- Contractual terms and conditions (in other words, penalties imposed for late delivery).
- Length of reporting periods. (For example, activities need to be tracked in an agile way based on days and not weeks.)

Enterprise Environmental Factors

This is reference data (usually through commercially available surveys) that can influence typical durations. If, for example, your company is embarking on configuring the many options available in Salesforce.com, a typical integration effort for a company of your size might be on the order of two man-months.

Organizational Process Assets

Your organization hopefully has kept a stockpile of information from other projects that can help determine activity durations. This may include the following:

- Historical information (for example, to document an online help guide for a typical project takes two man-months).
- Project calendars.
- Scheduling methodology and rules of thumb.
- Peers who can offer advice based on their experience.

BEST PRACTICE It is a good idea to cross-check duration estimates with more than one technique.

Tools required for the Estimate Activity Durations process are discussed in the following sections.

Expert Judgment

You'll want to rely on experience to derive practical duration estimates from a number of sources, including historical information (from organizational process assets), your experience, and your team's experience. PMBOK rightly specifies that if this expertise may not be credible (perhaps from a project so different that you are estimating durations "out of the blue"), then the resultant schedule will most likely not be credible.

> Didn't I cover analogous and parametric estimating before? Yep! Similar concepts, including Rough Order of Magnitude, are used in cost estimating (see the "Estimate Costs" section in Chapter 6).

Analogous Estimating

Sometimes called the *top-down method*, this is an estimate based on expert judgment and historical information to make a limited, quick estimate of overall durations.

What is great about this technique is that for most agile software projects, you'll be dealing with a management team outside of the development organization who will appreciate the idea of Sprints and iterative mini-deliveries, but they'll need to know a rough idea of the overall project schedule range up front. Analogous estimating is the perfect way to provide a schedule range. However, there is a distinct negative to this approach: Without detail, the resultant activity duration estimates may not be very accurate.

Parametric Estimating

Although not necessarily a good estimating technique for software, you can use a performance indicator to aggregate an overall schedule. If you have a firm belief that using lines of code is a good technique to estimate duration of work, then all you'd have to do is multiply estimated lines of code by some productivity factor for each activity to come up with duration estimates.

Alternatively, you could use Regression Analysis (also known as a *scatter diagram*) to plot a history of points (like time and lines of code) to try to adapt some sort of formula that can be used in estimating future activity durations.

There is also the benefit of assuming that the more often you do something (like write a set of test procedures), the more efficient you'll become. This *learning curve* variation of parametric estimating might imply that the tenth time you've written a set of test procedures, you should be able to do the eleventh more quickly.

Three-Point Estimates

This uses an average to calculate an estimate based on a range, as outlined in Table 7.17.

Table 7.17 Three-Point Estimates

Points	Description
Most likely	The realistic duration assuming that the resources will be available as planned. (This usually takes into account interruptions, dependencies, meetings, and other "distractions.")
Optimistic	Best-case scenario that considers the resources to be available and focused on the project. (This also assumes that the resources assigned are the best possible to perform the activity!)
Pessimistic	Worst-case scenario where the resources are not as available or productive as possible. (A case in point is where some of your better resources may be periodically required for urgent customer technical issues that are escalated for immediate attention.)

As an example, to perform an activity, a realistic estimate is three hours, the optimistic estimate is two hours, and the pessimistic estimate is eight hours. The result is a simple average:

```
Duration = Average(Most Likely, Optimistic, Pessimistic)
Duration = Average(3, 2, 8) which is 4.3 hours
```

You may have heard of the Program Evaluation Review Technique (otherwise known as PERT). Similar to three-point estimates, this provides a weighted duration estimate that places an emphasis on the most likely estimate:

```
Duration = (Optimistic + Pessimistic + (4 * Most Likely) / 6)
Duration = (2 + 8 + (4 * 3)) / 6 = 3.7 hours
```

Reserve Analysis

Finally, in recognition of schedule risk, you may wish to factor in an overall buffer that accounts for contingency reserves or management reserves. Generally, this additional duration is a range that may be one (or more) of the following:

- Percentage of the overall durations.
- Fixed number of duration periods.
- Developed by some schedule risk analysis (see "Perform Quantitative Risk Analysis" in Chapter 4).

Throughout the cyclical nature of an agile software project, you'll probably revisit and refine reserves.

NOTE What? One more? Yes, there is another technique not mentioned in PMBOK that is well worth mentioning here: *heuristics* (also known as rule of thumb). An example of a common heuristic is the "80/20 Rule," where 80% of an activity's duration estimate is based on 20% of the code to be written. This approach is surprisingly popular in software development.

The outputs for the Estimate Activity Durations process are as follows.

Activity Duration Estimates

These are quantitative estimated durations for a project's set of activities. Based on the example project, Figure 7.20 shows an extension to the activity estimating spreadsheet you have been building upon.

	Resource Calendar							Estimate Activity Durations		
ResId	Type	Name	ML	O	P	Period	Cost	Duration Min	Duration Max	Explanation
1	People	David	3	2	8	Hrs		4	5	Actual computed duration is 4.3 hrs, David has done this before
2	People	Crazy Max	8	12	24	Hrs		12	16	Actual computed duration is 14.7 hrs, Max is working on several other key customer priorities at the same time = Risk!
3	Equipment	QA Test machine					$2,500	$2,250	$3,000	Prices change every day (it appears), but as most equipment does, the price could even drop

FIGURE 7.20
Activity duration estimates example.

How this information is presented can vary, but it should include the following:

1. Duration estimate
2. Range (+/−, percentage, minimum/maximum, or whatever works)
3. Explanation (or as some would call it, the "evidence")

Project Document Updates

As a result of performing activity duration estimates, project documents may need to be updated. This includes documents like the activity attributes, activity resources, consolidated resource calendars, and so on.

Develop Schedule

Representing the largest number of inputs, tools, and outputs of the PMBOK processes, schedule development is one of the most important and complex. *I'm going to simplify this* process as much as possible. Once the activity duration estimates and network diagrams are complete, it is time to produce a calendar-based schedule.

Just about every input for the Develop Schedule process has been created in the previous schedule processes, so I won't spend much time describing them again:

- **Activity list and activity attributes:** Identify project activities and their characteristics.
- **Resource calendars:** Identify availability of resources.
- **Network diagrams:** Drawings that visually show the relationship of activities to one another.
- **Activity resource requirements:** The types and quantities of resources that are needed to perform the activities identified in the activity list.
- **Scope baseline:** Primarily the Project Scope Statement, the overall scope baseline clearly identifies the scope definition, project plans, and WBS. (Please pay attention to assumptions and constraints that would impact how the schedule is created.)
- **Enterprise environmental factors:** Anything in the market or in your company that can influence how the schedule is created.
- **Organizational process assets:** Lesson learned, templates, company-wide resource calendars, and policies and procedures all can help you create the best schedule possible.

Perhaps an even better way to present how all of the inputs fit into developing the final schedule is shown in Figure 7.21.

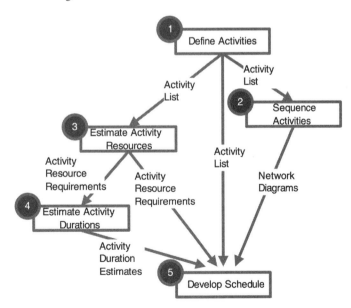

FIGURE 7.21
Processes and key outputs used to develop the project schedule.

The numbers in Figure 7.21 represent the sequence of schedule processes I've covered in this chapter. The Develop Schedule process, for example, is the fifth process. You can usually save time by performing these processes in parallel.

You can see how the various scheduling processes feed into the final Develop Schedule process.

NOTE

Before I go any farther, there are a few definitions you need to know about quantifying the amount of flexibility you have on an activity schedule. Slack, also known as *float,* is the amount of time that an activity can slip or be delayed without impacting the finish date of the project, milestone, or another activity. There are three kinds of slacks:

- **Total slack (total float):** This is the amount of time that an activity can be delayed without delaying an intermediate milestone. If your agile project has 30-day cycles and five-day rest periods between each cycle, you could say that the total float is five days.
- **Project slack (project float):** This is the amount of time a project can be delayed without delaying the company (or customer) expectation. For example, the project may be scheduled for release in November, but the company must ensure that the project is completed no later than the end of the calendar year (December). The project slack, in this case, would be one month.
- **Free slack (free float):** This is the amount of time an activity can be delayed without impacting its successor activity.

Of all the types of slacks presented, total slack is the one typically referred to with project management software. Slack is called *negative slack* if the project is behind. Conversely, a project can also have *positive slack*. For example, slack is −4 (negative slack) if the project is four weeks behind plan. Slack is +4 (positive slack) if you are four weeks ahead of plan.

The key tools and techniques used to create a project schedule are described in the sections that follow.

Schedule Network Analysis

Oddly enough, this refers to the use of any of the other techniques I'll describe to produce the project schedule.

Critical Path Method

Also known as CPM, Critical Path Method is the combination of activities that, if any are delayed, will delay the project's completion (finish) schedule. This method has two main purposes:

1. Calculate the project's expected finish date.
2. Identify the activities in the project schedule that can slip without delaying the project's planned release schedule.

> A project can have multiple critical paths and *near-critical paths* (which is close in duration to the critical path).

It's that simple! The critical path is defined as the following:

- It is the longest duration path through a network diagram.
- It determines the shortest time to complete the project.

The greatest risk to a project normally takes place on the critical path. If an activity on the critical path has no slack and it slips (or is delayed), it will push out the finish date. You'll have to pay close attention to activity relationships, path convergence, and path divergence.

BEST PRACTICE To minimize project risk, put your most-skilled talent on critical path activities.

Critical Chain Method

Based on the theories of Eliyahu Goldratt, the Critical Chain Method provides a unique way to view and manage project uncertainty. This technique can be summarized as follows:

1. Perform Critical Path Method.
2. Analyze resource constraints and probabilities for each activity.
3. Re-determine the latest possible start and finish date for each activity.
4. Add schedule buffers between activities.
5. Manage the project so that you never exceed those inter-activity buffers.

Using the Critical Chain Method can cause the original critical path to change.

Resource Leveling

You may wish to apply resource leveling to a schedule that has already been analyzed by the Critical Path Method. Resource leveling addresses the typical situation where resource availability doesn't match the needs of the project. In particular, you'll want to adjust resources to be a little bit more consistent across an activity (or activities), as shown in Figure 7.22.

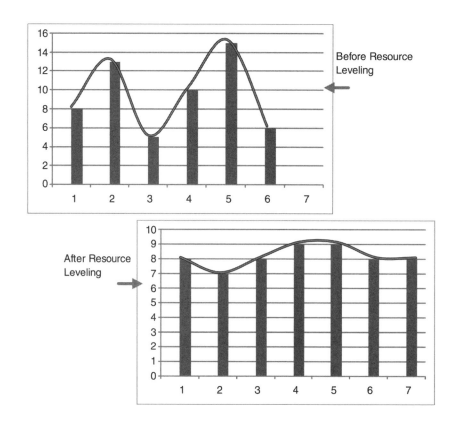

FIGURE 7.22
Resource leveling a sample project (before and after).

BEST PRACTICE Resource leveling will most likely alter the critical path, which ultimately impacts the schedule.

Before resource leveling, resources may be unrealistically varied by time period or by number of hours team members are expected to work per day. (Even though PMBOK suggests the possibility of planning longer hours, agile best practices do not recommend extended work hours.) In Figure 7.22, you can see the wide range of resource needs across six time periods. Once resource leveling is introduced, the use of resources can be adjusted accordingly to be more consistent across time periods. After applying resource leveling to your project schedule, it isn't unusual for the overall schedule to stretch out, as it did by one period in Figure 7.22.

What-If Scenario Analysis

You can also use tools like Monte Carlo Analysis to predict possible schedule outcomes based on calculating different activity durations and assumptions.

Schedule Compression

Simply put, you'll always need to look at ways to complete the project schedule early without impacting project scope. There are two types of schedule compression techniques:

■ **Crashing:** For those of you who, like me, don't particularly like the word "crashing," don't fear—in PMBOK-land, this is completely different! Crashing allows you to examine ways to get the greatest amount of schedule compression with the least amount of cost. Common techniques are as follows:

   1. Overtime
   2. Additional resources assigned to the project
   3. Paying for faster delivery (of equipment, not people)

   Crashing will not change your project's network diagram showing the relationship between activities.

   By the way, employing more resources to an activity may not actually increase project costs. If a project takes a single resource eight days to complete, doubling the resource could potentially get the work accomplished in half that amount of time: four days. By utilizing more resources, you have effectively improved calendar time (the schedule) dramatically.

   PMBOK spends a fair amount of effort discussing how to minimize risk, and frankly, taking risks can actually be a good thing. The schedule to create the movie *Toy Story 2* was originally planned to take 18 months; however, the wrong team was working on the project, and the schedule fell behind. Pixar's Ed Catmull in the *Harvard Business Review* tells it like this:

   "Finally *A Bug's Life* was finished, freeing up John, Andrew, Lee, and Joe to take over the creative leadership of *Toy Story 2*. ... but by then we had only eight [months] left to deliver the film. Knowing that the company's future depended on them, crew members worked at an incredible rate. In the end, with the new leadership, they pulled it off."

   Ed took on an incredible risk in changing the management team after the project had already started. Crashing, in this case, worked! Just having resources on a project may not be enough—they need to be the *right* resources, and sometimes augmenting a team with a creative, talented team can make a huge difference.

NOTE

Be suspicious of crashing—you may not always get the desired results (employee burnout, for example). Crashing can easily result in the opposite of what you want by introducing more risk and cost. Incentives, which I'll cover in Chapter 9, should be avoided at all costs!

■ **Fast Tracking:** The other schedule compression technique is *fast tracking*, where activities originally designated to be performed in sequence are performed in parallel. As a result, fast tracking will most likely change your project's network diagram relationship between activities. If you lined up your activities correctly (see "Sequence Activities" earlier in this chapter), you may find it difficult to use the fast tracking technique.

Fast tracking easily adds risk to any project that may jump-start without complete specifications, resulting in possible rework. The sheer amount of coordination required to handle additional "parallelism" is a risk that you shouldn't minimize. (There was probably a reason that you originally sequenced activities to begin with—so be careful.)

■ **Scheduling tool:** Without a scheduling software tool (a project management software application), projects of any size would require laborious, error-prone manual effort to create. It is always a good idea to perform a quick manual cross-check just to be sure that something wasn't entered incorrectly.

Outputs of the Develop Schedule process are shown in the following sections.

Project Schedule

Schedules can be presented in many different ways, but the best approach is to show a project schedule visually, as a chart. Typically, milestones or activity work completed is usually denoted by a dark fill, and those undone are not filled (in other words, white). Being time-based, the *as-of date* on the schedule signifies the current time on the schedule. Everything to the left of the as-of date signifies *progress to date*.

> The as-of date is analogous to "You Are Here."

There are several project schedule formats recognized by PMBOK.

■ **Milestone chart:** Key milestones are shown as diamond shapes (perfect to show an executive). This format, shown in Figure 7.23, doesn't show duration of work—just milestone endpoints.

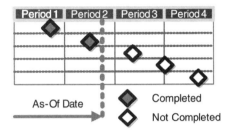

FIGURE 7.23
Milestone chart example.

■ **Bar chart:** Activity durations are shown as logical bars and typically only show high-level overall work groups (frequently called a summary schedule), as shown in Figure 7.24.

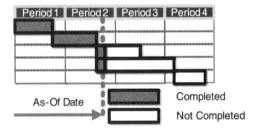

FIGURE 7.24
Bar chart example.

■ **Gantt chart:** A Gantt chart can present more detail of every activity along with resources and dependencies. This format, as shown in Figure 7.25, is most popular with project managers and software developers. If you want to get really fancy, this chart can show schedule durations, predecessor/successor relationships, number of resources, assigned resources by name, and so on.

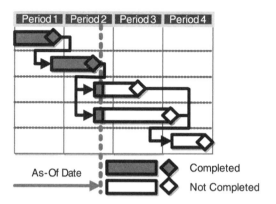

FIGURE 7.25
Gantt chart example.

Referring to the network diagram shown in Figure 7.14, you can easily export this to be imported as a part of another project's schedule with Microsoft Project, as shown in Figure 7.26.

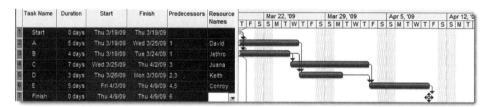

FIGURE 7.26
Sample project shown using Microsoft Project as a Gantt chart.

Originally called a *Harmonogram* by Karol Adamiecki in the late 1900s, Henry Gantt popularized Gantt charts in the early 1910s.

Although there are varying degrees of detail that can be captured using MS Project, it is fairly intuitive to establish and view activity relationships (the darkened cells on the left of Figure 7.26). The Gantt chart (to the right in Figure 7.26) automatically calculates the schedule (with arrows representing dependency relationships between activities).

Based on the success of web-based software solutions like Salesforce.com, a relative newcomer to project management systems software is LiquidPlanner out of Seattle. Their pragmatic approach toward dealing with uncertainty and enterprise-wide project scheduling is unique. Setting up a project is easy. You establish your project and resources and then enter in the Promise By date (see Figure 7.27). For each activity, you enter in the estimate as a range (best and worst case) for each activity.

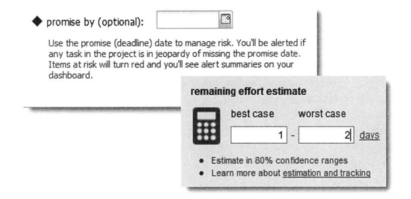

FIGURE 7.27
Establishing the promise date and an activity's level of effort with LiquidPlanner.

Finally, once you enter all of the information about the project, you can visually see the results in a Gantt chart (see Figure 7.28).

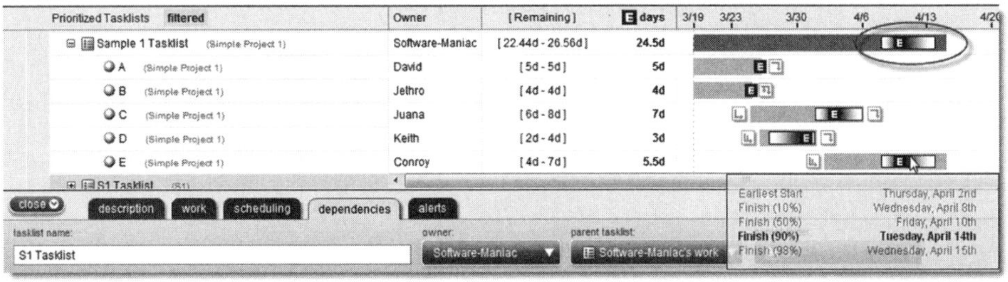

FIGURE 7.28
Viewing the current schedule as a Gantt chart with LiquidPlanner.

You may have noticed the range of dates and the letter "E" icon on the activity bars. The fuzzy gray bar around the "E" represents the 80% confidence range, and the end of the bar represents the suggested safe promise date (98% confidence). Pop-ups will display the expected activity completion date range, as shown below the cursor in Figure 7.28. If you set a promise date, the software will alert you if that date becomes at risk.

As LiquidPlanner learns more about your project's success to date, the expected dates are adjusted accordingly. In favor of agile software projects, LiquidPlanner provides a collaborative work environment where project notes are maintained "in the cloud," and individual team members can self-report their progress. The software is certainly not quite as feature-rich as other established project management software projects, but it definitely hits the sweet spot of what every agile project manager needs.

Schedule Baseline

This represents the accepted original schedule timeline to be executed against by the overall Project Management Plan. In the case where the customer is directly involved with the project, they will also approve it. The schedule baseline may also be augmented to reflect changes as approved within the overall Integrated Change Control process. With agile software projects, the overall schedule baseline should be developed with flexibility in mind (in other words, knowing that changes are going occur).

Schedule Data

Simply put, schedule data is the backup information used to develop the schedule. The schedule baseline may also include other supporting documentation:

- Alternative schedules
- Scheduling of contingency reserves (according to the timeline)
- Resources required (according to the timeline)

Project Document Updates

Key project documents may be updated based on finalizing the schedule. These include such documents as the following:

- Activity resource requirements
- Activity attributes
- Project calendar (used to report schedule progress on all projects being tracked)
- Risk Register

Once you have laid out a schedule, compare it to what management and the customer expect. If the schedule is too short, then you're done! Wait—that will rarely happen! If the calculated schedule is within a few days of the expected schedule, then great—you're probably done! Otherwise, if the schedule is too long, here are some alternatives you could consider. (All are planning tasks and are listed in the order of most probable benefit to your project.)

1. Remove or modify project scope.
2. Consider more concurrent activities or even add more resources. (However, this can be much more difficult to integrate and control.) Don't forget to look at how leads and lags can impact the schedule.

3. Decrease project risks that would impact the schedule immediately. (There are all sorts of things that you can do with managing risks.)
4. Force-fit the schedule to somehow make the expected commitment, hope for the best, and then quickly hunt for another job. (This option is only thrown in here to make sure that you were paying attention.)

Tips and techniques for handling the first three options are covered in Chapters 4 and 5.

TIME MANAGEMENT IN THE MONITORING & CONTROLLING PROCESS GROUP

Control Schedule

The Control Schedule process is performed throughout the entire project life cycle. Although change will undoubtedly occur throughout a project, your role is to minimize schedule impact as a result of those changes.

The PMBOK Fourth Edition has dramatically enhanced what's involved with controlling a project's schedule. Specifically, this includes keeping track of a few standard metrics:

BEST PRACTICE Avoid the subjective "percentage complete" guesses when controlling schedule progress.

---

1. **Earned Value Reporting:** Remember the cost calculation stuff? This is exactly how you can objectively measure a project's cost performance to date. See Chapter 6.
2. **Variances between planned and actual schedules:** As you evaluate progress, your team needs to determine just what has been completed, usually as a percentage. How to realistically measure progress varies by organization (and possibly by project), but here are some typical techniques:
   - **50/50 Rule:** An activity gets credit for being half complete (50%) once the work is in progress, but it doesn't get full credit (100%) until the activity has been totally completed.
   - **20/80 Rule:** An activity gets credit for being 20% done when the work begins and gets the last 80% once the activity has been totally completed.
   - **0/100 Rule:** There is no partial credit until the activity work is 100% complete. This effectively removes the shades of gray or "I'm almost done" interpretation of activity completion (and this is definitely my preference of the three).

It goes without saying that schedule control is strongly tied to scope control, discussed in the section "Ensuring Projects Stay on Scope" in Chapter 5.

Inputs for the Control Schedule process are outlined in the following sections.

Scope Baseline

The Project Management Plan is used to specify what you are to do if the schedule needs to be re-evaluated. The overall scope baseline includes the WBS and the WBS Dictionary, which is always good for reference purposes.

If there is such a thing, the Project Management Plan usually refers to the Schedule Management Plan, which details how schedule changes are to be implemented. Also, the scope baseline usually refers to the original schedule baseline.

Project Schedule

The most recent version of the schedule with annotations summarizing updates, completed activities, and activities in progress.

Work Performance Information

The result of regular status meetings where activity progress towards completion is being collected. See the section "Perform Integrated Change Control" in Chapter 4 for more information.

Organizational Process Assets

The assets available to the team that influence controlling the schedule, such as cost and schedule policies, guidelines, procedures, reporting methods, and which software scheduling control tools should be used.

Key tools and techniques to be used in the Control Schedule process are outlined in the following sections.

Progress Reporting

On a regular basis, use a standard presentation template to produce a "project dashboard" that shows the current status of a project. This could include the following elements:

1. Schedule baseline and current and forecasted schedule
2. Percentage complete of the current activities
3. Earned value showing work progress as it relates to schedule and cost ("Calculating Project Cost Performance Metrics" in Chapter 6)
4. Overall risk indicator (red, yellow, or green) and mediation plan

Not unlike a control panel used in sales force automation software, there is no reason that you couldn't adopt a way to report project progress that clearly pinpoints how the project is executing to the current plan.

Performance Measurement

In addition to earned value reporting, there are specific formulas that can be used to calculate schedule variance (SV) and Schedule Performance Index (SPI). Both are described in Chapter 6.

> PMBOK, for good reason, has defined a technique called schedule comparison bar charts—why not consider that part of the progress reporting stuff?

Your role is to decide if any schedule variance requires corrective action. As a rule of thumb, any major variance that impacts the critical path requires urgent attention. Otherwise, if there is a schedule variance for non-critical path activities, you may decide that the overall risk to the project is small.

Some software companies rely on measuring progress as a means for continuous improvement. Constantly measuring SV and SPI is considered a good way to track how well your teams and individuals perform. (Also, remember to keep this information for the project as an organizational process asset for valuable lessons learned!)

Variance Analysis

Using what you just learned about float (slack) in a schedule, you can examine the differences between start and finish dates and recommend corrective action where appropriate. This may seem very similar to the first two items in this list, but Variance Analysis only represents the act of comparing schedule information (forecast versus actual). This is why the network diagram is so indispensable—it quickly shows you where the gaps exist between what is and what *should be*.

Change Control System

This system defines whatever information is necessary (typically in a form, e-mail, or something).

NOTE

Any change due to a schedule adjustment must be handled by the Integrated Change Control process. Hopefully, you'll have a CCB (Change Control Board) that meets regularly to address change in a project's schedule.

BEST PRACTICE You'll use some of the same techniques to control a project schedule that you use to develop the schedule.

Schedule Adjustment Techniques

This category of techniques look at adjusting the project schedule based on the Variance Analysis being performed. This includes the following:

- **Resource leveling:** Distribute work evenly among resources (described earlier in this chapter). Leveling a project's resources usually extends a project, but it may paint a more realistic way to use available talent.
- **Adjusting leads and lags:** You can always adjust leads (where an activity can start before its predecessor completes) and lags (where there's a specific waiting period between activities) to see how that changes the schedule.
- **Schedule compression:** Use the various ways to compress your schedule (crashing and fast tracking).
- **What-if scenario analysis:** Typically, brainstorming a variety of different ways to approach the schedule and using Monte Carlo Analysis to plot out the possible durations in order to see the range of possible schedule outcomes. (An example is to consider outsourcing part of the work, which could save you time but could be costly while distracting key internal resources.)

Project Management Software

This is easy—you could track all of a project's activities manually or use project management software (like Microsoft Project) to do the work for you. Hopefully, you'll organize your project software into a hierarchy based on WBS work packages and then by activities. (You'll see why this is important in the work performance measurements output of this process.)

Outputs for the Control Schedule process are as follows:

- **Work performance measurements:** Since stakeholders in general may not care about specific activities, rolling up percentage completions of work packages is a good idea.
- **Change requests:** All of the tools and techniques identified in this process could result in one very important output—a change request due to a proposed schedule adjustment. Any schedule change should come with a couple of alternatives (and not just "the schedule has to slip" thing), will have to be reviewed, and run through the formalized Perform Integrated Change Control process.

BEST PRACTICE Try and anticipate a possible schedule change before it happens!

If you are a hands-off or a non-technical project/software manager, you may not even see possible schedule slips coming! On the other hand, you'll be in a better position to predict schedule adjustments if you use expert judgment, ask the right questions, have an awareness of lessons learned outcomes from similar projects, and are on top of the details of your project.

This is not an open invitation to obligate your team to non-stop team project review meetings—that would defeat the purpose of agile software methodology! Rather, being involved but also being a "fly on the wall" can be just as effective as holding frequent meeting marathons.

■ **Organizational process assets updates:** Take the time to maintain your own lessons learned regarding the history of schedule adjustments throughout your project. Any additional information (for example, reasons why the schedule was changed, why certain decisions were made, and so on) will make a real difference to a future project/software manager reviewing your project when he is facing similar schedule changes.

■ **Project document updates:** There are lots of documents that can be updated as a result of schedule adjustments, as shown in Table 7.18.

Table 7.18 Updated Project Documents Due to Schedule Change

Feature	Description
Schedule baseline	The original schedule baseline is maintained, and the new schedule baseline is adjusted as necessary.
Schedule Management Plan	Part of the Project Management Plan, this document indicates how project schedule changes should be handled.
Scope baseline	Update the scope if the schedule change impacts the scope (usually due to a change in resources).
Cost baseline	Update this document's cost structure if the schedule change impacts the cost (due to schedule compression, resource leveling, and so on).
Project schedule	An updated schedule should be regenerated to reflect changes in schedule data (for example, paths, floats, or durations may have changed in the network diagram).

TIME MANAGEMENT BEST PRACTICES

Let's put what you just learned into practice.

HOW TO REDUCE SCHEDULE RISK

What are some of the key elements that influence a project's schedule (in other words, time)?

■ Misjudging the level of effort to perform key tasks (could be positive or negative).
■ Resources are not available.
■ Introduction of out-of-scope requests (or removal/modification of planned scope).
■ The unknown (undiscovered risks that could impact the overall schedule).

> PMBOK places a great deal of emphasis on dealing with estimating, controlling, and reporting scheduled project time. Unfortunately, no one can stop time if a project gets behind.

Although you could view these time influencers as being largely outside of your control, it is *your* responsibility to manage them. The following five techniques can reduce time-influenced project risks:

1. **Use the best estimators:** Put your best estimators on the project at the beginning of its life cycle so that the estimates are accurate and realistic. It is not okay to underestimate or overestimate by more than the schedule range you are willing to accept. And by all means, get a complete cross-functional estimate to include testing, documentation, and integration (roll-out) in your total estimate. The worst thing you can do is get just the engineer's estimates while "ballparking" the rest of your organization's estimates. According to PMBOK, expert judgment is a key ingredient to a project's scheduling success.
2. **Focus your resources:** Ensure that resources are focused and available for the duration of the project. Although this might not be practical in all cases, don't be tempted to remove key staff members from the project until the project has been properly delivered. Just a friendly reminder: Resources are usually more than just *people*—*materials* and *equipment* also need to be taken into account as resources.
3. **Eliminate scope creep:** During a project's development, coordinate with Marketing and within your own department to stave off those nasty scope issues where scope is added to an already late project or is arbitrarily removed. Some level of scope adjustments will most likely take place on any project, but if it does and it impacts the schedule in any way, you have redefined a new project for yourself.

If you don't handle scope creep as a different project, the resultant delayed project will automatically be perceived as a schedule slip to your friends in Sales (even though they may have demanded the changes themselves).

4. **Prepare for the unknown by hunting for risks:** Preparing for unknowns is probably your most difficult task of the lot. As one software engineer smugly told me, "You never know the unknown until it hits you square in the face." (What he's really saying is, "How can you hold me accountable for a project I can't possibly predict?")

   Your best, most-experienced talent should have a good handle on avoiding unforeseen circumstances. Less experienced (and especially less talented) staff members may not see the unknowns coming. Always have the team ask itself, "What is going to stop us from getting to the next milestone?" Keep those risks on the top of your mind with risk mitigation planning. See Chapter 4, "Run Development as a Business," for more details on managing risks.

NOTE

A typical approach could be to "let the project manager come up with the project schedule, and we'll see what the schedule is once Microsoft Project spits it out." Perhaps this is a reasonable option for some industries, but *not* for software. (You may wish to re-read "Habit 5—Delegating Absolute Control to a Project Manager" in Chapter 1.)

5. **Make sure your team and stakeholders buy in to the schedule:** Failure to gain buy-in usually equates to project failure (perhaps not in features or fanfare, but certainly in the schedule). The Rough Order of Magnitude (ROM) approach should be used when planning for the overall schedule. You can refresh your memory on this topic in the "Estimate Costs" section of Chapter 6. You should get in the habit of estimating a schedule based on a time range for final release (even if the range is fairly large initially).

> You'll never be remembered for missing a feature, but you'll always be remembered for missing a schedule.

BIBLIOGRAPHY

Agile Alliance. *Manifesto for Agile Software Development* (www.agilealliance.org).

Agile Alliance. *Declaration of Interdependence* (www.pmdoi.org).

"Agility Counts." *The Economist.* September 20, 2001 (www.economist.com/displayStory.cfm?story_id=779429).

Arisholm, Erik, Hans Gallis, Tore Dybå, and Dag I.K. Sjøberg. "Evaluating Pair Programming with Respect to System Complexity and Programmer Expertise." *IEEE Transactions on Software Engineering.* Vol. 33, No. 2, February 2007.

Beck, Kent and Cynthia Andres. *Extreme Programming Explained: Embrace Change, Second Edition.* Boston: Addison-Wesley, 2005.

Catmull, Ed. "How Pixar Fosters Collective Creativity." *Harvard Business Review*, Sep. 2008: 65–72.

DeCarlo, Doug. *eXtreme Project Management: Using Leadership, Principles, and Tools to Deliver Value in the Face of Volatility.* San Francisco: Jossey-Bass, 2004.

deJong, Jennifer. "Taking the Extreme Out of Extreme Programming." *SD Times.* Feb 1, 2005 (www.sdtimes.com/SearchResult/28409).

Dr. Dobb's Portal. *The Agile Manifesto.* www.ddj.com. J. Wiley and Sons, 1994.

Goldman, Steven, Roger Nagel, and Kenneth Preiss. *Agile Competitors and Virtual Organizations: Strategies for Enriching the Customer.* New York: Van Nostrand Reinhold, 1995.

Johnson, Tony. *PMP Exam Success Series: Certification Exam Manual.* Carrollton, TX: Crosswind Project Management, 2006.

Jones, Capers. *Applied Software Measurement: Global Analysis of Productivity and Quality, Third Edition.* New York: McGraw-Hill, 2008.

Larman, Craig. *Agile and Iterative Development: A Manager's Guide.* Boston: Pearson Education, 2004.

Lui, Kim Man and Keith C. C. Chan. "Pair Programming Productivity: Novice-Novice vs. Expert-Expert," *International Journal of Human-Computer Studies.* September 2006, Vol. 64, No. 9. (September 2006), pp. 915-925. (www.cs.utexas.edu/users/mckinley/305j/pair-hcs-2006.pdf).

McConnell, Steve. *Rapid Development: Taming Wild Software Schedules.* Redmond, WA: Microsoft Press, 1996.

Meloche, Thomas, James Goebel, and Richard Sheridan. "Paired Programming in the Software Factory." The Menlo Institute. (www.menloinnovations.com/freestuff/whitepapers/paired_programming_q_and__a.pdf).

Mulcahy, Rita. *PM Crash Course.* Minneapolis: RMC Publications, 2006.

Newkirk, James and Robert C. Martin. *Extreme Programming in Practice.* Boston: Addison-Wesley, 2001.

Schwaber, Ken. *Agile Project Management with Scrum.* Redmond, WA: Microsoft Press, 2004.

The Standish Group. *Chaos Reports* (1994-2006) (www.standishgroup.com).

8 Deliver On-Time, Quality Products

Similar to the previous chapter that focused on scheduling processes, this chapter discusses the importance of project quality management. Investing in quality best practices is critical to your organization's success. There is a simple question for you to answer:

Q: How many times can you afford to deliver products to a customer that don't measure up to the degree of quality they expect?

A: Just once. You've lost that customer forever.

This chapter focuses on two key categories:

- Quality
- Continuous improvement

QUALITY? WHAT'S THAT?

This topic could take volumes of pages to define, but put down some ideas as to what constitutes your definition of quality:

1.
2.
3.

Some examples that might make sense are the following:

1. Validate that features work as they should.
2. Removal of defects.
3. Execute a planned set of tests that users would try.

DEFINING QUALITY

But let's try this simple definition according to PMBOK:

> "Overall quality is the degree that a set of characteristics fulfill requirements."

> Requirements (scope) were covered in Chapter 5.

There's another interpretation of that same definition that I particularly like (since I wrote it):

> Quality is how well the thing does as it was supposed to do.

Much better! Project quality management, the topic of this chapter, addresses quality policies, objectives, and responsibilities so that the project will ultimately satisfy customer and stakeholder needs.

REVISITING PLAN-DO-STUDY-ACT

This topic was covered in a couple of places already in this book (starting with the "Plan, Do, <Something>, and Act" section in Chapter 3), and it is worth repeating. According to W. Edwards Deming (personified as the father of modern-day quality methodology), the output of one step (Plan) becomes the input to the next (Do). This cycle, as adopted by the American Society for Quality (ASQ), is based on making small improvements and measuring how much improvement they make (Check) before you change your process to include them (Act). Traditionally, this was called PDCA. In later years, Deming changed the PDCA cycle slightly to the PDSA cycle, as shown in Figure 8.1.

It is the "Study" part that focuses on analyzing what your team has just created, and this is where quality is a key component of the work. Due to the cyclical nature of agile software development, PDSA fits well into rapid iterative development, inherent emphasis toward quality, and reinforces the notion of *continuous improvement.*

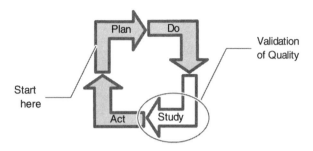

FIGURE 8.1
Plan-Do-Study-Act (PDSA).

In Sid Kemp's book *Quality Management Demystified*, the benefit of PDSA is that you can apply it over and over again, correcting course to achieve better and better results. Process continuous improvement, according to Kemp, can provide several benefits:

- Improve quality
- Increase effectiveness
- Increase efficiency

And all of this under the umbrella of quality management! All that is good, but there are a couple of situations you must ensure do not happen:

1. Overworking project teams can directly result in rework and employee attrition.
2. Rushed planned quality tasks may result in errors going undetected, resulting in product or service failures.

ENSURING QUALITY THROUGHOUT THE SOFTWARE LIFE CYCLE

Quality management is unique among all of the knowledge areas because of its sources of information from statistics, management, quality, psychology, and even law.

INTRODUCING THE QUALITY MANAGEMENT KNOWLEDGE AREA

The PMBOK knowledge areas have been slightly changed between the Third and Fourth Editions (basically process name changes). There are three quality processes defined by PMBOK (see Table 8.1).

Table 8.1 Quality Management Area Processes (PMBOK 4th Edition)

	Process Groups			
	Implementation			
Initiating	**Planning**	**Executing**	**Monitoring & Controlling**	**Closing**
	Plan Quality	Perform Quality Assurance	Perform Quality Control	

PMI's foundation for quality concepts is mainly from TQM, ISO 9000, Six Sigma, Cost of Quality, and many other sources that have gained in importance, generally since World War II.

> You may wish to go back and review the section "Introducing the Decision Pyramid" in Chapter 5.

Much of the thought process behind quality also reinforces the basic belief of customer satisfaction. What customer wants to purchase products or services that have quality issues? *No one that I can think of.* Yet the quality process is one that company management often suggests be reduced or done away with. If a project gets behind, one of the first thoughts is to cut out all of the quality checks, right?

KEY QUALITY TERMINOLOGY

There are several quality terms that need to be covered before proceeding through the PMBOK processes.

Total Quality Management

This is also known as TQM and was developed by W. Edwards Deming. In his book *Out of the Crisis*, he identifies 14 principles of management that are key to successfully providing quality products. These include the following that are most applicable to agile software teams:

- Cease quality as an inspection task to achieve quality—build quality into the product to begin with.
- By focusing on improving quality and productivity, you will ultimately decrease costs.
- Utilize leadership and accountability during project execution and do not focus on Management by Objective (MBO) by just measuring after-the-fact quality metrics as the sole means of measuring how good the quality is. For example, an objective could be to "not exceed 100 defects for this release," which could actually make management look good but still result in a project woefully late to market.

Kaizan

Otherwise known as *continuous improvement*, this is a Japanese management term that stresses small changes that result in constant process improvement. To remain competitive and to maximize the use of resources, most company cultures are readily adopting Kaizan principles of not accepting "things as they are" but adopting constant improvements.

Grade versus Quality

Quality deals with how well something works (it should have stability and predictability). *Grade* on the other hand is often misused as quality. Grade deals with the characteristics of the product or service and tends to represent the *level of functionality*. An installation software program may be considered low grade if it gives you no options but to install everything into a specific folder. Given this same example, a more feature-rich installation software program could employ tons of options (features to install, destination folder designation, and so on) and be considered higher grade. Nonetheless, grade is less important than quality—in other words, regardless of a product's grade, it must have high quality!

Just in Time

Also known as JIT, this is typically a manufacturing method that brings inventory close to zero levels to avoid any waste. If your company produces a shrink-wrapped software product, the last thing your Manufacturing department wants is to have misjudged the inventory and have to toss out or take back outdated software when a new version is released. You may have noticed that when Adobe is ready to announce a new version of a product (like Photoshop Elements), the current version on the store shelves has all sorts of price discounts. (This is usually a hint that something new is about to be released!)

Dell thrives on JIT with their made-to-order web mail order business. This gives them more flexibility, lowers inventory costs, and is generally a great way to do business, especially as the rapid rate of hardware innovation quickly makes components obsolete.

ISO 9000

This is a set of three quality standards established by the ISO (International Organization for Standardization):

1. **ISO 9000:** Presents quality definitions and terminologies.
2. **ISO 9001:** Using ISO 9000 as the guideline, this defines requirements and is used as the basis for certification purposes.
3. **ISO 9004:** Presents a set of guidelines to develop quality systems (policies, procedures, culture, tools, and techniques) designed to improve quality.

How does it work? Actually, quite simply. If due to customer, regulatory, or internal company needs you decide to create a Quality Management System (QMS), you must meet the requirements specified by ISO 9001.

In creating the QMS, you may wish to use the ISO 9000 definitions and the ISO 9004 guidelines. One of the first steps is to perform a *Gap Analysis*, which shows what you currently have in place versus what the ISO requirements are. Once you define the gaps, you get management approval and fill those gaps in order to solve the problem(s). You'll need an Internal Compliance Audit, and to make sure your QMS is fully compliant, you can get an independent ISO registrar to review and certify that your plan (the QMS) conforms to ISO guidelines and requirements.

What this process really means is that "you define what you'll do," and then you'll audit to make sure that "you do what you defined." That's it!

The lesson on ISO 9000 certification is that it is a very costly and time-consuming effort. Audits are *not* a one-time deal—you'll need to have Finance and management's commitment to audit periodically (once a year or two is typically necessary).

BEST PRACTICE Only go through the rigors of ISO 9000 certification if you and your management are committed to a multi-year, company-wide effort.

Accuracy versus Precision

Two key components of quality are often confused. *Accuracy* refers to a measurement goal toward a target. In software, if the goal for a series of disk writes is less than two milliseconds, accuracy would deal with how close the actual measurement is to that target. Thus, 1.9 milliseconds may not only be accurate, it may fit the quality goal that is required.

Precision, on the other hand, refers to consistency. Given the same example, through a series of disk write tests, precision has to do with how often the actual measurement meets the target. If all tests are within 5% of the target, that may be acceptable. However, if the test results vary between −50% and 200%, then it may not conform to the requirements.

Prevention versus Inspection

Prevention is a proactive approach that eliminates defects and potential defects. *Inspection*, however, is a reactive approach that fixes errors or defects as they are prioritized.

Standard Deviation

Also known as Sigma, this formula is defined as the following:

```
Sigma = (Pessimistic - Optimistic) / 6
```

There are varying degrees of Sigma, and each implies a certain degree of quality. Perhaps the diagram shown in Figure 8.2 will help.

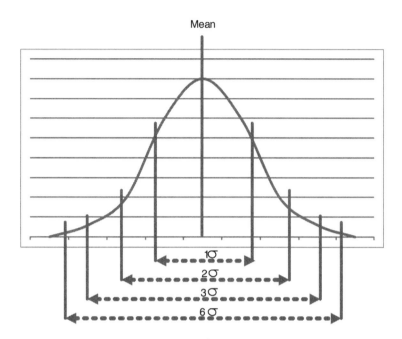

FIGURE 8.2
Standard deviation.

You read this as a distribution, and the larger the Sigma the higher the quality. One Sigma, or 1σ, equates to approximately 68% being the acceptable minimum for your process. In the case of setting up 100 computer systems, this means that as long as 68% of them work (68 systems), you have met One Sigma.

Two Sigma, or 2σ, jumps all the way to 95%. Given the same example, as long as you have fewer than five computers fail out of 100, you have met a Two Sigma quality rating. (Three Sigma is an even higher quality bar at 99.7%.) Six Sigma (a term you probably have heard) is the modern day target of quality; this represents 99.9% quality with less than one defect per 100 units produced. These are the steps to calculate the standard deviation:

1. Average all data points to create the mean.
2. Calculate the difference between each data point and the mean.
3. Square each of the differences and divide the sum of the squared differences by the number of data points minus 1.
4. Take the square root of that number to produce the standard deviation of the data set.

NOTE

Why care about all of this Six Sigma stuff? The greater the Sigma, the less rework and the least cost. Ever thought about tracking the number of acceptable defects while a software product is being developed? You could easily apply a standard deviation set of rules to your team and measure just how many defects are found by QA test engineers that should have been found and corrected by the software engineer who created the feature. The more you strive for Six Sigma, the better you attain continuous improvement.

You also want to limit the graph by keeping the bar with as little variation as possible. The tighter (smaller width), the better. A process with a lot of variability (spread), according to Michael George et al. in *What Is Lean Six Sigma?*, the more defects you'll have.

Lean Six Sigma takes Six Sigma a few steps farther by focusing on process improvement. To achieve Lean Six Sigma, you'll want to do the following:

- **Reduce defects:** Eliminate variation in quality and speed.
- **Delight your customer:** Improve process flow and speed.

Fitness for Use

Created by Joseph Juran, this quality term says that the needs of the customers and stakeholders are clearly defined. The quality program put in place is designed to ensure that the product or service satisfies their needs.

Capability Maturity Model Integration (CMMI)

Previously known as CMM, CMMI has recently been recognized as an internal standard as part of ISO 15504. CMMI is a five-level quality measurement hierarchy (yes, another pyramid!) that identifies quality processes, with the fifth level being the highest and toughest to achieve (see Figure 8.3).

FIGURE 8.3
CMMI levels.

Table 8.2 summarizes the five CMMI levels and how they impact leading and facilitating software teams.

Table 8.2 CMMI Level Descriptions

Level	Name	Description
1	Ad Hoc	Processes are typically undocumented, often chaotic, and reactionary. There is virtually no predictability possible (a waste of money to operate this way).
2	Repeatable	Some processes are repeatable with somewhat successful, consistent results. There is still risk of exceeding costs and time estimates.
3	Defined	Defined and documented standard processes with an emphasis on successfully attaining objectives. This is a great standard to aim for. (Most software companies aren't even close to this level.)
4	Managed	Using quantitative and other measurement techniques, measure performance, fix gaps, and make the process work for you by becoming predictable and controllable.
5	Optimized	An organization that relies on innovative, quantitative measurements to not only deliver as planned but also to advance with continuous improvement.

If you had to guess objectively, what would your organization's CMMI rating be? You may think that CMMI has become a methodology for the dinosaurs, but you'll find that many offshore software companies take great pride in achieving and claiming CMMI Level 4 or 5 status. In fact, it is generally regarded as a selling point. (The real trick is maintaining CMM level status.)

According to Dutton and McCabe in their excellent presentation entitled "Agile/Lean Development and CMMI," CMMI works well when you have a team with the right skills, a rapid training/learning atmosphere, open communications, and continuous improvement by executing to process. (Does that sound a little like agile? It certainly does to me!)

NOTE

It is also Dutton and McCabe's perspective that there is a major conflict between agile and CMMI concerning the role of empowerment and trust. CMMI's reliance on external audits undercuts agile's reliance on peer pressure as an internal team responsibility. In fact, you run the danger of focusing on compliance rather than letting the team police its own performance and effectiveness.

Your opportunity may be to find a good middle ground between jus' e'nuff CMMI adoption to help measure and control agile software projects.

QUALITY MANAGEMENT IN THE PLANNING PROCESS GROUP

PMBOK Third Edition had far fewer inputs (Project Scope Statement and Project Management Plan), but the Fourth Edition, through practical feedback from PMI members, has bolstered up the list.

Plan Quality

Inputs to the Plan Quality process are described in the following sections.

Scope Baseline

This is the set of documents that identifies the project's scope, including the Project Scope Statement, WBS, and WBS Dictionary. Together they represent the features, functions, and work required for the project to complete and to be verified that it is complete. Scope baseline has been discussed in just about all of the chapters leading to this one. Scope, and defining requirements in particular, is a key ingredient to "getting quality right." (Don't forget that the scope baseline also indirectly refers to the overall Project Management Plan.)

BEST PRACTICE If a project's scope isn't well defined, no amount of emphasis on quality will produce the desired results.

Stakeholder Register

This includes the list of project stakeholders—there is probably a subset of them that can provide feedback of the level of quality they expect. (It may not be enough to just have a quality product; they may expect something that outperforms your competitors.) This was discussed in Chapter 5 in the "Collect Requirements" section.

Cost Performance Baseline

First introduced in Chapter 6, the Cost Performance Baseline indicates how and when to measure the project's cost (actual versus planned).

Schedule Baseline

This baseline indicates the accepted performance start and finish dates. This was presented in detail in Chapter 7.

The inputs used for the Plan Quality process come from a variety of different process outputs in other knowledge areas—quality is a unifier among PMBOK knowledge areas.

NOTE

Risk Register

This list of risks (categorized and prioritized) is worthwhile keeping in your daily regimen (like a vitamin). Reviewing the top risks (and they should be adjusted as your project proceeds through its life cycle) may illuminate threats and opportunities that influence quality. The Risk Register was introduced in the "Identify Risks" section in Chapter 4.

Enterprise Environment Factors

You may work in a market where there is an expectation of quality adherence (for example, ISO 9000, UL, and so on), and strict adherence is required over and above the testing that you would normally perform.

Organizational Process Assets

There may be artifacts available by your company or department that may have an influence on quality processes. Examples include lessons learned, historical databases, policies, procedures, and guidelines. One of those may be a quality policy that sets the tone for the level to be exercised throughout the company. If and when stakeholders want you and your team to "ship anyway" without full quality validation, you can always refer them to the company's quality policy.

Tools and techniques are discussed in the following sections.

Cost-Benefit Analysis

Quality is an expensive proposition, and for startups it can appear like a luxury. However, quality activities should outweigh their costs, which typically include the following:

- Customer acceptance
- Stakeholder satisfaction
- Less rework
- Overall lower costs

The definition of your quality program and how much testing is to be performed should be included in the overall Quality Management Plan.

Cost of Quality

This important term is the cost associated with the following:

- Conformance to requirements.
- Steps taken to eliminate non-conformance to requirements.

The Cost of Poor Quality (COpQ) or the Cost of Non-Conformance generally implies that the company pays for quality in a reactive way, typically after the product or service has been released (see Table 8.3).

Table 8.3 Cost of Conformance and the Cost of Non-Conformance

Cost	Conformance	Non-Conformance
Inventory (e.g., packaged software)	Lower inventory needed	Excess inventory
Warranty support	Minimal, profitable	Excessive post-delivery, expensive
Training	Informed, part of the deliverable	No time, reactionary training "live" on the phones with upset customers
Product	Delivered, move onto the next one	Rework (perhaps even scrap)
Employee satisfaction	Pride in a job well done	Morale issue

Control Charts

These determine if a process is stable or has predictable performance. Maximum and minimum values are established to ensure that, if exceeded, they require corrective action. For example, control charts can help identify quality trends of incoming, corrected, and unfixed defects. If the incoming rate far exceeds the corrected rate, the project is not ready to be released. Control charts can be highly customized for your own needs and what is being used by other projects in your company's project portfolio.

A control chart is a good tool for keeping track of hours spent on a project over time.

Figure 8.4 shows an example where a control chart can be used to track defects by period.

This sample can be enhanced to include *deferred defects*.

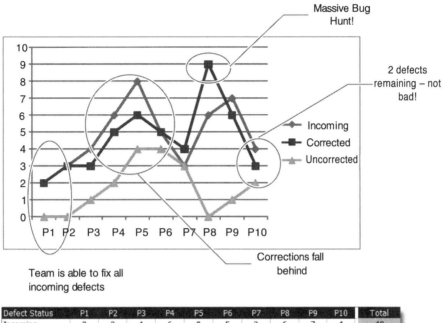

FIGURE 8.4
Sample control chart.

In this sample, there are 10 periods (otherwise known as Sprints), which initially show that incoming defects were corrected immediately. That didn't last too long because incoming defects far outpaced corrected defects in Sprints 3 through 6. Finally, in Sprint 8, "all hell broke loose," and with the aid of tofu pizzas (the project team are all vegetarians), the team corrected all defects. By Sprint period 10, however, two more uncorrected defects needed to be fixed.

The point is that during the planning stages, you may wish to engage the team to identify what the target maximum number of defects should be. All of these factors could be used to measure continuous improvement, but the best quality measure is to ensure that no serious defects exist upon any Sprint exit.

Benchmarking

This is where you can compare your actual project quality practices with other similar projects from your own company or through industry data. Based on historical record keeping, you may wish to target a software upgrade to have 20% fewer recorded defects than the previous version. Results will bring up all sorts of explanations, such as feature complexity, different staff, better unit testing, and so on.

Design of Experiments

Often known as DOE, this is a statistical method that allows you to explore different parameters to fully test the quality of the product. For web-based software projects, this may be writing a test plan that identifies how well the server application performs based on different concurrent user loads (10, 100, 1000, and so on). Software load test tools (also known as *stress tools*) can be invaluable in cases like this.

Statistical Sampling

If the sheer number of test cases is too overwhelming, you may need to examine a sampling of inspection/validation points that performs the most thorough test coverage possible. This is oftentimes aided by *test automation,* where tests can be scripted to reduce manual error and to save time.

Flowcharting

What? Flowcharting??? Introduced in the PMBOK Fourth Edition, by simply charting the flow or relationships of software algorithms, this form of visual quality planning can illuminate where tests *should* be performed. This is especially true for decision points, boundary conditions, and relationships between subsystems (that may or may not be directly linked together). They say that pictures say a thousand words, and it's amazing how test planning and even design reviews can benefit by diagramming the software's logic or workflow.

Quality Methodologies and Planning Tools

Also introduced in the Fourth Edition, the use of Lean Six Sigma, Capability Maturity Model Integration (CMMI), and others already described should be considered as quality management methodologies to be used in defining your Quality Management Plan.

The outputs for the Plan Quality process are discussed in the following sections.

Quality Management Plan

A key component of the overall Project Management Plan, the Quality Management Plan describes how the team will manage quality on your project. It is vital that everyone on your team (including the stakeholders) understand the standards and measurements you will use. Figure 8.5 shows an example of the beginnings of a Quality Management Plan.

BEST PRACTICE A Quality Management Plan should reduce costs by clearly defining what quality standards the project must use.

Goals for Project Metrics

Metric	Goal	Rationale	How We'll Do It
Schedule Variance	< 10%	Prior project had a 20% variance, continuous improvement need	Escalate key Risks that could impact any of the 30 day Sprints
How Defects are Categorized	3 Must Fix 2 Should be Fixed 1 Not critical	Since Defect repair is costly later in the life cycle, fix 2s and 3s immediately	Weekly defect status reviews with an emphasis on Defect prevention, track Defect rates and open communication to the team
How Defects are Prioritized	3 High priority 2 Medium 1 Low 0 Postpone	Defects will be evaluated based on both Priority and Category Only High Priority customer impacts will be automatically corrected, Mediums will be evaluated by the team	Weekly defect status reviews with an emphasis on Defect prevention, track Defect rates and open communication to the team
Test Plan Creation	Within 30 days of project inception	The overall Test Plan will provide the guidance for how the project work will be validated	Individual Test Cases will be created within five days for every Sprint by the team

FIGURE 8.5
Sample Quality Management Plan excerpt.

What is the benefit of this plan? *Glad you asked!* As long as the team accepts the plan, the Quality Management Plan can:

■ Reduce overall project cost.
■ Reduce the chances of a schedule overrun caused by rework.

Quality Metrics

Document how you'll be measuring your product or service quality during the project. This normally includes the following:

■ *What* formulas or measurements you will use.
■ *When* you will do the measurements.
■ *Why* these measurements are performed (in other words, the benefit).
■ *How* you will interpret the results.

Since there are tons of tools and techniques in both the upcoming Perform Quality Analysis process and the Perform Quality Control process, specify up front which of them you will be using, and stick with it throughout the life cycle. It is far better to identify the chosen few than attempt to measure everything—in practice, you may not be able to keep up.

Quality Checklists

Remember when you brought your vehicle in for service and the mechanic had a checklist that was used to ensure that everything was done? Well, a checklist comes in handy, especially if you need to ensure that a milestone is ready and all necessary validations have taken place. For example, to close every iteration in an agile software project, you may have a checklist of steps something like what's shown in Table 8.4.

Table 8.4 Quality Planning Checklist

✓ 1. Defect review meeting took place, quality met.

✓ 2. Technical and user documentation completed.

   3. Product management okay'ed feature set.

✓ 4. Software deployed to IT server for distribution.

✓ 5. Project status chart updated.

✓ 6. Customer feedback received.

✓ 7. Software and all documents backed up.

In this example, the third item still needs to be completed. A checklist can serve as a reminder that all components of an agile project's tasks for the current iteration have truly been completed. (With software projects being so complex these days, a good ol' checklist is a great thing!) A complete series of quality checklists can act as a test plan for your project.

Process Improvement Plan

Another part of the Project Management Plan, this document provides the guidance for eliminating anything that is wasteful, of little added value, or that results in low-quality outcomes.

Where most of us are just trying to deliver a project on schedule, the best organizations are looking for more ways to improve the project as it proceeds through its life cycle, which ultimately should benefit any and all future projects. Process improvement targets and results should be maintained in a historical reference (or lessons learned). As your agile project advances through mini-iterations, this plan (and the other outputs of this process) should be updated as necessary.

Project Document Updates

As usual, most any of the documents used as inputs or produced as outputs in this process can be updated to become the new baseline. One of the key documents that PMBOK mentions that could be updated is the Stakeholder Register. Active stakeholders need to buy into the overall Quality Management Plan. Make it simple when you communicate the highlights of the plan to them (like a two-slide PowerPoint presentation at most).

BEST PRACTICE Make sure that you communicate the Quality Management Plan to stakeholders up front.

Most likely, every stakeholder will agree to the plan. However, this agreement becomes important later if the project schedule needs to be revised in order to pass all quality metrics. (A simple reminder of everyone's commitment to quality should be all that is necessary.)

QUALITY MANAGEMENT IN THE EXECUTING PROCESS GROUP

The planning performed in the Plan Quality process and the results from the Perform Quality Control process drive the Perform Quality Assurance process.

Perform Quality Assurance

The lack of distinction between what goes on between Perform Quality Assurance and Perform Quality Control processes can appear confusing. To compound the differences even further, most software organizations don't have the luxury of distinct staff members performing these two functions.

> Just so you know, some PMP training books actually present the Perform Quality Assurance process after Perform Quality Control.

Surprisingly, Perform Quality Assurance is not about inspecting the product for quality or even measuring defects. This process is the application of overall systematic quality checks to ensure that the project employs all processes needed to meet the requirements. (Some might call this an auditor function.) *A necessary role? Is it a luxury role? You decide.*

BEST PRACTICE Removing inefficiencies should result in reduced cost of quality.

After the Plan Quality process is performed, you should start the Perform Quality Assurance process with the intent of overall continuous improvement through better attention to reducing quality risks. Inputs produced from the Plan Quality process are as follows:

- **Quality Management Plan:** Part of the overall Project Management Plan documents, this plan describes how quality assurance will be performed on the project.
- **Quality metrics:** This set of measurements provides the standards that the work will be measured against.
- **Process Improvement Plan:** Also a part of the overall Project Management Plan, this describes just how continuous improvement is going to be achieved. It is always a good feeling to be able to plan for some simple ways to reduce any waste and to stay focused. This usually goes hand in hand with quality metrics and could actually be one in the same (my recommendation).

    A simple example could be the fact that historically critical defects sometimes hitchhiked between iterations in the last agile project. This time, why not make it the goal that no critical defects will be allowed to be corrected in a subsequent iteration, thus keeping the team focused and reducing wasted energy by extending the amount of time that defects remain open?

> Some teams make sure that, if a build fails, the name of the offending software developer who caused it is made public. (*This is kinda mean but effective if you believe that there are too many defects being caused.*)

Another extreme example employed by Microsoft and many other software companies is the insistence that a product is built nightly, tested automated, and the results are communication with status e-mails (or some other mechanism) to the team. If you haven't deployed this technique, you'd be amazed at how your overall processes improve with reducing the time waiting for a build to be prioritized. Nightly builds are a hallmark feature of agile software projects. (Sometimes a team will kick off twice-a-day builds, depending on how long they take!)

Other inputs to the Perform Quality Assurance process are based on feedback from other knowledge areas, including the Perform Quality Control process (to be discussed in the next section).

- **Work performance information:** This is the result of gathering actual project status information that you'd normally be looking at on a frequent basis:
    1. Project status (percent completion, milestones finished, testing started, and so on).
    2. Schedule and costs progress. (This would allow you to calculate and communicate the completed project value to date discussed in the "Calculating True Project

Status with Earned Value" section of Chapter 6.) Believe me, Finance people love this stuff (even if you don't).

3. Technical performance measures (such as the latest application responsiveness to database queries).

4. Other information that can be tracked and measured (as appropriate).

Keep the number of items to a core set—better to track and analyze a few key measurements than track too many of mixed importance.

■ **Quality control measurements:** How well is the quality control performing, and do any of the quality activities need to be adjusted to meet project quality goals? This is almost like a feedback loop, where the results of testing are measuring up. For example, control charts can be used to spot a project's incoming and corrected defects. You can review what a typical control chart looks like in Figure 8.4.

NOTE

In the PMBOK Third Edition, change requests (both approved and implemented) are specified as key inputs because any change in scope or schedule can have an effect on a project's quality. Since this is no longer specifically stated in the Fourth Edition, keep the impact to quality in mind as change is introduced in your project.

BEST PRACTICE Performing quality assurance validates the quality *process* and not the *product*.

Tools and techniques that are recommended for Perform Quality Assurance process are as follows:

■ **Quality planning and quality control tools and techniques:** This is a simplified way of saying any tools and techniques that are used in Plan Quality and Control Quality processes can be used in quality analysis. There is a close relationship between the Quality Management, Cost Management, and Risk Management knowledge areas. For example, a great tool that can be used is the fishbone diagram (also known as Root Cause Analysis) first introduced in Chapter 4.

■ **Quality audits:** Audits help you verify compliance between actual results and expected results. Actual results are performed in the Control Quality process (defined in the next section), and expected results are defined in the Plan Quality process. *What do you do with this analysis?* Easy—record audit analysis as lessons learned as a key output of this process!

■ **Process analysis:** This is typically a "like to have" technique, but in the spirit of continuous improvement, by taking the Process Improvement Plan as your guide and using Root Cause Analysis, you and your team can find interesting ways to reduce wasted energy and improve quality. By interpreting the cause of problems, you can usually eliminate similar problems from occurring in the future. This is a great brainstorming technique, and the more "out of the box" thinkers you have involved, the better your ultimate decisions will be.

Outputs of the Perform Quality Assurance process are as follows:

■ **Change requests:** Changes may need to be requested as a result of the Perform Quality Assurance process. These are not automatic—they need to be submitted for approval using the Perform Integrated Change Control process.

Normal defect correction should be handled through regular software defect management techniques, but those defects or quality issues that impact the Triple Constraint (cost, time, scope, and, of course, quality) require formal escalation and approval through the Perform Integrated Change Control process described in Chapter 4 (also see Figure 8.6). This process should happen frequently enough to keep up with the pace of agile software projects and get the visibility with some sort of Change Control Board (CCB).

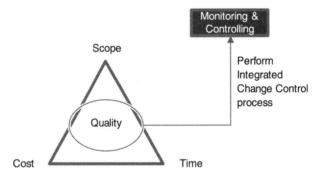

FIGURE 8.6
Quality issues that require change requests.

■ **Organizational process asset updates:** As a result of analyzing a project's quality procedures, process assets may have to be updated. As new information is gathered (like lessons learned), update as new practices are implemented.
■ **Project document updates:** Documents that are a part of the overall Project Management Plan may need to be updated to action taken from this process. This includes the Quality Management Plan, the Schedule Management Plan, the Project Scope Statement, and the Cost Management Plan. All of these, funnily enough, represent the Triple Constraint (see Figure 8.6)!

Unless you like to create multiple documents for everything, why not consider each of these plans to be sections within a single Project Management Plan?

QUALITY MANAGEMENT IN THE MONITORING & CONTROLLING PROCESS GROUP

And finally—this is where actual testing is performed.

Perform Quality Control

As a reminder, quality can be simplified and defined as the following:

How well the thing (software) does what it is supposed to do.

Before getting too far into the Perform Quality Control process, there are several pairs of quality terms that may be used interchangeably but have drastically different meanings. In Table 8.5, each row shows a pair of related terms along with a brief definition. (This table, by the way, is chock full of information, so don't just skip over it!)

Table 8.5 Quality Control Comparing Paired Terms

Quality Control Term	Compares to
Prevention: Keeping defects from taking place in the process. A very proactive approach required before source code is checked into the team's source code management system, it is unit tested and validated by a peer software engineer. (Sounds like an XP project, doesn't it?)	**Inspection:** Catching errors before they impact customers. Although more reactive than prevention, product and process inspections represent how the majority of software is tested and qualified by executing test cases. Inspection can be manual or automatic (or even both) and can augment prevention techniques.
Sample: How much an item is tested is determined. If you elect testing a sample, you must have confidence in the results. There should be a big enough sample set (and this may have to be continually adjusted as the project progresses).	**Population:** The number of quality items covered with tests. In the case of software, every test point, feature, and function point must be verified according to the test plan. If you can't possibly test every item, then adopt a sample set instead.
Attribute sampling: The result either conforms to what is expected or it doesn't. For example, the computation of state tax must result in an exact number.	**Variables sampling:** The measure of the degree to which the test results conform to expectations (usually within a continuous range). For example, as long as the software under test refreshes the next user interface window in less than three seconds, that meets the requirements.

(continued)

Quality Control Term	Compares to
Special causes: In the case of statistical tools and techniques (like control charts described in Figure 8.4), special causes are considered to be unusual events. Special causes are typically desired. An example is where a test script itself lets error conditions sometimes pass (implying that the test wasn't originally designed or implemented correctly).	**Common causes:** Where normal process variation is expected and is somewhat random. One of the best examples is where a DRAM manufacturer expects that out of 1,000,000 memory boards built, no more than 50 will fail (.005%) due to DRAM chip raw material defects.
Tolerances: Deals with the limits that have been set for product acceptance. For a scientific software project, you might require all calculations computed by the application to be accurate within three decimal places.	**Control limits:** Identifies thresholds that consider the project out of control if exceeded. As in control charts, you might draw a box around where all results plotted on the chart must lie for the test to pass.

What is a *function point?* Simply stated, an application can be measured by the number of function points it delivers to the user (customer). "How much testing is enough?" can be derived using Function Point Analysis (FPA). (See the bibliography at the end of this chapter for Alvin Alexander's online article about Function Point Analysis.)

There are many inputs, tools, techniques, and outputs with quality control—no surprise! And having some statistical and mathematical background is vital, according to PMBOK, in order to properly produce accurate quality control outputs.

Quality control takes inputs from many sources, as discussed in the following sections.

Quality Management Plan

A key component of the overall Project Management Plan, this document describes how quality control will be performed for the project.

The Quality Management Plan is also a key input for the Perform Quality Assurance process! (It goes without saying, but I'm going to say it anyway—the Quality Management Plan provides the blueprint for quality assurance and quality control.)

NOTE

Quality Metrics

This will be used to measure whether the project and product results meet the stated quality specifications defined by the Plan Quality process.

Deliverables

The previous two inputs are necessary for quality planning, but they don't mean much unless you have a product or service to test with. This is described in "Develop Project Management Plan" (see Chapter 4). Especially for agile software projects, the best thing is to always have a buildable product that can be tested early in the software development life cycle.

Quality Checklists

These are the steps (test plan) that are to be performed in product and project quality validation. The checklist can also reference actual test cases to be executed for each test in the plan.

Work Performance Measurements

Provide project status on what has been completed versus what was planned to be completed, including the following:

- Technical (features or scope) performance
- Schedule (or time) performance
- Cost performance

Say, wait a minute! Aren't those the same elements identified in the Triple Constraint? To make PMI proud that you put their teachings to good use, use the calculations (Earned Value, Planned Value, and Actual Value, respectively) to produce a concise status of project metrics. (These are presented in "Calculating True Project Status with Earned Value" in Chapter 6.)

Let's look at an example. If the project assumed that a properties feature in the UI was to be tested, yet this feature was still in design, you'd have to alter your testing scenario to conclude that this feature wasn't ready for validation.

NOTE

Work performance measurements are similar to publishing quarterly financial statements. These measurements document the actual versus expected quality results (much like your CFO would publish actual versus expected monthly financials). That is the purpose of the Perform Quality Control process.

As a reminder, because it can get confusing, the Perform Quality Analysis process does just like you'd expect—it analyzes the trends and the effectiveness of the quality program (just like a Finance guy would summarize and forecast a company's finances in a quarterly or annual report). In addition, work performance information refers to the actual results collected from the tests being run during the project's life cycle.

Approved Change Requests

Unfortunately, approved change requests will probably have an impact on scope, which would require timely modification of quality control tests to comply with the new definition of work.

Organizational Process Assets

Quality standards, defect reporting procedures, communication, and escalation policies are but a few of your company's standard modes of operation that may have an impact on the Quality Control process.

The tools and techniques used in the Perform Quality Control process are discussed in the following sections. (Go get some coffee—there's a lot of them.)

Charts and Diagramming Techniques

Also known as the Seven Basic Tools of Quality, or the Basic Seven, these were first defined by Kaoru Ishikawa, an engineering professor at Tokyo University, and adopted by the American Society for Quality (ASQ). (Their web site is www.asq.org.)

> ASQ isn't the only game in town—Software Quality Engineering (SQE) is a wonderful organization worth looking into (www.sqe.org). They are very committed to defining quality standards for agile software projects.

One or more of these tools can be used in the Perform Quality Control process:

- **Cause-and-effect diagram:** Also referred to as a fishbone or Ishikawa diagram, this tool uncovers how various factors may be linked to defects. You start with the defect (the effect) and then work backward by diagramming responses to repetitive questions "why" or "how," showing the relationships of the causes to one another (see Figure 8.7).

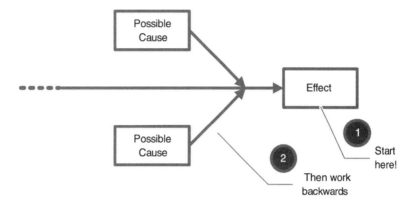

FIGURE 8.7
Creating a cause-and-effect diagram.

Here's a sample conversion between you and the team:

You: The defect is that the performance of this module is not acceptable—it doesn't meet the requirements. Anyone know why?

Team: Well, the code does what it should. I guess the design wasn't thought through.

You: Why?

Team: In order to keep up with the sprint, we only spent one day on it. I told you we needed more time, and now we're paying for it.

You: It should have taken no more than one day. How is it that a cache scheme wasn't used?

Team: What's a cache do? (*Oh oh . . .*)

You: (Frustrated now!) Is there more? How come it didn't get done?

Team: We couldn't get Gary off of the other project to help us in time.

You: Why is that important?

Team: Because he's done killer performance work like this before!

So there are a couple of root causes: A cache was never properly designed, and to do it right required Gary's involvement (see Figure 8.8). This team interaction gives you some additional information as to what happened. You also received team buy-in with the mitigation that needs to be taken.

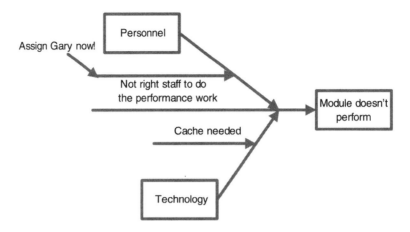

FIGURE 8.8
Sample cause and effect.

There are several rules with cause-and-effect diagramming that you should keep in mind:

1. The causal relationships do not have to be symmetrical.
2. You can intermix the "how" and "why" responses.
3. Get the team involved in this exercise—it may appear silly at first, but you'd be surprised how easily root causes can become identified by utilizing the collective wisdom of your team.
4. No possible cause is a bad one; go ahead—put it on the diagram (it may fuel other ideas).
5. There can be multiple derived causes (and not just one).

According to Kemp's *Quality Management Demystified*, the use of Ishikawa diagrams can teach you about overall quality best practices. Most problems can be solved if you break them down into pieces or components and don't avoid problems—root out the cause and get it resolved in time for the next quality control pass.

■ **Control charts:** Determine if a process is stable or less predictable. Control charts (also known as *statistical process control charts*) should answer the following question: "Are the process variables within acceptable limits?"

    ■ According to best practices recommended by PMBOK, the results should reside within Three Sigma (discussed earlier in this chapter under the "Key Quality Terminology" section). As an example, determine through execution of quality control tests if the number of software defects are within acceptable limits. Using the example in Figure 8.4, you would plot the result of quality tests over time. By monitoring fluctuating values, spikes, or gradual trends, you can determine if the results are putting the project at risk.

Let's go even deeper than PMBOK does in explaining how all of this should work by plotting the incoming defects using a control chart, as shown in Figure 8.9.

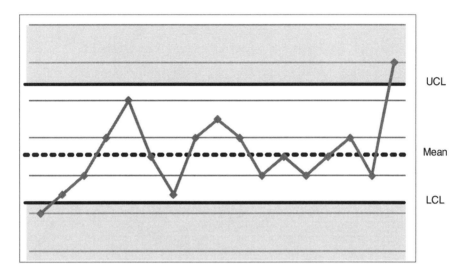

FIGURE 8.9
Control chart limits established for quality control.

The mean is created as the average of the sample of incoming defects and is shown as a horizontal dotted line on the control chart. Next you'll draw the Upper Control Limit (UCL) and the Lower Control Limit (LCL), which is generally Three Sigma (in either direction from the mean). This covers roughly 99.7% of the allowable range that defects should reside in.

So where does this lead to? PMBOK believes that control charts are a good visual representation of quality trends:

1. If measurements fall outside of the UCL and LCL, the process is understandably out of control. In this case, there are two points at the very beginning and at the very end that fall out of the range. This is hardly a trend—so hopefully the project is in pretty good shape.
2. Using a concept called the *Rule of Seven* (this isn't the same as the Basic Seven, by the way), if seven or more consecutive data points (incoming defects in this example) are on one side of the mean, then they should be investigated. If they are above the UCL or below the LCL, then chances are the project is at risk and theoretically out of control.

3. The control chart shows that the project is in control so far, despite two data points outside the control limits because the Rule of Seven indicates that incoming defects are close to the mean (as shown in Figure 8.10). In evaluating the best course of action using control charts, objective expert judgment is more important than optimism ("wishful thinking").

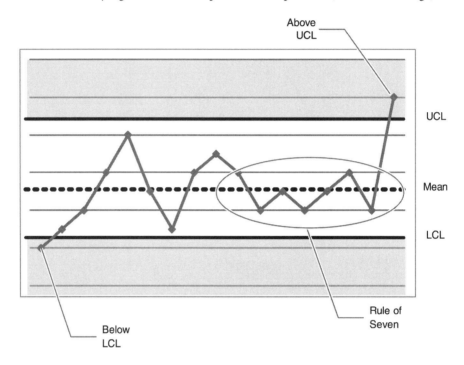

FIGURE 8.10
Interpreting a control chart under the Perform Quality Control process.

■ **Flowcharting:** Although losing its favor in the software world for more advanced visualization techniques, remember when you struggled getting a program algorithm or logic to work, and you spent a couple of hours thinking through it with a flowchart? The same is true when you are trying to predict where quality problems may happen, or when you need to verify that a failing process is being validated thoroughly.

In the sample flowchart shown in Figure 8.11, the outcome of the test procedure tested below minimum and expected value, but there was no test defined to validate the above maximum condition. A flowchart's purpose is to help you and the team visualize that all cases are truly being covered. For the purpose of continuous improvement, this test case should be augmented to ensure that all meaningful combinations of code paths are being properly qualified.

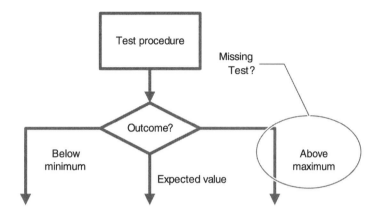

FIGURE 8.11
Flowcharting in quality control.

■ **Histogram:** This vertical bar chart shows the frequency of defects on a sample or population being measured. (The soon to be discussed Pareto chart is actually a form of histogram.) Figure 8.12 shows an example of when a histogram can be used to plot the incoming defects during 10 periods in a project's life cycle.

The importance of a histogram is that you can see trends—it isn't uncommon to also label each bar with percentages or even show a curve that identifies trends or cumulative value (for example, total number of defects to date).

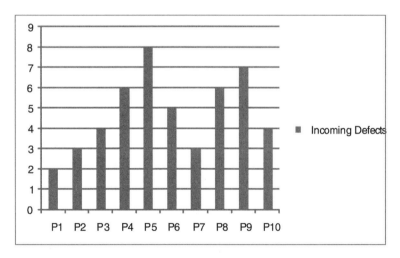

FIGURE 8.12
Histogram used to track incoming defects under quality control.

■ **Pareto chart:** This is a special histogram that typically shows how many defects were generated by type (or category), usually ranked from greatest to least. The intention of a Pareto chart is to focus on the issues most likely to change the results of the project. Normally, vertical bars represent types, categories, or subsystems and are ranked by importance (from left to right). Behind it is a cumulative percentage of the incoming defects (which should add up to 100%), as shown in Figure 8.13.

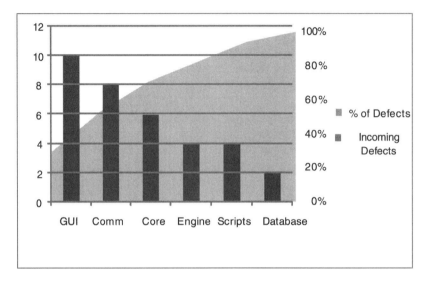

FIGURE 8.13
Pareto chart tracking incoming and total number of defects as part of quality control.

A Pareto chart is good for showing subsystem categories of defects—it does not always, however, indicate which are most important to focus on.

Notice that the cumulative area background (% of defects) levels out after the third subsystem (Core). This should imply that the subsystems to the left (GUI, Comm, and Core) represent the majority of defects that need attention. (Conversely, if the slope of the percentage cumulation doesn't level out, chances are all of the subsystem's defects are evenly distributed.) The phrase "choose your battles" comes to mind when using Pareto charts (and where you spend your time correcting the right defects).

Pareto's Law, otherwise known as the 80/20 Rule, states that 80% of the problems come from 20% of the causes. You will likely find that a few root causes are the source of the majority of the quality problems on a project.

■ **Run chart:** Similar to a control chart, this chart shows the history of quality as a series of snapshots. If all of your projects kept quality statistics collected as run charts, you'd have a fabulous set of assets for lessons learned purposes. A run chart can be used to analyze how quality trends over time, as shown in Figure 8.14. Note that the periods (P1, P2, and so on) represent Sprints. It is that simple! This is probably one of the most important tools you can use to communicate true status to stakeholders.

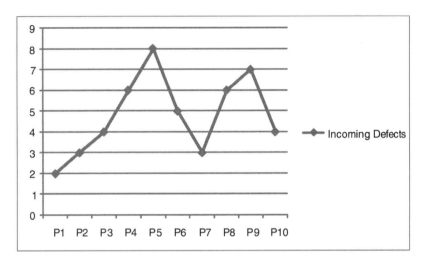

FIGURE 8.14
Run chart in quality control tracking incoming defects.

Run charts and control charts are usually assumed to be the same thing—they aren't—but you'd be surprised by the number of PMP study books that get it wrong. If in doubt, always refer to the official PMBOK guide.

BEST PRACTICE If you have to choose one tool to track defects during Perform Quality Control process, use run charts.

But wait! There's more. . . . Why not add just a little bit more information to your run chart with the addition of the number of defects accumulated over time? (See Figure 8.15.) Once the project ends, you'll be able to see not only defect trends but also the total number of defects spiked upward (or flattened). You can also use a run chart as a forecasting (predictive modeling) tool to estimate how many defects are yet to be discovered.

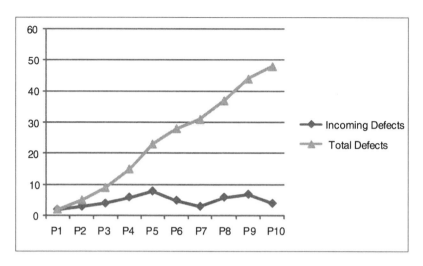

FIGURE 8.15
Addition of accumulated number of defects in a run chart.

■ **Scatter diagram:** This tool is an interesting one—scatter diagrams are helpful in comparing and showing a relationship (or pattern) between two items being tracked (which PMBOK calls variables). By periodically using this tool throughout a project life cycle, you can visually see if two variables are related or dependent (close together in the chart). Otherwise, the variables you are tracking might be totally unrelated or independent (not so close together in the chart).

Here's a perfect example where the trends "don't lie." Say your quality team has developed a set of new tests. You may want to use a scatter diagram to see if the number of tests passed have on the number of defects found over time, as shown in Table 8.6.

Table 8.6 Sample Set of Defect Logs for Display Using a Scatter Diagram

Defect Status	P1	P2	P3	P4	P5	P6	P7
Tests passed	5	10	13	18	20	30	35
Defects found	45	30	25	38	25	10	8

For a fast-moving iterative development project, you'd expect the number of defects to drop. Table 8.6 shows the facts for each Sprint (P1, P2, and so on), but there's nothing like a scatter diagram to show the overall trend (see Figure 8.16).

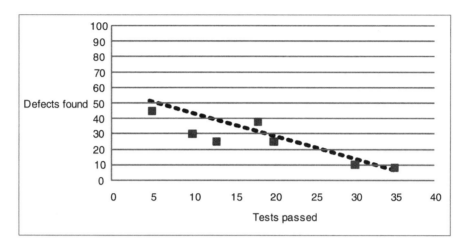

FIGURE 8.16
Sample scatter diagram showing data point correlation.

If you draw a trend line (the dotted line between the points), there is a direct correlation that clearly shows the impact new tests have by coincidentally reducing the number of defects found. This downward trend, by the way, is called a *negative linear correlation*. (Can you guess the name of a trend line going upward?)

> Information like this can really help lessons learned. Did adding more test cases help you find more defects?

Another variation on this example is when the number of tests passed varies period by period, and for some reason, there is an inconsistent number of defects found (see Table 8.7).

Table 8.7 Sample Set of Defect Logs for Display Using a Scatter Diagram

Defect Status	P1	P2	P3	P4	P5	P6	P7
Tests passed	5	10	13	60	20	45	35
Defects found	45	30	5	38	25	50	8

In fact, this set of data points may be more realistic. In Period 4, a bunch of defects were discovered, even though the number of tests passed was at its highest. In Period 6, there was a mad influx of defects that were closed prior to Period 7. The scatter diagram would look like Figure 8.17. As you can see, there is no clear pattern (upward or downward), resulting in a high probability that the project may be out of control. In this case, the scatter diagram has no correlation.

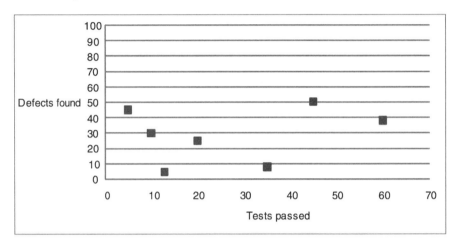

FIGURE 8.17
Sample scatter diagram (without any correlation).

That, by the way, is the last of the Seven Basic Tools of quality charts and diagramming techniques. *But we aren't quite done yets . . . there are three more!*

Inspection

Inspection can be defined in all sorts of interesting ways, based on the type of testing you do and certainly the industry you serve.

BEST PRACTICE If your requirements aren't correct, there is a high likelihood that quality control will not discover key defects.

For the purpose of discovering defects, inspection determines where the work conforms to the requirements. The execution of tests is a key ingredient of inspection—the more automated the better. The best software shops augment inspection through code reviews, peer reviews, unit tests (programmer self-tests), regression tests, and even audits.

As a reminder, inspection elements are all inherent features of XP and Scrum, described in the section "Agile Software Development Methodology" in Chapter 7.

NOTE

Statistical Sampling

If you can't test every possible case, use expert judgment to decide on a sampling of quality checks that validate key function points and special conditions. In the case of test execution, you may not have any choice but to use statistical sampling—especially if tests would otherwise take months to run!

Approved Change Request Review

Derived from *defect repair review* in the Third Edition of PMBOK, all approved change requests need to be validated as conforming to the updated requirements.

The outputs for the Perform Quality Control process are the following:

- **Quality control measurements:** During the Plan Quality process, it should have been specified how the project or services were going to be validated by the Control Quality process. It is unlikely that all of the tools and techniques listed here are going to be used on every project, so choose your weapons wisely. The most valuable measurements are those that can directly impact the delivery of quality as well as continuously improve quality through better detection of defects (in other words, test coverage) and reducing the number of defects.
- **Validated changes and change requests:** Software corrections are re-inspected and will either be
  - Accepted
  - Rejected (which will require rework and consequently re-inspection)

  Validated changes typically can be handled by the team and, if handled in a timely manner, won't need to be escalated to upper management. Change requests, on the other hand, *will be required* if the action (corrective, preventive, or defect repair) impacts the overall Project Management Plan. As an example, a key requirement states that your software product's performance has to improve at least 20% from the previous release. Through inspection, a couple of the product's new features (like Undo) resulted in the opposite effect.

  In certain circumstances, performance has slowed by at least 20%. This is an example of where going through the Integrated Change Control process works well. Everybody gets informed, they evaluate trade-offs, and a crisp decision is made. (Well, that's how it *should* occur.)
- **Validated deliverables:** The outcome of this process is that after a pass of quality control, you'll have deliverables (product or services) that have been validated. (Obviously, this will include some defects—but at least the true state of the deliverable is known.)

■ **Organizational process asset updates:** Of all the times PMBOK stresses this throughout all of the knowledge area processes, *this* is the one time when you need to take this output seriously. If checklists are used (inspection checklists, for example), make sure you update them during the project's life cycle. (It is too difficult to go back and update them after the fact.)

I've mentioned lessons learned throughout this process, and keeping track of continuous improvement, defect counts, number of life cycle passes, and so on becomes vital for postmortems and for use with other projects in the future.

■ **Project document updates:** Quality, above most anything else that can derail a project, has the greatest impact on the success of the overall project. As a result of quality control outcomes, there may be changes to the Quality Management Plan, Process Improvement Plan (optional), and other project documents.

BEST PRACTICE Even if your project has fewer features than expected, quality cannot ever be compromised.

USE CASES—WHY THEY ARE IMPORTANT FOR QUALITY

Use cases were previously introduced in the "MRDs and Use Cases" section of Chapter 5, but it is important to bring up the concept again as a key ingredient to succeed with quality processes. If, for example, your team needs to build a software product that has a complicated workflow, you should facilitate a set of design sessions that provide a vehicle to storyboard the flow. A perfect example is to use Unified Modeling Language (UML)—through the use of state transition mappings, you and your team can model the interactions between user scenarios.

> There is a wealth of UML and use-case information available on Jason Gorman's web site, aptly called www.parlezuml.com.

Visualization techniques like UML can provide a very user-centric (and hopefully non-technical) way to describe how the software should work (in other words, its behavior) prior to committing to any code. It also has the distinct benefit of making sure that all key stakeholders agree on how the software should interact with the user. For those middleware products that are popular in business-to-business (B2B), interactions between systems need clarity of definition, and product analysis is absolutely needed (even if there is no user interaction required). Emerging from the object-oriented programming world in the 1980s, use-case analysis has proved an effective way to present requirements from the view of the customer. A use case visually shows the *goal* (benefits) of using a *system* from the needs of an *actor* (see Figure 8.18).

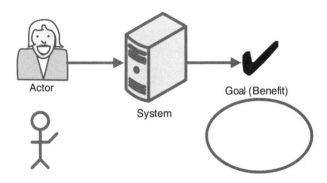

FIGURE 8.18
An actor (user) uses a system to accomplish a goal (which has benefits).

> Typically the actor is shown as a stick figure (easier to draw), and both systems and goals are shown as text inside of ovals.

An actor is the starting point and is external to the system that it needs to use to attain the goal. An actor can be a role, a person, or even a system; for example, in a B2B connectivity application, the actor can be a billing software application, and the system can be a parts inventory software application. They are related but not integrated. The most common type of actor is a user, and the system is the software that the actor is interacting with.

A *use-case scenario* (also known as a *usage scenario*) specifies the options that help solidify a requirement: The team involved with building use cases (and use-case scenarios are definitely powerful team-building exercises) needs to keep on asking questions like "then what?" or "what would happen with. . . ?" This approach should build up as many of the scenarios as can possibly be conceived.

BIBLIOGRAPHY

Alexander, Alvin J. "How to Determine Your Application Size Using Function Point Analysis." Devdaily.com (www.devdaily.com/FunctionPoints/FunctionPoints.shtml).

American Society for Quality. "Seven Basic Quality Tools" (www.asq.org/learn-about-quality/seven-basic-quality-tools/overview/overview.html). Excerpted from Nancy R. Tague's *The Quality Toolbox, Second Edition.* ASQ Quality Press, 2004.

Deming, W. Edwards. *Out of the Crisis*. Cambridge, Massachusetts: MIT Press, 2000.

Dutton, Jeffrey L. and Richard S. McCabe. "Agile/Lean Development and CMMI." *Systems and Software Consortium*. 9 Mar 2006 (www.sei.cmu.edu/cmmi/adoption/pdf/dutton.pdf).

George, Michael L., David Rowlands, and Bill Kastle. *What Is Lean Six Sigma?* New York: McGraw-Hill, 2004.

Gorman, Jason. *UML for Managers*. 7 Feb 2005 (www.parlezuml.com/e-books/uml-formanagers/umlformanagers_ch1.pdf).

Johnson, Tony. *PMP Exam Success Series: Certification Exam Manual*. Carrollton, TX: Crosswind Project Management, 2006.

Kemp, Sid. *Quality Management Demystified*. New York: McGraw-Hill Professional, 2006.

Praxiom Research Group Limited. *ISO 9000: An Introduction*. Last updated 2 Jan 2009 (www.praxiom.com/iso-intro.htm).

Software Engineering Institute. *Capability Maturity Model Integration (CMMI)*. Carnegie Mellon University (www.sei.cmu.edu/cmm).

Software Engineering Institute. CMMI Mappings and Comparisons. Carnegie Mellon University (www.sei.cmu.edu/cmmi/adoption/comparisons.html).

Thomsett, Rob. *Radical Project Management*. Upper Saddle River, NJ: Prentice Hall PTR, 2002.

Part

4 | People

The dreaded human element issues! With a well-defined set of knowledge areas that are dedicated to planning and processes, it is encouraging that PMBOK recognizes that you can have all of the technical stuff under control. But without considering how to motivate and inspire a project environment of open, truthful communication, you'll have less than successful results.

■ **Chapter 9, "Finding, Retaining, and Motivating the Best Talent":** I can't think of anything more important than finding, rewarding, and retaining the project staff. Surprisingly, PMBOK provides a very sound foundation for dealing realistically with the people issues that will typically confront any project. I'll supplement this material with all sorts of modern philosophies and psychologies of successful people. The included management tips and techniques should become a basis for people management best practices.

■ **Chapter 10, "Create a Winning Workplace":** One of the most important knowledge areas focuses on project communications. For some unknown reason, software developers tend to struggle at being able to communicate—and for that reason, you need to pick up that slack. PMBOK believes that you spend the vast majority of your time communicating. This chapter is designed to help you communicate effectively to motivate teams to perform.

9

Finding, Retaining, and Motivating the Best Talent

The best way to work with the human element with respect to project management is to take the PMBOK Human Resource Management knowledge area and break it down into meaningful best practices dealing with people. Specifically, we'll approach this topic as follows:

- Planning for people resources on your project
- Finding the best talent
- Retaining, developing, and motivating the best talent
- Effective ways to manage the project team

"IT WOULD BE SO MUCH BETTER IF I DIDN'T HAVE TO DEAL WITH PEOPLE!"

PMBOK believes that there is a critical human element tied to project success. I'll cover all sorts of theories, leadership, talent acquisition, and motivation. There is the belief that a project manager (or software manager) has a distinct advantage being the one in total control of a project and its resources. Oftentimes, it may appear that the team has total control, and you are just along for the ride.

Inspiration and motivation can either make or break a team's ability to deliver. As you are ultimately responsible for the success of the project, you'll be delegating that same responsibility to the team. The unspoken goal is that the team will return successful results, and you in turn will deliver to the customer (and the company) what they expect—a quality product delivered on time. The reality is that you and the team are actually dependent on each other.

This chapter coupled with Chapter 10, "Create a Winning Workplace," will form the foundation that you'll need to feel comfortable in dealing with the human side of project team management. Most important, you may wish to review the section "Functional Organizations" in Chapter 3 to determine the type of organizational structure being used. There can be a conflict if you, as a project manager, are imposing roles and responsibilities with personnel that are not under your direction.

BEST PRACTICE The roles and responsibilities of project and line management must never be confusing to project team members.

Line management (for example, the engineering manager) may assume that they direct all of the work assignments, and if the project manager starts directing work, the software engineer could easily become confused, wondering, "Who do I report to?" Clarity in management roles that properly support your organizational structure is critical for every project. Keep in mind that it is never black and white—roles and responsibilities among managers leading the team can be distinct, shared, or even slightly overlapped.

THE HUMAN LIFE CYCLE

PMBOK has defined four people-oriented processes in the Human Resource Management knowledge area.

OVERVIEW OF THE HUMAN RESOURCE KNOWLEDGE AREA

Table 9.1 shows the Fourth Edition PMBOK processes.

Table 9.1 Human Resource Management Knowledge Area Processes (PMBOK 4th Edition)

	Process Groups			
	Implementation			
Initiating	Planning	Executing	Monitoring & Controlling	Closing
	Develop Human Resource Plan	Acquire Project Team		
		Develop Project Team		
		Manage Project Team		

HUMAN RESOURCE MANAGEMENT IN THE PLANNING PROCESS GROUP

The first process helps you figure out which resources are needed and how you'll train, manage, and motivate them so that the project is successfully released on time according to the scope required.

Develop Human Resource Plan

As with all agile projects, the plan may initially provide an overview document that will, through discovery during the development life cycle, become more complete over time. This flexibility is important, as resource needs adjust as the project changes. Inputs are discussed in the following sections.

Activity Resource Requirements

Created in the Estimate Activity Resources process described in Chapter 7, this is composed of a list summarizing the people (and non-people) resources needed for the project. For an example, refer to Figure 7.17 in Chapter 7. The Develop Human Resource Plan process needs the resources identified and when they'll be needed, including the following:

- Start and finish dates (for example, Sep 10–20, 2008 for Sprint #2)
- Skill sets (for example, Adobe Flex programmer)
- Experience level (for example, senior level and above)

Enterprise Environmental Factors

Information that can influence the Human Resource Plan include current organizational structure, market conditions (for example, the availability of talent is limited), personnel policies and procedures (boring stuff but probably important to consider), and what internal personnel are available. Overall, enterprise environmental factors provide a perspective as to what is available in order for you to build a credible plan.

Organizational Process Assets

What stuff is available to help you make a better plan? Here are a few: job descriptions, templates (for organizational charts), and historical information (lessons learned) of organizational structures, or motivational techniques that have worked in the past.

Tools and techniques used in the Develop Human Resource Plan process are discussed in the following sections.

Organization Charts and Position Descriptions

There are three basic ways to depict the organization used for the project:

- Hierarchical
- Matrix
- Text

The *hierarchical chart* usually shows a top-down structure with the project manager at the top of a hierarchy of individuals identified based on some sort of breakdown hierarchy: by work package, department, or some other structure. All in all, the way the organization is structured should make sense to the team and to stakeholders.

Normally, there are very sophisticated HR systems that can be used to create a visual representation of your organization (not unlike the Resource Breakdown Structure shown in Figure 7.18 in Chapter 7).

> For project organization charts, you should include part-time staff as well as consultants. (It might be a good idea to visually distinguish those differences.)

Thus there's a simple way to construct an org chart using a tool that you probably already own: Microsoft Visio. Visio can import a Microsoft Excel spreadsheet to create an org chart, as shown in Figure 9.1. When your organization changes, simply update the Excel spreadsheet, answer a few questions using the Visio Organization Chart wizard, and voilà—org charts are magically re-created!

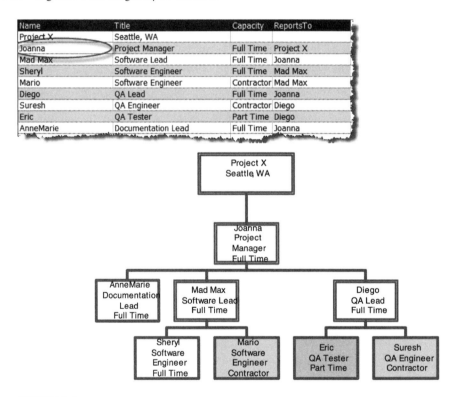

FIGURE 9.1
Creating an organizational chart from a spreadsheet.

A Resource Breakdown Structure (discussed in the "Estimate Activity Resources" section of Chapter 7) usually defines the project's resource organization to help track project costs and may include other information that can be used by your HR and Finance departments.

Matrix-based charts are typically simple spreadsheets (or tables) that summarize who is doing what on a project. An excellent tool for you to use with the team to establish roles and responsibilities for the project is a RACI diagram (also known as a RACI matrix). There are at least four roles that should be assigned to every team member based on the following:

- **Responsible:** Performs the work on the task. (There can be multiple team members with the responsible role.)
- **Accountable:** The person who approves the work.
- **Consulted:** Individuals whose opinions are sought (usually requiring two-way communication).
- **Informed:** One-way communication of project status.

BEST PRACTICE Avoid conflicts by clarifying roles and responsibilities throughout a project.

As a team-building process, you can ease team stress by clearly identifying each stakeholder's role and responsibility with a RACI diagram, shown in Table 9.2. (This is also a great team-building activity.)

Table 9.2 Sample RACI Diagram (R=Responsible, A=Accountable, C=Consulted, I=Informed)

Stakeholder	R	A	C	I	Explanation
Tom, QA	Y				Core team member
John, Engineer	Y				Core team member
Me, Lead		Y			Butt "on the line"
Sarah, Technical Writer	Y				Core team member
Gary, Chief Architect			Y		Technical guidance
Madhu, Marketing			Y		Feature decisions
Jon, Finance				Y	Budget awareness
Kirsten, Engineer	Y				Core team member

Once you set up the project's RACI diagram, do some simple role-playing activity with the team and speed through a fictional project life cycle to make sure that the team members know what their roles will be. It'll only take five to 10 minutes! This works as long as an individual's role doesn't change throughout a project's life cycle and if you have a small team.

Another more generic way to clarify RACI is with generic job duties in the form of a Responsibility Assignment Matrix (RAM). This is where you specify roles and responsibilities that may change during a project's life cycle (either by phase, work package, or in any way that is convenient for you to monitor). Roles are identified horizontally and the sequence vertically (in this case, key project phases). Responsibilities, shown in Table 9.3, are identified in the cells by a single letter.

Table 9.3 Generic RACI Diagram (R=Responsible, A=Accountable, C=Consulted, I=Informed)

Project Phase (Work Package)	PM	Arc	SE	QA	TW	EX	SEL
Document and approve scope	A	R	I	I	I	I	R
Create database	I	C	R	I			A
Sprint 1—feature subset A	A	C	R	R	R		R
Sprint 2—feature expansion of A	A	C	R	R	R		R
...							
Project release (or final handoff)	A	I	R	R	R	I	R

Legend:
PM: Project Manager
Arc: Architect
SE: Software Engineer
QA: Quality Assurance Engineer
TW: Technical Writer
EX: Executive (Finance)
SEL: Software Engineer Lead

Text-oriented formats can be used to maintain a list of personnel and what they will be doing on a project. Not quite as sophisticated as the hierarchical or matrix charts, they can be used to summarize job descriptions, titles, and the staff involved on the project (see Figure 9.2). This list format can be used as a template for other projects and can even help summarize the needs for recruiting staff for your project.

Position Description	Key Role	Specific Skills	Resource
Project Manager	Lead and facilitate project	PMP certified	Joana
Technical Lead	Manager, design, programmer	Hands-on software lead	Chris
Software Engineer	GUI programmer	C#, Java Script, DHTML, Flash	Enrique
Software Engineer	Business Logic	ETL, C#, C++, message queues	Mad Max
Test Engineer	Test plans, test runs, performance	Script languages, profiling	To be hired
Test Engineer	Run tests, validate installation/upgrade	Installshield, script languages	Joanna
Customer Support Engineer	Beta site, early adopter, knowledge base	Contractor	Marsha

FIGURE 9.2
Text-oriented format used for team personnel list.

Networking

Simply stated, networking is a technique where you communicate inside and outside your immediate organization to better understand how you will attract, motivate, and retain key talent. This includes (but isn't limited to) trade events, meetings, informal communications, and proactive contact of peers in the industry.

For example, Steve McConnell, CEO of Construx, hosts a regular monthly meeting with software development executives in the Seattle area. This interaction is exciting because we not only share "war stories," but we often discuss issues that have to do with human resources—our most complex responsibility (besides delivery of software on time).

Organizational Theory

It isn't enough just to lead and facilitate the "nerd herd," is it? You also must dig into the inner depths of what makes individuals and teams work. Although briefly presented in PMBOK, the most critical theories behind organizational dynamics include the following:

- Hierarchy of needs
- Importance of motivation
- Theories X and Y
- Performance review and career planning

> Some of the more complex, ongoing leadership and team challenges are covered in Chapter 10.

Abraham Maslow grouped human needs into five basic categories called Maslow's Hierarchy of Needs, shown in Figure 9.3. This is usually shown as a pyramid: The base is the lowest level (its foundation), and the pinnacle is what you want to achieve.

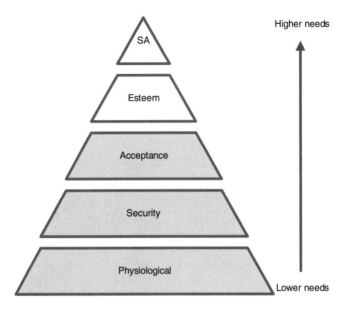

FIGURE 9.3
Maslow's Hierarchy of Needs.

Each of these categories, according to Maslow, must be achieved in order—the needs at the bottom must be satisfied before the needs at the top can be realized (see Table 9.4).

Table 9.4 Hierarchy of Needs Definitions (Shown Top to Bottom)

Need	Definition	Example
SA (Self-Actualization)	*Working to full potential*	Achieving to plan, "evangelistic," and they love their work.
Esteem	*Feeling of importance*	Given the choice assignments, being recognized, promotable or has a clear career path, a big contributor.
Acceptance	*Part of the team*	Accepted as a valuable teammate, participates with key decisions, "a part of something bigger than oneself."
Security	*Freedom from fear*	Company is growing, secure, stable management, and so on.
Physiological	*Basic biological needs*	A workplace, computer, software tools, and so on.

"So how does this hierarchy relate to your team?" For example, it is your responsibility that the QA team is treated as equal partners with software engineers. Another action you could take is to make sure that the team is learning and advancing with training (typically limited to software engineers in many organizations).

What happens if you don't act? If individuals don't feel acceptance, they'll want off the team. If individuals don't feel secure, they'll look for a different position elsewhere. You can't really expect everyone to be at the self-actualization level, but wouldn't it be phenomenal if your entire team were executing at that level? That's where empowerment, great communication, and incredible customer satisfaction are fundamental to a successful organization. (It is one thing to be excited about working on neat technology, but it is even better if you have the knowledge that what you are working on has tremendous benefits for paying customers!)

BEST PRACTICE Financial gain is not typically a motivational tool for software developers.

Another organizational theory that you should know about is Herzberg's Motivational-Hygiene Theory, which identifies two main areas that are motivating factors:

- **Hygiene:** Providing a safe work environment, basic tools to perform the work, and job stability (mostly financial in nature). (Hygiene bears no resemblance to "keeping clean," by the way.)
- **Motivating agents:** The opportunity to improve and do more, responsibility, and education (mostly non-financial in nature).

According to Herzberg, providing both of these motivates workers, and in most cases, "money is *not* a motivator." Similar to Maslow's theories, Herzberg believes that just having the presence of certain factors does not make someone satisfied, but the absence will definitely make someone dissatisfied at work. Tables 9.5 and 9.6 show key factors for both hygiene and motivation.

Table 9.5 Hygiene Factors

Present?	Factors
Yes	Company policies and procedures
Yes	Good direction and supervision
Yes	Working relationship with management
Yes	Good to great working conditions
Yes	Regular, competitive paycheck (the company is stable)
Yes	Security (long-term prospects are good)
Yes	Relationship with co-workers

Table 9.6 Motivating Factors

Present?	Factors
Yes	Achievement (individual, team, and company)
Yes	Recognition of a "job well done"
Yes	Work is interesting and challenging
Yes	Responsibility and delegation (not micromanaged)
Yes	Advancement and growth potential

Herzberg's theories assume that workers (in this case, software developers) want and expect to find meaning through their work. Consequently, hygiene factors must be present, but they do *not* motivate by themselves. Motivation factors will motivate, but without hygiene factors in place, you'll still have demotivated employees.

According to a recent article by Tracy Hall et al. entitled "What Do We Know About Developer Motivation?," the authors examined close to a hundred studies on motivating factors for software developers and found some interesting results (as shown in Figure 9.4). Your ability, as the manager, to motivate the project team has an immediate impact on productivity, quality of work, overall success, and employee retention.

FIGURE 9.4
Motivation has a tremendous impact on a project team's effectiveness.

Recent surveys indicate that there has been a substantial shift, where a team member's motivation has a lot to do with team relationships and working environment. According to Tracy Hall's study, the most important motivational factors to software developers are shown in Table 9.7.

Table 9.7 Most Important Motivational Factors for Software Developers

No.	Motivational Factor	Highlights
1	Identification with the task	Clear goals; team identifies with product quality produced.
2	Great (not just good) management	The direction is known; effective communication.
3	Employee participation	Involved; working with others is a positive.
4	Career path	Opportunities; knows what to do in order to advance.
5	Variety of work	Learning, making good use of skills, and being stretched.

> Perhaps not surprisingly, a similar study found back in the 1980s that software developers enjoyed learning and being challenged but had little need for socializing.

Another great motivational tool not mentioned in this particular study is *job enrichment*. According to Kliem and Ludin's *Project Management Practitioner's Handbook*, job rotation (moving people from one role to another) and job enlargement (increasing the number of tasks and responsibilities) can not only change one's daily pace but can enhance an employee's satisfaction. In summary, management must provide challenging tasks, recognize quality work, and give developers autonomy to perform their jobs.

McGregor's Theory X and Theory Y have been used since the 1960s to describe how two very different employee attitudes directly impact how management should motivate them. McGregor's belief is that companies follow one or the other approach when management is trying to understand and motivate workers (see Table 9.8).

Table 9.8 McGregor's Theory X and Theory Y

Need	Theory X	Theory Y
Staff members	Not motivated to work.	Very motivated; desire to work.
Management (you!)	Forced to micromanage.	Empowers the team to do the work.
Overall theme	Distrust between staff and management.	Trust between staff and management.

So, does your organization fall under Theory X or Theory Y? (Hint: You can't be both.) It's no surprise that a Theory X organization isn't going to attract and motivate software developers. Here's a summary of the key benefits of a Theory Y software organization:

- A Theory Y manager will remove barriers so that staff members can self-actualize their potential.
- When staff members want to do well at work, there is an "untapped energy" of creativity ready to erupt.
- Prevailing belief that there is a high degree of satisfaction in doing a great job.

There is actually a relationship between Theories X and Y and Maslow's Hierarchy of Needs (see Figure 9.5). McGregor's work, an extension to Maslow's Hierarchy of Needs, shows that the lower three "needs" (physiological, security, and acceptance) are what motivate the Theory X workforce, while the upper two (esteem and self-actualization) are key traits of a Theory Y workforce.

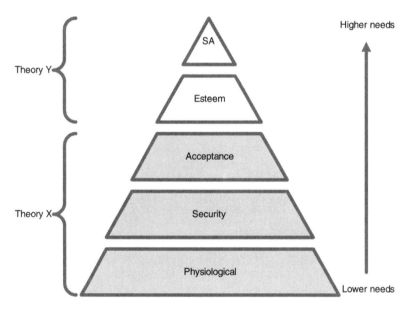

FIGURE 9.5
How McGregor's Theory X and Theory Y relate to Maslow's Hierarchy of Needs.

Stirring up some controversy, Geert Hofstede and Gert Jan Hofstede have determined through extensive research that organizational theories may even be influenced by cultural diversity. One of these dimensions that impacts the software organization in particular is how team-spirited an individual is (see Figure 9.6). This is known as *Hofstedes' Cultural Diversity Model*, and it uses an index range of between 0 and 100.

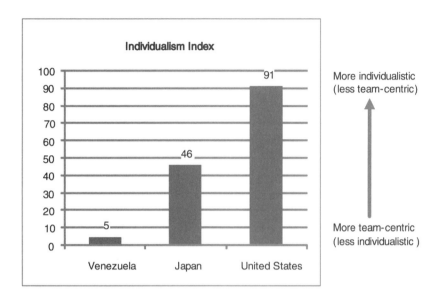

FIGURE 9.6
Collective versus individual factor (Hofstedes' Cultural Diversity model).

Based on the Hofstedes' research on education, culture, interviews, and work habits, the United States is almost 100% individualistic (teammanship isn't a first priority); but in Venezuela, there is a very small individualistic nature (value of 5). To Venezuelans, the needs of the *team* are generally regarded as more important than the needs of the *individual*. According to their research, Japan is right in the middle (wrestling between which is more important, the individual or the team). Another way to interpret this index is that 100 is the same as "looking out for number 1" and close to 0 demonstrates the philosophy that "we're all in this together." *Controversial? Certainly is. . .*

Let's look at one more chart regarding organizational theory. There is the constant battle for work/life balance that some companies preach (but aren't even close to living by). Some organizations claim that they have to work burnout hours just to survive, while others believe that companies should work a lot smarter (and that working long hours for extended periods of time is a sign of a broken company). The Hofstedes' research shows a real cultural bias based on masculine and feminine characteristics, as shown in Figure 9.7.

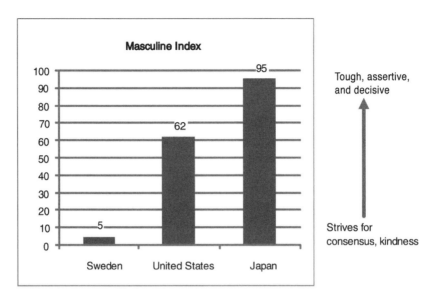

FIGURE 9.7
Consensus versus assertive factor (the Hofstedes' Cultural Diversity model).

Sweden, in this survey, has the least regard for masculinity (value of 5), and Japan is mostly (95) on the assertive, decisive side. The United States leans towards a more masculine value (62), but because it isn't far above the midpoint, there is a recognized value to consensus and collaborative style. In summary, a value of 100 means that you "live to work," and the closer to 0 the more you "work to live." *Where does your workplace lean?*

> The Hofstedes make the inference that a 0 in the masculinity index has more con-sensus (female) attributes, while 100 represents a more dominant (male) culture.

Now that I've presented some basic organizational psychology theories, there's another key ingredient regarding employee motivation and retention. Yep, you guessed it—performance measurement! Let's go through a very simple exercise: Select one employee on your project team, put yourself in their shoes, and honestly answer these questions in the checklist (see Table 9.9). Enter a yes or a no (there is no maybe in *this* survey).

Table 9.9 Sample Employee Performance Checklist

Yes or No	I, the Employee, . . .
	know how I am performing.
	know clearly what my priorities are.
	know how my project fits in the overall roadmap.
	know what I need to do to advance my career.
	have regular performance reviews with my boss.

Your employee should be well aware of how they are performing, and they should have a clear focus on their work. If you only have one (or two) items checked, you could be at risk with that employee: risk that the employee is not aware of their performance, risk that there is no apparent work focus, and risk that the employee (if given the opportunity) could leave for another company.

This is where the dreaded performance appraisals play an important part in employee motivation. Let's first explore why appraisals are so important. According to Bob Nelson and Peter Economy in *Managing for Dummies*, there are reasons why performance appraisals are necessary for employee motivation and retention:

- Chance to summarize past performance and establish new performance objectives.
- Opportunity for two-way, meaningful communications.
- Forum for career planning and development.
- Last, but not least, maintains a formal documentation of a person's performance.

If you've ever tried to terminate an employee "for cause," one of the very first things your HR department will ask you for is a documented history of performance issues. Without that information, no HR manager in his right mind is going to put an employee on "double-secret probation," a Performance Improvement Plan (PIP), or even attempt dismissal.

Every company has its own performance feedback standards, policies, and procedures, but here are a few effective, time-proven rules of thumb:

1. Never wait until the mandatory performance review process to prepare annual performance appraisals.
2. You can ask for self-appraisals until you are "blue in the face," but ultimately you need to have the information that has been kept throughout the review period (usually a year).
3. Communicate through regular performance reviews (I like monthly) that are designed to take no more than *20 minutes* of two-way discussion between the manager and the employee. *Don't believe a performance review can take that short a period of time?* Let's review a sample monthly performance review template. The first part identifies the employee's overall goal, as shown in Figure 9.8.

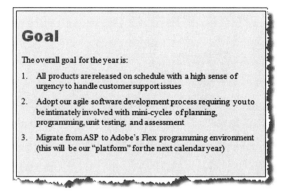

Goal

The overall goal for the year is:

1. All products are released on schedule with a high sense of urgency to handle customer support issues

2. Adopt our agile software development process requiring you to be intimately involved with mini-cycles of planning, programming, unit testing, and assessment

3. Migrate from ASP to Adobe's Flex programming environment (this will be our "platform" for the next calendar year)

FIGURE 9.8
Key activities that paired programmers should perform on a project.

This goal should provide an employee's focus for the entire year while reinforcing the company's overall mission. Next, you need to specify the top priorities for the upcoming review period (in this case, for the next month), as shown in Figure 9.9.

Performance Planning

February 2009

Pri	Tasks to be performed	Result (Overall __)
1	Design database access module and get Chief Architect's approval.	
2	Prototype database configuration UI and get QA and Usability Engineer's buy in.	
3	Attend Intro to Flex seminar, pass the summary test and write your first Flex test program (an assignment from the course).	
4		

Note: I will assign a QA Test Engineer to work with you starting by the middle of February. This should reduce risk.

FIGURE 9.9
Planning an employee's key tasks (from a sample monthly performance review).

As you can see, this is a pretty simple format for an employee's monthly performance objectives discussion. This prioritizes each task (the Pri column values in Figure 9.9) and indicates how the employee will be measured (the Tasks to Be Performed column). It is always a good idea to include special notes, indicating what you can do to help the employee succeed during the next review period (see the Note paragraph in Figure 9.9).

Finally, when it is time to review the employee's performance 30 days later, another 20-minute meeting is arranged (see Figure 9.10). In this example, the results for each task have been documented, the overall "grade" for that period is given (in this case, the employee achieved a Meets Expectations, ME, for the month), and you have laid out the goals for the next month (March 2009).

Performance Planning

February 2009

Pri	Tasks to be performed	Result (Overall <u>ME</u>)
1	Design database access module and get Chief Architect's approval.	**Achieved. Gary approved with comments (which you incorporated).**
2	Prototype database configuration UI and get QA and Usability Engineer's buy in.	**Yes, also achieved, you also got Support's feedback. Wonderful!**
3	Attend Intro to Flex seminar, pass the summary test and write your first Flex test program (an assignment from the course).	**Did not attend – priority 1 and 2 took a tremendous effort.**
4		

Note: I will assign a QA Test Engineer to work with you starting by the middle of February. This should reduce risk. **Jeremy is now assigned and will start working with you March 1, 2009.**

March 2009

Pri	Tasks to be performed	Result (Overall _)
1	Implement first phase of the database access module.	
2	...	

FIGURE 9.10
Performance results 30 days later (from the sample monthly performance review).

BEST PRACTICE All it takes is about 20 minutes a month to manage an employee's performance expectations.

And what about the weekly status reports management normally requires (but seldom reads)? Chuck 'em! Unless there is a pertinent amount of detail that needs to be written, you owe it to yourself (and the employees) to keep the amount of meaningless paperwork to a minimum.

Status reports are typically not read, and as long as you keep monthly performance reports focused to the right set of priorities, that should be all you need. (Don't skimp and make it so slimmed down that *anyone* can succeed—the objectives must support the needs of the project, which should be somewhat of a stretch to accomplish.) This simplified monthly performance report approach I've presented takes little to no time and ensures effective two-way communications, clarity of assignments, clarity of priorities, and regular performance feedback. At the end of the yearly review period, you should have 12 documented performance reviews making the annual performance appraisal "grind" effortless! In addition, you have greatly reduced project risk by making sure you are managing your team's individual performance.

All of this for a measly 20 minutes a month! Pretty good investment of time, heh? Ready for the output now?

The sole output for the Develop Human Resource Plan process is the Human Resource Plan. In PMBOK's infinite wisdom, the Human Resource Plan is a new term that includes three other planning documents that were separately identified in the Third Edition (see Figure 9.11).

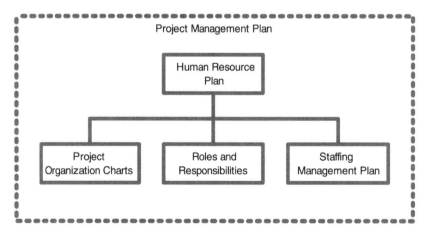

FIGURE 9.11
Components of the Human Resource Plan.

Like most other planning documents, the Human Resource Plan is a key part of the overall Project Management Plan. These documents are as follows:

■ **Project organization charts:** Organizational charts tell all stakeholders how your team is structured. This can be a highly detailed summary of the team associated with the project. It can also be as simple as identifying each team member's name. A sample is shown back in Figure 9.1.

■ **Roles and responsibilities:** The RACI matrix, shown in Tables 9.2 and 9.3, provides a simple-to-read tool with everyone's roles and responsibilities on your project.

■ **Staffing Management Plan:** The Staffing Management Plan details how and when the project will be staffed, released, and optionally trained. As part of the Staffing Management Plan, a resource histogram (see Figure 9.12) is a perfect visual way to show how resources are to be applied. (Remember, this is a plan and not actual fact!) Notice that in this example, resource demands vary week by week.

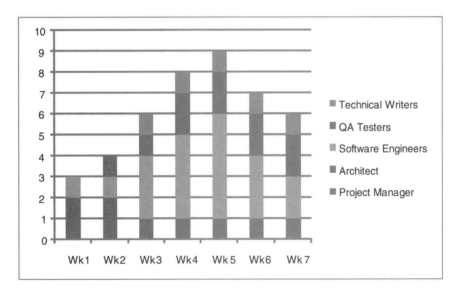

FIGURE 9.12
Sample resource histogram.

Don't forget vacations, holidays, and other time constraints that may impact the allocation of resources during the lifetime of a project.

You may wish to document how resources will be released to other projects (for example, what kind of notice they'll need), as well as any training needs. Although not necessarily a part of the Staffing Management Plan, PMBOK recommends identifying clear criteria for any rewards, merit, and award systems to be employed during the project's life cycle. Last, but not least, make sure that compliance to any regulations (or company guidelines) is identified. In the case of a union shop, there may be restrictions that staff members cannot exceed 40 hours of work per week. Overall, the resource histogram should be very closely aligned to the scheduling process described in the "Estimate Activity Resources" section in Chapter 7.

One last thing—the Staffing Management Plan should also include training, feedback, and motivational strategies that you can use during the Develop Project Team process (see the "Develop Project Team" section later in this chapter).

HUMAN RESOURCE MANAGEMENT IN THE EXECUTING PROCESS GROUP

There are three distinct processes in the Executing process group to be performed:

- Acquire project team
- Develop project team
- Manage project team

Although these processes are organized as a sequence to be performed one after the other, the reality is that these three processes usually overlap and can cycle back to update the Human Resource Plan.

Acquire Project Team

Confirming and obtaining the project team is the focus of the Acquire Project Team process, and depending on the organization structure, that can be easy or it may be difficult (especially in a matrix structure where you need to fight to build a team). Considerations in selecting resources include ability, experience, subject matter expertise, and interest. (In the case of contractors, cost can be a huge determining factor.) The Acquire Project Team process inputs are discussed in the following sections.

Human Resource Plan

This is the guiding plan that clearly identifies the following:

- **Roles and responsibilities:** These describe the positions and expertise required to fulfill the needs of the project.
- **Organization charts:** These define the number of folks performing specific functions (for example, engineering, QA, and so on) and the reporting structure (which clarifies how personnel will be managed and who makes final decisions).
- **Staffing Management Plan:** This outlines when resources are needed during the proposed life cycle of the project.

Enterprise Environmental Factors

Factors that can influence acquiring a team include resources that are (and are not) available, administration policies (for example, how to acquire the talent without upsetting everybody!), and the talent pool organization charts from which to draw on. There may also be relationships already established with outsourcing vendors to streamline the use of non-company resources. Of course, to effectively attract new talent requires upfront planning, since it can be quite time-consuming to post positions, interview, hire, and train.

Organizational Process Assets

There may be forms, policies, procedures, and templates that can be used to officially form the team. If you are working with outside recruitment firms or hiring using standard job boards, chances are that your company has strict guidelines you'll need to adhere to. Working closely with the HR and Finance departments is critical especially when the impact of performance reviews and project cost accounting need to be tracked.

Tools and techniques in the Acquire Project Team process are discussed in the following sections.

Pre-Assignment

Under certain circumstances, most project managers already have people in mind to assign to a project team. This is especially true when specific resources are identified in the Project Charter or SOW as being required for the project to be successful. (Keep in mind that your project may be already at risk if most of the team is new or has never worked together before.)

Negotiation

Perhaps one of the most difficult roles you have to perform is negotiating for resources. Prime folks you'll have to negotiate with are as follows:

- Functional managers
- Other project management teams
- External organizations

For the first two sources, you may need executive assistance, especially if there is concern over which project is most important. This is also where the Decision Pyramid should be used to referee for scarce resources. Hopefully, your task for allocating talent will be easier if the schedule needs in the resource histogram (refer to Figure 9.12) can accommodate everyone's schedules. Speaking of schedules, you may have to re-evaluate the critical path if talent availability impacts when work is accomplished (see both topics, "Sequence Activities" and "Estimate Activity Resources," in Chapter 7).

Acquisition

To use external hiring assistance, you'll need to use all sorts of techniques to clearly articulate the people you are looking for, when you need them, and how skilled they need to be in order to complete the work. Job boards can work, but there is an ever-growing trend that some of the more localized web-based sites (like Craigslist.com) are becoming the place to find talent.

BEST PRACTICE Create job postings that will "yank" someone who is not otherwise looking for a job to want to interview with your company.

Using Table 9.10 as a guide, do your job postings meet the criteria checklist?

Table 9.10 Job Posting Criteria Checklist

Explain the position and need?

Make someone want to contact you immediately?

Discourage unqualified people from applying?

Communicate a sense of levity (in a stressful role)?

Position the company in a positive light?

NOTE The fourth item in the list is most important. For every one hundred résumés you receive, how many are really qualified?

Twenty?

Ten?

<gasp>Three?

In surveys that I've done with audiences throughout the United States over the past 15 years, the unanimous consensus is somewhere between one and five. So, if there is something you can do to improve on that statistic, do it up front in the job posting!

Consider two example job postings shown in Figure 9.13.

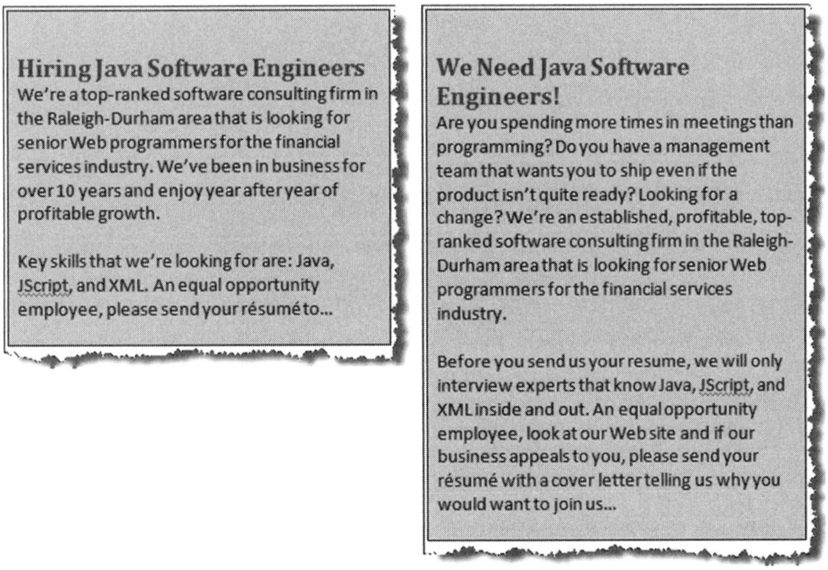

Hiring Java Software Engineers
We're a top-ranked software consulting firm in the Raleigh-Durham area that is looking for senior Web programmers for the financial services industry. We've been in business for over 10 years and enjoy year after year of profitable growth.

Key skills that we're looking for are: Java, JScript, and XML. An equal opportunity employee, please send your résumé to...

We Need Java Software Engineers!
Are you spending more times in meetings than programming? Do you have a management team that wants you to ship even if the product isn't quite ready? Looking for a change? We're an established, profitable, top-ranked software consulting firm in the Raleigh-Durham area that is looking for senior Web programmers for the financial services industry.

Before you send us your resume, we will only interview experts that know Java, JScript, and XML inside and out. An equal opportunity employee, look at our Web site and if our business appeals to you, please send your résumé with a cover letter telling us why you would want to join us...

FIGURE 9.13
Sample job posting (before and after).

The "before" job posting on the left does a nice job presenting a summary of the role and the individual you are trying to hire. The style is similar to what you'll find in most job postings. How does it fit with the checklist shown in Table 9.11?

Table 9.11 Before Job Posting Criteria Checklist

✓	Explain the position and need?
	Make someone want to contact you immediately?
	Discourage unqualified people from applying?
	Communicate a sense of levity (in a stressful role)?
✓	Position the company in a positive light?

Is this posting engaging? Is it going to get someone excited about contacting you? *Not at all!* The "after" posting on the right is more effective because it fulfills the rest of the checklist without a whole lot more words (see Table 9.12).

Table 9.12 After Job Posting Criteria Checklist

✓	Explain the position and need?
✓	Make someone want to contact you immediately?
✓	Discourage unqualified people from applying?
✓	Communicate a sense of levity (in a stressful role)?
✓	Position the company in a positive light?

> Of course, you might have a little bit of a challenge getting your Human Resource department to go along with non-traditional advertisements!

What about getting some help in the hiring process? In dealing with recruiters (also affectionately known as "headhunters"), they can provide an alternative energy and valuable resources if, and only if, they reduce your efforts to find qualified talent. We've all gotten excited working with a recruiter who initially said that he "has just the right candidate" (of course, it wasn't). Before long, you are spending as much time reviewing résumés and dealing with the recruiter as you would have working the job boards through your own HR department. Just for fun, I created a spreadsheet that prioritizes the most critical requirements that measure if a recruiter is a good source of talent (see Figure 9.14).

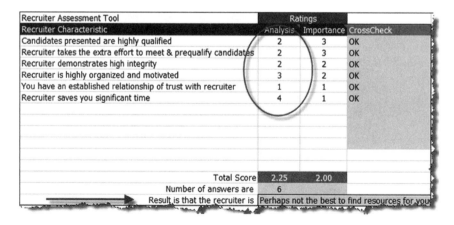

FIGURE 9.14
A home-grown recruitment assessment tool.

> Another criterion you may want to consider is how connected the recruiter is. Does he have a huge Rolodex? Is he specialized in my industry?

The Recruitment Assessment tool (don't make this into an acronym, okay?) is a great way to compare the services among recruiting agencies, and it is easy for you to create your own tool. There are six key characteristics that are listed from most important to least important (the Importance column). By entering a value in the Analysis column (1 through 7, with 7 being the best score), you can see how the overall tally (2.25 out of 7) produces a somewhat subjective result, which, in this example, concludes that this specific recruiter is "Perhaps not the best to find resources for you."

BEST PRACTICE The recruiter's only role is to find the best qualified talent in the least amount of time.

Although you would probably have different characteristics, a great recruiter needs only to present highly qualified candidates to you. Those who have taken the effort to talk to, and hopefully meet, candidates (preferably, face to face) have a higher chance of finding you the best talent in the least amount of time. And isn't that what you want a recruiter to do for you?

At least in the United States, recruiter fees can range anywhere from 15% to 35% of a new hire's first year's salary. When times are tough and there's plenty of recruiter competition, you shouldn't have to pay more than a 20% fee. Ever.

What about the candidate interview process itself? This is where many organizations fall flat and miss out on getting the best talent. Even in a tight job economy, the best talent will always be tougher to grab if you don't act quickly and decisively. Here are some basic rules of thumb:

1. Perform a phone interview introducing the candidate to the company and the position, and gauge each other's interest. This is a good time to "come clean" about the company's culture, upsides, and struggles. No company is perfect, and it helps to be candid up front. (They'll find out anyway when they become an employee.)
2. If you decide to bring the applicant in for an interview, schedule it as soon as you can—preferably the following day. If possible, arrange for an intense half day of interviews and schedule with a good cross-department set of interviewers.
3. Have everything ready for the interview: an application form, company information, benefits, and a copy of the job description. Most important, make sure that each of the interviewers knows the schedule and that they keep to the schedule.
4. During the interview, never leave the applicant alone. Each interviewer should arrive on time. (Don't forget to schedule a bathroom break after two hours!)

Some signs that the applicant isn't engaged or the right fit are that the applicant hardly asks any questions, doesn't make eye contact, watches the clock, or can't answer questions directly.

5. During the day, have every interviewer submit their written feedback (e-mail is okay) to the hiring manager without biasing their thoughts with other interviewers. At the end of the day, the hiring manager closes out the interview with the applicant and clearly indicates the next steps and approximate timeframe for an answer.

6. At the end of the day, the interview team should get together and discuss the positives (and concerns) about the applicant. If the applicant isn't the right fit, get back to the applicant right away. If the team agrees that the person is the right fit for the organization, "get on the stick" and start reference checking. Extend an offer to the applicant within two to three days (provided that references check out).

Of course, sometimes a second interview is required (with management or other senior technical folks). But with a second interview, if you are sold on the individual, it is an amazing opportunity to present an offer (based on positive feedback, of course) at the end of the second round. *I promise—the applicant will be amazed!* It shows that you and your team have a sense of urgency and, despite common wisdom, you do not have to take weeks to make a decision—time is your enemy when it comes to finding the best talent for your company.

What about aptitude tests or programming tests? It's always a good idea to have an applicant respond to hypothetical questions and have them present, either on a white board or piece of paper, the algorithms or approaches they'd recommend.

On the other hand, that's what reference checking is for! According to DeMarco and Lister in their book *Peopleware*, aptitude tests are typically left-brain oriented, yet things that an applicant does in the future will most probably be more right-brain oriented to a greater degree. That is because, as the individual grows in his position, his ability to perform "holistic thinking, heuristic judgment, and intuition based upon experience" becomes more important. A test may give you a perspective of the applicant in the short term (for the next couple of years), but the results have little to do with how that applicant will perform for the long term (say, the next 20 years).

Virtual Teams

Over the years, technology companies are working together without necessarily being in close proximity. Through the use of great applications over the Internet, this remote collaboration is becoming more common. Given great project management along with battle-hardened, experienced talent, this style of communication can work quite well. With key applications that are available on practically every home PC or laptop, you can do most anything (see Table 9.13).

Table 9.13 Virtual Team Tools of the Trade

Use This	To Replace This (or to Do a Specific Function)	Benefit
VoIP (Voice over IP)	The telephone	Low to no cost
Instant Messaging (IM)	Ad hoc hallway conversation	Instant dialog any time
Video conferencing (built in on most laptops now)	Expensive video conferencing systems	No expensive rental or scheduling required
Remote desktop	Having to send resources on site to solve issues	Instant access to software and data on a remote computer
E-mail	Letters, faxes, inter-office mailers	The ubiquitous 24/7 paperless office
FTP (VPN)	Backup, restore, transfer, and sharing of common information	Moves lots of data fast, accesses shared project assets, and no travel costs

Some software companies are built on the basis that their staff of experts are spread out and work exclusively from home offices. Many open source projects are created exactly on this model.

These tools (and others) provide the ability for teams to work in a geographically distributed manner. This is beneficial for the following team working arrangements:

- From home offices.
- Remotely, for those who have mobility handicaps.
- Different shifts or hours.
- A common language (for example, English) that isn't the chosen spoken language, but basic written English and software code become the "language of choice."
- Energy efficiency and travel expenses. (Travel is quickly becoming a luxury.)

All of these virtual office benefits can be quite a management, coordination, and motivation challenge. Personal contact and motivational tips and techniques presented earlier in this chapter become vital for you to energize folks and to encourage collaboration. E-mail, for example, can be heartbreaking when the content is misinterpreted by the receiver. In addition, e-mail and IM can easily become a crutch when non-actionable chit chat messaging becomes constantly disruptive. For this very reason, it is wise to not encourage e-mail to be a team member's number-one method of communication. If a situation is urgent, consider another form of communications (like the telephone or face to face).

You'll need to take more care to ensure that the virtual team is truly performing, and according to PMBOK, this includes resolving conflicts, making buy-in decisions by the team, and sharing the credit (where credit is due).

When acquiring talent, there are a couple of key theories that look promising but also have a very "dark side" (see Table 9.14).

Table 9.14 Halo and Expectancy Theories

Theory	Positive Assumption	Downside
Halo Effect (also known as **Halo Theory**)	A great technical talent will become a great manager (if someone is good at one job, they'll be good at another).	The best programmer will often be promoted to a management role, but if they don't have leadership skills, the company lost a great programmer and gained a lousy manager. Mitigation? Train them to be successful!
Expectancy Theory	The employee who works continuous long hours on the project assumes that they'll be appropriately rewarded.	The tester working nonstop hours might expect a reward relative to the amount of effort. They'll be extremely disappointed when the project is done. Mitigation? Set realistic expectations up front.

Outputs of the Acquire Project Team process are as follows:

■ **Project staff assignments:** This is the primary output of this process. This document (or set of documents) should indicate *who* is assigned to *what* key activities and *when* they are assigned. (You may not want to broadcast an individual's role six months before you need it!)

This list should also be available in a team e-mail address list so that electronic correspondence can be directed to the entire team as a whole using a single name. Needless to say, this list will probably change as resources change during a project's life cycle.

For fast-paced, ever-changing agile projects, keeping staff assignments updated and visible enables stakeholders to always be aware of everyone's roles.

■ **Resource calendars:** Already identified as important inputs to other processes (see the Procurement knowledge area sections in Chapter 6 and the Estimate Activity Resources process in Chapter 7), the resource calendar documents the time period that resources are available.

   If your organization is focused on consulting project work, the resource calendar becomes invaluable to help manage the ever-changing assignments as customers and unplanned business relationships change. (And you can't avoid that!) If, on the other hand, your workload tends to be fairly static and the resources are already product-oriented, this becomes less important.

■ **Project Management Plan updates:** Where PMBOK Third Edition indicates that only the Staffing Management Plan is updated, the Fourth Edition rightly assumes that any part of the Project Management Plan may be impacted with changes made in the Acquire Project Team process. Specifically, the components of the Human Resource Plan (refer to Figure 9.11) may have to be updated according to how well you acquire resources for your project (and which resources are going to be available). Not having the right staffing available when required will usually have a direct impact on the project schedule (see Chapter 7, "Master the Art of Scheduling").

BEST PRACTICE It is your job to make sure that you have the right resources available at the right time to meet the project schedule.

Develop Project Team

How you develop the team and improve your team's performance is really one of the most important of the Human Resource Management processes, and yet it can be the process on which you spend little or no time.

BEST PRACTICE Develop your team by keeping the members motivated.

Inputs to the Develop Project Team process are as follows:

■ **Human Resource Plan:** This plan, specifically the Staffing Management Plan, should include strategies and plans for developing the team members on the project. This should include rewards, performance feedback, and additional training, all with the purpose of motivating and focusing your staff. Whatever tools and techniques that are designed in the plan, they should be simple and reasonable to implement—it doesn't help to plan for all sorts of things that you won't have time to follow up with.

Plan on frequent performance feedback sessions, even if you simply list the top two or three tasks that each individual must perform. Going over these weekly, bi-weekly, or monthly is important for you, the project, and especially the individual.

This technique reduces project risk, gives the individual constructive guidance and feedback, and also provides overall feedback that can be used when you need to fulfill the dreaded annual performance review.

Even if the team member doesn't report to you, coordinate with the functional manager so that at least one of you is delivering regular individual performance feedback.

■ **Project staff assignments:** Created from the Acquire Project Team process, you need a list of who the team members are and a brief overview of what they are working on. (Don't forget to keep this updated as the project goes on.)
■ **Resource calendars:** Last but not least, it is always good to know the availability of talent for the project. This helps you plan for events or whatever you plan to do to develop the team.

Tools and techniques for the Develop Project Team process are shown in Table 9.15.

Table 9.15 Develop Project Team Tools and Techniques

Tools and Techniques	How to Use Them
Interpersonal skills	Also known as "soft skills," or "general management skills," you can reduce project issues by adopting a style that emphasizes listening, empathy, influence, anticipating and handling concerns, and so on. Do not underestimate the importance of developing these skills (even with software developers).
Training	Whatever can be reasonably afforded (time and cost), you should ensure that the team members get the opportunity to enhance their competencies, which in turn benefits the team. Formal, planned training can be online, computer-based, and in a classroom. Informal, unplanned training tends to focus on mentoring, on-the-job communication, observation, conversation, and performance feedback.

Tools and Techniques	How to Use Them
Team-building activities	This is any activity that enhances the cohesiveness of the team. This usually doesn't happen naturally (unless the team has a long-standing working relationship), so it needs development (hence, this Develop Project Team process). As a project progresses, team-building usually becomes more important. Team-building, if forced, will undoubtedly fail. Team-building, if performed on a regular basis, can be incredibly successful, especially when you've created a shared goal and the entire team is involved.
	Team-building can take place as a special topic in a regular meeting (like a "bug hunt," prioritizing and discussing key defects impacting getting to the next milestone). It can also take on a special event (dinner out for the team, a milestone achievement party, and so on).
	To be successful, you'll need management support and the commitment of the team members. It isn't unusual for a team to go through several stages of development, as discussed in "Understanding Team Dynamics" in Chapter 10.
Recognition and rewards	As originally planned in the Staffing Management Plan (of the Human Resource Plan), the goal is to provide a ***win-win*** recognition and reward environment.
	A ***win-lose*** environment is one where, for example, you encourage what you think is a team-building contest, but there is a winner and a loser. Not good. Another is when you mistakenly publicly recognize someone for heroic acts of performance, but the reality was that it took the entire team to create that success. You effectively rewarded the individual and alienated the rest of the team. Even worse.
	A ***lose-lose*** environment is where both the project and the team lose. This can happen when you attempt to entice the team to go "above and beyond" with a reward system, but instead set them up for failure. Don't believe it? See the note immediately following this table.
	There are many publications and studies performed regarding recognition and rewards. I've already presented some organizational theories in this chapter in the section entitled "Develop Human Resource Plan." In addition, Chapter 10 discusses all sorts of motivational techniques focused on communicating with your team.

(continued)

Tools and Techniques	How to Use Them
Ground rules	Ground rules? Does this sound a little like kindergarten? According to PMBOK, having a few ground rules can establish proper expectations of team behavior. For example, a ground rule may be that everyone on the project is responsible to protect the intellectual property (IP) of the project. Another ground rule might be that all team members are required to attend team meetings and that the dialog must be centered around transparency, honesty, and (most of all) facts. Another ground rule might be that if someone gets "hot under the collar" toward another team member that they will never, ever throw a phone at them. (It only happened once.)
	As a project progresses and the team gets used to working together, the ground rules will change. If you find it necessary, keep these rules published (although most teams would consider that ground rules are mostly common sense). Whatever you do, don't go overboard with ground rules that discourage effective team-building.
Co-location	Very clearly a benefit of some agile software methodologies (see "Why XP Has Transformed the Agile World" in Chapter 7), placing team members in close proximity can make a huge difference in improving team morale and communication while reducing project risk.
	Common co-location methods include putting everyone in a war room where all the team members work. If the project is being directed toward a specific customer, it isn't too unusual to set up shop at a customer's site. (This can be required if the project is with the government, and there are significant security requirements. Most of us know all about those stints, especially if you work in the Washington, D.C. area!) One common characteristic of a co-located project is that it tends to be temporary for that project (or for a phase of a project).

NOTE

If you incentivize your project team to meet a milestone by a specific (usually unattainable) date and if the team doesn't achieve the commitment, what do you, as the project/software manager, do? Reward them anyway? Establish yet another goal? Punish? Opportunities like this may accidentally work once in a career, but after-the-fact awards are significantly more effective at motivating key individuals.

Dangling incentives may work for individual sales people, but the practice definitely can backfire with software development teams. You thought you were *developing* the team, and instead you accidentally *demotivated* the team!

BEST PRACTICE Awards are significantly better than rewards from incentives. And private awards (unless you are recognizing the entire team) have the best result.

Outputs for the Develop Project Team process are discussed in the following sections.

Team Performance Assessments

Evaluate how the team performs as a unit. While avoiding "touchy-feely" surveys that unscientifically test a team's morale, it is best to validate the team based on objective project-oriented criteria. As a result, you should be able to assess how the team is developing.

BEST PRACTICE High-performance teams are characterized by their ability to achieve results according to plan.

High-performing teams usually have great communication and trust. To assess if you have a high-performing team, validate the following:

1. Are objectives being met?
2. Is the project on schedule?
3. Is the project on or under budget?

If the answer to one or more of these is no, then you and the team should identify root causes and team development activities in order to correct them. Table 9.16 shows some common issues that require development of the team.

Table 9.16 Developing the Team to Improve Performance

Possible Root Cause	Development Opportunity
Team attrition	Find out why members are leaving and turn that around.
Defocused	Align (and continue to reinforce) the team to a common purpose and avoid distractions.
Need training	Add technical mentors, sign up immediately for training, or do whatever it takes to get the team confident of the skills needed to complete the project.
Communications breakdown	Make sure communication techniques are useful, consistent, and effective (see Chapter 10 for more guidance).

Overall, treat the team performance assessment as development of the team based on continuous improvement (starting with using the tools and techniques identified in this process to develop the team). See Figure 9.15. And, as usual with agile, iterative software projects, repeat this cycle throughout the project on a regular basis.

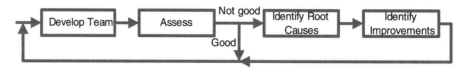

FIGURE 9.15
Assess and test overall team performance.

As you assess and test the team's performance, make sure that you document what you encounter and what works (and doesn't work). This information is invaluable as a lessons learned benefit for future projects.

Enterprise Environmental Factors Updates

You'll need to ensure that personnel administration records are updated, including employee training records, skills developed, and performance assessments.

Manage Project Team

Once you have assessed the team's performance and have hopefully identified the improvements that should be introduced, you need to monitor and control the human resource aspects of team management. This will mean that you have to mentor, guide, give feedback, and possibly issue change requests as a result of personnel issues relating to how well the Human Resource Plan is being tracked.

It may seem ridiculous to associate inputs, tools, techniques, and outputs to the process of managing a software development team, but having a sound baseline can always assist you in managing the most difficult, time-consuming, and sometimes exasperating component of any project—its personnel! Inputs to this process are discussed in the following sections.

Project Staff Assignments

This identifies who is on the team and how they will be used for the project.

Human Resource Plan

This plan is created in the Develop Human Resource Plan process and includes three key components:

■ **Roles and responsibilities:** What each individual (or the type of role) will be expected to be accountable for (typically visualized as a RACI diagram).
■ **Project organization charts:** Summarizes the hierarchical structure of the team members.
■ **Staffing Management Plan:** Provides how and when the project will be staffed, released, rewarded, and trained (among other things pertinent to planning for effective use of personnel on the project).

Team Performance Assessments

These are assessments of the project team's performance based on how well the project is progressing, the identification of personnel-related root causes, and actions required to resolve those issues. This is a key output of the Develop Project Team process.

Performance Reports

A key output of the Communications Management's Report Performance process (see the section "Report Performance" in Chapter 10), the latest project status reports and forecasts can help in determining the proper next step in recognizing and adjusting to human resource needs. This can include but isn't limited to the following:

■ Future staffing needs
■ Recognition, awards, and rewards
■ Updates to adjust the Staffing Management Plan (a part of the Human Resource Plan)

> Performance reports should clearly and objectively indicate just how well the project is progressing versus the expected costs, time, and scope (in other words, the Triple Constraint).

Organizational Process Assets

Assets you may wish to take advantage of include the following:

■ Certificates of appreciation (a form used for recognition)
■ Bonus request forms (a form used for awards and rewards)
■ Personnel performance reports (for performance feedback, good and bad)

The tools and techniques of the Manage Project Team process are discussed in the following sections.

Observation and Conversation

Generally informal techniques by which team members are monitored to make sure that they are progressing toward goals. This can take many forms, including noticing motivational levels, demeanor, interactions, attitude, and so forth. Management by Walking Around (MbWA) is a great technique to lighten the "management assessment" stigma by regularly speaking to, questioning, mentoring, and listening to team members. The overall goal is to learn more about work processes taking place, but also to encourage two-way communication between team members and management. Intangible by-products of MbWA that can assist in highlighting human resource accomplishments and issues include the following:

- Team members enjoy telling about their accomplishments.
- Personnel issues may become more apparent (so that management can proactively repair things).

Project Performance Appraisals

A key component of your job, in a managerial position, is to evaluate a team member's performance. There can be many ways to communicate performance with team members, but the three that are most popular are shown in Figure 9.16.

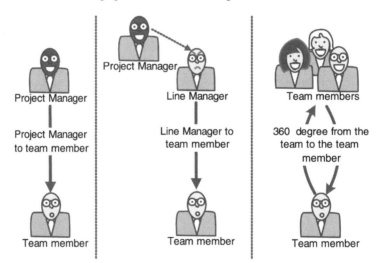

FIGURE 9.16
Communicating performance appraisal feedback.

The diagram is subdivided into three groups. The group on the left shows the role where you, as the project manager, deliver performance feedback to each team member. The middle group shows the project manager informing the functional manager of a team member's performance (more like "whispering"), who then ultimately delivers performance feedback to the team member. (Not the most efficient use of time, but this may be the way it should be done in a matrix organization.)

Finally, the group to the right in Figure 9.16 can be performed not only by the project manager, but also by the entire team, using a format commonly known as *360 degree feedback* (or *multirater feedback*). This is where a team member has the opportunity to receive performance feedback from other team members, including yourself.

The feedback is usually submitted with an assessment form. The most effective 360 degree technique provides feedback based on behaviors typically required for the customer and the team. Ultimately, the purpose of the 360 degree feedback is to assist each individual to understand the strengths and weaknesses that can be acted upon to improve his or her personal development. The 360 degree technique encourages a degree of transparency found only in the best-run organizations.

According to the American Society for Training and Development (ASTD), which annually reviews the training and personnel development practices of more than 750 firms, 55 of them are regarded as leading-edge and high-performing organizations. In fact, according to ASTD, the 55 best organizations are steadily increasing their investment in these systems (see Figure 9.17). Perhaps due to peer pressure, the best-performing companies that ASTD monitored dramatically increased their use of 360 degree feedback. Regardless, more and more companies are seeing the benefit of two-way performance review processes. An individual's annual performance review should include a personalized development plan and well-integrated 360 degree feedback.

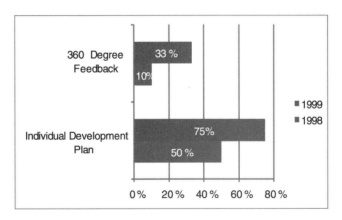

FIGURE 9.17
Adoption of individual development plans and 360
feedback (ASTD).

According to Susan M. Heathfield in her article "360 Degree Feedback: The Good, the Bad, and the Ugly," 360 feedback offers some substantial benefits and some real negatives (see Table 9.17).

Table 9.17 360 Feedback Positives and Negatives

Benefits (Positives)	Negatives
Improves feedback from more sources than just the manager.	Insufficient information to help you improve; follow-through requires a change management plan.
Develops teams to work more effectively with each other.	If the feedback isn't directed toward the goals of the organization, the results may appear to be scattered and disconnected.
One of the best methods to understand personal and organizational development needs.	Becomes a "feeding frenzy" toward the negative and weaknesses.
Assists in career development.	Without sufficient training, consolidating the feedback may artificially inflate (or deflate) results.
Reduces discrimination risk.	
Improves customer service.	

> 360 feedback can highlight organizational disconnects that aren't readily apparent. There is a personal story I can't avoid telling you about. After I set on-time delivery goals with the team, they performed a "360" on me. The first feedback they gave? "Why should you hold us accountable when no one else in the company was being held to *their* goals?"

If performed correctly, it turns your organization into a truly transparent, performance-driven team. But if started haphazardly, it could create a disaster that could destroy team manship, as well as confidence in management, and require a long time to recover (possibly months). There are a few rules that can improve the odds of having a successful 360 feedback session:

1. Feedback gathering and communication should be administered by someone trained and experienced in 360 feedback techniques.
2. All team member feedback should be anonymous in order to spare hurt feelings and to encourage more constructive criticism.
3. There must be a plan (or template) that guides each team member to adopt this feedback into a positive course of personal development action.

NOTE

The use of 360 degree feedback can also be used with contractors, part-time employees, and even vendors.

Conflict Management

Keeping conflict in check helps raise productivity (performance) and enhance working relationships (morale). According to Robert Bolton's *People Skills*, experience should dictate that conflict is unavoidable, and you need to anticipate it. Conflict often becomes detached from its initial causes and easily escalates until it consumes the entire team unless you control it immediately.

Differing opinions is a good thing (a desired thing) for any project and can result in increased creativity and better decision making. (Some of the best ideas can occur when the team is forced to "think outside of the box!") This is the positive side of conflict. This is echoed by noted author of the book *Overcoming the Five Dysfunctions of a Team*, Patrick Lencioni, who states the following:

> "If team members are never pushing one another outside of their emotional comfort zones during discussions, then it is extremely likely that they're not making the best decisions for the organization."

According to PMBOK, there are several stages of handling conflict, as shown in Figure 9.18.

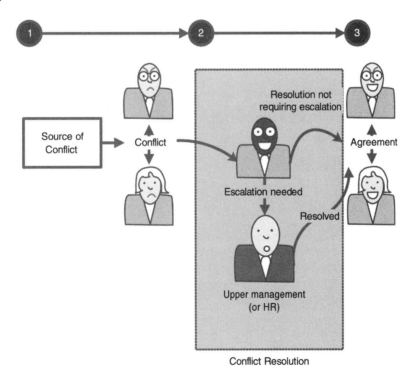

FIGURE 9.18
Conflict handling flow.

Viewing Figure 9.18 from left to right, the source of conflict initiates where two or more team members have a conflict. What is typically the source of conflict?

1. The source of conflict can come from many sources, resulting in two or more team members being at odds. According to Tony Johnson (author of *PMP Exam Success Series: Certification Exam Manual*), the biggest source of conflict starts when scheduling and resources expectations are set, as early as the planning stages. Contrary to popular belief, personality is the least source of conflict.
2. If the conflict is major, it needs to be resolved by you. There are two possible outcomes: You resolve the conflict without escalation, or you need some assistance requiring upper management or, if that fails, the Human Resource (HR) department.
3. Finally, the conflict is resolved among all parties.

> According to Andy Crowe's *The PMP Exam*, even though conflict may occur among team members, it is usually between project and functional management.

It is rarely that easy. PMBOK provides guidance to both recognize individuals' styles as well as techniques for resolving conflict. In fact, some styles are constructive to resolve conflicts, and some are destructive and may offer little to no value in conflict resolution (see Table 9.18).

Table 9.18 Team Members' Styles (or Roles) That Impact How Conflicts Are Handled

Constructive	Destructive
Initiators—Actively initiate ideas.	*Aggressors*—Openly hostile and opposed to the project or achieving any resolution at all.
Information seekers—Open communicators and dig into the facts (the why); positive but can be a little frustrating for others.	*Blockers*—Attempt to interrupt the communication flow or block access to pertinent information.
Information givers—Great knowledge and openly communicate it.	*Withdrawers*—Most likely to not participate (or even appear disinterested), which usually impacts overall team morale, especially when you need everyone "pumped up" to perform.

(continued)

Constructive	Destructive
Encouragers—Able to be positive and communicate what is possible (not on what is impossible).	Recognition Seekers—"What benefits me?" typifies this style, which can ultimately jeopardize the success of the project.
Clarifiers—Want to make sure that everyone's "on the same page." (Tend to be intuitive if they notice not everyone is understanding.)	*Topic Jumpers*—Constantly changing the subject or bringing up irrelevant facts. (Sometimes bad use of humor is introduced.)
Harmonizers—To increase the understanding, they will enhance the information with more useful facts.	*Dominators*—When one person dominates the discussion, other great ideas become less important (also known as the "class bully"!).
Summarizers—When content can be overwhelming, this style oftentimes requires re-communication to increase understanding.	*Devil's Advocates*—Enjoy taking a contrarian view to most statements or suggestions made, and although this can be a positive, if not controlled, it discourages open communication and stalls forward progress.
Gate Keepers—Draw people in by encouraging participation by all who should be involved.	

Referring back to the wonderful book *People Skills*, Robert Bolton has identified the following steps he calls the *conflict resolution method*:

1. **Treat the other person with respect:** Sometimes the tone of discussion, your body movements, and even eye contact can signal if you are open to discussion or already have your mind made up. To kick off conflict resolution (especially those started via e-mail), don't attempt to respond initially the same way. It is far more effective to get face to face or call on the telephone (if the parties aren't in close proximity).

2. **Listen until you "experience the other side":** The importance of showing empathy and that you understand the other person's viewpoint is critical to reaching resolution. The author believes it is never a good idea to make the superficial comment, "I know how you feel." Instead, listen and reflect out loud what you think you heard. Once you get the acknowledgement from the other party, you can move to step 3. (Hopefully, this step begins to reduce the emotional side of the conflict.)

3. **State your views, needs, and perception:** You are the mediator and facilitator, and it is important for you to express the view, goals, requirements, and overall perception. This step may be unnecessary, but briefly stating your view on the situation will help frame up the resolution.

4. **Come to a common understanding:** There are several techniques I'll discuss in the next few paragraphs that can be used, depending on the circumstances and your style.

This simple set of steps can provide an easy-to-remember process when you have to resolve a conflict. Your role as a leader is to pick up on these behavior dynamics and to perform the following actions to ensure that you come to the appropriate conflict resolution:

- For *constructive* behavior, encourage that this behavior is best suited to achieve resolution.
- For *destructive* behavior, you should try to diminish or even eliminate that behavior.

There is no single technique that will work for all types of conflicts but, according to PMBOK, a more proactive leadership approach is preferable over a reactive approach (see Table 9.19).

Table 9.19 Conflict Resolution Techniques

Technique	Description
Withdrawal (avoidance)	Ignore the problem and hope it goes away. This is reactive and not a suggested technique, since a timely resolution rarely takes place. For example, "Joseph is difficult to work with. Perhaps he'll get frustrated and leave the team soon."
Smoothing (accommodating)	Downplay the conflict instead of dealing with it head on. Typically, smoothing doesn't solve the problem; it merely attempts to diminish it. For example, "Even though this project is much more complicated than the previous one, let's use the same design technique and hopefully it will work." Conflicts that are smoothed tend to require more attempts later to solve (thus frustrating everyone).
Forcing	A direct order or threat is used to resolve a conflict or issue. It brings to bear whatever force or power is necessary and typically doesn't resolve the underlying problem. It reduces team morale and is never a good, long-term solution. Do you want your department to be known as an organization that forces decisions (regardless of the circumstances)? No! For example, "You keep on bringing up how difficult it is to solve this algorithm. You've already been given two days; if you don't solve it by tonight, I'm pulling you off the project."

(continued)

Technique	Description
Compromise	This is an activity where both parties sacrifice something in order to reach an agreement. The idea is that "somewhere in the middle" there must be common ground. Arriving at a compromise is oftentimes viewed as a "lose-lose," resulting in a less than satisfying solution.
	For example, "Beth, you want this new feature included, and Joseph, you don't want the feature included at all—in fact, you have the concern that this breaks up the simplified flow we've always strived for in this product. For example, "I know—we'll add just one core subfeature and see what our customers think. Beth, you get part way there, and Joseph, we haven't compromised the product much at all. You like? Great! Okay. Good meeting!" Yuck. That dialog doesn't feel so good, does it?
Problem solving (confrontation)	By definition, solving the problem involves constructive confrontation to address the problem. Since you are driving at the root cause, it must never become personal! For a great, personalized example of a problem solving situation, see the note that follows Figure 9.19.

To summarize techniques used to handle conflict resolution, there are always cases where you need to adapt a specific technique to the situation, but Figure 9.19 shows the range of techniques from the least amount of effort (on your part) to the most amount of effort.

FIGURE 9.19
Conflict resolution techniques require varying amounts of effort.

Withdrawal and smoothing techniques rarely resolve the conflict, forcing may work occasionally but is absolutely the worst type of conflict resolution, compromise doesn't really satisfy anybody, and true problem solving is the best technique.

Ultimately, the conflict should get resolved (and not necessarily to everyone's satisfaction). The negative side of conflict can occur if the conflict escalates with little to no resolution for an extended length of time.

NOTE

In summary, what is the best way to address team conflict? Use expert judgment by addressing the issue early (do not let any conflict linger!), keep it private (not everybody needs to be dragged into it), stick to the facts, and use an open, direct yet collaborative approach to achieve a resolution that reinforces the project's common goal. If you need to take it beyond the team itself, use your Decision Pyramid (see the section "Introducing the Decision Pyramid" in Chapter 5.)

I remember years ago our technical writing team wanted to restructure the documentation from one massive book into several smaller books. The reasoning was that binding costs for a mammoth "700 pager" were too much, and it allowed three books to be owned by three different writers (instead of three writers fighting with each other working on a single book).

Of course, some of the managers didn't like the change at all. During the course of the meeting, the technical writing manager was standing her ground, and you could tell folks were getting really frustrated. The customer support manager, who had been noticeably quiet, was asked for his opinion. He said, "Customers are going to be frustrated, and our field service people will undoubtedly forget one of the three books, so they'll be calling us for assistance. We'll end up being their live manual, and the service calls could go on for hours."

Good information.

However, we almost went ahead and just sided with the technical writer's point of view when one of the engineering managers blurted out, "Say, I thought our number-one priority was satisfying the customer? The one-book idea is what will work best for customers, and the stupid [she was always blunt] three-book idea serves our own internal needs best. What gives?"

She was right—case closed! I remember to this day how I closed the meeting:

"Thank you all for the feedback, and although dividing the manual into smaller manuals is an innovative idea, none of us can justify doing that if this negatively impacts customers. For that reason, we will keep the single-book concept."

It was the right solution for our customers and customer-facing staff members.

According to Patrick Lencioni's *Overcoming the Five Dysfunctions of a Team*, in order to validate that you have successfully resolved a conflict, the following three points need to have occurred:

1. The decision has clarity and is understood among the appropriate stakeholders.
2. Facts are facts—the reasoning behind the resolution is factual, avoiding subjective (and oftentimes emotional) assumptions and ambiguity.
3. The decision has buy-in but does not have to require consensus.

In the book *Leading Geeks*, Paul Glen makes a special point regarding your role in supporting conflict resolution. First off, recognize that there is a difference between *conflict* and *debate*.

Your role is to ensure that forums are open-minded and as egoless as possible. When a debate erodes into conflict, it is always best to let the individuals arrive at a solution among themselves. When that isn't possible, separate individual beliefs into what is best for the project. You, as a leader, should illuminate the trade-offs (sometimes technical, sometimes business, and sometimes both). This tool is exactly like the Decision Pyramid (which is mentioned often throughout this book) and can help objectively resolve the conflict.

Once self-interested politics become the norm, it can be difficult to change this evolving culture into a more positive one.

Interpersonal Skills

With greater emphasis in PMBOK's Fourth Edition, it is recognized that project managers should use the appropriate interpersonal skills and expert judgment to ensure that the team is working to its full potential. This involves three interpersonal skills you'll use the most with your team throughout the project (see Figure 9.20).

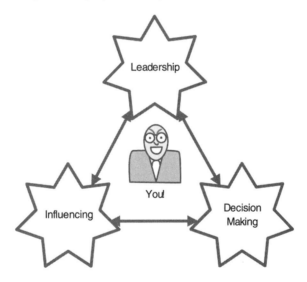

FIGURE 9.20
Balancing interpersonal skills throughout a project.

■ **Leadership (including inspiration):** Successful projects require strong leadership skills. You being excited, evangelistic, and positive about the project's goals can't help but rub off on the team. (If, on the other hand, your style is interpreted as "just another project," your team will typically take on that same less-than-positive perspective.)

■ **Influencing:** Your ability to influence team members (and stakeholders) in a timely manner is important. Does influencing have to be synonymous with politicking? Nope. Influencing has the following positive characteristics:
1. Clearly communicating with the team.
2. Persuading to get buy-in (even if you can't get to consensus).
3. A listener who is considerate of other viewpoints.
4. Maintaining mutual trust (which oftentimes encourages a team's commitment).
5. Gathering relevant and critical information to address important issues.
6. Taking a fact-based approach (for example, "this feature will bring us an additional $200K of revenue if we do it according to specifications") and never relying on emotional responses (for example, "just do it—it is what I want").

■ **Decision making:** The ability to negotiate and make the best, timely decision. This is typically harder than you think, but your team relies on you to direct overall decision making. (Otherwise, a team wouldn't need any management at all!) Some key ingredients to making effective decisions include the following:
1. Focus on goals the team is collectively serving. (Remember the Decision Pyramid?)
2. Follow a decision-making process. (Hopefully you have one, and every decision doesn't take on a different approach.)
3. Make sure you know the environmental factors that influence your team's decision. (For example, investing in an export feature that will support a file format that is about to become an evolving standard might be important for customer and competitive reasons.)
4. Develop personal qualities of the team members. (For example, delegating where you'd normally make the decision yourself will go a long way.)
5. Stimulate team creativity. (For example, even though you might have an architect on board, why not get a subset of the team to design a subsystem and use the architect to critique and mentor them?)
6. Most important, proactively manage opportunity and risk. (Remember, risks can be either negative or positive.)

Issue Log

As conflicts and issues arise throughout a project, a log provides a trail that identifies who is assigned the work and what the final resolution is (see Table 9.20).

Table 9.20 Issue Log

Date	Human Resource Issue and Resolution
Jan 10, 09	The chief architect disagreed with the approach taken for the Undo subsystem. The requirements state only one level, but according to Johan, the software architect, it took no more work to design a multi-level Undo feature. Was resolved 10 days later, once the product manager and the lead engineer reviewed his concerns. The technical design was modified to everyone's satisfaction. In fact, we'll enable one level with this project and enable multiple levels in a subsequent release as a new feature!
. . .	. . .

Why maintain yet another document? Once again, keeping track of what human resource conflicts and issues take place may be very helpful for lessons learned and performance review purposes. By the way, keeping this information in a document is just as good as a small database or a spreadsheet.

> Bear in mind that some conflict information should not be as publicly accessible as others!

Outputs to this process have definitely changed between the PMBOK Third and Fourth Editions, as discussed in the following sections.

Change Requests

There are many reasons that staff (human resource) issues can impact the project so much that change requests have to be escalated. These include the following:

- Team could be dysfunctional, and perhaps some drastic changes in personnel are required.
- Team member's skills could overall be underqualified (can't keep up) or even over-qualified (completely bored, resulting in less than quality results).
- Understaffed—you need additional help that was unplanned (and quite possibly not able to fit into your project budget).
- *And many others. . . .*

What could happen as a result of change requests? You could...

- Move resources to different assignments (or even different projects).
- Outsource (or contract) the work.
- Replace nonperforming team members.
- As a result of burnout, give stressed workers some much-needed time off.

Ultimately, we are dealing with a "people business," and any organization should be used to handling issues like these. You'll need to immediately enter into the Integrated Change Control process.

The more proactive you can be to avoid having to react to human resource issues, the better. An example identified in PMBOK is the cross-training of team members with key skills (especially if only one engineer knows how to implement a core feature). Also, any recommended corrective actions that may help a team perform as planned include awards used, changing staff members, and training. If you notice that some software developers struggle at maintaining regular attendance, you (and the team) may wish to enforce standard *core hours* so that the team benefits from the much-needed access of staff. (A signal that this could become a serious problem is when it is difficult to accommodate everyone's schedule to plan for meetings during the work week.)

Project Management Plan Updates

Any component of the Project Management Plan (costing, schedule, and scope) may have to be adjusted to react to human resource actions. Almost all of these will impact the Human Resource Plan (in other words, the Staffing Management Plan, roles and responsibilities, and project organization charts).

Enterprise Environmental Factors Updates

Organizational factors that may require updates include team members' skills and performance appraisal feedback.

Organizational Process Asset Updates

Lessons learned documentation is probably at the heart of how you've handled critical human resource situations. There may also be templates, policies, and procedures that could be adjusted based on what you've learned on your project.

BIBLIOGRAPHY

Bolton, Robert. *People Skills: How to Assert Yourself, Listen to Others, and Resolve Conflicts.* New York: Simon & Schuster, 1979.

Crowe, Andy. *The PMP Exam: How to Pass on Your First Try, Third Edition.* Kennesaw, GA: Velociteach, 2008.

DeMarco, Tom and Timothy Lister. *Peopleware: Productive Projects and Teams, 2nd Edition.* New York: Dorset House Publishing, 1999.

Emmons, Jon. *Management By Walking Around.* March 28, 2006 (www.lifeaftercoffee.com/2006/03/28/management-by-walking-around).

Glen, Paul. *Leading Geeks: How to Manage and Lead the People Who Deliver Technology.* San Francisco: Jossey-Bass, 2003.

Hall, Tracy, Helen Sharp, Sarah Beecham, Nathan Baddoo, and Hugh Robinson. "What Do We Know About Developer Motivation?" *IEEE Software,* July/August 2008, 25(4), pp. 92–94 (http://ieeexplore.ieee.org/xpl/freeabs_all.jsp?arnumber=4548414).

Heathfield, Susan M. "360 Degree Feedback: The Good, the Bad, and the Ugly." About.com Human Resources Guide (http://humanresources.about.com/od/360feedback/a/360feedback.htm).

Hofstede, Geert and Gert Jan Hofstede. *Cultures and Organizations: Software of the Mind.* New York: McGraw-Hill, 2005.

Johnson, Tony. *PMP Exam Success Series: Certification Exam Manual.* Carrollton, TX: Crosswind Project Management, 2006.

Kliem, Ralph L. and Irwin S. Ludin. *Project Management Practitioner's Handbook.* New York: AMACOM, 1998.

Lencioni, Patrick. *Overcoming the Five Dysfunctions of a Team: A Field Guide for Leaders, Managers, and Facilitators.* San Francisco: Jossey-Bass, 2005.

Nelson, Bob and Peter Economy. *Managing for Dummies.* Foster City, CA: IDG Books Worldwide, 1996.

Project Management Institute, Inc. *A Guide to the Project Management Body of Knowledge: PMBOK Guide, Third Edition.* Newton Square, PA: Project Management Institute, 2004.

Project Management Institute, Inc. *A Guide to the Project Management Body of Knowledge: PMBOK Guide, Fourth Edition.* Newton Square, PA: Project Management Institute, 2008.

Spolsky, Joel, ed. *The Best Software Writing I.* New York: Springer-Verlag, 2005.

Spolsky, Joel. "The Joel Test: 12 Steps to Better Code." 9, August 2000 (www.joelonsoftware.com/articles/fog0000000043.html).

Wikipedia.org. *Theory X and Theory Y* (http://en.wikipedia.org/wiki/Theory_X_and_theory_Y).

10 Create a Winning Workplace

Now that you've seen almost all of the knowledge areas, I've saved the best for last! You've now hopefully mastered all of the planning and process tools and techniques. And based on the prior chapter, you should have a good handle on the all-important people needs on a project. According to Rita Mulcahy's *PM Crash Course*:

Q: What is the number-one employee complaint about their management or project?

A: Poor communication.

She goes on to say that the secret to effective communications is to plan for it. This chapter presents the Communications Management knowledge area as you've never seen it before. Here are the concepts will be covered:

- Why communication is so critical.
- Planning for effective communication (emphasizing collaboration instead of competition, as well as developing your own style of communication).
- Distributing the right amount of useful information to the team and stakeholders.
- Managing stakeholder expectations.
- Reporting project performance in one page or less.
- Living by the PMBOK "Code."

WHY IS COMMUNICATION SO IMPORTANT?

Communication, as it relates to software and project management, is simply the tasks that disseminate information. Communication can be both written and oral and is never performed by inference ("I thought you knew. . ."). You must take your role in communication to heart because according to PMBOK,

"The majority (90%) of your job is to communicate."

It isn't enough that you just communicate—you need to be incredibly *effective* at communication. There are many organizations that can help improve the effectiveness of your communication style: Toastmasters, Association of Training and Development (ASTD), and the Society of Technical Communicators (STC), to name a few. Communication is definitely multidimensional. First, who is the audience you need to communicate with?

- **Internal:** Within a project to the team.
- **External:** Outside the project to customers, media, management, other project teams, and so on.
- **Vertical:** Up and down the organizational structure.
- **Horizontal:** With peers.

BEST PRACTICE Communication is never "one size fits all"—tailor what is communicated to be beneficial and specific to the audience.

Then what type of communication is actually performed?

- **Formal:** Reports, memos, briefings, SOW, and presentations (typically unidirectional communication).
- **Informal:** E-mails, meetings, hallway chit-chat, and ad hoc discussions (usually two-way meetings).
- **Official:** Newsletters, white papers, and annual reports.
- **Unofficial:** Off-the-record comments.

All of these communication categories can be either written, oral, or both. And there are the ever-present verbal and non-verbal dimensions where your body language (crossing of arms) and voice inflections (raising your voice) can impact how the listener receives the information you are communicating. PMI strongly believes that proactive and thorough communication is a key ingredient to a project's success. But these aren't the only key ingredients to effective communication.

So, How Often Do You Communicate?

I bet you think you spend a fair amount of time communicating. Being totally honest (don't worry, your boss won't see this), how do you spend your time on average every work day communicating?

Percentage	Doing What?
	In meetings (with peers, management, and so on)
	Communicating with the project team
	Miscellaneous time unaccounted for (time flies?)
	Behind closed doors (writing reports, planning, . . .)
	Other. . .
	Total (should add up to 100 percent)

How you fill in this simple survey says a lot about your style and that of the culture of your organization (which more often than not influences your style).

If you belong to a startup where action and "sweat equity" (meaning you don't sleep much) prevail, you might find yourself with the profile shown in Figure 10.1. The profile of a startup environment shows that the vast majority of time is spent with the team, and the rest of the time primarily in meetings (which probably occur late in the day and into the evening).

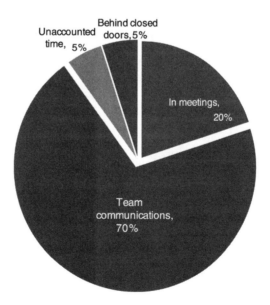

FIGURE 10.1
Time devoted to communication in a fast-paced startup environment.

What about e-mail (behind closed doors)? You could say that is communicating, and perhaps it is. (And perhaps it is required, especially dealing with remotely distributed team members.)

But all too often, assuming that sending an e-mail fulfills the act of communication is stretching the truth. Especially with important and time-sensitive information, an e-mail should always be followed up with personal contact of some kind (telephone call, meeting, and so on).

What about the communication required if you are with a larger company or perhaps one that is laden with meeting-itis (not a real word; see Figure 10.2). In this case, communication is also prevalent; however, the amount of time you spend with the team may not be quite enough.

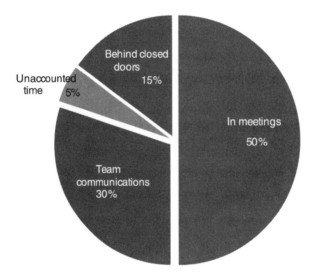

FIGURE 10.2
Communication based on a more bureaucratic,
meeting-bound culture.

Lastly, there might be a common ground that depends on the culture of the company, the team dynamics, and your own communications style (see Figure 10.3). With about half of your time spent communicating with the team, 30% in meetings, and the remainder spent working behind closed doors (planning, e-mail, and other activities), there is no available time left. In fact, I'd venture to say that you are constantly trying to catch up in order to stay on top of things.

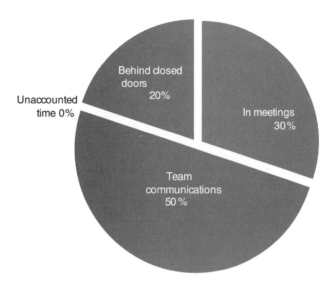

FIGURE 10.3
Balanced communication geared toward agile project development.

One additional communication scenario (not shown in a figure) is where you, as the leader, are basically introverted and don't enjoy spending more than a quarter of your time communicating with stakeholders or the team. (Don't laugh—I've met many managers in the software field who prefer to minimize the amount of time communicating.)

Table 10.1 is a summary of the four communication scenarios. I took the approach where the In Meetings and Team Communications values can be added together to represent active communication. The remaining values (Unaccounted Time plus Behind Closed Doors) represent non-communicating time. For the first three situations, all are greater than 80%, which is what you would expect a project or software manager to do. The main difference is that only the startup and the agile styles are team-centered communications. The bureaucratic style may have a lot of communication, but it is probably mostly formal and written content to upper management.

Finally, enter your own percentages that you filled out at the beginning of this section and see how you compare with the other scenarios.

Table 10.1 How Much of Your Day Do You Communicate?

Doing What	Startup	Bureaucracy	Agile	Introverted	Your Score
A. In meetings	20%	**50%**	30%	20%	
B. Team communications	**70%**	30%	**50%**	25%	
C. Unaccounted time	5%	5%	0%	5%	
D. Behind closed doors	5%	15%	20%	**50%**	
TOTAL	100%	100%	100%	100%	
Communicating (A+B)	**90%**	**80%**	**80%**	45%	
Non-communicating (C+D)	10%	20%	20%	**55%**	

WHAT COMMUNICATION SKILLS SHOULD YOU DEVELOP?

You might think that the communication skills you'll need to develop center around your ability to present statuses and to have that "gift of gab." Not exactly true. Let's go through the list that PMBOK suggests (and I'll add a few of my own based on historical lessons learned):

- **Being prepared with the information:** Before you communicate, know the project status and have the facts. (This enhances your credibility.)
- **Listening:** Cutting people off, hearing yourself speak, and not taking what you are hearing seriously is *not* the role of a successful project or software manager. Actively and effectively listen to what your team and stakeholders are saying.
- **Questioning and probing:** Without being obnoxious, your job is to ask the right questions to be sure that you understand ideas and situations fully.
- **Educating:** Through mentoring and guiding the team, you may even convince software developers to rise up to become a project or software manager, too!
- **Fact-finding:** Part of your job is to make it easier for the team to do their job, right? Right! Whenever some research needs to be done, rather than automatically load it on a busy developer's plate, you should take it on yourself. This may be as simple as locating another PC for the QA team, identifying software component libraries that do specific functions the team needs, or running interference with upper management to get technical training approved.
- **Setting and managing expectations:** Your team may be saying that it will take two days to complete a task (and that is probably what the product manager wants to hear), but you owe it to the team to plan on contingencies and risks, so you may have to set a schedule range that gets communicated to stakeholders. (You know, there's nothing wrong with coming in early on a schedule!)

■   **Persuading and negotiating:** Achieve mutually acceptable agreements or take action to get things done. Consensus building is an excellent technique, but it can be exhausting, especially if the team gets stuck brainstorming different approaches rather than getting things done. Keeping everyone on the team aware of the Decision Pyramid is always a good idea. You need to do your best to keep personal bias out of the decision making.

■   **Resolving conflicts:** If there is any issue that can upset the progress of a project or the team somehow gets entangled in a battle of wills, your role is to resolve the conflict as quickly as possible, using all the communication styles and expert judgment you can. (For more time-proven tips and techniques on managing conflict, refer to the "Manage Project Team" section in Chapter 9.)

■   **Communicating status and next steps:** Probably your most important communication skill to develop is the ability to ensure that the team and stakeholders understand the current project status and what is coming next.

THE CONUNDRUM OF EFFECTIVE COMMUNICATION—HOW MUCH IS ENOUGH?

In Ed Yourdon's superb *Death March*, he states that the ideal communications culture is one where the manager is "transparent" with information—total disclosure on current information that impacts the schedule, including project status, risk, constraints, and so on. (Full transparency is an agile requirement.)

BEST PRACTICE Effective communication must be timely, with the intent to build trust and loyalty among team members and stakeholders.

Since building trust is so important for the manager, the counterpoint to this approach is that the project/software manager could be shielding the team from anything that could possibly distract them. The solution that Yourdon proposes is that you present the basic information that is necessary to the project team. If questions are asked about information that wasn't covered, answer them as truthfully and honestly as you can (some information, of course, might be confidential).

In most cases, team members appreciate being spared the politics and other non-pertinent information. The key is to engage in as much open communication as you can without getting stuck with all of the details that can frequently derail or demotivate team members who need to remain focused on their work.

COMMUNICATING FOR SUCCESS

The PMBOK Communications Management knowledge area provides a rich set of processes to ensure that you properly disseminate information to all of the stakeholders. In many ways, communication is where everything on a project comes together.

OVERVIEW OF THE COMMUNICATIONS MANAGEMENT KNOWLEDGE AREA

PMBOK Fourth Edition has rearranged the processes and even added a new process (Identify Stakeholders) at the very beginning of a project's life cycle, as shown in Table 10.2.

Table 10.2 Communications Management Area Processes (PMBOK 4th Edition)

Process Groups				
	Implementation			
Initiating	**Planning**	**Executing**	**Monitoring & Controlling**	**Closing**
Identify Stakeholders	Plan Communications	Distribute Information Manage Stakeholder Expectations	Report Performance	

The Communications Management set of processes is composed of information gathering and reporting that is completely dependent on inputs and outputs from other knowledge area processes. Superb communication is vital for the success of agile software projects because so much is dependent on fast planning, fast execution, and fast reaction without the use of mounds of documentation.

COMMUNICATIONS MANAGEMENT IN THE INITIATING PROCESS GROUP

Never underestimate the role of a stakeholder on a project.

Identify Stakeholders

A *stakeholder* is anyone who is actively involved with your project. This includes (but isn't limited to) the following:

- Customers
- Sponsors
- Performing organization (the team)
- Upper management

Back in the "Collect Requirements" section in Chapter 5, there was a reference to something called a Stakeholder Register, and that is what is produced in this process!

Understanding what motivates the stakeholders early in the project will help maximize their positive influences and hopefully mitigate any potential negative impacts (see Figure 10.4).

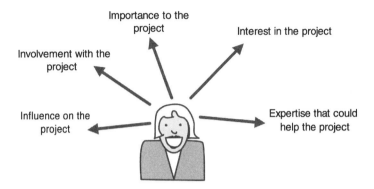

FIGURE 10.4
Stakeholder's role in a project.

With the potential for so many stakeholders needing to be informed on project status, understanding how to prioritize your interactions will help optimize your time and ensure that your attention is given to the stakeholders who can help your project become successful. The Identify Stakeholders process commences immediately during the initiation of a project.

Inputs to the Identify Stakeholders process are as follows:

■ **Project Charter:** This overview document should provide information about the parties that would be involved in some capacity with your project.

■ **Procurement document package:** Remember the various types of procurement documents mentioned in Table 6.19 in Chapter 6? Even though these documents aren't really produced until the Planning process group (in the Project Procurement Management knowledge area), you should at least have a good idea at project initiation if a soon-to-be-selected third-party provider will become another stakeholder to the project.

■ **Organizational process assets and enterprise environmental factors:** As you've seen throughout all of the knowledge areas, the organizational process assets should be taken advantage of, including Stakeholder Register templates, lessons learned, and any other material that has been used in other projects. The use of existing templates not only saves you from re-inventing the wheel, but it also ensures that the documents you prepare are consistent with others used in your organization.

The enterprise environmental factors that can influence this process include company culture, policies, and procedures, as well as those within your department or even the industry you serve (for example, government regulations).

Organizational process assets are used in every one of the Communications Management knowledge area's processes.

Tools and techniques used in the Identify Stakeholder process can be a little complicated. It's hard to believe, but there may be some stakeholders who do not want you and your team to succeed, especially if they didn't want the project to be funded at all. The converse is also true. The perspective of what each stakeholder expects from you will certainly influence what you communicate. For example, some stakeholders (like investors) don't need the level of detail that another stakeholder may require. Knowing how to fine-tune your communication appropriately to each stakeholder (or stakeholder group) is important for your project's success. Regardless, you owe it to every stakeholder to always communicate the truth about the project in a timely manner.

> Refer to the "Stakeholders" section in Chapter 3 for a summary of positive and negative stakeholder characteristics.

Stakeholder Analysis

This is a three-step process used to gather and analyze information about stakeholders so that you can use your influence and relationship-building skills to enhance your project's chance of success. (By the way, this is *not* politicking!) The steps are as follows:

1. Identify all stakeholders and project-relevant information about their influence on the project (for example, who is actively involved, assist in getting more resources if required, and so on). This information actually forms the basis of the key output of this process: the Stakeholder Register.
2. Evaluate the potential impact each stakeholder has in order to define an appropriate communications strategy for them. There are several techniques I'll be going over in just a moment.
3. Assess how key stakeholders are likely to react or respond to various project situations in order to win their trust and support. You'll want to mitigate any potential negative impacts.

There's a simple diagramming technique that can be used to classify stakeholders as either actively involved in the project or not as active (or possibly quite passive). I call it *target practice*, as shown in Figure 10.5. The drawing on the left shows the two circles that will be used: the inner circle (active) and the outer circle (passive). In this example, stakeholders are assigned a unique number (A through K) and placed in the appropriate circle. All but four stakeholders (in the center ring) are active.

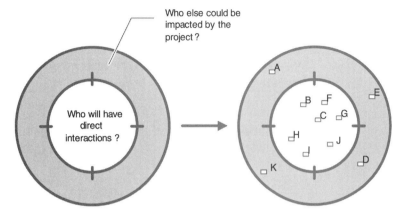

FIGURE 10.5
Target practice—identifying active stakeholders.

Stakeholders in the center ring are more active and will most likely require a different level of communications than those in the outer ring. There are several other more quantitative tools that you could use, and most have to do with creating a four-part grid. Like the target practice example, the idea is to plot each stakeholder on the grid, as shown in Figure 10.6.

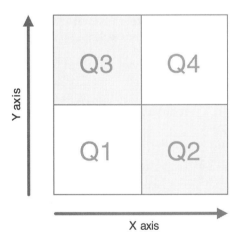

FIGURE 10.6
The use of four-part grids in stakeholder analysis.

The grids most commonly used in stakeholder analysis are power versus interest, will versus skill (primarily used for sales people), influence versus impact, heart versus head, and power versus influence.

In the case of power versus interest stakeholder analysis, you would assign a one through seven range for each stakeholder as it relates to their power (ability to get things done) on the project. If a stakeholder has minimal power (an observer, for example), they might rate a 2. Assign values (one through seven) the same for each stakeholder based on interest. Repeat for every stakeholder and then plot the results, as shown in Figure 10.7.

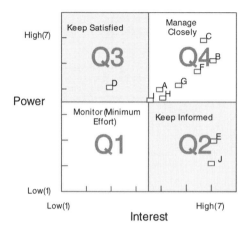

FIGURE 10.7
Power/Interest grid used to analyze
stakeholder involvement in the project.

Use Table 10.3 to interpret how you should communicate to stakeholders using their placement on the grid (shown in increasing level of importance). If stakeholder D is a general manager of another peer software department, he may have incredible power (to make things happen), but because he has his own projects to worry about, he may have little interest in your project. Stakeholder J is a very important VP of one of your client companies and may have very little power (to make things happen) but has a high interest that the product is successful and satisfies his company's needs.

Table 10.3 Communication Strategy Using the Power/Interest Grid

Grid	Power/Interest	Communication Strategy
Q1	Low power, low interest	Keep them informed (but nothing more).
Q2	Low power, high interest	Inform and they may be able to help.
Q3	High power, low interest	Have a stake in the project, keep informed.
Q4	High power, high interest	Have the biggest stake, your biggest ally.

In either case, you would typically *not* communicate the same level of project status to them. Stakeholder D may want to know that the project is on schedule (because he lent you a couple of great programmers, and he will want them back). Stakeholder J will want to know when his favorite features are being implemented so that his team can participate in trying them out prior to final product delivery. (That customer involvement represents the agile way!)

BEST PRACTICE Always communicate the *right* information that benefits the needs of the stakeholder.

Consider updating stakeholders with the project status by providing a brief summary of highlights tailored to each communication group (by quadrant) as an e-mail. Don't forget to attach a full project report (usually geared to those in quadrants Q3 and Q4), as shown in Figure 10.8.

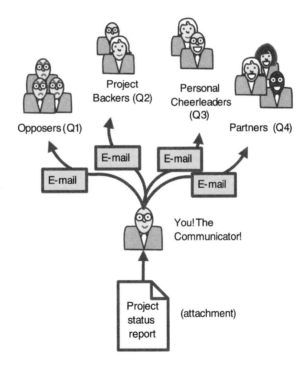

FIGURE 10.8
Tailoring the communications to stakeholder groups.

In summary, assess how key stakeholders are likely to react or respond to various project situations in order to win their trust and support. You'll want to use stakeholder analysis as a way to mitigate any potential negative impacts.

Expert Judgment

Use expert judgment by seeking feedback from individuals, groups, and resources that can assist in making decisions based on collective expertise and experience. Access to Subject Matter Experts (SMEs) can dramatically lessen the possibility of negative risks and help you fine-tune additional facts when you communicate. Expert judgment can be obtained through one-on-one meetings, interviews, focus groups, surveys, and any other technique that gets you the information you need to be successful at communicating.

Outputs for the Identify Stakeholder process are discussed in the following sections.

Stakeholder Register

This includes information about each stakeholder, along with other characteristics that may help determine how best to communicate with each stakeholder during the rest of the communications management processes (see Figure 10.9).

		Stakeholder Information		Assessment Information				Classification		Power / Interest	
ID	Name	Position	Contact Info	Knowledge	Expectations	Power/Interest	Influence	Int/Ext	Supporter	Power	Interest
1	Stanley	Dir of Finance	stan@swco1.com	Basic	Under budget	Keep satisfied	No	I	Neutral	5	5
2	Al	VP of Sales	al@swco1.com	Basic	Get out on time	Keep satisfied	Yes	I	Supporter	6	7
3	Sandra	GM A1 Division	sandra@swco1.com	Yes	Get out on time	Manage closely	Yes	I	Supporter	7	7
4	Thomas	GM A2 Division	thomas@swco1.com	No	I don't care	Monitor	No	I	Resistor	5	3
5	Bill	Investor, Board Member	bill@swco1.com	Basic	Raise company's	Keep informed	Possibly	E	Supporter	3	7
6	Jason	QA Lead	jason@swco1.com	Yes	Automate tests this time	Manage closely	Yes	I	Supporter	6	7
7	AnneMarie	Technical Writer	spiritual@swco1.com	Yes	Update docs only	Manage closely	Yes	I	Supporter	5	6
8	Gautam	Software Engineer	gautam@swco1.com	Yes	This will be a challenge!	Manage closely	Yes	I	Supporter	5	5
9	Eddie	Systems Architect	fasteddie@swco1.com	Yes	Needs to be scalable	Manage closely	Yes	I	Supporter	5	5
10	Al	VP, beta customer	albert_s@cust2.com	Yes	I need these features!	Manage closely	Yes	E	Supporter	2	7
11	Jordan	Project Manager	jordan@swco1.com	Basic	This will probably fail	Monitor	No	I	Resistor	1	1

FIGURE 10.9
Sample Stakeholder Register.

BEST PRACTICE The Stakeholder Register contains information that can be highly sensitive—you may wish to control its usage and availability.

Each entry in the Stakeholder Register is divided into the following sections:

- **Stakeholder information:** Identifies a unique stakeholder identifier (ID), name, position, title, and contact information. (In case you were wondering, the names and e-mail addresses aren't real.)
- **Assessment information:** Assesses a stakeholder's knowledge, expectations (driving factors), Power/Interest quadrant, and whether the stakeholder has influence on the project. (You can always define your own information, but these represent the stakeholder analysis described in the past few pages.)
- **Classification:** This is an indicator of a stakeholder's involvement with the project and the company, including internal (employee) or external (consultant) and whether they support the project. Other useful information can be maintained in the Stakeholder Register, including specific assessment values (for example, Power/Interest grid assessments are shown in Figure 10.9).

Stakeholder Management Strategy

This strategic plan identifies stakeholders (possibly by group) who have significant impact (quite possibly the Influence column in Figure 10.9), suggested level of participation, and their organization (for example, management, SMEs, the team, and so on). This approach is designed to increase stakeholder support and minimize negative impacts throughout the project's life cycle.

NOTE

It was astute of PMI to introduce an entirely new process for identifying stakeholders in the PMBOK Fourth Edition. Getting a clear understanding of who the stakeholders are at the very start of a project's initiation reduces the negative effects of statements like, "Oh, I didn't know you were interested in this project?" or "If only I had let Gina know the status—her guidance could have helped us past that major obstacle that set us back by a month."

This process, however, is more than just identifying stakeholders—you are *classifying* them in a way that allows you to maximize exactly how you need to communicate with them. It bears repeating—the vast majority of your role (some say close to 90%) is based on some form of communication.

This strategic document could also be included as part of the Communications Management Plan (which is created in the next process of the Communications Management knowledge area, the Plan Communications process). Alternatively, the document could also be a static document that is used as a template for all projects.

COMMUNICATIONS MANAGEMENT IN THE PLANNING PROCESS GROUP

Now that you've successfully identified your project's stakeholders (or, steakholders, for you meat eaters), let's plan for the communications that will be necessary for your project.

Plan Communications

An integral part of the Project Management Plan, the Plan Communications process basically defines a communications approach to be used throughout a project's life cycle.

In Connolly and Rianoshek's *The Communication Catalyst*, nowhere is the importance of effective communications more important than when a company is involved with a merger and acquisition (in other words, the blending of two different companies and cultures). According to the authors, by combining studies from notable "change consultancies" like Mercer, McKinsey, and PricewaterhouseCoopers, effective communications is a key part in the success or failure of mixing two cultures together.

BEST PRACTICE Without the use of extensive paper specifications (that aren't usually read), agile software projects rely on effective communications.

Look at the statistics shown in Figure 10.10. The surveyed companies that participated in mergers and acquisitions (also known as M&A) experienced a less than stellar success rate, with 90% achieving less or equal value than they had before. According to the same book, although there are many factors that go into the success (or failure) of M&A, there is a dramatic impact due to stakeholders misunderstanding the overall benefits and value. Communication has an important role if all parties involved can't assign meaning and subsequently take appropriate action, and if stakeholders can't create meaningful, trusting relationships.

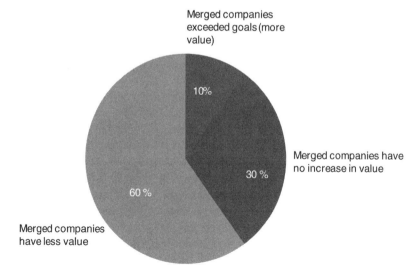

FIGURE 10.10
Effective communications can have a dramatic impact on the results of an M&A.

PMBOK states that effective communications should possess the following attributes:

- **In the right format:** If the audience has little time to read detailed reports, reduce details (for example, make them one page or less) and make them readily accessible. (For example, placing your communication's content in the body of an e-mail, rather than as an attachment, not only reduces keystrokes, but it is more likely to be read.)
- **Timely:** Stale news is almost as bad as no news at all!
- **Impactful:** Some project managers pride themselves on a style that uses lots of unnecessary explanations, big words, and so much ambiguity that it is almost impossible to determine what a project's real status actually is. In Figure 10.11, the top example is very typical of a project status report you've undoubtedly seen before. You can never expect the reader to understand the overall status buried in the text (for example, "although 30 days later than expected"). The second version gets the attention of the reader with a crisp heading (for example, "Schedule Is at Risk") and provides a clearer description of the project status in the corresponding text. The second example even has an action plan to attempt to remedy the situation. *Now that's project leadership!*

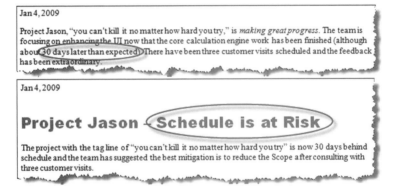

FIGURE 10.11
Two sample project schedule status report updates.

Inputs to the Plan Communications process are as follows:

- **Stakeholder Register:** Identification and characteristics of stakeholders that will have some level (even if minimal) of impact on your project.
- **Stakeholder management strategy:** Based largely on having a Stakeholder Register, this document indicates how to communicate with key stakeholders. (This document may be overkill and unnecessary.)
- **Organizational process assets and enterprise environmental factors:** There may be templates, lessons learned, and historical information that can provide guidance as to how best to communicate projects status. There may be corporate or industry assets that have a bearing on your communications planning. If your customer is a government agency, there may be a strict form of communication that is expected.

PMBOK Fourth Edition doesn't mention the scope baseline (Project Scope Statement and Project Management Plan) as inputs. There may be constraints and assumptions in those documents that dictate how communication should be handled.

Tools and techniques of the Plan Communications process are discussed in the following sections.

Communications Requirements Analysis

There needs to be some analysis performed to determine *who* gets communicated to, *what* communication should be created, *how* they should receive it, and *how often* it should be published.

There are all sorts of factors that help identify all of this. Let's start by identifying who gets communicated to. Figure 10.9 showed a simple overview of directly communicating to four groups of stakeholders. You can take this to an extreme by calculating the number of *communications channels*. The total number of communications channels is a good indicator of just how complex a project's communications strategy can be. PMBOK suggests the following algorithm to determine just how many distinct communications channels there are based on the number of stakeholders or stakeholder groups (the variable n):

```
Communications channels = n (n - 1) / 2
```

If you have four stakeholders that require communication, the total number of possible communications channels can be calculated as follows:

```
Communications channels = 4 (4 - 1) / 2
Communications channels = 4 (3) / 2
Communications channels = 6
```

Figure 10.12 shows lines drawn between every stakeholder (and in this example, there are six of them—thus, there are six communications channels). The number of channels dramatically increases with even as few as 10 stakeholders (resulting in 45 communications channels). In the case of too many communications channels, there may have to be a hierarchy where there is an official channel of communication established for key stakeholders, and then the information is further filtered to other stakeholders.

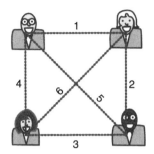

FIGURE 10.12
Calculating the number of communication
channels with four stakeholders.

Does this sound mean or bureaucratic? Not at all. Let's say your role is to communicate to
key stakeholders, which includes your product manager. Even though the Sales department
may also be stakeholders, they may be viewed as secondary to your project, and it may be best
to let the product manager communicate the project status to them. (In fact, there may be
many reasons for this to take place so that the Sales team focuses on selling what is currently
being shipped rather than a project that is still going to be in development for another three
months.)

According to Clark Campbell's provocative book, *The One-Page Project Manager*, there
are three types of communication that need to be considered:

1. **Up:** To upper levels of management, which typically implies less frequent, more
   formal, and less detailed status communication.
2. **Down:** Usually to people who work for you and to the team. (Whether you directly
   manage them or not, they tend to look to you for guidance, leadership, and mentoring.) The style of communication tends to be very frequent, less formal, and
   more detailed.
3. **Outward:** To peers, colleagues, and other organizations perhaps not tightly connected
   to your project. The style of communication depends a lot on the culture and rules of
   thumb set up in your organization (although it tends to be less formal than the Up
   crowd and more formal than to the Down crowd).

Why even worry about communications channels and types? Referring to Figure 10.12, the
number of relationships helps you understand that not only do you have to worry about how
you communicate to stakeholders, you need to also plan for the possibility that stakeholders
will communicate between themselves.

Need a refresher on what constitutes effective communications? Then review
PMBOK's recommended attributes identified in this section.

Although communication content to stakeholders may be tuned for specific audiences (or, more appropriately, stakeholder groups), they will undoubtedly talk among themselves, and your messaging must be consistent, accurate, and timely. The last thing you want is for one stakeholder to feel like he is receiving the optimistic view early and another is receiving the actual facts later (which may not be quite so "rosy").

This situation could ultimately destroy you and your team's integrity and credibility. PMI is very clear about the importance of these characteristics for each and every PMI member that earns PMP certification (discussed near the end of this section). In fact, the PMBOK exam has several trick questions testing how well you understand your ethical responsibility as a PMP.

Communications Technology

There is no single way to communicate in all circumstances. Communications technology, according to PMBOK, is dependent on a number of factors:

- **Urgency:** If project status takes a critical turn (for better or worse), do you wait to communicate this to stakeholders next week when your project status report is released? Probably not! Be clear on how you will communicate status changes that require urgent attention.

- **Technology availability:** Remember the inter-office mail envelopes or even the telephone? We've turned into a paperless society where too much information is communicated too easily (regardless of its importance). Quickly type it, then click Send. Now we're all bombarded with unnecessary information that can bog down any software development organization. What can work better is making use of information that is most efficient for stakeholders to access on their own terms.

   A perfect example is the use of Microsoft Sharepoint (or any other collaboration software product), which uses an internal intranet site to keep track of pertinent project status. The use of a single shared server location makes it easy for any stakeholder to access a project's current status. (Another benefit is that you can assign privileges for updating content as well as easily maintain a history of project status information reports.)

- **Compatibility with staff:** If new staff has been added, do they need training to understand how communication is to occur? Geography (offshore) and language can become big issues. Communication is much easier when staff members have a certain degree of compatibility.

- **Project duration:** If the project has a long duration, is there a chance that the Communications Management Plan created in this process going to change? For example, if you are converting from Sharepoint to another system midstream, you should plan for a migration and possible stakeholder training.

- **Environment (working conditions):** It isn't unusual for software developers to abhor face-to-face contact but overall, upon project kickoff, make sure the team members (and other stakeholders) get together to commit to effective and efficient mechanisms to collectively ensure that the team is focused and project status is properly being discussed. More and more companies are transitioning to virtual organizations where voice and visual conferencing tools are becoming more commonplace.

Communication Models and Methods

There is a basic model of communication, regardless of the medium, that is important to understand. There are three mandatory components that comprise your communication model that are important to understand:

- **Sender:** Initiates the communication and is responsible for encoding the message and communicating it.
- **Message:** The information content that is placed on some medium (like a network, paper, and "air" for verbal).
- **Receiver:** Receives the message from the sender and either asks for further clarification or acknowledges the message.

> The PMBOK Fourth Edition has moved these tools to this process from the Distribute Information process.

The most common model is one-way, where information is created and published (encoded) and then ultimately received (after being decoded). Figure 10.13 should clarify how this works (the smiling lady on the left is the sender, and the man with the protruding ears is the listening receiver). But there is a problem. Is the sender really sure that the receiver received the message and understood it?

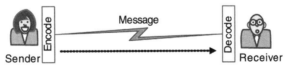

FIGURE 10.13
One-way communication model—send a message to a receiver.

Effective communication is usually a two-way form that assumes the sender will expect a confirmation from the receiver: Either the message was properly received or that it needs to be resent (implying that there is a corresponding encoding, this time by the receiver), as shown in Figure 10.14. This two-way protocol requires that the sender and receiver change hats.

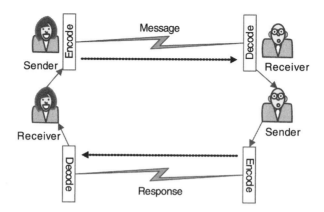

FIGURE 10.14
Two-way communication model—receive message and respond.

Two-way communication is a critical component of ensuring that communication really "sticks." The sender is responsible for creating a message that is clear and complete, as well as ultimately confirming that it was understood by the receiver. The receiver is responsible for making sure that the information is received in its entirety, understood, and acknowledged.

Communication blockers (or *noise* as PMBOK calls it) refers to anything that gets in the way of the receiver's ability to interpret the sender's communication. This could be all sorts of things, including language misunderstandings, unclear assignments, ambiguous feature set definitions, and so on. You have a responsibility to remove communication blockers as quickly as you can.

Speech and listening interactions require a certain amount of intuition, patience, and experience in order to have successful two-way communication exchanges (see Table 10.4).

Table 10.4 Two-Way Communications Interactions

Interactions	Description
Active listening	Receiver asks for clarification or provides feedback to the sender.
Effective listening	Receiver observes visual and vocal cues while providing feedback to the sender.
Feedback	Sender responds to a receiver's feedback by several means: asking questions, visual and vocal cues, and repeating the message (but in slightly different terms).

Interactions	Description
Nonverbal	Primarily body language (facial expressions, posture, hand motions, and so on) interactions that signal if the message is truly being received properly. According to Tony Johnson's PMP *Exam Success Series: Certification Exam Manual*, nonverbal communication can easily account for at least 50% of the total communication on a project. For that reason, a good listener must recognize nonverbal "signals."
Paralingual	As an extension to nonverbal communications, the inflection, volume, and pitch of the voice can have implications as to the type of interaction recognized (by the sender or the receiver).

There are many challenges to proper handling of the "round trip" exchange of information (sender to receiver and receiver to sender). *And you thought just being technically skilled and PMP certified would be enough? Ha!*

NOTE

This "round trip" (sender communicates and then the receiver interprets and subsequently responds) is a real dilemma for software teams. There is an overwhelming perspective among software teams that "as long as I sent the e-mail, I did my part"—you fulfilled your obligation and communicated.

Nothing could be further from the truth! E-mail has become one of the most efficient and convenient forms of communication for any technically savvy organization. It has allowed us to instantly communicate anywhere in the world at any time, reduced any need for administrative assistants (who has those anymore?), improved our typing skills, saved money and hassle by not using the phone or fax nearly as much, and improved our overall connection with stakeholders. On the other hand, e-mail has some noticeable deficiencies. You can't hear the tone and intonations of the sender, and active listening can't be used to clarify the understanding of the message you are trying to communicate.

How about some hints for successful e-mail communication?

- Short, simple, and clearly communicated text that fits on one screen page.
- Has a meaningful Subject line (boy, have I messed that up many times).
- Clearly indicates priority and action requested.
- If you have more detailed information, create that as an attachment.
- If the action required is really serious, follow up an e-mail with two-way communication.

I've discussed the communication models; there are several communication methods to share information among project stakeholders:

- **Interactive communication:** A multidirectional exchange of information among two or more stakeholders. These are usually in the form of conference calls, video conferencing, and meetings.

- **Push communication:** A unidirectional exchange of information among two or more stakeholders who need to know the information, but there is no validation that it is actually reached or was understood by the receivers. This includes letters, e-mails, faxes, Internet site announcements, and reports.
- **Pull communication:** Large volumes of information generally designated for large audiences that require the receivers to access the content at their own discretion. This is typically PDF documents, product downloads, knowledge repositories, e-learning material, and so on. About the only interaction you'd expect with this method is that the receiver should provide some sort of contact information when registering to access the material. This could, of course, turn into an opportunity to follow up with two-way communication (for example, a presales lead contact that turns into a bona fide customer).

You should decide the method (or methods) to employ when creating the communications plan for your project. *Speaking of "the plan"* . . . the output for the Plan Communications process is discussed in the following sections.

Communications Management Plan

The primary output of this plan is up to you as long as it benefits the needs of the project. The document or set of documents is a key component of the overall Project Management Plan. Its content can be formal, informal, detailed, or not detailed—whatever makes sense for your stakeholders.

BEST PRACTICE In order to decide what to communicate, put yourself in a stakeholder's shoes and ask yourself "Now, what would I want to know about this project?"

Although PMBOK defines a laundry list of items that the Communications Management Plan should include, you may as well keep it simple and hopefully similar to other projects' plans. Minimally, the plan should include the following items:

- *Who* should receive project communications.
- *What* communications they should receive.
- *Who* should send the communications.
- *How* the communications will be sent.
- *How often* communications will be sent and updated.
- Optionally, *definitions* used in the communications.

If this list sounds familiar to you, the components of the plan are mostly derived from performing a communications requirements analysis.

Project Document Updates

The entire set of communications management processes is iterative and will most likely change throughout a project's life cycle. This conforms to the agile way of thinking that the life cycle is a continuous set of discoveries and adjustments. Documents that may need to be updated include the following:

- **Project schedule:** May have to be adjusted, possibly due to communication snafus.
- **Stakeholder Register:** The list and roles of stakeholders may change, thus impacting how information is to be communicated.
- **Stakeholder management strategy:** Perhaps the way communication was supposed to work doesn't work!

COMMUNICATIONS MANAGEMENT IN THE EXECUTING PROCESS GROUP

There are two processes in the Executing process group:

- **Distribute information:** Make project information available to stakeholders.
- **Manage stakeholder expectations:** Manage stakeholder needs and communication.

Distribute Information

If you haven't started it already, this is where you start actually communicatin' and working with stakeholders. Where the Plan Communications process lays out how communications will be handled, the Distribute Information process carries it out. Just to be clear—the Distribute Information process refers to the act of distributing project information to stakeholders and *not* to the creation of the information (which is in the upcoming "Report Performance" section).

The sole output of this process is the updating of organizational process assets. Inputs to the Distribute Information process are discussed in the following sections.

Communications Management Plan

In the PMBOK Third Edition, this was the only input into the process. This plan should define how information will be distributed and what you are to do if you need to change how communication takes place.

Performance Reports

Performance reports are created from the Report Performance process. As agile projects cycle, these reports include current status, project performance to date, and forecasts of what it will take to complete the project (or project phase).

> You can measure performance in terms of schedule, but that probably isn't enough. Use the Earned Value Technique (EVT) as an objective measure of a project's true health.

Organizational Process Assets

This includes policies, procedures, guidelines, templates, and, of course, historical (lessons learned) information.

The tools and techniques employed during the Distribute Information process are discussed in the following sections.

Communication Methods

The sky is the limit in terms of the medium you choose to communicate information, but it can include the following:

- Meetings (group and one on one).
- Conferencing (video, audio, both).
- Computer chats. (For example, instant messaging—not sure this is a viable mechanism, but it certainly can augment team interactions with real-time messaging.)
- Letters. (Well, *somebody* must still write letters to stakeholders, right?)

Information Distribution Tools

This refers to how you choose to distribute information, including the following:

- Paper. (Yes, some people still like it—make sure it is recyclable.)
- Active electronic communications (e-mail, fax, voice mail, telephone, video/web conferencing, recordings, and so on).
- Passive electronic tools (portals, shared electronic databases, repositories, intranet like Microsoft Sharepoint, and so on).

Organizational Process Assets Updates

There is a single output, but whew—this is a big one. In this case, *assets* refers to most anything communicated to stakeholders (from any knowledge area) that needs to be recorded for posterity. This includes the following:

- **Project reports:** Project status reports, lessons learned, issue logs, project closure reports, and reports that would be of interest to stakeholders.
- **Project presentations:** Any formal (or informal, for that matter) presentations shown to stakeholders that you feel are relevant to save.

■ **Project records:** This may be asking too much, but pertinent memos, e-mails, and other material that may have importance to the project should be saved. If you are going to apply for a patent, keeping any records of correspondence that would support early patent ideas being considered might be very important. This could also include information from unlikely sources not typically associated with the project (like, for instance, board member feedback).

■ **Lessons learned:** Any information that sheds some light on causes of issues and corrective action taken would be very helpful, not only for postmortems but to aid future projects if they encounter similar situations.

Keeping process asset information in a shared repository is better than in your personal e-mail folder for a number of obvious reasons (especially as people come and go on projects).

A real-world need is tracking and documenting the point of technical feasibility. You will most likely want to know when this occurred on your project, how it was justified, and how much effort will be expended to project closure (in other words, product release). Finance needs to track this for expense capitalization according to FAS 86 guidelines. (Remember, the Finance department folks are your friends!)

Manage Stakeholder Expectations

The distinction between the Manage Stakeholder Expectations process and both the Distribute Information and the soon-to-be discussed Report Performance processes can be quite confusing. (It does beg the question why the Manage Stakeholder Expectations process wasn't folded in under one of those other two processes to begin with.) To add to the confusion, PMBOK Fourth Edition has moved the Manage Stakeholder Expectations process from the Monitoring & Controlling process group into the Executing process group (which is odd because this process is concerned with *validating* that stakeholders are getting the information they need).

You've distributed project information, but does your role stop there? Nope! This process is focused on issue and change management working with stakeholders. The inputs to this process are as follows:

■ **Stakeholder Register:** This is a list of stakeholders that are to some degree associated with the project. This list defines, among other attributes, the key stakeholders that are most important to focus your energies on. The Stakeholder Register is created by the Identify Stakeholders process.

■ **Stakeholder management strategy:** Coupled with the Stakeholder Register, this strategic planning document identifies the stakeholders' goals and objectives. This is used to determine strategic initiatives (I prefer to call them "weapons") to manage stakeholder expectations. The stakeholder management strategy document is created by the Identify Stakeholders process.

- **Communications Management Plan:** This all-encompassing communications planning document provides an overall understanding of stakeholder goals, objectives, and most important, the level of communication required throughout the project's life cycle. The Communications Management Plan is part of the Project Management Plan (actually a subsidiary document).

- **Issue and change logs:** Not keeping track of outstanding issues detected or requested changes can result in team members and stakeholders losing confidence that necessary closure is taking place. It is that "90% done" or "I thought you fixed that" type of dialog that is typical of software organizations without a pronounced project management acumen. Using Bugzilla or other issue/change control systems to keep track of prioritizing, categorizing, status, and ultimate resolution is necessary for any software project.

- **Organizational process assets:** Just as your company's marketing manager prepares and presents marketing material that complies to corporate communications standards and procedures, so should you (with the project's stakeholders). This might include any historical lessons learned information that records how similar issues were handled on other projects. In addition, there are probably organization standards, templates, policies, and procedures that should be used regarding communications requirements, procedures for handling issues, and change control procedures.

There are three primary tools and techniques used in managing stakeholder, which are discussed in the following sections.

Communication Methods

Use the methods that support the Communications Management Plan. This includes ensuring that project status is communicated to the stakeholders in the most appropriate way (possibly tailored to the way the stakeholders will most benefit from project information).

Interpersonal Skills

You are responsible for using your interpersonal abilities to manage stakeholder expectations. This should not be interpreted as being political—on top of being the leader and overall facilitator of the project, you need to act as the press secretary to ensure that all of the stakeholders are getting the right information at the right time. Some of the most important skills that you need to consider are as follows:

- Building trust among all stakeholders.
- Resolving conflict based on project merits without ever turning "personal."
- Active listening. (If you find that your mouth hurts at the end of every work day, that might be a signal that you do far more yappin' than listening.)
- Building consensus and an overall feeling of *realistic confidence* (not too pessimistic and not too optimistic).
- Overcoming resistance to change or new ideas.

Management Skills

As a project or software manager, you aren't *one of the guys* any longer—you need to demonstrate the ability to direct and control a group of wildly different individuals to perform toward a common goal. For this to take place, you need to provide the right information at the right time. (I've said this before.)

> Being raised in the southern part of the United States, I developed this horrible habit of opening doors for women and calling everyone "guys" regardless of gender. Sorry, can't help it.

Hopefully, you have an ability and a strong desire to write and present information with the idea of making sure all stakeholders are "on the same page." I've seen too many software development managers, executives, and project managers who are superb at their craft (software programming and design, for example) who shy away from being able to effectively communicate. They prefer to work alone in their office while zinging out e-mails, or they prefer to hear themselves "pronounce their technical brilliance all day" (without really bothering to listen).

If you enjoy the art of effective communication, your stakeholders will appreciate it. (This does *not* imply that you should over-communicate by establishing lengthy team and stakeholder meetings each and every day.) The beauty of agile software methodology is that the role of crisp, frequent, and short communication can be highly effective!

The following sections discuss the outputs to the Manage Stakeholder Expectations process.

Change Requests

At the top of the list are change requests that may need to be escalated for resolution that includes corrective or preventive action. In an ideal world, interactions with stakeholders can be contained within the team, but the reality is that certain changes may impact scope, schedule, or cost, and those usually need more visibility with upper management.

Project Document Updates

There may be a number of project documents that, as a result of communicating with stakeholders, need to be updated, including the Communications Management Plan, Stakeholder Register, stakeholder management strategy, and the issue log.

Organizational Process Assets Updates

The background behind decisions that are made when communicating with stakeholders is invaluable for other projects as lessons learned (and to show the progression of decisions throughout a project's life cycle).

COMMUNICATIONS MANAGEMENT IN THE MONITORING & CONTROLLING PROCESS GROUP

The Report Performance process is where the material to be communicated is collected and prepared.

Report Performance

This process has a strong relationship to the Control Costs process, since the cost management analysis uses the same information that you need to report on a project's performance.

> See the "Control Costs" section in Chapter 6 for more information.

Inputs to the Report Performance process are discussed in the following sections.

Project Management Plan

Since this process is involved with reporting on project performance status, and specifically, gaps between planned and actual performance, the Project Management Plan should shed some light on the current scope baseline, schedule (aka time), and cost (the infamous Triple Constraint). As software projects iterate and adjust, so too will the Project Management Plan.

Work Performance Data and Measurements

Figure 10.15 shows the inputs, tools and techniques, and outputs of the Control Costs process. The two circled items in this process are used in project performance reporting. Work performance information, an input to the Control Costs process, is needed because it includes results like deliverables status, schedule progress, and costs incurred to date. Work performance measurements, an output from the Control Costs process, report on the project's performance. This set of measurements summarizes planned versus actual schedule results, planned versus actual cost results, and planned versus actual scope product (feature) results.

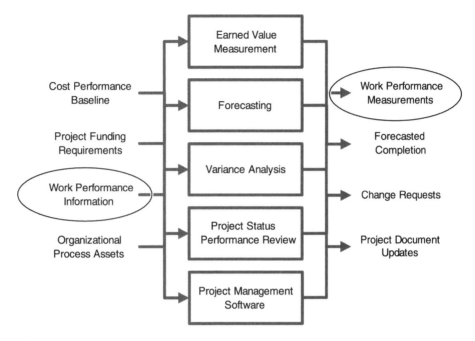

FIGURE 10.15
Control Costs process revisited.

Organizational Process Assets

Your organization should have a library of report templates, policies, procedures, and even some standard variance limits that, if exceeded, require executive management intervention. These assets are important in order to maintain consistency with reporting performance formats used with other projects.

The tools and techniques for the Report Performance process are discussed in the following sections.

Variance Analysis

Compare the current baseline against the actual performance results to date. The Variance Analysis tends to focus on the Triple Constraint elements of a project: scope, schedule, and cost. (You must be sick and tired of me repeating what the Triple Constraint is.) Refer back to "Control Costs" in Chapter 6 for more information on Variance Analysis.

Forecasting Methods

Although forecasting is typically a cost control activity, there are several methods that can help predict the future performance of the project:

- **Time series methods:** By keeping track of historical information, you can estimate future outcomes primarily of earned value.
- **Judgmental methods:** By using the Delphi method, forecasting by analogy, and other techniques, you can incorporate intuitive and expert judgment to help forecast future outcomes.
- **Other methods:** This is an odd catch-all that includes simulation or probabilistic forecasting to forecast future outcomes. If you remember LiquidPlanner's project management system, their software takes advantage of probabilistic forecasting to predict future schedule performance.

NOTE

If there ever was a time to keep track of lessons learned information, it is in the results of forecasting methods.

Communication Methods

Status review meetings can be used as a meaningful two-way communication setting to exchange and analyze performance information concerning a project's progress. You are the one who should organize and run the meeting, and according to PMBOK, a push communications technique is a good way to distribute performance reports. However, keep in mind that it is actually in the previous Manage Stakeholder Expectations process where actual meetings are administered.

Reporting Systems

You'll need a tool (usually computer software) that can be used to capture and maintain historical records, and even distribute information (the output of this process) to stakeholders.

They say that pictures say a thousand words—so the more visual and less wordy the better. A reporting system ensures that project information isn't lost in someone's e-mail system (or their memory). Instead, the information is maintained for postmortems and lessons learned.

The outputs to the Report Performance process are discussed in the following sections.

Performance Reports

Once your project's performance analysis tools and techniques are completed, select the best format to present the results to your stakeholders. As an example, you might want to produce a simple one-page performance chart for project sponsors and executive management, while your team may need a comprehensive report instead. As a reminder, it may be appropriate to tailor a different message for those stakeholders who are only mildly interested versus those who are relying on the release of the project for their own success (for example, your boss).

Remember to use the tools and techniques covered earlier in the chapter in order to tailor the message to benefit stakeholders (refer to Figure 10.8).

Performance reports represent the sole most important output of all the Communications Management knowledge area's processes. The ingredients of a successful performance report should include the following information:

- Review of past performance.
- Current status. (Identify key risks that would impact any part of the Triple Constraint.)
- Forecasted project completion that is usually based on schedule (time) or cost.
- Most important, how your project release status relates to the overall product roadmap—this keeps the team's work in perspective with the goals of the organization and the company.

Reports may have to be customized depending on the stakeholder grouping (in the Communications Management Plan). The team may wish to see only project milestone information, whereas upper management may only wish to see a couple of bar charts showing Key Performance Indicators (KPIs), such as the values shown in Table 10.5.

Table 10.5 Key Performance Indicator Reporting

Measurement	Description
Planned Value (PV)	The planned work that should have been performed.
Earned Value (EV)	How much work was actually completed.
Actual Cost (AC)	The actual cost spent so far.

> KPIs generically represent Earned Value Management. This was covered in detail in the section "Calculating Project Cost Performance Metrics" in Chapter 6.

Change Requests

Besides critical defects (discussed in Chapter 8, "Deliver On-Time, Quality Products"), change requests are a typical result of the Report Performance process. These changes must be factored back into the Integrated Change Control process in a timely manner. These recommended corrective actions should hopefully bring the project back in line with the Project Management Plan, whereas recommended preventive actions should reduce the probability of future negative consequences to a project's performance.

Organizational Process Assets Updates

This process more than most should provide plenty of historical information for future projects as lessons learned concerning performance reporting.

FOOLPROOF COMMUNICATIONS TECHNIQUES

Believe it or not, we're done with all of the PMBOK processes! Now, let's get to the fun stuff. The "Identify Stakeholders" section earlier in this chapter demonstrated the importance of not only identifying all of the stakeholders but also categorizing them according to some grouping (usually in four categories visualized in a grid).

UNDERSTANDING STAKEHOLDERS AND SPONSORS

To be an effective communicator, your only measure of success would be if each stakeholder is getting the information they need to assist you in a successful project. Does this mean that you need to establish four different communication plans? (Refer to Figure 10.8.)

KEEPING COMMUNICATION SIMPLE AND CONSISTENT

You are the only one responsible for the project's communication to its stakeholders. Software developers, it seems by their very nature, abhor communicating. In keeping with the agile philosophy that less is better, keep what you communicate simple and consistent so that it is effective (used by the team and the project's stakeholders). Communication is not a *negative* thing—it is a *necessary* thing. Here's an example of e-mail correspondence between a project manager and a software engineer that is summarized from an article I read some 15 years ago:

> *Project Manager:* We are getting behind on the project and a number of people on the team are concerned about your design.

> *Software Engineer:* My design? No one has sent me an e-mail on it.

> *Project Manager:* That's because sometimes you come across as being a little defensive and not open to feedback.

> *Software Engineer:* That's crazy. I'm very approachable.

> *Project Manager:* Then I'll schedule a meeting for Thursday with you and the team.

> *Software Engineer:* You mean a sit-down meeting? Why can't they just send me an e-mail about it?

> *Project Manager:* Yes, of course. Real people in a room—together.

> *Software Engineer:* I'd rather respond to an e-mail than waste time in a meeting.

> *Project Manager:* That is exactly why this project is in the shape it is in.

MANAGING MEETINGS

According to DeMarco and Lister's insightful book *Peopleware*, when a meeting is invoked with some number of attendees, expect that everyone provides a purpose. The long-winded diatribes, needless banter, and people glancing at the clock are all clear indications that your meeting has become meaningless. There are many theories on meeting best practices, but the following sections outline a few golden rules.

BEST PRACTICE When you set up and lead a meeting, you, and only you, are responsible for its success.

Meetings Should Benefit All Attendees

First and foremost, if you are interested in having meetings because that's the "thing to do," then have them only when absolutely necessary. Attendees (stakeholders) need to contribute and derive benefits from each meeting, since the intent is to make and communicate decisions. If a meeting tends to be geared toward one-way communication, there are better mechanisms for that than a meeting (including e-mail). A common mistake, according to Andy Crowe's *The PMP Exam*, is to invite those who will not actively participate or receive little to no benefit.

Meetings Require Agendas

Sounds like common sense, but if you look back at the meetings you had last week, how many of them actually had the following defined beforehand?

- Goal (the *reason* for the meeting in the first place).
- Topics to discuss (the *what*).
- Maximum time frame (*how long*).
- Benefits to attendees (the *why*).

If a meeting, including those that you host, doesn't have an agenda—KILL IT! If you finish the agenda early, close the meeting early. If the agenda takes a little bit longer than planned, finish the meeting anyway.

Be Prepared

Reminiscent of the Boy Scouts' famous motto, showing up to a meeting unprepared is the ultimate "kiss of death." Not only is it embarrassing and impacts your credibility with the attendees, it is expensive. (Multiply the time wasted by everyone's salary and loss of productivity.)

Take the approach documented by Connolly and Rianoshek's *The Communication Catalyst*. Prepare a meeting checklist that identifies for each attendee the following information:

1. Attendee's name and title.
2. Purpose (their role in the organization).
3. The value they bring (to the meeting).
4. Concerns (their perspective to the meeting's goals).
5. Relationship status to the team. (This can actually be in the form of the stakeholder groupings you choose to use to classify stakeholders in the Identify Stakeholders process.)

> The use of a preparation checklist may be overkill for most meetings, but it can be very helpful in planning for a difficult meeting.

A meeting is a serious activity and, once again, if attendees are unprepared—KILL IT!

Listen, Foster Creative Thinking, and Drive Toward Making Decisions

Although you don't want to stifle interactions during the meeting, you do want to inspire communication, acknowledge constructive input, make sure that everyone contributes, and ensure the team makes a solid decision (remember the Decision Pyramid). The balance of listening while guiding discussions is an important skill for you to develop—you want the attendees to think back at how successful the meeting was to reaching decisions without being railroaded into a predetermined conclusion. (Even if you had your mind made up before the meeting, you never want to force your hand.)

Be Clear

What does that mean? Well, if you've led a meeting, thought you got closure, and then found that attendees had different perspectives of the meeting's outcome, you'll have to have another meeting, or you'll have to race around and re-explain the outcome to everyone. According to Patrick Lencioni's *Death by Meeting*, "it is shocking and yet understandable that intelligent people cannot see the correlation between failing to take the time to get clarity, closure, and buy-in during a meeting and the time required to clean up after themselves as a result."

Be Interesting

What? Be *interesting?* According to Donald Kirkpatrick's excellent *How to Conduct Productive Meetings*, the creative use of flip charts, handouts, and presentations can turn a boring meeting into something a little bit more visually stimulating. (If you aren't careful, you might develop a reputation where people may *want* to come to your meetings!)

Be Organized

There's nothing worse than being at a meeting where the leader (you) jumps around "all over the place." Not only is it hard to focus and stay on time, it eventually will impact your ability to get people interested in even attending your meetings. Using *How to Conduct Productive Meetings* as a good foundation for leading effective meetings, Kirkpatrick recommends the following steps:

1. **Set the tone with a short, focused introduction:** Welcome everyone to the meeting, state the meeting's objectives, why it is important to have the meeting, and why the attendees will benefit from the results of the meeting. Last but not least, quickly summarize what the meeting will cover and what their participation needs to be.

> Make sure that before you go to step 2, everyone understands what you stated in the introduction (step 1).

2. **Present the body of the meeting's information:** Use an outline if you have to, but use clear and simple language, be specific, use aids effectively, and make sure that you are making that all-important eye contact. This is the point where you balance one-way and two-way communication techniques. Taking the time to listen and not rush through quick decisions is a great leadership characteristic. Also, bringing back wayward, too-detailed conversations (as is often the case with technical people) to the focus of the meeting is your job.

   For those folks who can provide great feedback yet are resistant to openly communicating, you need to effortlessly bring them into the conversation (without embarrassing them). Don't forget to acknowledge opinions throughout the meeting.

3. **Use aids effectively:** During visual presentations, it is always best to minimize the use of words, use diagrams whenever possible, limit the amount of information per page (slide or flip chart), and don't say exactly what is written—ad lib! You may want to make handouts available, but it never ceases to amaze me how people leave handouts laying around after the meeting (which I have to pick up). (Not to mention this is a waste of paper.)

4. **Conclude the meeting with a vengeance:** Review the overall objective of the meeting (again!), the main points discussed, paying particular attention to key comments that could introduce risks, and finally, summarize the action items and final decision made.

You initially *welcomed* everyone to the meeting—so don't forget to *thank* everyone for attending. Last but not least, make sure that everyone knows if and when there is another meeting.

Document the Meeting

Document the highlights and especially the decisions the team arrives at and distribute the results soon after the meeting (so that the material is "fresh" in people's minds). If you wait a week to communicate the results, it must not have been that important to have the meeting in the first place. What is really amazing is if you can document the notes electronically while the meeting is going on (without slowing down the meeting, of course!) and then publish it immediately after the meeting has been concluded! WOW!

Are there any other major impacts to how meetings are effectively led? You bet! Once again, in *Death by Meeting*, Patrick Lencioni summarizes the impact of badly organized and inconclusive meetings:

> "They generate real human suffering in the form of anger, lethargy, and cynicism… and also impact people's self-esteem, and their outlook on life."

Other bad, bad, bad meeting impacts include the following:

- **You didn't invite all of the right stakeholders:** You make a decision for the team and the project you feel good about, and then. . . <wham!> another stakeholder who has pertinent information was not considered, and it might require the team to rework the previous decision. If this happens more than once on a project, you could easily lose trust among the team in your ability to lead. (Building trust is exactly what effective communication is all about.) Lessons learned—it is your responsibility to have the right decision makers in your meetings.
- **You tried to gain consensus:** The goal of a meeting is to get a unified decision by meeting attendees. If everyone buys in, then you have reached consensus—ultimately a project manager's holy grail. Generally, software teams have a wide variety of interesting viewpoints and opinions, so your best bet is to get buy-in even without consensus. If you try to force consensus, chances are high that you will have to rework your decision again and again. And if that happens, you lose credibility as someone who cannot make a decision. (And you thought you were doing everyone a favor by reaching a unanimous decision!)

    How do you make a decision if you can't reach consensus? Easy—employ the use of the Decision Pyramid to keep the decision-making process from becoming personal (or forced).
- **The meeting never really ends:** You know you have the basis of an unsuccessful meeting if afterward, attendees are huddled together in small groups, regurgitating the same topics (oftentimes with frustration). These after-the-meeting conversations can leave everyone with that "empty feeling in the pit of the stomach" that the meeting wasn't able to reach an agreed-upon decision.

    This situation doesn't help to stimulate a work environment where meetings are viewed as positive events rather than the "time wasters" perception prevalent in modern-day business. Advice? Immediately stop the hallway chit-chat, host an emergency meeting, apologize for the prior meeting not being successful, and get a decision made with everyone's input.

IS A PROJECT KICKOFF MEETING REALLY NECESSARY?

In the first two processes of the Communications Management knowledge area, there was virtually no mention of a kickoff meeting. This is a valuable mechanism endorsed by PMBOK that should take place prior to the project entering into its first Executing process group cycle.

BEST PRACTICE The project's kickoff meeting officially sets the project in motion!

In fact, once the Project Charter (refer to Chapter 4) is established, you need to get the team (and key stakeholders) together to communicate the project's goals, communication plan, and so forth. According to Crowe's *The PMP Exam*, the kickoff meeting has the following benefits:

- Brings the team together with the key stakeholders, sponsor, customer, and senior management to discuss the overall project's plan and charter.
- Provides a wonderful forum to share lessons learned from other projects with everyone.

PROJECT CLOSURE AND LESSONS LEARNED

This topic was first brought up in the "Close Project or Phase" section of Chapter 4, and it bears additional discussion. In Rita Mulcahy's *PM Crash Course*, in addition to the importance of lessons learned, there are a couple of techniques she uses to get the participation necessary for a successful meeting.

To increase meeting participation, she invites an executive manager or key sponsor to the project kickoff, key milestone meetings, and to the project closure meeting. In addition to getting close to 100% attendance, it gives the special guest time to interact with the team. (It also benefits the team in that they can get more insight into what upper management thinks about the importance of their project.)

The other technique is to issue assignments to attendees to prepare a presentation or report for a subsequent meeting. In the case of lessons learned, this could include topics like the following:

- What went right
- What could have done differently
- What was learned

The benefit is two-fold: It gives the team members the opportunity to "strut their stuff," and it makes the meetings dramatically more interesting.

UNDERSTANDING TEAM DYNAMICS

BEST PRACTICE High-performing teams typically go through tough team dynamics during a project's life cycle.

The dynamics of team interactions, communications, and relationships can be a complex situation for anyone in a leadership position. Without getting deep into team psychology, there is a model popularized by Bruce Tuckman back in 1965 that still holds true today. It is called, for lack of any other term or acronym, Forming-Storming-Norming-Performing (see Figure 10.16). What you must remember with this model is that this is a team-building effort. Each stage is achieved after a previous stage, and there's no guarantee that a team will go through all five stages.

Hey! There are five stages, yet the name for this team development doesn't include the Adjourning stage. (Why? Tuckman added this stage later.)

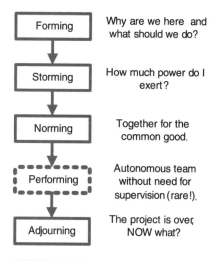

FIGURE 10.16
The Tuckman model of five stages of team development.

Before you go hunting through PMBOK to locate this Tuckman stuff, there is now a brief summary in the Fourth Edition (though there was no mention in the Third Edition). You might disagree with the model or even with the fact that there is such a thing, but the Tuckman model is still a valuable tool even though it was originally developed and became popular in the "dark ages" of the 1960s.

What does this sequence of team development actually mean? Your role is mostly directive (educating and setting the team direction), *but your communication and leadership style will have to adjust, depending on the stage the team is in.* Should you subscribe to the Tuckman model, it isn't such a bad idea to educate the team on the model itself. That level of team transparency develops trust among the team members and with you.

The Forming Stage

Tuckman believes that a "healthy" team goes through these phases, and you, as the overall team leader, facilitator, and communicator, need to adapt to these changes in order to build a performing team. The first stage of team development is *Forming* (see Table 10.6). The team is formed, they learn and buy into the project objectives, and they start to perform the tasks. Unless the team has worked together before, they begin to get used to each other and slowly but surely start to build trust even though at this early stage, team members are used to operating independently. Your role is to be *directive* and get the team thinking like a *unified* team.

Table 10.6 Tuckman Model Forming Stage

Team Dynamics	Your Communication Style	Description
Risk avoidance, acceptance	Directive	Team meets on the opportunity, agrees on the project's objectives, and begins to perform the tasks you lay out. The team is learning about each other, and the level of trust starts to develop.

Team members are usually on their *best behavior* in this stage—you wouldn't want to start off a new project with a bad impression, now would you? A team that understands the common set of a project's objectives will be less apt to stray from the needs of the project. For example, a rallying cry for a major update release for your product may be to focus all of your energies on performance throughput improvements. In this case, spending valuable time on new features isn't in the best interest for the project and represents gold plating (which, in this case, is not a good thing).

BEST PRACTICE Every team member should be able to recite the project's objectives in a 30-second "elevator speech."

The Storming Stage

This is characterized by the team "feeling their oats" through competition and sometimes erupting in conflict. In the *Storming* stage (see Table 10.7), the team members are feeling a little more confident; they open up to each other, oftentimes being very forceful with their views on approaches and decisions that should be made. This stage, if properly led and facilitated, can come to a quick resolution, or the team may, unfortunately, never get out of this "anarchy."

Table 10.7 Tuckman Model Storming Stage

Team Dynamics	Your Communication Style	Description
Conflict, anxiety, and open expression of ideas	Listening (with directive reinforcement)	Frustrated and confused team members doubt the goals, decisions, roles, and other team members' abilities. Who's got the power?

This stage is necessary for team development and, ultimately, can produce better software products. However, you have a couple of obstacles to overcome:

- There is usually great benefit to what the most vocal team members express, but the way their message is being communicated can become personal, unprofessional, and destructive.
- Team members who are less assertive may clam up and hope this tidal wave subsides, or they may attempt to divert the conversation to less controversial (and, consequently, less important) topics.

Regarding your communication style. . . your role is to be respectful of differing opinions, focus on constructive resolution, and remind the team of what had already been decided in the Forming stage. When you face conflict, here are some tips from *The Team Handbook* (by Peter Scholtes, et al.):

- Control overbearing and dominating participants by balancing "meeting hogging" and validating facts. (Do not rely on emotional responses, no matter how convincing.)
- Encourage interaction with reluctant participants.
- Take the time to resolve (or postpone) decisions if you are running out of time.
- Avoid at all costs personal attacks (attribution) and stick to the facts.
- Redirect and assist those comments that are simply "plops" (appear as out of nowhere comments) or discounted perspectives (where one team member denounces another's ideas).
- Bring meetings back to focus when members get into too much detail or go off on tangents.

- Take feuding team members aside outside of a meeting setting and adjust the destructive behavior immediately. (It is very important not to punish them publicly—chances are bad blood existed *before* your project started.)

If you let the Storming stage continue too long, the team will become disillusioned and unmotivated. You can't let the team's progress get out of control. The more mature team members can usually help provide technical wisdom and experience to move the most vocal individuals along to the next stage. The best advice I can give you is to *listen*!

> If you never quite exit the Forming stage with a unified direction, the Storming stage will usually have to re-establish Forming all over again. Yikes!

The Norming Stage

Ah, the team is aligned with a common purpose (Forming), you've gotten past the angry period (Storming), and now the team *wants* to work and succeed together. The *Norming* stage encourages leadership at all levels of the organization (see Table 10.8). Progress is being made, teamwork is strengthened, and trust and confidence abound. The team is operating as a team should. Making team-based decisions tends to be easier for a team working toward common objectives.

Table 10.8 Tuckman Model Norming Stage

Team Dynamics	Your Communication Style	Description
Leadership is shared, trust and relationships gel	Participative (with feedback cross-checks)	Team members adjust their behavior in order to share with collective milestone attainment. Trust and team accomplishments begin to take shape.

Your communication style should become more participative in decisions, getting feedback (public and private), hosting team-building events, and even surprising the team with special outings, unplanned perks, and milestone celebrations. Your everyday role is very important for the success of the team at this stage.

Maintaining the Norming stage typically requires special attention in order to avoid slipping back into the Storming stage:

- Make sure you are taking every opportunity to bond the team together. Ensuring that everyday meetings, if you are doing Scrum, are effective is one way. If you work with geographically distributed software development sites, you need to take extra steps so that they truly feel like part of the team.

■ Cross-check with proactive feedback techniques so that individuality and innovation aren't being stifled for the benefit of not making waves. This may indirectly result in increased frustration, but you need to encourage contrarian feedback for the overall good of building better products.

To achieve team consensus, *The Team Handbook* once again offers some great advice:

■ Make sure you have allowed enough time and don't rush to force consensus.
■ Listen carefully.
■ Encourage all members to participate.
■ Seek out differences of opinion and search for alternatives that meet the goals of all members.
■ Avoid changing your mind in order to avoid conflict.
■ Make sure there is enough time.
■ Revalidate the final decision and explain why it is the best decision.

This is a great time to get more customer and executive sponsorship visibility, not only for the team's progress but also to the team members themselves.

The Performing Stage

After the Norming stage is achieved, a team can become a well-oiled machine—almost Radar-like energy (remember the TV show *MASH*?)—when team members anticipate what to do in order to succeed with milestone attainment (see Table 10.9). Only *some* teams will reach the Performing stage.

> Teams that have a long-standing history of working together will be more likely to reach the Performing stage.

Table 10.9 Tuckman Model Performing Stage

Team Dynamics	Your Communication Style	Description
Intuitive, self-directed unity	Participative	High-performance results with the team functioning as a unified unit. A characteristic of the team is that teammates run almost without guidance—team is knowledgeable and confident. As a result, your role is a combination of participant, cheerleader, and "obstacle remover."

What characterizes a project team that achieves the Performing stage?

- Motivated.
- Knowledgeable.
- Thirst for problem solving and pitching in to help other team members.
- Dissent is expected and allowed as long as it doesn't take on a "life of its own."
- Intuitive and able to make decisions even without supervision.
- Likely to complete tasks at a faster-than-expected pace.

NOTE

Don't laugh, but DeMarco and Lister's *Peopleware* and Mihály Csíkszentmihályi's *Finding Flow: The Psychology of Engagement with Everyday Life* preach the almost "euphoric" concept of *flow*. If there is anything close to this in software development, it is the Performing stage of team development.

Flow is a highly satisfying condition for the individual and the team that is defined as having clear team objectives (Project Charter!), intense concentration (check e-mail three times a day, not every minute!), lack of interruptions and distractions (intercom paging and cubicles are definitely not allowed!), a sense of challenge, and immediate feedback.

The Adjourning Stage

Although added later as a final, fifth stage, the *Adjourning* stage (also known as *Mourning*) can be traumatic for a tightly knit team (see Table 10.10). This stage is the point where lessons learned are documented and discussed with the idea of improving the organization's future tactics. *Blame tossin'* should not be allowed during this discussion. Ensure that you have a transition plan already arranged for each team member and, above all, celebrate the completion of the project.

Table 10.10 Tuckman Model Adjourning Stage

Team Dynamics	Your Communication Style	Description
Team disbandment (positive or negative)	Proactive	Project closure tasks are performed, including lessons learned. Possible sense of loss after the team completes its mission.

You must be *proactive* and *decisive* in your communications style. With any awards situation, it is important to recognize all team members. (There are plenty of opportunities to provide additional recognition with key performers privately, as was discussed in the previous chapter.)

WHAT IS THIS PMI "CODE" THING?

Although every professional organization has some sort of code of ethics, when you become a PMP (Project Management Professional, remember?), you are obligated to commit to the "PMI Code of Ethics and Professional Conduct" that is published in the *Project Management Professional (PMP) Credential Handbook*. This document is not part of the PMBOK (*Project Management Body of Knowledge*) reference guides, but it is available from the PMI web site www.pmi.org/PDF/pdc_pmphandbook.pdf. Click on the Credential Terms of Use bookmark, and then select the PMI Code of Ethics and Professional Conduct link. (Please note that PMI can change these links at any time.)

Besides the normal "Thou shalt not steal or lie" and other expected guidelines, there are some key elements of the code relating to software management that you should keep in mind:

- **Grow project management as a profession:** As far as social and career responsibility goes, PMI requests that you "spread the word" and help grow project management as a true profession. Did you know that in 2007, the International Organization for Standardization (ISO) recognized PMI, and specifically the PMP, as an accredited credential program as ISO 17024? This gives your PMP certification worldwide endorsement by 85 countries (and growing) as a globally accepted benchmark.
- **Help team members:** Just because you might already be a genius at project management doesn't mean your project management and software management colleagues are. You have an obligation to first and foremost accomplish the work of the project. But along the way, PMI wants you to make every conceivable effort to help and mentor others. *A very noble goal!*
- **This is a professional practice:** Not unlike CPAs, lawyers, or doctors, you are expected to practice the skills and art (yes, art!) of project management in a professional manner. Leave your ego at the door. You don't have to parade your PMP certification around your neck. The extended project team will know that you are a talented project manager by your deeds and how you interact with said stakeholders.
- **Avoid culture battles:** Assuming that you are working in a global environment, it could be a fatal mistake not to be mindful of cultural differences, perceptions, lifestyles, and biases. Looking from the outside in, be aware that you have a responsibility to educate your partners of cultural nuances that are inherent in your shop or surroundings. As a unifying world separated only by distance and language, cultural patience and empathy go both ways. Nonetheless, you need to maximize the collective potential of all parties that make up the project.

NOTE

This same cultural professionalism applies within your own site, where team members and stakeholders are typically from different backgrounds and all parts of the world.

■ **Comply with policy, copyright, license agreements, and the law:** It goes without saying but you must comply with industry, company, and government law when acting as a representative of PMI. If you expand your laboratory and authorize the electrical and HVAC work without the proper permits, *that is a violation.* Here are some examples that might explain compliance. If company policy states that no software can be released with severity level 1 defects, and you hide the fact and deliver it anyway, *that is a violation.* If your team incorporated and enhanced some source code that you thought was public domain or freely available, you may have inadvertently exposed your own software rights as no longer being protected intellectual property. Using technology that requires a run-time license, and yet you don't establish a timely mechanism to "pay what you owe," *is a violation.* If you witness something illegal or not compliant, you have the obligation to report it in a timely manner.

According to a recent article by Alex Handy in *SD Times*, General Public License (GPL) looks like a pretty harmless way to encourage the creation and adoption of open source to counter years of proprietary software solutions. In fact, the famous *copyleft* policy of GPL may inadvertently encourage a software provider to incorporate any GPL code without monetary compensation or legal entanglements. To further complicate the GPL ecosystem, derivative works from GPL sources must themselves be resubmitted in the open source community under the terms of the GPL. I can hear it now: "You mean my application that uses GPL components becomes available in source format, too?"

You can read more information by downloading "A Practical Guide to GPL Compliance" from www.softwarefreedom.org/resources/2008/compliance-guide.html. (Again, that specific link might change!)

■ **Be very sensitive to conflicts of interest:** The perception or actual infraction of a conflict of interest hurts all parties. Most organizations have corporate guidelines that admonish any hint of conflicts of interest as a key part of corporate governance.

Think you're immune? Perhaps not. . . . An example might be where a relative of yours becomes the technical field engineer to a supplier of yours. What should you do?

A third-party software supplier invites you to a lavish weekend at a local resort *supposedly* to talk business, but the main "work" appears to be playing golf, which, by the way, any self-respecting software leader wouldn't be interested in, right?

If in doubt, talk to upper management if situations like these come up. PMI believes that just the *perception* that you (or your team) take advantage of something that appears to favor some other entity is just as bad as actually being caught doing something that "crossed the ethical, common business practice line."

■ **Accurate status reporting:** Although open for interpretation, you must take responsibility for reporting true project status as objectively as possible. For example, if you delivered and closed a product for customer delivery but didn't go through the agreed-upon release checklist, you weren't acting responsibly. If five priority level 1 (severe) defects were discovered earlier in the week, and you don't report it in either the next team meeting or CCB, *you weren't behaving responsibly.*

BEST PRACTICE Armed with the facts, you must report truthful project status in a timely manner regardless of the consequences.

BIBLIOGRAPHY

Billows, Dick. "Post-Project Reviews: Lessons Never Learned" (www.4pm.com/articles/Project_lessons_learned.pdf).

Campbell, Clark A. *The One-Page Project Manager: Communicate and Manage Any Project with a Single Sheet of Paper*. Hoboken, NJ: John Wiley & Sons, 2007.

Connolly, Mickey and Richard Rianoshek. *The Communication Catalyst: The Fast (But Not Stupid) Track to Value for Customers, Investors, and Employees*. Chicago: Dearborn Trade Publishing, 2002.

Crowe, Andy. *The PMP Exam: How to Pass on Your First Try, Third Edition*. Kennesaw, GA: Velociteach, 2008.

Csíkszentmihályi, Mihály. *Finding Flow: The Psychology of Engagement with Everyday Life*. New York: Basic Books, 1997.

DeMarco, Tom and Timothy Lister. *Peopleware: Productive Projects and Teams, 2nd Edition*. New York: Dorset House Publishing, 1999.

Handy, Alex. "A Guide for GPL Compliance." *SD Times*. Sep 15, 2008.

Huffman, Libby. "Power/Interest Grid." Office Arrow (www.officearrow.com/forums/templates-documents/931-power-interest-grid-word.html).

Johnson, Tony. *PMP Exam Success Series: Certification Exam Manual*. Carrollton, TX: Crosswind Project Management, 2006.

Kirkpatrick, Donald. *How to Conduct Productive Meetings: Strategies, Tips, and Tools to Ensure Your Next Meeting Is Well Planned and Effective*. Baltimore, MD: Victor Graphics, 2006.

Kuhn, Bradley M., Aaron Williamson, and Karen M. Sandler. "A Practical Guide to GPL Compliance." Software Freedom Law Center. Aug 26, 2008 (www.softwarefreedom.org/resources/2008/compliance-guide.html).

Lencioni, Patrick M. *Death by Meeting: A Leadership Fable About Solving the Most Painful Problem in Business*. San Francisco: Jossey-Bass, 2004.

Mulcahy, Rita. *PM Crash Course: A Revolutionary Guide to What Really Matters when Managing Projects*. Minneapolis: RMC Publications, 2006.

Project Management Institute, Inc. *A Guide to the Project Management Body of Knowledge: PMBOK Guide, Third Edition.* Newton Square, PA: Project Management Institute, 2004.

Project Management Institute, Inc. *A Guide to the Project Management Body of Knowledge: PMBOK Guide, Fourth Edition.* Newton Square, PA: Project Management Institute, 2008.

Scholtes, Peter R., Brian L. Joiner, and Barbara J. Streibel. *The Team Handbook, Third Edition.* Madison, WI: Oriel, 2003.

Seningen, Scott. "Learn the Value of Lessons-Learned." The Project Perfect White Paper Collection. June 27, 2005 (www.projectperfect.com.au/downloads/Info/info_lessons_learned.pdf).

Tuckman, Bruce. "Developmental Sequence in Small Groups." *Psychological Bulletin 63* (1965): 384-399.

Yourdon, Edward. *Death March.* Upper Saddle River, NJ: Prentice Hall PTR, 1997.

Index

D

E